TURKEY AND THE HOLOCAUST

Turkey and the Holocaust

Turkey's Role in Rescuing Turkish and European Jewry from Nazi Persecution, 1933–1945

Stanford J. Shaw

NEW YORK UNIVERSITY PRESS
Washington Square, New York

Copyright © 1993 by Stanford J. Shaw

First published in the U.S.A. in 1993 by
NEW YORK UNIVERSITY PRESS
Washington Square,
New York, N.Y. 10003

Library of Congress Cataloging-in-Publication Data
Shaw, Stanford J. (Stanford Jay), 1930–
Turkey and the holocaust : Turkey's role in rescuing Turkish and
European Jewry from Nazi persecution, 1933–1945 / Stanford J. Shaw.
p.   cm.
Includes bibliographical references and index.
ISBN 0–8147–7960–3
1. Holocaust, Jewish (1939–1945)   2. World War, 1939–1945—Jews–
–Rescue—Turkey.   3. Jews—Turkey—History—20th century.
4. Refugees, Jewish—Turkey.   5. Jews, Turkish—Europe.
6. Righteous gentiles in the Holocaust—Turkey.   7. Turkey—Ethnic
relations.   I. Title.
D804.3.S54   1993
940.53'18—dc20   92–354
                                                              CIP

Printed in Hong Kong

Contents

List of Plates

1. The Staff of the Turkish Consulate-General in Paris at the celebration of Turkish Republic Holiday in 1943. L.-R: Germaine Guicheteau, Local Clerk Refik Ileri, Consul-General Fikret Özdoğancı's daughter Mina (later Mina Türkmen); Consul-General Fikret Özdoğancı, his wife Nüzhet Hanım, Vice Consul Namık Kemal Yolga, Tcherna Frisch, Local Clerk Nerman Özdoğancı, niece of the Consul-General, Recep Zerman and Janine Bousquet. (Photo courtesy of Namık Kemal Yolga)
2. The Staff of the Turkish Consulate-General in Paris on the occasion of the celebration of Turkish Republic Holiday (*Cumhuriyet Bayramı*) in 1941. L.-R: Chancellor Namık Kemal Yolga, Consul-General Dülger, and local clerks Guicheteau, Frisch, and Zerman. (Photo courtesy of Namık Kemal Yolga)
3. Jewish Turks standing in front of the Turkish Consulate-General in Paris in 1943 waiting to get passports and visas to enable them to return to Turkey. (Photo courtesy of Namık Kemal Yolga)
4. Jewish Turks standing in front of the Turkish Consulate-General in Paris in 1944 waiting to get passports and visas to enable them to return to Turkey. (Photo courtesy of Namık Kemal Yolga)
5. The Sirkeci Terminal railroad tracks of the Orient Express, where Jewish refugees coming from Europe arrived in Istanbul. (Photo by Stanford J. Shaw)
6. The Sirkeci Terminal building in Istanbul. (Photo by Sebah)
7. The Sirkeci Synagogue. (Photo by Stanford J. Shaw)
8. Istanbul University main gate. (Photo by Stanford J. Shaw)
9. The Haydarpaşa railroad station, terminus of the Anatolian and Syrian railway system used by Jews going by land to Palestine.
10. The Haydarpaşa synagogue. (Photo by Stanford J. Shaw)
11. Exterior of the Chief Rabbinate in Istanbul. (Photo by Stanford J. Shaw)
12. The Tokatlian Hotel (Istanbul). (Photo by Abdullah Frères)
13. The Pera Palas Hotel (Istanbul), center of Jewish Agency operations to rescue East European Jews during World War II. (Photo by Stanford J. Shaw)
14. Bebek on the Bosporus where many Jewish refugees in Turkey lived during World War II. (Photo by Stanford J. Shaw)

vii

Photographs of Documents

Preface and Acknowledgments

I first became aware of Turkey's role in rescuing thousands of Jews from the Holocaust during my research for *The Jews of the Ottoman Empire and the Turkish Republic* (Macmillan, London, and New York University Press, New York, 1991). Most of the extant documentation on these tragic but moving events became available to me only after the manuscript of that book had gone to press, however. Starting with a visit to the offices of Jak V. Kamhi, head of the Quincentennial Foundation and President of the Profilo Corporation of Istanbul, retired ambassadors Tevfik Saracoğlu and Behcet Türemen, historian Naim Güleryüz, and the Foundation's Administrative Director Nedim Yahya, who showed me copies of a number of letters exchanged between Jewish Turks resident in wartime France, the Turkish Consulate in Paris, and German diplomats, Gestapo officers, and concentration camp commanders as well as French officials involved in the persecution of Jews at that time, I began a search for more comprehensive documentary evidence. I found such evidence in the archives of the Turkish Foreign Ministry in Ankara, the Turkish Embassy and Consulate-General in Paris, and the Archives of the United States Department of State in Washington, D.C. and of the French Ministry of Foreign Affairs, as well as in numerous published and unpublished studies and memoirs by, and personal interviews with, people who were involved. Obviously more study is needed in the German archives as well as in the local and Turkish diplomatic archives surviving from Nazi-occupied countries other than France, such as Belgium and Holland. In addition, the author would appreciate it if readers with personal knowledge of the events described in this book would share their experiences with him so that subsequent editions may be enriched and added to in the light of their contributions.

For their assistance in obtaining access to archival collections, I would like to thank H.E. Kürtçebe Alptemoçin, Foreign Minister of Turkey at the time I made use of the Ministry's archives in Ankara; Director of its Research Department Cenk Duatepe and his predecessor, now Ambassador to the Philippines, Erhan Yiğitbaşıoğlu; Turkish Ambassador to France Tanşuğ Bleda; Turkish Consul-General in Paris Argun Özpay, now Ambassador to the Republic of Mongolia; retired Ambassador Kâmuran Gürün, Member of the Turkish Historical Society, for many years Secretary General of the Turkish Foreign Ministry; Bilâl Şimşir, former Turkish Ambassador to Albania and later to China, also an active member of the

Turkish Historical Society, who as a young Turkish Foreign Service officer catalogued the Embassy archives in Paris, London and elsewhere in Europe; Hayim Eliezer Kohen, Director of Protocol at the Chief Rabbinate in Istanbul, who during World War II was involved with those charged by Istanbul's Jewish community with receiving and caring for Jewish refugees arriving from western Europe; Vidar Jacobsen, of the *Centre de Documentation Juive Contemporaine* in Paris; the staff of the archives of the *Ministère des Affaires Étrangères*, Paris, and Maitre Serge Klarsfeld, the brilliant and energetic 'Nazi hunter' based in Paris, who made available to me a number of documents on Jewish Turks in Nazi-occupied Europe which he and his wife Beate found in the German archives during the course of their pioneering researches on the Holocaust.

English translations of many of these sources are presented in this work, with copies of the originals deposited in the Simon Wiesenthal Holocaust Center and University Research Library, University of California, Los Angeles, the United States Holocaust Memorial Museum, Washington, D.C., the *Centre de Documentation Juive Contemporaine* in Paris, and the Zülfaris Museum of Turkish Jewry in Istanbul.

I would like to thank my wife's mother and father, Seniha and Emin Kural, whose accounts of their relations with Jewish refugees along the border between Greece and Turkey during World War II first opened my eyes to Turkey's role in rescuing European Jewry during the Holocaust; His Eminence Rabbi Haim Nahum Efendi, last Grand Rabbi of the Ottoman Empire (1909–1920) and later Chief Rabbi of Egypt (1923–1960), who first stimulated me to undertake research into the history of Ottoman Jewry during conversations in Cairo in the winter and spring of 1956; Professor Avram Galante, pioneering historian of Ottoman and Turkish Jewry, with whom I had fruitful conversations on Heybeliada in Istanbul in 1956, particularly regarding the difficult relations between Ottoman Jews and the other minority communities; Mrs. Mina Türkmen, daughter of Fikret Şefik Özdoğancı, Turkish Consul-General in Paris during World War II, who as a young woman was resident in the Consulate-General on Boulevard Haussmann; Ambassador Melih Esenbel, for many years Turkish Ambassador to the United States, who served as third secretary in the Turkish Embassy at Vichy during World War II; Ambassador Namık Kemal Yolga, Turkish Vice Consul in Paris during the war and later Secretary General of the Turkish Foreign Service, to whom I am particularly grateful for the permission which he granted for me to include in this study the photographs which he supplied of the Paris Consulate-General and its staff as well as of the Jewish Turks who came to him and his colleagues for assistance during the war; Ambassador Necdet Kent, wartime Vice Consul at the Turkish Consulate-General at Marseilles, which later moved to Grenoble following the German occupation of southern France, all of whom related their experiences in helping Jewish Turks who applied for assistance against persecution by the French as well as the Germans; and to Jak V. Kamhi of Profilo Holding as well as to Ishak Alaton and Üzeyir Garih, co-owners of the Alarko Corporation, Istanbul, who told me about the experience of their relatives who were saved from the Holocaust by the Turkish government. My particular thanks go to my wife, Professor Ezel Kural Shaw, of California State University, Northridge, and to my Graduate Research Assistants for this study at the University of California, Los Angeles, both citizens of Israel, Ms. Ruth Barzilay-Lombroso and Mr. Oded Neuman, and to the U.C.L.A. Academic Senate Research Committee and Von Grunebaum Center for Near Eastern Studies, as well as the United States Fulbright Commission, which provided financial support for my research in Turkey during the Academic Year 1990–1991.

Turkey's role in helping European Jews during the Holocaust has been largely ignored or deprecated in studies and conferences on the subject, if for no other reason than that the number of individuals involved, both those killed by the Nazis and those who survived, was a very small percentage of the six million Jews exterminated by the Nazis and their sympathizers. Searching through the monumental studies of the Holocaust by such eminent scholars as Yehuda Bauer, Raul Hilberg, Serge Klarsfeld and others uncovers scant mention of Jewish Turks or of Turkey's role, either in helping Jews in France and other parts of western Europe, or in facilitating the activities of Jewish rescue organizations operating in Eastern Europe from offices in Istanbul.

Even in the numerous memoirs written by members of these agencies or by people who were rescued, hardly anything is mentioned about Turkey's role other than that it was there, and that its officials occasionally caused them trouble as a result of bureaucratic problems of one sort or another. Gratitude is conspicuously lacking in these accounts, and disdain for Turks, whether Jewish or Muslim, seems always to be present. No-one seems to realize that during the years in question Turkey itself was in imminent danger of invasion by the Nazi armies that had already overrun Yugoslavia and Greece and were camped on its borders while making substantial demands of all sorts, including not only the ending of Turkey's role as a base to help the Jews of Nazi-occupied Europe, but also the shipment of all the Jewish refugees who had reached Turkey to Germany for extermination, demands which the Turkish government ignored or rejected.

Ira Hirschmann, executive at New York's Bloomingdale Department Store, who was sent to Turkey by President Franklin Roosevelt in 1944 as an agent of the newly-created War Refugee Board to help rescue East European Jews, a task which could not have been carried out without the encouragement and assistance of the Turkish government, thus displayed great prejudice against his hosts by such ignorant remarks as 'The Turks are not mechanically trained, with the result that they fumble with gadgets and machines',[1] referring to one Turkish official with whom he was negotiating as 'this sad-eyed little Turk',[2] stating that Turkey's capital Ankara 'was really nothing more than a mountain village, and it offered few of the amenities of civilized life', and going on to disparage Turkey's role in providing excellent positions for the refugee scientists and professors who had been brought from Germany to Turkey in the 1930s by stating that these were 'A few men of outstanding caliber, artists and scientists that any nation would have been glad to number among its leaders . . . ,'[3] implying that Turkey should have been honored to rescue them. When discussing negotiations when Turkish ship owners were asking substantial rental fees in return for sending their ships to pick up refugees from Eastern Europe and carry them to Palestine in Black Sea and Mediterranean waters patrolled by Russian, German and British warships trying to stop them, he concludes that the ships that were being offered were 'old tubs',[4] that the fees the owners were asking in return for placing their ships in jeopardy were 'outlandishly exorbitant' or 'piratical',[5] and that the owners' requests that their boats be replaced if sunk were inappropriate. It is remarkable that he was not expelled, but the Turks at least knew that his mission was too important for that.

Even at the famous Second Yad Vashem International Historical Conference held in Jerusalem on April 8–11, 1974 on the subject of *Rescue Attempts During the Holocaust,* the important paper presented by Dalia Ofer on 'Activities of the Jewish Agency Delegation in Istanbul in 1943'[6] was entirely ignored in the subsequent discussion of the several papers presented in her panel,[7] while the statement by Chaim Pazner, official in the Geneva office of the Jewish Agency during the war, that the Turkish government had intervened with German and French authorities to rescue thousands of Jewish Turks in Vichy France who had lost their Turkish citizenship because of their acquisition of French citizenship and failure to register with Turkish

---

1. Ira Hirschmann, *Lifeline to a Promised Land* (New York, Vanguard, 1946), p. 64.

2. Hirschmann, p. 66.

3. Hirschmann, p. 137.

4. Hirschmann, p. 60.

5. Hirschmann, p. 64.

6. *Rescue Attempts during the Holocaust: Proceedings of the Second Yad Vashem International Historical Conference, Jerusalem, April 8–11, 1974* (Jerusalem, Yad Vashem, 1977), pp. 435–450.

7. *Ibid.,* pp. 451–463.

consulates in France[8], was actually *denied* by Joseph Friedman, who after admitting that 'I am not a historian nor am I involved in research', went on to reply :

> I must admit that I know nothing about the 10,000 Turkish nationals. In fact this is the first time I have heard there were 10,000 Jews in France who were Turkish nationals. It seems to me that there must have been a mistake and that the number was not more than 1,000. As far as the matter itself is concerned, as I mentioned, I know nothing. [9]

The documents which I have consulted for this monograph are tragic and moving. One cannot help but be overwhelmed by the desperate appeals for help against persecution and impending deportation at the hands of the Nazis or of the Vichy government made to the Turkish diplomats by Jewish Turks resident in Nazi-occupied and Vichy France, particularly by those who had previously abandoned their Turkish citizenship when they thought it would be more profitable for them to become French Jews, only to discover after the arrival of the Nazis that it was far better to remain, or resume being, Jewish Turks; by the letters of gratitude sent to the Turkish diplomats by those who were rescued; and by the letters from relatives describing the sad fate of those for whom help came too late, particularly due to Nazi determination on many occasions to deport and exterminate Jewish Turks before the Turkish diplomats could act to save them.

The actions of the governments of France (Vichy) and Great Britain during the war to prevent the rescue of many Jewish refugees because of the danger which such action might pose to their own interests stimulates particularly negative emotion for someone like myself, who had in the past admired both nations for their liberalism and enlightenment. The disinclination of some Ashkenazi Jews today, along with a number of non-Jewish groups who, for their own reasons, wish to suppress all mention and recognition of Turkey's important role in assisting Jews during the Holocaust, also is a cause for regret. May this account of Turkey's role in rescuing Jews from the Holocaust stimulate a realization which will encourage a willingness to perceive history in the light of the story it presents rather than through the distortion of encrusted prejudice.

Stanford J. Shaw

---

8. On Turkey's intervention to save these Jews see p. 13 of this work.

9. *Ibid.*, pp. 649, 653. For the facts as to how Turkey intervened with the Vichy government to prevent it from shipping these Jews off to Germany for extermination, see page 127.

1

Turkey and the Jews, 1933–1945

Neither the people of the Republic of Turkey nor those of Europe and America fully realize the extent to which Turkey, and the Ottoman Empire which preceded it, over the centuries served as major places of refuge for people suffering from persecution, Muslims and non-Muslims alike, from the fourteenth century to the present. In many ways the Turks historically fulfilled the role subsequently taken up by the United States of America beginning in the late nineteenth century.

The Turks' first encounter with persecuted minorities came as the Ottoman Empire was being created. Starting in the early years of the fourteenth century, Osman and his successors rose up to capture the lands of the decrepit and degenerate Byzantine empire in Anatolia and southeastern Europe. During these conquests, the Jewish minorities who had survived centuries of Byzantine persecution actively assisted the invaders and contributed to Ottoman victory and conquest in the certain expectation that they would be given the same toleration and freedom under Muslim Ottoman rule that their ancestors previously had received under the rule of the Abbasids of Baghdad and the Umayyads of Spain.

In later centuries the Ottomans received thousands of Jewish refugees from Christian blood libel attacks throughout western Europe and from persecution at the hands of the Inquisition in the Iberian Peninsula and Italy. The Ottoman role as primary place of refuge for the persecuted continued afterwards. In the sixteenth and seventeenth centuries, the sultans gave refuge to thousands of Marranos and Moriscos, Jews and Muslims respectively who had converted to Christianity in Spain under the force of the Inquisition, but who had continued to be subject to persecution because of suspicions that they had not in fact abandoned their former religions. In the late seventeenth and early eighteenth centuries, the Ottomans provided refuge for thousands of Muslims and Jews who survived the Habsburg invasion of Serbia and Bulgaria following the failure of the second Ottoman siege of Vienna in 1683 and the Cossack massacres of Jews in the Ukraine under the leadership of Boghdan Chmielnicki. In the eighteenth century the Ottomans gave refuge to thousands of Muslims fleeing from repeated Russian invasions of the Rumanian principalities and from the destructive and bloody Russian invasion and conquest of the Crimea and the lands of Central Asia north of the Black Sea.

During the nineteenth century the Ottomans received over one and a half million Muslim and Jewish refugees fleeing from massacre and persecution in the Christian provinces of southeastern Europe as they revolted and won their independence from Ottoman rule,[10] a situation which seems destined to be repeated, insofar as Jews are concerned, in the last decade of the twentieth century as the nations of the Soviet Union and its satellites in Eastern Europe recover their independence after seventy years of Communist rule, in the process allowing the revival of anti-Semitism which seemingly had been forgotten during the interval.

The persecution and massacres began with the Greek Revolution early in the nineteenth century when Greek insurrectionists against the Sultan hunted out and slaughtered every Jew and Muslim they could find, starting in the islands of the Aegean sea and continuing into the Morea and the Greek mainland. The slaughter of all those who did not fit into national ambitions continued later in the century in Rumania, Serbia and Bulgaria, constituting a true genocide which the world still does not recognize because it was carried out by Christians in the name of liberation from Muslim rule.

As Russia extended its 'Eastward Movement' across Central Asia to the Pacific during the middle and late nineteenth century, enveloping the Muslim Tatar Khanates which had remained there since the days of Genghis Khan, thousands more Muslim Tatars and Turkomans as well as Jews who had lived in the area since they had fled Byzantine persecution came to refuge in the Ottoman dominions.

As France took over North Africa and Britain moved into Egypt and Cyprus during the late nineteenth century, and as Austria occupied Bosnia

---

10. Stanford J. Shaw, *The Jews of the Ottoman Empire and the Turkish Republic* (Macmillan, London, and New York University Press, New York, 1991), pp. 188–199.

in 1878 and annexed it in 1909, more refugees fled into the ever-shrinking dominions of the Sultan. Nor were all of these Muslims and Jews. The Ottomans took in hundreds of Christian refugees from the conservative suppression in western and central Europe which followed the Congress of Vienna in 1815 and after the suppression of the liberal revolutions that took place in 1848. The Ottoman Empire became a major source of refuge for Jews subjected to terrible pogroms in Russia starting in 1881.

The Greek occupation of Ottoman western Thrace and Salonica in 1912 during the First Balkan War led to new persecutions of the Muslims and Jews living there. Many of the survivors fled into Ottoman territory, particularly after the Muslim and Jewish quarters of Salonica were burned in the great fire of 1917, after which the Greek government refused to allow anyone but Greek Christians coming from Anatolia to resettle in their homes, while the ancient Jewish cemetery of Salonica was desecrated as it was covered over by the construction of the new Greek University of Salonica.[11]

The brutal Russian invasion of eastern Anatolia in the early years of World War I caused those who survived to flee westward into the territories still controlled by the Ottomans. The Bolshevik Revolution and the Russian Civil War that followed led to new migrations of thousands of Jews and Muslims as well as Russians who fled across the Black Sea following attacks on them by both Reds and Whites.

During the Turkish War for Independence, which went on at the same time, from 1918 to 1923, Istanbul and the Marmara islands were crowded with thousands of refugees in flight from southern Russia, with the Allied armies then in occupation of the old Ottoman capital doing little to alleviate the suffering while preventing the weak government of the sultan from providing help on its own initiative.

Through all these centuries, however, Turkey faced no greater challenge, nor responded more nobly, than it did in response to Nazi persecution of the Jews of Europe starting in 1933 and continuing until the end of World War II.

---

11. D. J. Delivanis, 'Thessaloniki on the Eve of World War I', *Balkan Studies* XXI/2 (1980), pp. 191–201; A. Angelopoulos, 'Population Distribution of Greece today according to Language, National Consciousness, and Religion', *Balkan Studies*, XX/1 (1979), pp. 123–132.

TURKEY SHELTERS PROFESSIONALS
DISMISSED BY THE NAZIS IN THE 1930s

The Turkish republic took in hundreds of refugees from Nazi persecution during the 1930s, including leading professors, teachers, physicians, attorneys, artists and laboratory workers as well as thousands more less well known persons.[12] For the most part they were brought to Turkey and given senior positions within six months of their dismissals by the Nazis. Most were appointed to major professorships in Istanbul University, then being intensively reformed and modernized, and in the newly-established faculties of Ankara University. Others were given the opportunity to found and direct important scientific research institutes, where several generations of Turkish scholars and scientists were trained. [13]

Much of the work of arranging the invitations was carried out by the *Notgemeinschaft Deutscher Wissenschaftler* (Emergency Assistance Association for German Scientists), established in Zürich, Switzerland in March 1933 by Dr. Philipp Schwartz to help Jewish and other professors

---

12. Horst Widmann, *Exile und Bildungshilfe: Die deutschsprachige akademische Emigration in die Türkei nach 1933* (Bern/Frankfurt, 1973), translated into Turkish as *Atatürk Universite Reformu* (Atatürk's University Reform) (Istanbul, 1981); Fritz Neumark, *Zuflucht am Bosphor* (Frankfurt, 1980), translated into Turkish as *Boğaziçine Sığınanlar: Türkiyeye Iltica eden Alman Ilim Siyaset ve Sanat Adamları* (Those who Fled to the Bosporus: German Scientists, Politicians and Artists who fled to Turkey) (Istanbul, 1982); Faruk Hakan Bingün, *Nazi Almanyasından Kaçarak Türkiye'ye Sığınan Alman bilim Adamı ve Sanatçılar* (German intellectuals and artists who fled from Nazi Germany to Turkey) (Ankara Üniversitesi Sosyal Bilimler Enstitüsü Uluslararası İlişkiler Anabilim Dalı, Yüksek Lisans Tezi, 1990); Jan Cremer and Horst Przytulla, *Exil Türkei: Deutschprachige Emigranten in der Türkei, 1933–1934* (Karl Lipp, 1981); Cevat Geray, *Türkiyeden ve Türkiyeye Göçler ve Göçmenlerin İskânı* (The Migrations to Turkey and Settlement of the Migrants) (Ankara, 1962). On the reception of these academic refugees into the United States, Britain and elsewhere see Robin Rider, 'Alarm and Opportunity, Emigration of Mathematicians and Physicists to Britain and the United States, 1933–1945', *Historical Studies in the Physical Sciences* XV (1984), pp. 107–176; Max Pinl and Lux Furtmuller, 'Mathematicians under Hitler', *Leo Baeck Institute Yearbook* XVIII (1973), pp. 129–182; and Donald Fleming and Bernard Bailyn, eds, *The intellectual migration. Europe and America, 1930–1960* (Cambridge, Mass., Harvard University Press, 1969).

13. Avner Levi, 'The Jews of Turkey on the eve of the Second World War and During the War', (in Hebrew) *Pe'amim*, no. 29 (1986), p. 34.

being driven out of Germany following the Nazi rise to power. The society started with an office in the building of the *Neue Zürcher Zeitung* and later expanded into larger quarters with the help of Swiss sympathizers who provided money and served as volunteers. The Academic Assistance Council started to undertake similar activities at the same time in England, and tried to get the Swiss society to join it there, but the latter preferred to continue its work independently in Switzerland. Professor Schwartz first established contacts with Turkey in July 1933, arranging financial support to help the first refugee professors go to Istanbul. Along with Professor Rudolf Nissen and Professor Albert Malche, of the University of Geneva, he visited Turkey between 5–7 July 1933 and convinced Istanbul Mathematics Professor Kerim Erim and Education Minister Reşit Galip that the refugee Jewish professors could help the reforms then being introduced at Istanbul University. The committee left a list of refugee professors with the latter, who soon afterwards persuaded Turkish President Mustafa Kemal Atatürk to give the project his personal support. Schwartz also talked with Minister of Health Refik Saydam, who agreed to invite some of the refugees to work in the Ankara Nümune Hospital and other medical facilities in Turkey.

The refugee scholars who were brought to Turkey after 1933 included some of the most important professionals in Germany and Austria before the Nazis came to power, most of whom had been dismissed from their positions because they were Jewish, though some had left because of opposition to Nazism or because, though they themselves were not Jewish, the Nazis had uncovered a Jewish ancestor somewhere in the past.[14] Most came with their families and some with their professional assistants. Among others there were labor economist **Alfred Isaac,** professor at the Nürnberg Polytechnic school of Economic and Social Sciences, who directed the business course at the Faculty of Economics at the University of Istanbul from 1937 to 1951; Economist and Sociologist **Alexander Rüstow,** a Socialist activist in Weimar Germany, administrative director of the German Machine Manufacture Society and Dozent at the Berlin Higher Trade School when the Nazis came to power, who tried to organize a last desperate resistance to Hitler before fleeing to Turkey in 1933, where he taught Economics, Economic Geography and Philosophy at Istanbul University, at

---

14. More detailed biographies of these and other professors and scientists brought to Turkey during the 1930s are to be found in Appendix 5 of this volume

the same time joining the anti-Nazi activities of some of the refugees and others in Turkey;[15] Roman philologist **Leo Spitzer**, Professor of Roman and Comparative Philology at Cologne University, who founded the School of Foreign Languages at Istanbul University, later taken over by **Erich Auerbach**, Professor of Roman Philology at Marburg University from 1929 to 1935, who served as Professor of Roman Philology at the Faculty of Arts of Istanbul University, where he wrote *Mimesis*, a major study of European literary criticism; **Andreas Schwartz**, Professor of Roman Law at Zürich University and later at Freiburg University in Germany, who taught Roman and Civil Law courses at the Istanbul University Law Faculty and made important contributions to Turkey's adoption of western law during the 1930s, as well as helping train two generations of Turkish attorneys, judges, and legal scholars; **Richard Hönig**, Professor of Criminal Law, Philosophy of Law, and Church Law at Göttingen University before being dismissed by the Nazis in 1933, who served as Professor of the Philosophy of Law and History of Law at Istanbul University through the 1930s and most of World War II; **Walter Gottschalk**, Head of the Oriental Section of the Prussian State Library in Berlin (1923–1935), who served as Library Specialist at the Istanbul University Library starting in 1941, cataloguing that library's major manuscript and book collections, most of which came from the famous Yıldız Palace library of Sultan Abdülhamid II, and also serving as Professor of Library Science at Istanbul University from 1941 until 1954; **Ernst Hirsch**, who taught first at Göttingen and then at Frankfurt before he was forced to leave Germany in 1933, and who in Turkey specialized in international trade law and legal philosophy at Istanbul University;[16] the sociologist and economist **Gerard Kessler**, Professor of Sociology and Economics at Leipzig University, who trained hundreds of Turkish students in labor economics at Istanbul University and who joined some of them in helping found the first Turkish labor unions following World War II; **Ernst Reuter**, former Socialist mayor of Magdeburg and later Mayor of West Berlin during the Berlin airlift following World War II, who taught urban planning while in Turkey

---

15. See Barry Rubin, *Istanbul Intrigues*, pp. 42–44 for a more detailed biography based on interviews with Alexander Rustow's son, Professor Dankwart Rustow, of the City University of New York.

16. Hirsch's memories of Turkey are found in his *Üniversite Kavramı ve Türkiyedeki Gelişimi* (The Concept of the University and Reform in Turkey) (Istanbul, Fakülteler Matbaası, 1979); and *Hâtıralarım* (My Memories) (Ankara, 1985).

from 1935 until 1946;[17] and economist and financial expert **Fritz Neumark**, Professor of Economics at Frankfurt University, who served as Professor of Economics and Finance at Istanbul University from 1933 to 1953.[18] **Albert Einstein** also was invited to teach at Istanbul University, and rejected the offer only at the last minute when he was appointed as Professor at the Institute for Advanced Studies at Princeton.

There were the architects **Gustav Oelsner**, City Architecture Director at Hamburg/Altona when dismissed by the Nazis in 1933, who in addition to teaching architecture and city planning at the Istanbul Academy of Fine Arts (*Güzel Sanatlar Akademisi*) played an important role in Turkey's municipal planning programs; **Rudolf Belling**, Professor of Sculpture at the Fine Arts Academy in Berlin before coming to direct the Sculpture Department of the Academy of Fine Arts in Istanbul from 1937 until 1951, subsequently teaching Architecture at the Istanbul Technical University, **Clemens Holzmeister**, Administrator of the Architectural Section of the Fine Arts Academy in Vienna before 1938, who then served as the Director of the Architectural Section of the Istanbul Technical University and Professor of Architecture from 1940 and 1954 and constructed many Turkish government buildings in Ankara, including the new Grand National Assembly (1938) as well as the ministries of Agriculture (1934), War (1931), Interior (1932) and Trade and that of the Turkish General Staff (1930); and **Bruno Taut**, who built the Faculty of Language, History and Geography (*Dil ve Tarih-Coğrafya Fakültesi*) in Ankara in 1937. In addition the French painter **Léopold Lévy** helped develop the school of modern painting at the Academy of Fine Arts in Istanbul after his arrival from France in February 1937, remaining as its Director until the end of 1949.

At Ankara University there were the Assyriologist **Benno Lansberger** (Leipzig) and the Hittitologist **Hans Güterbock** (Berlin), who organized and led major archaeological excavations in Anatolia before and during World

---

17. Reuter's letters written during his years in Turkey are published in Ernst Reuter, *Schriften–Reden, Zweiter Band: Artikel, Frief, Reden 1922 bis 1946*, ed. Hans J. Reichhardt (Berlin, 1973), pp. 453–687. See also Fritz Stern, *Ernst Reuter* (Berlin, 1976)

18. For Neumark's fond remembrances of his years in Turkey see his memoirs, Fritz Neumark, *Zuflucht am Bosphor* (Frankfurt, 1980). Translated into Turkish as *Boğaziçine sığınanlar: Türkiye'ye iltica eden Alman Ilim Siyaset ve Sanat Adamları, 1933–1953* (Those who took refuge on the Bosporus: German scientists and scholars who fled to Turkey) (Istanbul University, 1982).

War II, and who subsequently joined the Oriental Institute at the University of Chicago after helping to develop an entire generation of Turkish archaeologists; Classical Philologist **Georg Röhde** (Marburg), who in addition to training Turkish philologists worked with Minister of Education **Hasan Ali Yücel** during World War II in developing a major program of translation into Turkish of the major works of classical and European literature, still widely circulated a half century later;[19] and the Sinologist and Sociologist **Wolfram Eberhard** who, following the war, joined the faculty at the University of California, Berkeley.

In the Arts, renowned composer **Paul Hindemith** (Frankfurt) assisted in the creation of the Turkish State Conservatory in Ankara, which included among its faculty famous German theatrical producer **Carl Ebert** (Berlin), who founded the Theatrical Department in the Turkish State Conservatory and directed the Turkish State Theater in Ankara between 1941 and 1947 before moving on after the war to Los Angeles; and conductor Dr. **Ernest Praetorius**, who founded and led the President's Philharmonic Orchestra in Ankara.

Among major scientists brought to Turkey in the 1930s were botanists **Leo Brauner** (Jena) and **Alfred Heilbronn** (Münster), geologist **Wilhelm Salomon-Calvi** (Heidelberg) and chemist **Otto Gerngross** (Berlin). Jewish physicians invited to teach and direct university institutes included the micro philologist and epidemiologist **Hugo Braun** (Frankfurt), radiologist **Friedrich Dessauer** (Frankfurt), internist **Erich Frank** (Breslau), chemist **Fritz Arndt** (Hamburg), biochemist **Felix Haurowitz** (Prague), hygienist **Julius Hirsch** (Berlin), pediatrician **Albert Eckstein** (Dusseldorf), who directed the establishment of a series of clinics throughout Turkey; ophthalmologist **Joseph Ingersheimer** (Frankfurt), dental surgeon **Alfred Kantorowicz** (Bonn), gynecologist **Wilhelm Liepmann** (Berlin), pharmacologist **Werner Lipschitz** (Frankfurt), histologist **Karl Loewenthal** (Frankfurt), surgeons **Edward Melchior** (Breslau) and **Rudolf Nissen** (Berlin),[20] and physiologist **Hans Winterstein** (Breslau). In all, at Istanbul University the refugees were appointed to direct nine of the twelve institutes

---

19. Among the classics of foreign literature published in this translation series between 1940 and 1950 were literary works from Germany (76), France (180), England (46), Latin (28), Russia (64), Ancient Greek (76), Italian (13), and Persian and Arabic (23).

20. Nissen describes his refuge in Turkey in Rudolf Nissen, *Erinnerungen eines Chirurgen,* ed. Helle Blatter–Dunkle Blatter (Stuttgart, 1969).

at the Faculty of Medicine and six of the seventeen clinics established under its supervision.[21]

The professors were hired on contracts of two, three or five years. They were allowed to teach with translators at first, but were required to learn and teach in Turkish during the period of their first contract. They were obliged to write textbooks and manuals to be translated into Turkish for their students. In return they were paid a much higher salary than that of equivalent Turkish professors in addition to being provided with the cost of their transportation and moving of household goods and books along with the right to bring along a number of foreign assistants.

While the Turkish government did all it could to make the refugee professors comfortable and to assist their research, providing them with tax exemptions and free housing, and many with Turkish citizenship, this influx of highly-paid and privileged foreign specialists was not without its problems. The American Embassy in Istanbul reported in 1936 to the Secretary of State in Washington :

> The authorities at Ankara have attempted to give the German professors every possible facility for carrying on their work. Enormous sums have been spent on equipment for laboratories and hospitals. One now sees in Turkey hospitals equal in equipment to any in the world. In addition, more or less adequate appropriations have been made for operating these physical plants. It is understood that strong advocates and protectors of the professors exist in high circles in Ankara, and that any complaints which are made against them fall on deaf ears in the Capitol.[22]

The refugee professors and scientists were, indeed, resented by many Turkish professors, not only those who had been dismissed as part of the reforms, but also those who remained but who reacted to a situation in which the newcomers were paid four or five times as much as they. In addition to the assistants the newcomers were entitled to bring from

---

21. Barry Rubin, *Istanbul Intrigues*, p. 43.

22. Report by S. Walter Washington, Second Secretary of the American Embassy (Istanbul), 'Memorandum regarding German-Jewish Professors in the University of Istanbul', enclosed in J. V. A. MacMurray to Secretary of State no. 73, 14 July 1936. Department of State Decimal File 867.4016 JEWS 20 at the National Archives, Washington, D.C.

Germany, they also were given Turkish assistants, but the latter for the most part were persons who would otherwise have been appointed to the professorships turned over to the refugees, so they also had little liking for their nominal superiors and often ignored or sabotaged their activities and instructions. Thus the American Embassy went on to comment about the difficult relations that existed between many of the newly arrived scholars and their Turkish counterparts and assistants.

> Considerable friction . . . has existed in Istanbul. This was no doubt inevitable when a large group of foreigners of such note was introduced into an institution already established and staffed largely with citizens of this country. On the one hand, the Turkish manner of conduct has not led to the cooperation and effort to which German professors are accustomed on the part of their associates and subordinates; and, on the other hand, it is natural for the Turkish professors to feel that good positions and high salaries, which could have been enjoyed by themselves, have been given to outsiders. The medical professors are supported in their dislike of the Germans by the entire medical fraternity of Istanbul. Although the German professors are prohibited from engaging directly in private practice, any resident of Istanbul may go to the clinics operated by them and receive free of charge treatment of a standard so much higher than that provided by the local doctors that the latter find that their patients are decreasing in number. Moreover, patients who are willing to pay high fees have no difficulty in finding Turkish doctors who will agree to summon the German professors in consultation, which is a permissible means of circumventing the rules prohibiting private practice.

Few of the refugees knew Turkish when they came. Many lived together in Bebek on the Bosporus, Istanbul's choicest residential suburb, and did little to make the contacts with Turkish society and colleagues that alone could have rapidly improved their knowledge of the language and people. Until the refugees managed to learn Turkish, they taught in German, with assistants translating into Turkish for the students, creating considerable problems of communication. Most learned enough Turkish to fulfill their obligation and taught formally in the language, though many spoke Turkish so poorly that their students demanded that they continue to lecture in German while relying on assistants for translations. Others, however, failed to learn at all, and a few of these were dismissed as a result, leading to bitter feelings after their arrival in Britain and the United States, where they blamed the Turks who had in fact given them refuge when no other country would. Part of the problem was in attitude. Most of the refugees had been leading figures in Germany and elsewhere in western Europe and had treated even their German students with considerable arrogance, something which the democratically-minded Turks simply could not accept. Many of the refugees shared the centuries-long prejudice maintained against Muslims, particularly Turks, and including Jewish Turks, by the Germans and local Christians, and for the most part refused to join the anti-Nazi activities of Turkey's Jewish community. This caused considerable resentment and anger on the part of Muslim and Jewish Turks alike:

> The most conspicuous among the exiled Jews are the thirty-five professors in the University of Istanbul, some of whom were formerly leaders in their professions in Germany. The sentiments most frequently heard expressed by these scholars and scientists, however, are not those of revenge against the regime that is responsible for their exile, but of dissatisfaction at being in any country other than Germany whose customs and habits are theirs and where their forebears have lived for generations . . . . In spite of the fact that all of these men are in this country because of their dissatisfaction with conditions at home, their culture is German and some of them were in fact leaders in German scientific and scholastic thought during the postwar period. Their disagreement with the political regime in their home country has in no way changed their fundamental thought processes, and they show many evidences of their allegiance to the German nation, if not to the present government . . . . A great source of trouble for the Germans is language. Although interpreters were to be provided for three years, all of the contracts maintained clauses obligating the German professors to learn Turkish and to be prepared to lecture in that language after the termination of this period. During the three years which have just come to an end,

some of the professors have picked up a smattering of Turkish, some do not easily learn languages or are too old to do so, and all have found that they have been kept too busy to devote much time to language study. Turkish students do not generally understand German; but both those who do and those who do not often find that the subject matter of the lectures is made clearer when the professor speaks in German and has his remarks translated into Turkish by an expert interpreter than when he speaks Turkish badly. One professor has said that when he tried to speak Turkish to the students they stamped and yelled until he changed back into German. On the other hand, it would obviously be advantageous if all the professors could lecture in the native language of the students, and the fact that most of them are not prepared to fulfill this clause in their contract is a vulnerable spot of which their critics have not failed to take advantage . . . . [23]

Even Victor Maurer, Istanbul representative of the Nazi newspaper *Völkische Beobachter*, reported to Hitler's anti-Semitic propagandist, Alfred Rosenberg, on 18 December 1933 regarding the first Jewish professors who arrived in Turkey:

Many of the German professors invited to teach at the University (there are Jews among them) have been greeted in a friendly manner by Turkish public opinion, contributing thus to the propaganda of German culture, while most have not manifested their anti-Nazism, complicating the problem of the attitude which should be taken regarding them by the German side.[24]

The refugees were friendlier with each other and even with Turks, however, than they were with most Germans living in Istanbul. Many accepted Turkish citizenship when it was offered to them. Only those whose

---

23. J. V. A. MacMurray, United States Embassy, Istanbul, Turkey, to the Secretary of State, no. 74, 14 July 1936. (State Department archives Decimal File 867.4016).

24. J. Billig, *Alfred Rosenberg dans l'action idéologique, politique et administrative du Reich hitlérien: Inventaire commenté de la collection de documents conserves au Centre de Documentation Juive Contemporaine provenant des Archives du Reichsleiter et Ministre A. Rosenberg* (Paris, 1963), no. 595, p. 186.

connections with the Nazis were known or suspected were denied citizenship when they applied. Most of them had little contact with the official German establishment in Istanbul and Ankara which supported the Nazis–the German Consulate, the Teutonia club at Tepebaşı, opposite the American Consulate-General (which still often served as the Embassy), the German *Lise*, and official German newspapermen and their organizations.

The only German establishments where both sides came together were the German Archaeological Institute (*Alman Arkeoloji Enstitüsü*) located on the slopes of Siraselviler Caddesi near Taksim square in Beyoğlu (Pera), a major center of research and scholarship,[25] the nearby German Hospital,[26] and the German Protestant church. But aside from such interludes there was considerable conflict and rivalry between the two groups as time went on. The battle also extended to the Christian minorities, with some Armenians and Greeks supporting the Nazis against the refugees because of their long-standing anti-Semitism and rivalries with the native Turkish Jewish community, and in particular their fear that continued Jewish immigration would enable the Jews to strengthen their commercial and political influence in the country.

The German government officially revoked the citizenship of all the Jewish refugees in Turkey and demanded that they be returned to Germany for punishment, along with all Jewish Turks. The Turkish government consistently resisted all such demands, however, despite the many threats that accompanied these demands during the course of the war.

German Ambassador Franz von Papen related one of these incidents in his *Memoirs*, attributing the Turkish refusal to his own intervention:

> Hitler ordered me to withdraw passports from all the German émigrés in Turkey and deprive them of German citizenship. I resisted this order and informed Ribbentrop that the majority of the émigrés had left Germany with the full permission of the Government, and many of them had taken up posts in Turkish

---

25. In 1990 the Institute moved to modern new quarters in the nearby German Consulate-General.

26. The hospital was founded by German missionaries in the nineteenth century. It had been occupied by the American Hospital during the Allied occupation of Istanbul following World War I, but had been returned to the Germans in 1929 when American interests built the new Admiral Bristol Hospital in the Şişli section of the city.

universities . . . . I could not see my way to carry out his instructions, and told him that the Turkish government would consider such a step inexplicable. Not a single émigré was molested in any way . . . . [27]

Despite these difficulties, however, most of the refugees remained to make important contributions to Turkish academic and intellectual life.

SUPPRESSION OF NAZI-INSPIRED ANTI-SEMITIC MOVEMENTS IN TURKEY DURING THE 1930s

Istanbul's German community for the most part supported the efforts of Nazi ambassadors, journalists, merchants and spies to undermine Turkish faith in the loyalty and ability of the refugees as well as of Jewish Turks in general, often allying with local Christian nationalist groups in efforts to take advantage of wartime tensions and Axis threats against Turkey to eliminate Jewish competition and drive the Jews out of Turkey once and for all.[28]

The most virulent anti-Semitic newspaper in Turkey that resulted from this Nazi influence during the 1930s was *Anadolu* (Anatolia), published in Izmir by C. R. Atılhan, which was circulated widely in western Anatolia and eastern Thrace. It was suppressed, however, on 5 September 1930 by a group of soldiers led by Fethi Okyar, one of Atatürk's closest associates, most likely at his instigation, because of its threat to public order as well as to the rights of Jewish Turks. Okyar was rewarded by being named deputy to the Grand National Assembly for the district of Gümüşhane.[29]

Atılhan then went for a time to Germany at the invitation of the notorious Jew-baiter and racist Julius Streicher. He returned to Turkey in May 1934 and established another newspaper, *Milli İnkilâp* (National Revolution), which stimulated anti-Semitic feelings at Edirne and elsewhere in eastern Thrace, an area that was particularly susceptible to this sort of

---

27. Franz von Papen, *Memoirs* (London, 1952), pp. 521–522.

28. Johanes Glasneck, *Methoden der Deutsch-Faschistestchen Propagandatigheit in der Türkei vor und Während des Zweites Weltkrieges* (Halle, 1966).

29. *Vakıt, Hakimiyet-i Milliye,* and *Milliyet,* 6 September 1930.

appeal due to such feelings that had been nourished and expressed for centuries by its large Greek population before it was evacuated as part of the population exchange between Greece and Turkey which followed World War I.[30]

The result was the transformation of a governmental order to clear the border area of 'foreigners' into the circulation of rumors that Jewish Turks were plotting against the Republic with the help of the world Zionist movement, and the wide circulation of Turkish translations prepared in Germany of the notorious *Protocols of the Elders of Zion*, which had in fact been invented by the Czarist Secret Police in the late nineteenth century to provide a pretext for pogroms. Local orders for 'foreigners' to leave the border areas, coupled with violent attacks against local Jews, followed starting on 24 June 1934, causing most to flee to safety in Istanbul. News of the attacks was kept out of the national newspapers for a time due to the concurrent visit to the country of the Shah of Iran, Riza Pahlevi, but it finally was published for the first time on 4 July 1934.

Prime Minister Ismet Inönü had been traveling in Anatolia with the Iranian Shah, but as soon as he heard what had happened in Thrace he returned to the capital and immediately ordered the closing of most pro-Nazi political groups as well as *Milli Inkilâp*. On 5 July 1934 Inönü delivered a powerful speech to a special session of the Grand National Assembly, condemning anti-Semitism and defending the rights of Jewish Turks:

> I am obliged to discuss a recent regrettable incident. I have learned that a number of Jewish citizens in Thrace, because of certain regional measures, have been obliged to leave their homes and that many of them have taken refuge in Istanbul. In Turkey every individual is under the protection of the laws of the Republic. Anti-Semitism is neither a Turkish product nor part of the Turkish mind. At certain periods, it penetrates our country from foreign countries, but we reject it. This disturbance is most likely a contagion of this sort.

---

30. Avner Levi, 'The Jews of Turkey on the Eve of the Second World War and During the War', (in Hebrew), *Pe'amim* no. 29 (1986), p. 35; on the incidents in Thrace, see also the article by Avner Levi in *Pe'amim*, no. 20 (1984), pp. 111–132.

We shall never permit currents of this kind to be produced in Turkey. (applause) I have learned of this matter on my return to Ankara, and upon the express orders which I have given, this anti-Semitic movement has been completely stopped. Jewish citizens who have gone to Istanbul are free to return to their homes. Those responsible will appear before our tribunals. I have directed the Minister of the Interior to proceed to the places effected in order to make inquiries. Those responsible will be severely punished.[31]

Immediately after the meeting, he released a firm statement to the official Anatolian News Agency for distribution to the Turkish press and public:

I have just heard that a certain number of Jews has arrived in Istanbul from different parts of Thrace. Complaints directed to the President of the Council of Ministers indicate that they have been forced to leave their homes as a result of a series of local attacks. I am in the process of ordering an inquiry into the true character of the incident. But I wish to recall that all initiatives against the laws of the Republic will fail in themselves under the severe constraint of the law. My present declaration constitutes moreover an answer to the complainants. I advise the Jews, first and foremost, to have recourse to justice to secure their rights and pursue their attackers.[32]

Interior Minister Şükrü Kaya headed to Thrace in the company of the Commander of the Gendarmes to make a personal investigation of the situation. Returning to Ankara a week later, he presented a detailed report to the Council of Ministers, chaired by President Mustafa Kemal Atatürk himself, which on 12 July declared publicly:

Having returned from his inspection trip in Thrace, Minister of the Interior Şükrü Kaya Bey has submitted his report to the

---

31. Reported by Robert A. Skinner, United States Embassy (Istanbul) to Secretary of State, 6 July 1934. National Archives (Washington, D.C.), State Department Decimal File 867.4016/JEWS/10. See also T.C.B.B. *Zabit Ceridesi, Devre IV, cilt XXIII*, pp. 454–458, 6 July 1934.

32. *Ulus*, 13 July 1934.

Council of Ministers. It appears that Anti-Semitism began in Thrace during World War I and it continued during the Armistice and the fight for Independence. After having been suspended for a time during the early years of the Republic, it has penetrated the country once more during the last few years with more vigor and following new formulas obtained from different parts of the world. Anti-Semitic articles published recently in certain journals have troubled the relations of Turks and Jews. There are reciprocal complaints; one notices not only all the political, economic and national elements of Semitic and international anti-Semitic literature, but also a social peculiarity in Turkey, that the Jews persist in preserving a foreign language and culture, causing a presumption which against some of them that they are spies, and dangerous to the security of the country in the demilitarized zones. On the other hand, Jewish intellectuals, after having justly alleged that the question of national culture resulted from a fault of the Empire, have added frankly that their desire to assimilate Turkish culture is real and sincere, that the rumors put into circulation with respect to their duties and fidelity as citizens are unjust and without foundation. Rumors also were put into circulation throughout the Republic, beginning about the middle of June, to the effect that the Government desired to dislodge the Jews of Thrace but preferred that the movement should not be accomplished in the broad light of day, but by means of combinations and pressures. It appears to be the fact that the closing of Jewish accounts and the removal of Jews to Istanbul commenced in these conditions on June 24th at Çanakkale, and on June 30th in other regions in Thrace. The Central Government, having learned these various facts on the 3rd and 4th of July, sought by categorical orders to intervene in order to put a stop to this state of affairs. The incidents which have occurred up to now may be summarized as follows:

a. Of the 13,000 Jews, foreign and domestic, in Thrace and Çanakkale, 3,000 in all left for Istanbul.

b. Attempts to set up a boycott took place in the rural districts and at Edirne, and an attempt was also made to bring into this movement children in the schools.

c. Marauding elements went into action on the night of the 3rd and 4th of July at Kırklareli, where they attacked, violated and pillaged Jewish houses. The pillage was stopped before it extended to the market and to the shops. However, sixty-five houses were pillaged.

d. In the course of these events one gendarme was killed and one Jew wounded.

In consequence of these events, the present situation is as follows:

i. Everywhere the spirit of the bureaucrats has been freed from influence exercised by propaganda of every sort, and they have been put in a position to actively dominate the situation. Judicial and administrative measures have been taken against officials whose actions have been deemed to be insufficient during the course of these events and against those who have been indulgent against the violators of the law . . . .

ii. The authors of the events at Kırklareli are being pursued with the utmost vigor. More than 75 per cent of the objects taken and stolen from Jewish houses on the 3rd and 4th of July have been found and returned as a result of administrative and judicial investigations. The authorities have arrested the promoters and aggressors and have begun action against them. Jewish citizens who were frightened by the incidents and left are returning to their homes.

iii. In other localities, the government has explained to those who left out of fear or after having liquidated their affairs that there is no obstacle to their return. All transactions regarding commerce, debts and credits, with the exception of the pillage of Kırklareli, are considered by the Government as to be settled exclusively by action of the Ministry of Justice.

After thus exposing the actual situation and the events that took place, the Government has the duty of repeating and explaining below the line of conduct which it will follow, so as to give no place to hesitation:

1. The Government will prevent pressure for emigration and boycotts, no matter what the reason or the manner in which it is undertaken.

2. All offenses brought to the attention of the judiciary will be judged speedily.

3. Opposition to the return of Jews who have left other towns will not be permitted.

4. The most important question before the Government is to recreate an atmosphere of accord and security among its citizens. The Government considers the open and secret assistance provided by the majority of Turks for the Jews, the efforts exerted to protect the Jews against extremist propaganda, and the disgust felt as a result of the acts of aggression as factors destined to ameliorate the situation promptly.

5. The government will not permit in Turkey any provocations or suggestions of enmity against citizens. It expects the press to show prudence with regard to contagions susceptible of sowing discord amongst citizens.

6. Public officials will exert all their strength to achieve the line of conduct desired by the Government.

The General Secretariat of the People's Party is in the process of undertaking an inquiry into the subject of the regional committees who have not accomplished their task satisfactorily. It will take all measures necessary regarding those who have abused their functions. The organizations of the People's Party will support the efforts of the officials in their duties in carrying out the point of view of the government. In thus exposing the events and measures taken, the Government declares that there remains no matter which should inspire fear among its citizens.[33]

Hundreds of soldiers and gendarmes were sent to Thrace in order to restore order. The Mayor and police chief of Kırklareli were dismissed from their positions and arrested for their roles in spreading the rumors and for their failure to suppress the resulting agitation before damage was done. The District Mayor (*Kaymakam*) of Uzunköprü, located on the Greek border, issued an open invitation to the town's Jews to return, adding: 'It is my duty to protect your security, and I will do it with all my strength'.[34]

---

33. Robert Skinner, Embassy of the United States (Istanbul) to Secretary of State, no. 328, 16 July 1934. Department of State Archives, Decimal File 867.4016b. JEWS/11.

34. *Ulus*, 5 July 1934; *New York Times*, 16 July 1934.

Continued ferment in Thrace due both to Greek religious attacks and Nazi propaganda among Muslims, continuing into World War II, however, caused most of its Jews who had fled to remain in the more tolerant and liberal atmosphere of Istanbul and Izmir, while the Great Synagogue of Edirne, built on the model of that of Vienna in the early years of the twentieth century when the city's Jewish population was bolstered by the arrival of thousands of refugees from Germany and Russia, and by far the largest synagogue in Turkey, was allowed to fall into the ruined condition in which it remains today.

During World War II *Milli Inkilâp* was repeatedly suppressed by the government. Atılhan was arrested and sent to jail along with his comrades in anti-Semitic campaigns, and the government publicly promised the Jewish community that it would continue to protect Jews against all attacks and to treat them equally with all other Turkish citizens.[35]

At least partly in reaction to the Nazi-inspired movements and propaganda, Jewish Turks began to participate actively in national and local politics for the first time starting in 1934.[36] Dr. Abravaya Marmaralı was elected to the Grand National Assembly as a liberal independent, the first Jewish member of that body, while other Jews participated widely in local governments where they lived. In reaction to the widespread Turkish resentment against their continued use of Judeo-Spanish, Jewish men in particular began to use Turkish in their daily lives, as well as engaging in the wider stage of Turkish-language cultural activities as novelists, journalists, poets, playwrights and artists. Jews enthusiastically embraced Atatürk's urgings for everyone to adopt last names, with the novelist Abraham Nahon changing his name to Ibrahim Nim at the same time that he followed Marmaralı into politics, and the writer and philosopher of Turkish

---

35. Avner Levi, 'The Jews of Turkey on the Eve of the Second World War and During the War', (in Hebrew), *Pe'amim* no. 29 (1986), p. 36.

36. The Treaty of Lausanne (1923) had specified special seats in the Assembly to Turkey's Jews, Armenians and Greeks. The Jews, however, immediately surrendered this right, and other special privileges, trusting in the promises of equality provided in the new Turkish Constitution, and fearing that continuation of the special privileges provided in a Treaty signed with foreign powers would undermine their desire to become equal citizens in the new secular Republic. The other non-Muslim communities subsequently followed this lead. See Stanford J. Shaw, *The Jews of the Ottoman Empire and the Turkish Republic* (London and New York, 1991), pp. 245–246.

nationalism Moise Kohen assuming the old Turkish name, Tekinalp, at the same time undertaking a campaign among his fellow Jews to encourage them to learn and use Turkish.[37] The emergence of open clashes between Jews and Arabs in Palestine was widely published in the Turkish press, moreover, but the Turkish government did nothing to hinder contacts between Turkish and Palestinian Jews, including participation of the Istanbul Jewish sports society *Bar Kochba* in the Maccabee games held in Palestine in 1935, an invitation to the Jewish Palestinian soccer club *Hakoah* to play in Turkey at the same time, and permission for Jewish Turks to participate in the various World Jewish Congresses held during the late 1930s.[38]

Starting in 1937 German propaganda activities in Turkey increased considerably, with emphasis on anti-Semitism, as was the case with similar German propaganda efforts,[39] but with much less success due to strong opposition on the part of the Turkish public and government. The German Information Office was opened in the center of old Istanbul, on the Divanyolu near the Aya Sofya and Sultan Ahmed mosques and the city's publication center at Cağaloğlu.[40] Nazi propaganda also was published in the subsidized German-language daily newspaper *Türkische Post* as well as in the pro-Nazi daily *Cumhuriyet,* owned and edited by Yunus Nadi, who was provided special business concessions in Germany to secure his editorial

37. Avner Levi, 'The Jews of Turkey on the Eve of the Second World War and During the War', (in Hebrew), *Pe'amim* no. 29 (1986), p. 38. See also Jacob Landau, *Tekinalp–Turkish Patriot* (Leiden, Brill, 1984).

38. Avner Levi, 'The Jews of Turkey on the Eve of the Second World War and During the War', (in Hebrew), *Pe'amim* , no. 29 (1986), p. 39.

39. Amnon Netz, 'Anti Semitism in Iran, 1925–1950', (in Hebrew), *Pe'amim* no. 29 (1986), pp. 5–31; Nissim Kazzaz, 'The Influence of Naziism in Iraq and anti Jewish activity, 1933–1941', (in Hebrew), *Pe'amim* no. 29 (1986), pp. 48–71; Yair Hirschfeld, *Deutschland und Iran im Spielfeld der Machte, Internationale Beziehungen unter Reza Schah, 1921–1941* (Dusseldorf, 1980).

40. A detailed study of Nazi propaganda efforts in Turkey can be found in Johanes Glasneck, *Methoden der Deutsch-Faschistestchen Propagandatätigheit in der Türkei vor und Wahrend des Zweites Weltkrieges* (Halle, 1966). See also Lothar Krecker, *Deutschland und die Türkei im Zweiten Weltkrieg* (Frankfurt, 1964).

support for Turkish cooperation with the Axis, resulting in his gaining the nickname 'Yunus Nazi' among many Turks.[41]

The Nazis attempted to stimulate nationalism among Turks and Armenians living in Nazi-occupied Europe as well as in Turkey as part of its campaign to destabalize both Turkey and the Soviet Union and undermine their resistance to German invasion. Nazi efforts to revive the ambitions of Turkic nationalists to unite the Turkic territories of southern and central Russia with Turkey in a restored pan-Turkic empire, with the goal of placing the Baku oil fields under German control, were quite successful among many Turkish exiles from the Soviet Union who had been driven out of their homelands when the Bolsheviks took over their incipient republics during and after the Bolshevik Revolution. These Turkic nationalists were quite active in Germany and its allied countries throughout the war, but within Turkey they were kept under close scrutiny and control by the Turkish government, in fulfillment of the tradition left by Atatürk of 'peace at home, peace in the world', with several leaders of the movement being imprisoned near the end of the war.

The appeal met with considerably more success, however, among some ethnic Armenians in Turkey as well as elsewhere in western Europe, who were impressed and honored by Alfred Rosenberg's declarations in the 1930s that they were, indeed, full Indo-Europeans, or Aryans.[42] In addition to their long-standing and historic anti-Semitism and their resulting sympathy for the Nazi attacks on Jews, which had begun to manifest itself in Germany during the late 1930s, they saw in Hitler's invasion of Russia a golden opportunity to liberate what they considered to be 'Historic Armenia' from Soviet as well as Turkish rule, alarming Jewish Turks and Muslims alike.[43]

The British Ambassador to Turkey Hughe Knatchbull-Hugessen thus reported to London that:

---

41. Barry Rubin, *Istanbul Intrigues*, p. 45 and Wallace Murray, United States Embassy (Istanbul) to Secretary of State no. 774, 6 August 1938: State Department Decimal File no. 867.4016 JEWS/27.

42. See above, page 27

43. Patrik von zur Mühlen, *Zwischen Hakenkreuz und Sowjetstern: Der Nationalismus der Sowjetschen Orientvölker im Zweiten Weltkrieg* (Dusseldorf, 1971), 106. Also reports of Turkish Ambassador to Berlin Hamdi Arpag, in archives of Turkish Embassy (Paris), dossier 6127.

. . . the Armenians are extremely fruitful ground for German activity and as a result the non-Muslim elements with their pre-Kemalist mentality are always viewed with mistrust by the Turkish authorities.[44]

The Nazi propaganda stimulated the publication of some anti-Semitic articles and books by extreme right-wing Turkish political groups.[45] Writings such as these were, however, ignored entirely or vigorously condemned by Turkish public opinion and by most journalists and their newspapers, led by Zekeriya Sertel, editor of *Tan,* and the *Dönme* Ahmed Emin Yalman whose series of editorials led to the Government's closing of the German Information Office in late 1939 after it violently criticized Turkey's signature of treaties of alliance with Great Britain and France.[46]

The Germans responded by organizing a boycott of *Tan* by leading German companies and merchants doing business in Turkey, including Bayer Pharmaceuticals and the Daimler Benz motor car company. Even *Cumhuriyet* protested against this campaign against freedom of the press, however, along with several other Istanbul newspapers, but the German efforts against *Tan* and other newspapers that supported its campaign continued for some time during the war.

In response to the activities of German and British agents in Turkey, the government was compelled to maintain strict controls over all foreigners resident in country, who were compelled to register with the police wherever they lived or travelled, while being subjected to constant supervision by agents stationed wherever they lived or worked.

Following the arrival of large numbers of Jews in flight from increased anti-Semitic persecution in Poland, Hungary and Rumania during the late months of 1937, the German anti-Semitic propaganda increased, leading to efforts made in the Grand National Assembly to limit Jewish immigration

44. Great Britain , Public Record Office, FO 371/30031/R5337.

45. Kemal Karpat, *Turkey's Politics* (Princeton, 1959), pp. 264–270.

46. See *Tan,* 2 August 1939 and 20 November 1939. Also Zekeriya Sertel, 'Tan'ın Kazandığı Büyük Dava', *Tan,* 15 May 1939; 'Almanlar, Türk-Sovyet Dostluğunu Bozmak İçin Uğraşıyorlar', *Tan,* 8 December 1939; 'Türkiyede Alman Propagandasının Gizli Faaliyeti', *Tan,* 9 December 1939. Also Cemil Koçak, *Türkiyede Milli Şef Dönemi* (Ankara, 1986), p. 428–433, and M. Zekeriye Sertel, *Hatırdıklarım, 1905–1950* (What I have remembered, 1905–1950) (Istanbul, 1968), pp. 209–217.

from central and western Europe.[47] These proposals were denounced,
however, on 11 January 1938 in *Ulus*, official newspaper of Atatürk's
Republican Peoples' Party:

> The bases of our doctrine concerning national security, solidarity
> and cultural union are contained in the Constitution and other
> laws. However, one of the bases of the Kemalist Regime is to
> make decisions only according to national conditions and interests
> and to defend the principle of independence of all institutions
> against outside influences. Our measures for defending the right,
> honor, dignity and the interests of Turkish citizens living in the
> country are satisfactory and sufficient to render absolutely useless
> extreme proposals such as those which have been rejected. It is
> fair to say that these proposals, with regard to the rejection of
> which there was no doubt, presented other inconveniences in the
> nature of false interpretations to which they might have given rise.

The proposals were quickly defeated in the Grand National Assembly
by overwhelming votes. Robert Kelley, Chargé d'Affaires at the American
Embassy in Ankara, reported to the State Department:

> I have the honor to report that on January 10, 1938, the
> Committees of the Interior and of Foreign Affairs of the Turkish
> Grand National Assembly examined two bills introduced by
> Deputy Sabri Toprak, one restricting the immigration of non
> Turks into Turkey and the other requiring all Turkish citizens to
> speak the Turkish language. Both bills were admittedly directed
> against Jews.
>   The first bill would prohibit the immigration of Jews into
> Turkey, though it made exception for people in certain
> professions, such as in the fine arts, science and industry. The
> second bill provided that all persons who wish to adopt Turkish
> nationality must agree to learn to read and write the Turkish
> language within a year's period and be subject to deportation if

---

47. See *Ulus*, 11, 12 and 15 August 1939, *Tan*, 12, 15–18 August, 5 September 1939, 13
January 1940. *Cumhuriyet*, 13 January 1940, 1 April 1940.

they have not learned it at the end of that time. The exact provisions of this bill have not been published, but it is said that, if enacted into law, it would have affected not only Jewish immigrants but also the 80,000 Jews, mainly Spanish speaking, who now reside in the country and who have already acquired Turkish citizenship.

The Committee of Foreign Affairs rejected the bill relating to immigration into Turkey on the ground that the Government had already the power to take any measures desired in regard to immigration and that such a law was unnecessary. The Committee of the Interior in rejecting the bill relative to the use of the Turkish language declared that there was no reason for enacting such a law since there already existed legal provisions relative to the use of the Turkish language in the country. [48]

Prime Minister Celal Bayar further declared:

There is no Jewish problem in our country. There is no minority problem at all. We do not intend to artificially create a Jewish problem because of external influences. We will not allow external currents to influence us. [49]

Soon afterwards, however, the Istanbul police began to arrest and deport German and Italian Jews resident in Turkey because their own governments had revoked their citizenship and since, according to Turkish passport and residence laws recently introduced, stateless persons could not reside in Turkey. When the Istanbul Jewish leaders informed the government what was happening, however, and that the Jews in question would be persecuted if they were forced to return to their former countries, the deportation orders were revoked, and those already arrested were given new residence permits which allowed them to remain in Turkey for five years, with the possibility of renewal if necessary.

---

48. Robert F. Kelley, Chargé d'Affaires, a.i., United States Embassy, Ankara, to Secretary of State, no. 493, 13 January 1938. State Department Decimal Archives 867.4016 JEWS/25.

49. *Cumhuriyet*, 11 January 1938; *Journal d'Orient*, 3 November 1937, 26 and 28 January 1938.

Hüseyin Cahit Yalçın, a close associate of Atatürk, deputy from Çankırı to the Grand National Assembly, and editor of the influential daily newspaper *Sabah*, also wrote a strong editorial directly inspired by the new President following Atatürk's death, Ismet Inönü, who was to guide his country's policies with distinction for the next twelve years:[50]

THERE IS NO JEWISH QUESTION IN TURKEY

We are faced today with an important Jewish problem in which the whole world is interested. A small mistake by our police. A New Passport Law (8 December 1938) and new Law on residence of foreigners in Turkey (5 January 1939) was applied so as to order expulsion of Italian and German Jews resident in Turkey who had been deprived of their citizenship because of anti-Semitic legislation. The order was subsequently revoked.

To start with, we can say at once that there is no problem at all regarding Jews who are Turkish citizens. The Constitution of the Turkish Republic gives full political rights for Jews who have been living and working in Turkey for centuries. The Constitution of the Republic makes no distinction among its citizens in regard to religion and race. All the native sons of this country enjoy equal liberty of conscience and the right and duty to contribute together to the happiness and welfare of the fatherland of all. Though the welfare and good of the nation require that the affairs of the Republic be carried out by a single party (The Republican Peoples' Party), this principle has been applied in a very generous manner, since there are independent deputies in the Grand National Assembly who do not belong to this party, and among them are some who adhere to the religion of Moses.

All the schools of the state are open to Turkish citizens who are Jewish. They can attend them in full freedom and in large numbers. They may also hold all kinds of official positions, travel in all parts of the country, and publish newspapers. In sum, they can live in this country without being considered separately from the mass of citizens who are Muslims. These words are not a problem nor a wish, nor do they have any particular objective.

---

50. *Sabah*, 27 January 1939, reprinted in *Journal d'Orient*, 29 January 1939.

They express the simple reality of today. This is so much the case that it would have been useless to even raise the question if there were not a Jewish question causing anxiety in the world.

It cannot be supposed that the Constitution which until now has assured equal rights to all citizens of the Republic without discrimination because of race or religion, and which states their duties, should be changed. Such a feeling cannot be considered in the mind of any Turkish citizen. I am authorized to make this declaration most categorically. I am therefore not expressing a personal opinion or private idea. I write this with a firm conviction born out of opinions expressed by our most famous and authoritative officials in Ankara. As to Jews of foreign nationality, since there does not exist in Turkey any feeling of animosity of either an individual or collective nature toward Jews, we view the Jewish problem in the world from a humanitarian point of view.

The fact that among the foreign professors hired by the University, several are Jewish, shows that the frontiers of Turkey are not closed as a hostile barrier to the Jewish race. Seeing that Jewish professors invited to Turkey consider our country as their second homeland, that they combine honesty and devotion in their efforts to develop the minds of Turkish youths and contribute to the progress of science, inspires us with a sentiment of gratitude for their great character and sincerity.

During the 1930s and in reaction to Nazi propaganda, as was the case in the Ottoman Empire during the nineteenth and early twentieth centuries, it was not so much Turkish Muslims but, rather, Christians, who persisted in their anti-Semitic attitudes and activities. Some Armenian nationalists in Turkey, as in Germany and elsewhere in western Europe and the Middle East, were seduced by the declarations of the principal ideologue of Nazi anti-Semitism and reviver of the notorious *Protocols of the Elders of Zion,* Alfred Rosenberg, who in his *Der Mythus des Zwanzigsten Jahrhunderts* (Berlin, 1935–1941), which declared the 'Aryan race' to be the origin of all civilized culture and values and the Jews as their principal corrupters, as well as in the racial interpretations of the Nazi *Reichstelle fur Sippenforschung,* correctly pointed out that Armenians were, indeed, Aryans and thus members of the 'master race', entitled to dominate 'lesser peoples' of eastern Anatolia and the Caucasus if only Germany prevailed.[51] As a result, a few of Turkey's Armenians joined Germano-Turkish friendship societies set up in Istanbul and worked behind the scenes to convince Turkey's Jewish community to leave the country, greatly concerning other Turks, both Muslims and Jews. This tendency came to a climax in 1938, when it appeared that the 'New Order' might dominate Europe, when the Nazi flag was openly flown from the famous Tokatlian Hotel in the Beyoğlu (Pera) section of Istanbul as well as from its summer headquarters at Tarabya on the upper Bosporus.

The resulting Jewish boycott of both hotels was bitterly opposed by Yunus Nadi and his son Nadir Nadi in their newspaper *Cumhuriyet*, with a series of very critical editorials beginning on 20 July of that year:

WHAT IS IT TO OUR JEWS?

A strange boycott movement by our Jewish fellow countrymen in our city has attracted attention. The situation is this: the owner of the Tokatlian hotel in Beyoğlu and Tarabya, M. Medovich,[52] is an Austrian German. For some time this person, who has Austrian nationality, has on holiday and vacation days flown the Austrian flag with the Turkish flag. Following the Anschluss, Medovich became a German citizen and began flying the German flag.

Our Jewish fellow countrymen, who previously had comprised the largest group of patrons of the hotel and restaurant, were said to have been irritated by this and to have started a boycott against this institution. Now the famous habitués of the Tokatlian salon are not to be seen.

---

51. *Nationalsozialistische Deutsche Arbeiterpartie, Reichsleitung, Rassenpolitisches Amt (1938–1944)*, EAP 250–d–12/3, 4, 5, 6, 8, 10. See also in the same Archive: BUE 66, Nazi Party *Hauptamt Wissenschaft* folder of material on Professor Otto Gros, author of a Guide to Rosenberg's work, *Erlauterungen zum Mythus des XX. Jahrhunderts* (Berlin, 1939). The inclusion of Armenians was not generally accepted by most Nazi leaders, who preferred to lump the Armenians and Jews together, until Rosenberg, assisted by the Armenian National Council, convinced Hitler to the contrary despite the objections of the General Staff, which doubted their ability to make a military contribution.

52. *Author's note*: Medovich was in fact not the owner but the manager of the hotel, which was locally owned.

This strange sensitivity shown in this country against the actions of a subject of a foreign country which is undergoing political changes is seen as very strange in many quarters of this city. . . . An event invites us to think regarding some important problems, however much it may be painful for our Jewish citizens.

You will read in our issue of today that the Jewish Turks of Istanbul have declared a boycott against a hotel whose owner is a German subject. Those who previously constituted a substantial portion of its patrons now do not step foot in it. It is as if all the Jews of Istanbul have united and after long discussions have together excommunicated it. We do not know what the hotel owner will do.

The situation of this institution is not directly related to us. There are laws which stipulate the methods of activity of foreigners living within the borders of the Turkish Republic. It is a quite natural thing for a foreigner who conforms to them to do business in our country. We think it is quite natural. Even if as a result of any sort of national feeling, people may undertake agitation against this or that foreign institution, our government has no other duty to interfere beyond providing our protection within our borders. It is entirely natural for a German institution to work in Turkey and on holidays to fly its own flag beside that of the Turkish flag. Germany is a friendly country which maintains normal relations with us. Our countrymen operate hotels and restaurants and engage in other activities in the great German cities like Berlin and Vienna. When they fly our flags on holidays in these institutions no-one says anything to them.

However simple may be the reasons for our Jews to proclaim a boycott against a German subject working in Istanbul, this is cause for thought.

It is well known that in the world there is a thought and spirit of Jewishness. We are not here going to analyze the good and evil aspects of this spirit. The enemies of Jews' greatest weapon is the claim that these people whose noses are trade-marked are without a nation.

The Jews have secured minority rights in some nations. It is thus among us. But four or five years ago they underwent a

national crisis as a result of this. They cried out with a force which
startled all of us: 'What sort of word is minority. We are children
of this homeland, we are the product of this soil. We are Turks
with all our hearts.'

The gesture was beautiful enough to moisten the eyes of
people. In truth, according to the meaning explained by
Kemalism, the only condition to become a Turk is to sincerely feel
Turkish. And while there is nothing extraordinary in the
Turkishness of a fellow countrymen whose mother and father are
Turkish, it is worthy of our praise and honor for someone of
foreign origin to identify himself with this society. But one cannot
be a Turk only in words, it is necessary to demonstrate it. While
the Republic was proclaimed almost fifteen years ago, our Jewish
fellow countrymen have not stepped forward toward our society
even fifteen *centimes*. That broken French and Spanish which they
speak among themselves still continues to scrape our ears. Now
they have added to these a kind of German.[53] Occasionally we say
'When are these people going to learn Turkish?'

The other day a friend of mine said: 'It would be much more
suitable to say: It's better that they don't learn, sir. As if they were
really useful to those areas where they learned the language.
Their remaining foreign to our society will protect us from many
troubles in the future.' In reaction to the recent boycott event, the
words of our friends invite us to think, however painful it may be
to our Jewish fellow countrymen, about some important
problems. Nadir Nadi.

The Nadis' close connection to the German embassy, and their receipt
of financial and other favors from German officials, was described in a
report from the American Embassy sent to Washington later the same year:

I have the honor to report that during the latter part of July the
Istanbul press published several articles regarding the Jewish
problem. Although the discussion lasted only a few days, it served

---

53. *Author's note*: Nadi here is trying to raise opposition to the German and Yiddish-
speaking Ashkenazi refugees then arriving in Turkey from central and eastern Europe, but he
was not successful.

as a reminder that there is an important Jewish minority in Turkey offering opportunities for manifestations of anti-Semitism. The recent outbreak was initiated by the journalist Yunus Nadi, who published an article in his daily papers, the Cumhuriyet, and its French edition La République, attacking the Jews for boycotting the Tokatlian hotel in this city. He accused the Jews of boycotting what was formerly one of their favorite rendezvous because, following the Anschluss, its Austrian manager had hoisted the German flag alongside the Turkish flag. Other newspapers took up the discussion, asserted that no boycott had been organized against the Tokatlian Hotel, and accused Yunus Nadi of trying to stir up anti Semitism. The articles of Yunus Nadi were rather weakly written, and though he referred to the question during several days he made little effort to provide proofs of his sweeping assertions. It is possible and even probable that many Jews have avoided the Tokatlian hotel since the management commenced to fly the German Swastika, but there is no evidence that there has been any organized effort to boycott the hotel.[54]

A widely discussed aspect of the incident concerns the motives which may have prompted Yunus Nadi to try to stir up popular feeling over a question which has not before been a grave issue in Turkey. Various articles published by him during the last year have shown a strong pro-German bias, and reports have for some time been current regarding the receipt by him of certain material consideration for his pro-Nazi writings. Suspicions regarding this are encouraged by the knowledge on the part of numerous private commercial interests of all nationalities doing business in Turkey, that Yunus Nadi has on many occasions offered them his journalistic support 'for a fair price.' Interested persons have therefore been inquiring into the possible connection between Yunus Nadi and the German Embassy. It is now reported to a member of my staff from a reliable source that he has been receiving remuneration in the form of certain

---

54. *Author's note:* my discussions with leading Jewish Turks whose fathers were active in community affairs in the 1930s lead me to believe that there was, in fact, an organized Jewish boycott of the Totaklian and that this ultimately led to the hotel's demise following the war.

customs or quota facilities for the exportation to Germany of Oriental carpets. Whatever may be the motive which prompted Yunus Nadi to initiate a discussion of this problem, the Jewish colony in Istanbul is considerably perturbed over the possible future consequences. In former years the Jews have escaped much of the criticism, discrimination, and even persecution, to which other minorities in Turkey have been subjected. Recently there have, however, been several danger signals. When the question of the Turkish language has been under discussion, for instance, as it has been several times during the past year, there have been articles, generally from the pen of Yunus Nadi, calling attention to the fact that the members of the long-established Jewish colony in Turkey prefer to speak the Spanish language rather than Turkish. Concern over the situation is accentuated at this moment by the serious illness of President Atatürk and the feeling that he himself has been largely responsible for the tolerant and liberal attitude of the Turkish Government toward non-Moslem elements in the country. Parenthetically, it may be said that all the minority and opposition groups in Turkey are concerned at this moment over the possibility of the death of Atatürk. The Jews, however, are the most agitated, largely because of the probability that General Ismet Inönü may be powerful in the succeeding government, and they consider him to be violent in his prejudice.[55] The most enthusiastic journalistic support has, moreover, always come from Yunus Nadi, who, at the time of the crisis terminating in Ismet's fall from power last autumn, was more outspoken in deploring the change than were the other Turkish journalists.[56]

---

55. *Author's note:* this statement does not seem to be supported by the evidence. Inönü as prime minister stamped out the anti-Semitic violence in the areas of Turkey bordering Greece during the 1930s, and according to leading Jewish Turks, always was quite friendly with many of them. Inönü may have agreed to the enactment of the *Varlık Vergisi* in 1942, but this disaster was not the result of anti-Semitism, as is shown on p. 39 and *passim*, and he was directly involved in its abolition the following year.

56. J. V. A. MacMurray, American Embassy, Istanbul, Turkey to Secretary of State, no. 4, 6 August 1938. Confidential. State Department Decimal Archives 867.4016 JEWS/27.

Most other Turkish newspapers, led by the Kemalist evening paper *Tan*, edited by Zekeriya Sertel, vigorously opposed *Cumhuriyet* and condemned Nadi's remarks, and he finally was ordered to stop them by President Inönü himself after an appeal was made to him by leaders of Istanbul's Jewish community.[57] The Jewish boycott of the Tokatlian continued with increased strength, however, as a result of general Turkish support, and it ultimately caused the hotel to close following the war, transformed into an office building, as it has remained to the present day.[58]

TURKISH JEWRY DURING WORLD WAR II

Turkey managed to remain neutral during World War II.[59] The sympathies of President Ismet Inönü and most other Turkish leaders were clearly with the western Allies, with which alliances had been signed shortly before the

---

57. The Nadis also published similar editorials in *Cumhuriyet*, 22 July 1938, pp. 1, 7: 'Bir Yahudi davasına tahammul edemeyiz' (We cannot bear another Jewish case) and *Cumhuriyet*, 23 July 1938, p. 3: Peyami Safa, 'Iki Cins Yahudi (Two kinds of Jews)'. Editorials condemning these statements were published in: *Son Telgraf*, 20 July 1938: 'Istanbulda bir Yahudi meselesi ve onların boycotu mu var?' (Is there a Jewish problem and a boycott by them in Istanbul?); *Son Telgraf*, 21 July 1938: Burhan Cevad, 'Yahudi Meselesi' (The Jewish problem); *Tan*, 21 July 1938: Burhan Felek, 'Yahudi Meselesi'? (The Jewish problem?) *Son Telgraf*, 22 July 1938: 'Türkiye yahudileri Almanlar aleyhinde mi?' (Are the Jews of Turkey against the Germans?); *Son Telgraf*, 23 July 1938, p. 1: 'Yahudiler parti ve hükumete muracaatı düşünüyorlar.' (The Jews are thinking of appealing to the party and to the government); *Son Telgraf*, 23 July 1938, p. 6: 'Yahudiler Partiye müracaat edeceklermiş' (The Jews are said to be going to appeal to the Party); *Kurun*, 25 July 1938: 'Bizde Yahudilik meselesi varmı dır?' (Is there a Jewish problem here?) *Kurun*, 1 August and 2 August, 1938: Asım Us, 'Yahudi Meselesi' (The Jewish Problem); *Kurun*, 8 August 1938: M. Nermi, 'Türkiye yahudileri hakkında' (About the Jews of Turkey). Yunus Nadi's son Nadir Nadi, who took over *Cumhuriyet* following his father's death, ignores the entire episode in his memoires, *Perde Aralığından* (Istanbul, 1964), and is said to have become quite friendly with Jewish businessmen in Turkey before his death in 1991.

58. *Cumhuriyet*, 20 July 1938; J. V. A. MacMurray, United States Embassy (Istanbul) to Secretary of State, no. 4, 6 August 1938, Department of State, decimal archives 867.4016, JEWS/27; A. Messersmith, Department of State, to Secretary of State, Washington, D.C., 27 August 1938, in Department of State decimal archives 867.4016, JEWS/29. Yunus Nadi persisted in his pro-Nazi activities, however, during World War II.

59. Selim Deringil, *Turkish Foreign Policy during the Second World War* (Cambridge, and New York, Cambridge University Press, 1989), and Edward Weisband, *Turkish Foreign Policy, 1943–1945* (Princeton, N.J., Princeton University Press, 1973).

war began, but the latter's clear inability to provide assistance if an open war declaration had led to a German invasion from Greece, combined with vivid memories of the disastrous sufferings resulting from World War I and its aftermath, caused the Turks to maintain an uneasy neutrality, with the support of the Western Allies, with whom the Turks co-operated from behind the scenes, until Germany's impending defeat finally led Turkey to join the Allies late in 1944, thus emerging from the war among the victors, as Greece had been forced to do near the end of World War I.

While many Jews in most countries occupied by the Nazis in western Europe were able to conceal themselves throughout the war with local assistance, and while the Italians assisted the Jews to escape deportation and death in the territories that they occupied jointly with German forces,[60] because of the overwhelming anti-Semitism which continued to predominate in most of Greece,[61] Yugoslavia,[62] and Rumania,[63] the Nazis and their local

60. See, for example, Ivo Herzer, 'How Italians rescued Jews', *Midstream*, XXIX (1983), pp. 35–38; and Daniel Karpi, 'The Jews of Greece in the Holocaust period (1941–43) and the behavior of the Italian occupation authorities' (in Hebrew), *Yalkut Moreshet* XXXI (1981), pp. 7–38, which shows that the Italians protected Greek Jews so long as they were there, but that the local Greeks cooperated with the Nazis in identifying and deporting the Jews after Germany occupied Greece.

61. See, for example, Alexandros, Kitroeff, 'Documents: The Jews in Greece, 1941–1944: Eyewitness Accounts', *Journal of the Hellenic Diaspora* XII/3 (1985), pp. 5–32; and Steven Bowman, 'Jews in Wartime Greece', *Jewish Social Studies* XLVIII/1 (1986) 48(1), pp. 45–62, reprinted in *The Nazi Holocaust*, ed. M. R. Marrus, vol. 4. *The Final Solution Outside Germany, volume 1* (Westport and London, Meckler, 1989), pp. 297–314. Anti-Semitism seems to have been less strong in Athens than in Salonica and the rest of Greece, where it was endemic.

62. Zdenko Löwenthal, *The Crimes of the Fascist Occupants and their Collaborators against Jews in Yugoslavia* (Belgrade, 1957); Menahem Shelah, 'The Holocaust in Yugoslavia-the Communities in Serbia and Croatia', *Pe'amim* no. 27 (1986), pp. 31–61; and Jenny Lebel, 'The Holocaust in Yugoslavia-the Communities in Macedonia, Pirot and Kosovo', *Pe'amim* no. 27 (1986), pp. 62–76. Bulgaria was a special case. It defended its own Jews against Nazi demands that they be persecuted and sent off to Poland for extermination, but it subjected the Jews of occupied Macedonia to extreme persecution in order to secure Nazi permission to retain these territories.

63. This long–standing anti-Semitism is documented in Stanford J. Shaw, *Jews of the Ottoman Empire*, pp. 188–194 and Zvi Ankori, 'Greek Orthodox-Jewish Relations in Historic Perspective: The Jewish View', *Journal of Ecumenical Studies*, XIII (1976), pp. 17–57. On the other hand, Rumania at times did attempt to prevent the Nazis from deporting and exterminating all its Jews, according to Oliver Lustig, 'In Romania 'The Final Solution' could

puppets there were largely able to exterminate the Jewish minorities, thus culminating the persecutions begun in these countries following their achievement of full independence during the nineteenth century.[64] On the other hand, neutral Turkey defended its Jews and rejected Nazi demands for them to be deported for extermination in the death camps.[65] In the face of constant German pressure, however, it did appear to try to satisfy them in some respects and avoided a German invasion like that which had pulverized Greece by measures such as limiting the entry of Jewish Turks into military schools and segregating Jewish conscripts in the army into labor battalions rather than assigning them to regular military units.[66]

In the darkest days of World War II, moreover, after German forces had occupied Greece. Hungary, Rumania, Yugoslavia, and Bulgaria and pushed to the Turkish borders in Thrace, as the Turkish government was contemplating the evacuation of Istanbul in response, as each new German

---

not be applied', *Romania: Pages of History* XIII/3 (1988), pp. 205–221, and Asher Cohen, 'Petain, Horthy, Antonescu and the Jews, 1942–1944: Toward a Comparative View, *Yad Vashem Studies* XVIII (1987), pp. 163–198. Greek cooperation in the Nazi-led extermination of Greece's Jewish community is documented in M. Molho and J. Nehama, *In memoriam* (3 volumes, Thessaloniki, 1948–1953, republished in a single volume in 1980). See also David A. Recanati, ed. *Zikhron Saloniki: Grandezi i Destruyicion de Yeruchalaim del Balkan* (2 volumes, Tel Aviv, 1971–2). Greek cooperation with the Nazis policy of deporting Jews for extermination is documented in Daniel Carpi, 'Nuovi Documenti per la Storia dell'Olocausto in Grecia: L'atteggiamento degli Italiani (1941–1943),' N. Michael, *On the History of the Jews in the Diaspora* VII (1981), 119–200.

64. It is interesting to note, however, that in contrast with the general popular support given to Nazi measures against the Jews in these countries, the partisan guerrilla forces fighting against the Nazis provided significant assistance to escaping Jews, perhaps because many of the latter joined the partisans in their struggles. On the situation of the Jewish minorities in Southeastern Europe at this time, see American Jewish Committee, *The Jewish Communities of Nazi Occupied Europe* (New York, Fertig, 1982). See also Benjamin Arditti, *Vidni Evrei v Bulgaria/The Jews of Bulgaria during the Nazi Occupation, 1940–1944* (in Hebrew, Jerusalem, 1962); Frederick Chary, *Bulgarian Jews and the Final Solution, 1940–1944* (Pittsburgh, Pa., 1972); Carol Iancu, *Les Juifs en Roumanie* (Universite de Provence, France, 1978); and T. Lavi, *Yeudei Romania be Mouvak al ha Atlala* (Jerusalem, 1962);.

65. Lothar Krecker, *Deutschland und die Türkei im Zweiten Weltkrieg* (Frankfurt, 1964); Fritz Neumark, *Zuflucht am Bosphor* (Frankfurt, 1980).

66. Avner Levi, 'The Jews of Turkey on the Eve of the Second World War and During the War', (Hebrew), *Pe'amim* no. 29 (1986), p. 43.

advance led to the arrival of hundreds more refugees flooding into Edirne and Istanbul, and as Muslim and Jewish Turks alike wondered where Hitler would move next, across the English channel against England, or eastward against Turkey as the first step toward overrunning the Middle East,[67] rumors were spread by Balat's Christian inhabitants and neighbors that as soon as the Nazis arrived in Istanbul they would use the ovens of the local Balat bakery, called *Los Ornos de Balat* by the Jews, to cremate Turkish Jews. This created considerable anxiety and alarm among Balat's Jews in particular, causing many move elsewhere in Istanbul and to go to Israel following the war, though the story was entirely without foundation. The bakery was torn to the ground soon after the war came to an end in order to remove the Jews' last memories of the horrible threats that it represented.

The German propaganda campaign against Turkey's Jews and in support of efforts to secure Turkish adherence to the Axis was directed by the German Embassy and Consulate located at Taksim square in the Beyoğlu (Pera) section of Istanbul. Leading the campaign was Paul Leverkühn, Middle East agent of Admiral Wilhelm Canaris's *Abwehr,* who had earlier engaged in business both in Turkey and Syria and was considered an expert on the entire area. Under his direction, agents were sent throughout the country and elsewhere in the Middle East to spread Germany's message as well as to gather information, coordinated largely through facilities provided by several Arab mercantile families based in Iskenderun as well as by the Armenian Revolutionary Federation (*Dashnaks*) and in particular the Ayvazian family and its resort hotel, located in southeastern Turkey near the Syrian border.[68]

The most powerful Nazi society in Turkey was organized and controlled by the Gestapo agents stationed at the Consulate and the nearby Divan Hotel. Members of the German colony were organized into the *Teutonia Club,* whose massive headquarters was located across the street from the American Consulate in the Tepebaşı district overlooking the Golden Horn and Old Istanbul. All members of the German colony were compelled to join the *Arbeitsfront,* which secured jobs for members and arranged for the dismissal of Germans who failed to cooperate and to provide service and funds when ordered. Germans in Istanbul were also

---

67. Faik Ahmet Barutçu, *Siyasi Anılar, 1939–1954* (Istanbul, 1977), pp. 174–176.

68. Rubin, *Istanbul Intrigues*, pp. 57–58.

encouraged to join and participate in the activities of the Nazi *Sturm Abteilung* and *Sturm Staffel* in Istanbul along with the Hitler Youth, the *Bund der Ausland Deutschen*, the *Sportsverein*, the *Turnverein* and the *Allemania* Club, the latter formerly a reputable society formed by German businessmen in Istanbul, but subsequently made subordinate to the Teutonia Club for those unable to pay the rather substantial membership fee required by the former.[69] German males of military age were subjected to regular military exercises and discipline, with funds for organizations and propaganda provided by local German businesses as well as by the German government and the Nazi party.

Nazi propaganda efforts in Turkey during World War II attracted few Turks other than the pan-Turkic exiles from Central Asia who were entranced by the possibility of restoring their homelands with German assistance rather than by the German anti-Semitic appeals. The only significant Turkish convert to Nazi anti-Semitic ideas during the war was the pan-Turkist ideologist and racist Nihal Atsız, a high school teacher who, modeling himself after Hitler in word and dress, advocated an alliance with Germany as the first step toward '. . . ridding ourselves of Jews, communists, and freemasons'.[70] Turks such as Atsız who did succumb to the Nazi appeal were suppressed by the Ankara government, and many were thrown into jail, but the Nazis did manage to attract some Armenian nationalists to join their military and propaganda activities as well as their occupation of southern France and invasion of the Soviet Caucasus in the hope of creating an Armenian state in the East, making many Turks fear a repetition of the events in World War I, when, they believed, Armenian uprisings around Lake Van starting in 1914 led to the destructive and devastating Russian invasion of Eastern Anatolia in the years before the Bolshevik Revolution. [71]

---

69. 'Report on Nazi Activities in Turkey', by J. V. A. MacMurray, United States Embassy, Istanbul, sent in a report to Secretary of State, 14 July 1936, U.S. State Department Archives 867.4016. Text in Appendix 9.

70. Hasan Ali Yücel, *Davam* (Ankara, 1947), p. 16, quoted in Kemal Karpat, *Turkey's Politics* (Princeton, 1959), p. 266.

71. On the *Armenian Hossank Nazi Party*, the Armenian *Tseghagron* racist movement stimulated by Alfred Rosenberg, the Armenians who broadcasted anti-Semitic propaganda on Radio Berlin, and the Armenian 812th Battalion of the Wehrmacht see Patrik von zur Mühlen, *Zwischen Hakenkreuz und Sowjetstern: Der Nationalismus der sowjetischen Orientvölker im Zweiten Weltkrieg* (Düsseldorf, Droste, 1971), particularly pp. 105–6; also James Mandalian, 'Geregin Nezhdeh', *The Armenian Review* I (1957) and 'Dro–Drastamat

THE VARLIK VERGISI DISASTER

With Nazi troops on the border with Greece, only forty miles from Istanbul, the Turkish government faced severe financial problems caused by

---

Kanayan', *The Armenian Review* II (1958). Reports from Turkish Ambassador Hamdi Arpag (Berlin), years 1941 and 1942, in archives of the Turkish Embassy (Paris), file 5623.; NSDAP, Aussenpolitisches Amt, (Bonn) Amt Osten, EAP 250–d-18–10/FT 1–10, Folder 7. Peter Gosztony, *Hitlers Fremde Heere* (Vienna, 1976); A.A. Gretschko, *Die Schlacht um dem Kaukasus* (Berlin, 1969); Adolf von Ernsthausen, *Wende im Kaukasus. Ein Bericht* (Neckargemünd, Germany, 1958); Jürgen Thorwald, *The Illusion: Soviet Soldiers in Hitler's Armies* (New York and London, 1974), pp. 44, 66, 71–73, 105–118, 220, 223, 232; Sarkis Atamian, *The Armenian Community. The Historical Development of a Social and Ideological Conflict* (London, 1955), pp. 400–405; Andreas Hillgruber, *Die Räumung der Krim 1944* (Frankfurt/Main, 1959); Eberhard von Mackensen, *Vom Bug zum Kaukasus: Das III. Panzerkorps im Feltzug gegen Sowjetrussland 1941/42* (Neckargemünd, Germany, 1967); and David Wingeate Pike, 'Les Forces Allemandes dans le Sud–Oest de la France, Mai–Juillet 1944', *Guerres Mondiales et Conflicts Contemporaines*, XXXVIII/152 (1988), p. 8. The foreign volunteers in the German army, comprisong some 72 battalions in all, were considered to be supplementary troops (*ersatzpersonal*), and were generally divided into two groups, the *Caucasians*, including the Christian Armenians and Georgians and others who came from west of the Volga, and the *Mongols*, or "Asiatic Peoples', mostly Muslims, who were less highly considered and assigned to more menial tasks. The former were sent principally to two theaters of operations, the Southeast (Italy), and the West (France, Belgium and Holland), where they helped round up Jews for shipment to Auschwitz, while both groups were sent to Central Asia and the Caucasus. See David Wingeate Pike, 'Les Forces Allemandes dans le Sud–Oest de la France, Mai–Juillet 1944', *Guerres Mondiales et Conflicts Contemporaines*, XXXVIII/152 (1988), pp. 20–23; Carlos Caballero Jurado, *Foreign Volunteers of the Wehrmacht, 1941–1945* (London, Osprey, 1983). On the cooperation of some Armenians with Nazi propaganda activities in Europe and the Middle East see Paul Leverkuehn, *German Military Intelligence* (London, Weidenfeld and Nicolson, 1954); David Kahn, *Hitler's Spies* (New York, 1978), pp. 236–237; Barry Rubin, *Istanbul Intrigues*, pp. 56–61; Julius Mader,, *Hitlers Spionagegenerale sagen aus: Ein Dokumentarbericht über Aufbau, Struktur und Operationen des OKW–Geheimdienstamtes Ausland/Abwehr mit einer Chronologie seiner Einsätze von 1933 bis 1944* (Berlin, 1974), pp. 96–97, 26, 46–47, 361–362 and *passim*; Heinz Höhne, *Canaris* (New York, Doubleday, 1979), pp. 482–3; H.D. Schmidt, 'The Nazi Party in Palestine and the Levant, 1932–1939', *International Affairs* XXVIII/4 (October 1952), pp. 460–469; Bernest Bramsted., *Goebbels and National Socialist Propaganda, 1925–1945* (London, 1965). The exact connection between the 1914 Armenian revolt at Van and the Russian invasion of eastern Anatolia later the same year remains to be studied.

depressed economic conditions, wild inflation, shortages of food and other necessities due to an almost complete cessation of imports from the outside world, and the very substantial budgetary deficits caused by wartime mobilization measures adopted because of the fear of an imminent Nazi invasion.[72] Mobilization of its army alone caused its expenditures on national defense to increase from T.L. 164 to T.L. 542 million by the early months of 1943, while normal taxes paid for no more than one-third of this amount. At the same time the conscription of thousands of cultivators into the army reduced food and industrial production, leading to severe shortages of the basic necessities of life and rapid price increases for the goods left on the civilian market, a situation ready-made for businessmen and farmers who made the situation even more difficult by hoarding the remaining supplies and increasing prices substantially in the face of popular demand. The prices of raw materials rose from a base price of 100 in 1938 to 306.8 in 1942 and 453.3 a year later, while consumer prices in Istanbul rose from a base of 100 in 1938 to 132.5 in 1941, 211.5 in 1942 and 289 in 1943,[73] despite price controls, resulting in tremendous popular agitation against these 'war profiteers' who were making fortunes while the mass of people were suffering.

To solve these problems the Turkish government initially introduced rationing and price controls, but in the face of the tremendous economic and political pressures as well as inefficiency in enforcing the regulations, these were largely unsuccessful as the shortages and inflation mounted. Starting in the late months of 1942, therefore, the government undertook a series of drastic tax increases which staggered all parts of the economy even more than the conditions which had led to them. Following enactment of a series of huge increases of excise and income taxes, on 11 November 1942 the Grand National Assembly enacted the most disastrous of these, the *Varlık Vergisi*, or Wealth Tax, program which in order to raise the equivalent of some $360 million to pay for the extremely large army being maintained against the possibility of a German invasion through Greece, taxed the capital of those who had property and were thought to be making large

---

72. Turkey's tremendous budgetary problems during the war and the desperate efforts made to solve them are detailed in Ertuğrul Baydar, *Ikinci Dünya Savaşı Içinde Türk Bütçeleri* (Turkish Budgets during the Second World War) (Ankara, 1978).

73. *Istanbul Ticaret ve Sanayi Odası Mecmuası,* LX/1 (January 1944), and LX/2 (February 1944).

profits as a result of the war emergency.[74] Added advantages of the tax were to be its role in stifling the support which it was felt that the Nazis were gaining among Christian businessmen in Istanbul as well as in limiting the role of non-Muslims in the marketplace and withdrawing excess currency from circulation, which, it was hoped, would lead to a decrease in prices. [75]

The tax in itself was a fairly common practice in Europe at the time, but it was administered in such a way to bear most heavily on the easily accessible wealth of urban merchants, many of whom were non Muslims, who seemed to be the only ones in the country who had ready cash available to contribute to the national emergency.

A total of 114,368 individuals were determined to be subject to the tax, owing T.L. 465.4 million. Local assessment commissions (*mahalli takdir komisyonları*) of Finance Ministry officials and local merchants and notables were organized to assess and levy the taxes in each district. Their decisions could not be appealed, and the amounts due had to be paid within a very short period of time, as little as two weeks in many cases. As it turned out, the assessments were based on very limited information and were therefore often crudely assessed and collected, taxing some far more than they had and others far less.[76]

Those who lacked financial liquidity and were required to pay the tax at once had to sell everything or declare bankruptcy and even work on government projects, particularly at the labor camp at Aşkale, in eastern Turkey near Erzurum, in order to pay their debts, in the process losing most or all of their properties. The first train caravan carrying delinquent taxpayers from Istanbul to Aşkale left on 27 January 1943 with 32 men; there followed ten more caravans carrying 410 men during the first five months of 1943. A total of 2,057 persons were sent to holding camps for transportation

74. Law no. 6/4067. See TBMM *Zabıt Ceridesi, Devre 6, i4, cilt 30, 23 inikat,* 4 January 1943 and *Ulus,* 1 January 1943. *Varlık Vergisi hakkında kanun,* no. 4305. 11 Teşrinisani 1942. *Sicilli Kavanin* no. 23 (1942), pp. 901–907. See also the details in Şevket Süreyya Aydemir, *Ikinci Adam: Ismet Inönü, 1938–1950* (Istanbul, Remzi, 1967), pp. 228–236; Cemil Koçak, *Türkiyede Milli Şef Dönemi,* pp. 367–373; and Rıdvan Akar, *Varlık Vergisi* (Istanbul, 1992).

75. Rıdvan Akar, *Varlık Vergisi* (Istanbul, 1992).

76. The criticisms are given in detail in Ahmet Emin Yalman, *Yakın Tarihte Gördüklerim ve Geçirdiklerim* (4 volumes, Istanbul, 1971), III, 375–391, summarized in *Turkey in My Time* (University of Oklahoma Press, 1957), pp. 205–208; also Cemil Koçak, *Türkiyede Milli Şef Dönemi,* pp. 530–544, and Faik Ökte, *Varlık Vergisi Faciası* (Istanbul, 1951).

to Aşkale, but many of these paid their debts when they saw the government was serious in collecting what they owed, so only two-thirds of that number actually went.[77] Out of a total of 1,400 persons sent to Aşkale during 1943, 1,229 came from Istanbul, and 21 died while there.[78]

The eminent Turkish journalist Ahmet Emin Yalman, himself a crypto-Jew, or *dönme*, led those who criticized the law and its application, even as he justified its enactment and enforcement:

> The government, misled on the one side by financial difficulties, on the other by a misconception of 'social justice,' established a Capital Levy (*Varlık Vergisi*) levied on all those in the country who had property. It was true that huge amounts of illicit money had accumulated during the war in the hands of a few at the expense of the general public and in disregard of the spirit of our laws. It was also true that much of this money was in the hands of minorities and foreigners, who predominated in certain commercial fields. Many of these people, not entrusted to share in the defense of the country in armed military service, were not proving themselves loyal citizens. Pressed by the costs of keeping a million men under arms, the government was obliged to establish a capital levy; and it was entitled to do so, especially after leading commercial circles displayed a reluctance to share the nation's financial burden. Many businessmen even refused to subscribe to government bonds, which bore high interest rates.
>
> The Varlık was announced and carried out under such conditions that, while it did bring in some revenue, it was highly detrimental to the government's moral and material credit both at home and abroad. To begin with, the tax law prescribed no scale. Local commissions could use their judgment in making assessments. Then, there was no right of complaint or appeal. If the commission thought you had one million and chose to assess you for eight hundred thousand, while in reality you had only five hundred thousand, you were still indebted for three hundred thousand after paying all you had, and you could also be exiled for

---

77. See, for example, the report in *Ulus*, 28 January 1943, and *Tan*, 20 and 23 January 1943.

78. Cemil Koçak, *Türkiye'de Millî Şef Dönemi*, p. 541.

nonpayment of the rest. Data for Varlık assessments were gathered in unusually well-guarded secrecy. A good job had been done in establishing files on the sources of wealth of a long list of individuals, and considering the almost limitless possibilities of bribes, relatively little corruption was involved. Still, the data were inadequate, and discriminations of a political or religious character were often made, so that much injustice resulted. Above all, the scheme disregarded constitutional guarantees and was in open contradiction to fundamental principles of the regime. When exceptions, based on rights guaranteed in various conventions and treaties, were made for foreign residents as a result of complaints from their embassies and legations, Turkish victims of the tax openly resented less favorable treatment in their own country than foreign residents received. This was particularly bitter to the Turkish mind because it recalled the days when the Capitulations existed and foreigners' privileges were above native laws and regulations.

The tax was enforced in an atmosphere of terror which made open criticism impossible. I could only venture some indirect hints; and I tried to show the good sides of the tax in private discussions with foreign friends, who were furiously indignant. In the long run, the arbitrary application of the tax levy, the injustices, and the loss of moral and material credit at home and abroad left me no choice. I began to attack the whole scheme more and more boldly. By then, the government also had seen its error and had started to ease the burden. First, the tax on salaried people was abolished, so the honest ones who had paid were in fact penalized, in contrast to those who had not paid, and whose debt was now entirely wiped out. Then, the whole tax was abolished and all remaining indebtedness arising from it was erased, resulting in a further injustice to those who had paid and benefiting only those who had refused to pay.[79]

---

79. Ahmet Emin Yalman, *Turkey in My Time,* pp. 205–206. See also his *Yakın Tarihte Gördüklerim ve Geçirdiklerim* III, 375–383 where he discusses the tax in even more detail.

In the end the Wealth Tax produced revenues amounting to approximately T.L. 318 million, which greatly helped the government solve its financial difficulties, but the collections were far short of the expected T.L. 463 million,[80] and the law met with widespread criticism from throughout the political spectrum in Turkey as well as outside.[81]

The inconsistent and unequal application of the law by local councils and the bureaucracy hurt Muslims and non-Muslims alike, but the latter were particularly hard-hit and the economy was devastated. Within a few months of its enactment, therefore, the government saw the futility of removing people from their ability to produce the wealth that the Treasury was trying to tax, so as a result of the direct intervention of President Ismet Inönü all those sent to Aşkale were pardoned and returned to their homes in September 1943, and the tax was entirely annulled by a law enacted on 15 March 1944. [82]

The virtual exclusion of agriculture from the tax was so glaring, moreover, that soon afterwards the Agricultural Produce Tax Law (*Toprak Mahsulleri Vergisi Kanunu*) was enacted on 15 May 1943.[83] This tax bore very heavily on the cultivators, almost all of whom were Muslims, but the legislators had learned from the Wealth Tax disaster so that this law was much more fairly and efficiently administered, and the result was to secure considerably more revenue for the war effort without the kind of negative effects produced by the Wealth Tax.

That the Wealth Tax was not directed primarily against Jewish Turks, moreover, is shown by the fact that it was never accompanied by any sort of organized, government-sponsored anti-Semitic propaganda such as that which the Nazis spread through Germany and the German occupied

---

80. Yahya Tezel, *Cumhuriyet Döneminin Iktisadi Tarihi, 1923–1950* (Economic History of the Republican Period, 1923–1950) (2nd edn, Ankara, 1986), pp. 225–226; Giacomo Saban, 'Ebrei di Turchia (2): Gli Anni Difficili', *La Rassegna Mensile di Israel* LVI (1990), pp. 172–173.

81. For example, Ahmet Emin Yalman, 'Harp Kazançlarından Alınacak Vergi', *Vatan*, 29 May 1942; Zekeriye Sertel in *Tan* on 10 June and 11 June 1942.

82. *11 Teşrini Sani 1942 tarihli Varlık Vergisi Kanununa ek Kanun* (Supplementary law to the *Varlık Vergisi* law of 11 November 1942), *Sicilli Kavanin* 24 (1943), p. 740; *Varlık Vergisinin bakayasının terkinine dair kanun, no. 4530*, 15 March 1944, *Sicilli Kavanin* 25 (1944), pp. 97–98.

83. Yahya Tezel, *Cumhuriyet Döneminin Iktisadi Tarihi, 1923–1950* (Economic History of the Republican Period, 1923–1950) (2nd edn, Ankara, 1986), pp. 226–227.

countries at the same time, that most Muslim Turks themselves never showed anti-Semitism either before, during or after the program was in force, and that Jewish youths continued to join their fellow Muslim citizens in accepting conscription and serving in the armed forces with enthusiasm.

Most Turks were in fact impressed by the strong support of the British and American war efforts by Zionists in Europe and America, a fact which in combination with the historic identity and brotherhood of Turks and Jews in the Ottoman Empire, may well have provided the principal motivation for the efforts of the Turkish government and its representatives in Nazi-occupied Europe to rescue Jewish Turks from Nazi persecution and, despite numerous protests by both the British and the Nazis, for its granting permission to the Jewish Agency and other Zionist immigration groups to operate freely in Istanbul throughout the war and to send many of the refugees on to Palestine.[84]

Jewish Turks not affected by the tax continued their lives normally, concluding that while a very few of their number were suffering inordinately, even they were, at most, being sent to labor camps, while the Turkish government was saving all Jews in the country, and many Jews elsewhere in Europe, from the far more devastating fate of their co-religionists at the hands of the Nazis.

The famous Jewish historian Avram Galante was in fact elected as a deputy from Istanbul to the Grand National Assembly in 1943, shortly after the Wealth Tax was put into effect, while one of its principal advocates and defenders, Yunus Nadi, who had openly supported the Nazis in his newspaper *Cumhuriyet*,[85] was publicly excoriated by President Ismet Inönü on the train platform of the Ankara railroad station because of his open support of Nazi causes,[86] and in the same election soon afterwards was deprived of his seat in the Grand National Assembly as deputy from Muğla, while publication of his newspapers was suspended for several weeks.[87]

---

84. See p. 257 of this volume and *passim*.

85. See p. 28 of this volume.

86. Metin Toker, *Demokrasimizin Ismet Paşalı Yılları, 1944–1973: Tek Partiden Çok Partiye, 1944–1950*, (3rd edn, Istanbul, 1990), p. 22; Rubin, *Istanbul Intrigues*, p. 45.

87. *Cumhuriyet, Tan, Son Posta*, 1 March 1943. Laurence Steinhardt to Secretary of State no. 379, 1 March 1943. Department of State Archives Decimal File 867.00/3229.

American Ambassador Laurence Steinhardt thus reported to Washington on 9 March 1943:

> The election returns published this morning for the new Grand National Assembly disclose that the candidates known to be outstandingly friendly to the United States were reelected whereas Yunus Nadi, owner and publisher of the leading pro-Nazi newspaper was defeated . . . . There is a general feeling that his defeat may be largely attributed to his outspoken pro-Axis sympathies but another and perhaps more important reason was his failure to remain on good terms with the Party largely as a result of the embarrassment he has caused it by a tactless manifestation of his pro-Axis feelings on critical occasions.[88]

Many of those Jewish Turks whose families were most severely effected by the tax and its enforcement remain proud that their payments materially assisted Turkey in resolving its financial difficulties caused by the Nazi threat and that their country did more than any other country in Europe to save Jews from the Nazis. Most who suffered remained in Turkey following the war, moreover, rebuilt their businesses and fortunes, and continue as prosperous members of Turkish society to the present day.

---

88. Laurence Steinhardt to Secretary of State no. 301, 'Reporting Results of National Elections to Seventh Grand National Assembly', 9 March 1943: Department of State Archives Decimal File 867.00/3243. Also Barry Rubin, *Istanbul Intrigues*, p. 45.

2

Turkey's Role in Rescuing Jews from the Nazis during the Holocaust

JEWISH TURKS IN FRANCE AT THE START OF THE GERMAN OCCUPATION

Just as important as providing a haven for Jews who had lived in the Ottoman Empire for centuries was Turkey's role in helping rescue many Jewish Turks who were resident in Nazi-occupied western Europe during the Holocaust. At the start of World War II, about ten thousand Jewish Turks lived in France,[89] out of a total Jewish population of slightly over three hundred thousand, and probably an equal number of Jewish Turks lived in the remainder of western Europe. Of the 113,467 Jews over fifteen years of age resident in Paris, out of a total population of 1.7 million, approximately one-third were born outside France, including 3,381 in Turkey.[90] Of these, not surprisingly, 13.2 percent were in some sort of industry and 33.8 in commerce, while 48.4 percent, mostly housewives, were

---

89. This figure excludes Turkish Jews who had taken up French citizenship and were no longer carried on the roles of the Turkish consulates.

90. Annie Benveniste, *La Bosphore à la Roquette: La communauté judéo–espagnole à Paris (1914–1940)*, Jacques Adler, *The Jews of Paris and the Final Solution* (New York and Oxford, 1987), pp. 8–10. In the German-sponsored census held in the Fall of 1940, the numbers of foreign Jews resident in Paris were: Poland, 26,158; Russia, 7,298; Rumania, 4,382; Turkey, 3,381; Hungary, 1,926; Germany, 1,703; and Greece, 1, 642. Of course many of those listed as French citizens were in fact born in the Ottoman Empire or Turkey but had given up their citizenship.

not listed as having any occupation.[91] Jews constituted, however, very large proportions of the professionals in France. They were 12.5 percent of the physicians, fifty-seven percent each of the bankers and furriers, sixty-one percent of the shirtmakers, forty-five percent of the diamond merchants, and forty-three percent of the hat makers, a situation which stimulated a good deal of anti-Semitism among their French competitors as well as others in the country.[92]

Some of the Jewish Turks or their parents or grandparents had settled in France as long before as late Ottoman times, particularly those who had been trained in French culture at the schools established in the empire during the nineteenth century by the Paris-based *Alliance Israélite Universelle*, and who had feared what would happen following the dethronement in 1909 of Sultan Abdülhamid II, long a friend of the Jews.[93] Some had accompanied the French army which had occupied parts of Istanbul and southeastern Turkey following World War I, and which was evacuated in 1920 as a result of a separate treaty signed with the leaders of the Turkish War for Independence, going for the most part in fear of a triumph by the Greek army which had taken Izmir and advanced well into the southwestern part of the country, persecuting, massacring and attacking Jews as well as Muslims as they went.[94] Many others had gone in the 1920s when the newly established Turkish Republic was just beginning its radical reforms under the leadership of Mustafa Kemal and the future seemed very uncertain. Most had settled in the *Faubourg Saint Antoine* area of the 11th District in Paris, where they formed a 'little Turkey', speaking Turkish and/or Judeo-Spanish as well as French and practising the same occupations they had in the Ottoman Empire.[95]

According to Article 88 of the Turkish Constitution enacted in 1923, all persons living permanently in Turkey were Turkish citizens, and they remained citizens even if they lived outside the country for any length of time, as did their children, so long as they were properly registered with the

---

91. Adler, *Jews of Paris*, p. 18.

92. Adler, *Jews of Paris*, p. 20

93. Aron Rodrigue, *French Jews, Turkish Jews The Alliance Israelite Universelle and the Politics of Jewish Schooling in Turkey, 1860–1925* (Bloomington, Indiana, 1990); also Stanford J. Shaw, *The Jews of the Ottoman Empire and the Turkish Republic* (London and New York, 1991), pp. 163–166; Benveniste, *Roquette*, p. 43; Michel Roblin, *Les Juifs de Paris* (Paris, Picard, 1952).

94. Shaw, *ibid.*, pp. 238–240.; Benveniste, *Roquette*, pp. 36–37, 43–49.

95. Benveniste, *Roquette*, pp. 64–65, 89–124, 165–171.

nearest Turkish consulate. However because of the tendency of many of those resident abroad to lose all contact with the country, and in fact to assume citizenship of the country in which they lived, new Turkish citizenship laws enacted in 1935 decreed that those who had not returned to Turkey to take part in the Turkish War for Independence, or within five years following its conclusion, would automatically lose their Turkish citizenship; while those who had gone to live outside the country subsequently had to register with the consulates where they lived every five years, so that the latter could care for their interests, or their citizenship would end as well. While some did register, most Jewish Turks living in Europe did not see any need to do so, since most of them were now citizens of France and other west European countries, thus causing their Turkish citizenship to lapse in 1940, just as the Nazis occupied most of Europe.

PERSECUTION OF JEWS IN FRANCE DURING THE OCCUPATION

On 20 May 1940, almost immediately after the German conquest of France and the Low Countries, a German ordinance decreed by the *Militärbefehlshaber in Frankreich* (Military Commander in France) established the principle of German control over all enterprises in the conquered countries by military administrators to assure the provisioning of their people and maintenance of economic life.[96] On 27 September 1940, the German military administrator in occupied France promulgated a series of measures against its Jews, who were defined as being persons currently belonging to the Jewish religion who had more than two Jewish grandparents.[97] In the same month, a census was ordered of all Jews in occupied France. The Third German ordinance against the Jews, issued on 26 April 1941, stated that anyone who had three Jewish grandparents was considered to be Jewish, as well as anyone whose grandparents were Jewish

---

96. Association Les Fils et Filles des Déportés Juifs de France, *Les Juifs sous l'Occupation: Recueil des Textes Officiels Français et Allemands 1940/1944* (Centre de Documentation Juive Contemporaine, Paris, 1982) (hereafter referred to as LJSO), pp. 15–17.

97. LJSO, pp. 18–19, modified in the Third Ordinance regarding Jews, issued on 26 April 1941: LJSO, pp. 41–44, and the Fourth Ordinance regarding Jews, issued on 28 May 1941. LJSO, pp. 47–49; Also Warren Green, 'The Fate of Oriental Jews in Vichy France', *Wiener Library Bulletin* XXXII/49–50 (1979), pp. 40–50; and Warren Paul Green, 'The Karaite Passage in A. Anatoli's Babi Yar', *East European Quarterly*, XII (1978), pp. 283–287.

and was a member of the Jewish religion or married to a Jew.[98] This definition was repeated in *Statut des Juifs* issued by the Vichy government on 3 October and, in revised form, on 2 June 1941.

In occupied France, Jews were required to register in their sub-préfectures and not to leave their homes without permission, with those who had left for unoccupied France being prohibited from returning. They were not permitted to engage in any sort of trade or commerce,[99] and where Jewish owned shops were turned over to Christians for operation, signs had to be posted in both German and French designating them as Jewish establishments.[100] Starting with a decree issued on 18 October 1940, Jewish establishments were ordered to be 'Aryanized' by a commission directed by one of the occupation forces officials in charge of economic affairs, Dr. Blanke. They were to be turned over to Christian French administrators and subsequently sold by them, at minimum prices, to Christians, preferably Aryans, with the receipts being turned over to the *Caisse des Dépôts et Consignations,* nominally at least for the use of the former owners, though in fact the latter were to receive no more than annual interest payments of two and one half percent without being able to withdraw the principal.[101]

Starting on 4 September 1940, the Germans began to open Jewish safe deposit boxes in occupied France and to confiscate the contents. French banks in turn began to insist on receiving certificates of non-Jewishness from Christian customers and to close out the boxes of all those who did not comply. Many Armenians, like the Karaites, had secured exemption from the anti-Jewish laws, though by claiming they were Aryans instead of Turks, as the latter had done.[102] The Armenians had, indeed, been certified as

---

98. Serge Klarsfeld, *1941: Les Juifs en France: Préludes à la Solution Finale* (Paris, 1991), p. 22.

99. LJSO, pp. 94–95; French Foreign Ministry (Vichy) to Turkish Embassy to Paris (Vichy) no. 101, 13 January 1943; Archives of the Turkish Embassy (Paris).

100. LJSO, pp. 67–67. German ordinances of 27 September 1940 and 16 October 1940.

101. LJSO, pp. 17–18, 114–127. German ordinances of 20 May and 18 October 1940 and 26 April 1941. Turkish Consul-General (Paris) to Turkish Ambassador to Paris (Vichy) no. 82, 3 March 1941, Archives of Turkish Consulate-General (Paris). The process is described in a report from Turkey's Paris Consulate-General to the Ambassador to Paris (Vichy), 12 February 1941, no. 176–122–6127, in the Archives of the Turkish Embassy (Paris).

102. The Karaite Jews were for the most part exempted by the Germans from the anti-Jewish laws. The Germans accepted the Karaite claim that they were not racially Jewish, that they were in fact Turks, descendants of the Turkish Khazars of Central Asia, and that they therefore had no ethnic relation to the Jews of Europe: *See* Warren Paul Green, 'The Nazi Racial Policy toward the Karaites', *Soviet Jewish Affairs,* VIII (1978), pp. 36–44, Philip

Aryans by the German racial authorities of the *Reichstelle fur Sippenforschung*, and even had entered the Nazi armed forces, both by enlistment and by conscription and to serve among the 'Europeans,' unlike Turks and others who were consigned to the 'Mongols,' auxiliaries destined for menial duties. At times, however, in Paris they still were mistaken for Jews, so they went to great lengths to secure certificates of Aryanism from the German Embassy or of non-Jewishness from the Turkish Consulate-General[103] or from the *Commissariat Général aux questions Juives* (CGQJ), assisting the latter in return.[104]

On 29 March 1941, the latter was established under the initial direction of the virulent anti-Semite Xavier Vallat to constitute a Central Office in order to 'recognize and eliminate Jews from all interference in the vital domains and publish law, and then to administer the Jews and their properties under central direction until they are evacuated', thus to organize and direct German and French policies relative to Jews.[105] It subsequently proposed to the government 'legislative and measures needed to carry out the government decisions in principle regarding the Jews, their civil and political capacity, their right to exercise functions, employment and professions . . . to assure the coordination needed between the different departments of government to apply these laws and decisions, to arrange the administration and liquidation of Jewish properties and businesses, as

---

Friedman, 'The Karaites under Nazi rule', *On the Track of Tyranny* (London, 1960), pp. 97–123, and *Roads to Extinction: Essays on the Holocaust,* eds Philip Friedman and Ada June Friedman (New York and Philadelphia, Jewish Publication Society of America, 1980), pp. 153–175; Shmuel Spector, 'The Karaites in Nazi-occupied Europe as Reflected in German Documents', (in Hebrew) *Pe'amin* no. 29 (1986), pp. 90–108; Joseph Billig, *Le Commissariat Général aux Questions Juives* (2 vols, Paris, 1957) II, 158–164. *Also* the monumental study of Patrik von zur Mühlen, *Zwischen Hakenkreuz und Sowjetstern: Der Nationalismus der sowjetischen Orientvölker im Zweiten Weltkrieg* (Düsseldorf, Droste, 1971), pp. 50–51.

103. Request of Behar Deroyan to Turkish Consulate-General (Paris) for certification that he is not a Jew. Report of Turkish Consulate-General (Paris) no. 1943/1848, 26 May 1943. Archives of Turkish Consulate-General (Paris).

104. Ministère des Affaires Etrangères (Vichy), Service des Etrangères, 14 May 1942 to Ministry of the Interior, Secretary General of the Police, and Commissariat General aux Questions Juives, in Archives of Ministère des Affaires Etrangères (Quai d'Orsay), *Guerre 1939–1945, Vichy, Europe, serie C, 140*, fol. 48; Asher Cohen, 'Le Peuple Aryen vu par le Commissariate General aux Questions Juives', *Revue d'Histoire de la Deuxieme Guerre Mondiale et des Conflits Contemporains*, XXXVI/141 (1986), pp. 45–58.

105. Joseph Billig, *Le Commissariat Général aux Questions Juives* (2 vols, Paris, 1957) II, 158–164.

prescribed by law, taking into account the needs of the national economy, and to designate agents for these operations as well as supervising their activities, and to ultimately provoke police measures regarding Jews'. In fulfillment of this mission, among other things, it organized anti-Semitic exhibitions in Paris and elsewhere in France.[106]

To facilitate the rapid confiscation of Jewish properties, on 2 June 1941 a census of Jews was carried out in both occupied and occupied France.[107] Seizure of Jewish-owned apartments, shops and factories followed.[108] As a first step the law of 22 July 1941 decreed that enterprises belonging to Jews had to be provided with temporary Christian administrators as a first step toward 'eliminating all Jewish influence in national life'.[109] To carry it out, on 17 November 1941, the CGQJ was authorized to appoint French provisional administrators to take over all Jewish industrial, commercial and artisan enterprises as well as living quarters, both houses and apartments, and all equipment, goods, furnishings and the like within these properties.[110]

Even as these efforts went forward, Reinhardt Heydrich, chief of Hitler's Security Police, including both the Gestapo and the *Sicherheitsdienst* (SD), which controlled the concentration camps, obtained from Hermann Göring a new decree enlarging his anti-Jewish mission to include not only eliminating the influence of Jews by evacuating them from Europe, either by force or by urging them to emigrate to other countries, as ordered on 24 January 1939, but also by replacing the previous policy to one of annihilation, thus formally beginning execution of the Final Solution.[111] Between 20 and 25 August 1941, the German military held the first of a series of forced raffles among the Jews of Paris in which the 'winners' were arrested and sent to concentration camps on their way to Auschwitz for extermination.[112] Himmler followed on 23 October 1941 with regulations prohibiting all Jewish emigration from Germany, German-occupied areas, and Vichy France in order to facilitate their arrest and shipment to the death camps.[113]

---

106. Klarsfeld, *1941:*, p. 19; Michael Marrus and Robert Paxton, *Vichy France and the Jews*, pp. 71–115.

107. Published in the *Journal Officiel* on 14 June 1941.

108. LJSO, p. 53, 129–133.

109. LJSO, pp. 62–66; Klarsfeld, *1941*, p. 57.

110. Published in the *Journal Officiel* (Paris) on 1 and 2 Dec.1941.

111. Klarsfeld, *1941*, p. 57.

112. Klarsfeld, *1941*, p. 59.

113. Klarsfeld, *1941*, p. 80.

On 12 August 1941 a newly-built apartment complex in the Paris suburb of Drancy was turned into a concentration camp[114] intended mainly for foreign Jews being prepared for transportation to Auschwitz.[115] The *Camp d'Internement de Drancy,* since 1946 restored as a housing complex and renamed *Cité de la Muette,* was operated by the French police under the command of the *Préfecture de Police, Direction des Étrangers et des Affaires Juives* from its establishment until June 1943. The SS guards who patrolled within the camp were commanded at first by Theo Dannecker, *Judenreferat* (Jewish Expert) of the occupation authorities in France and Chief of the Service IV of the Gestapo, then by *Obersturmführer* Heinz Röthke from July 1942 until the end of 1943. Finally it was put under the direction of Alois Brunner, who was in charge of putting the Final Solution policies into full force at the camp during 1943–1944, bringing to an end the overall control previously exercised by the French police, coercing some Jews into serving to help annihilate their co-religionists, and in particular targeting children and French Jews for extermination so that twenty four thousand Jews were deported from Drancy to the death camps during his period of command.[116] The guards outside the camp were always French, and they were said to have behaved in an even more brutal fashion against the Jewish inmates than the SS guards within.[117]

For the Jewish Turks at Drancy, even more serious than the brutal treatment meted out by French gendarmes[118] and German SS guards alike,[119] the semi-starvation and ravages of the black market run by Jews, the illness and deaths by suicide or brutality as well as natural causes,[120] and the like, was the division of the inmates by nationality and the persecution to

---

114. Maurice Rajsfus, *Drancy: Un camp de concentration très ordinaire, 1941–1944* (Paris, 1991), pp. 83–128.

115. Rajsfus, *Drancy,* p. 146–147; Philippe Bourdrel, *Histoire des Juifs de France,* p. 215.

116. Mary Felstiner, 'Commander of Drancy: Alois Brunner and the Jews of France', *Holocaust and Genocide Studies* II /1 (1987), pp. 21–47.

117. For details regarding Nazi persecution of Jews in France, see the monumental works of Serge Klarsfeld as well as the archives of Marc Jerblum, one of the leaders of the Jewish resistance in France during World War II, in the Yad Vashem Central Archives (Jerusalem), no.p-7.

118. Rajsfus, pp. 83–103.

119. Rajsfus, pp. 215–275

120. Turkish Consulate-General (Paris) to Turkish Embassy (Berlin) no. 1942/5, 6 January 1942; Turkish Consulate-General (Paris) to Turkish Foreign Ministry (Ankara) no. 109/42, 9 March 1942, no. 192, 28 April 1942. The miserable conditions of life in the Drancy camp are vividly described in Rajsfus, *Drancy,* particularly on pp. 46–92.

which they were subjected by the French Jews in the camp, many of whom had assimilated the vicious anti-Turkish and anti-Muslim prejudices which had been so prevalent in Christian Europe since the Middle Ages:

There were there Frenchmen, Poles, Turks, and the like. I was chief of the room and I never succeeded in being able to place myself between the yiddishists and the hispano-Turcs, who constantly intrigued for a few more bits of bread . . . . [121] They lived by nationality, by groups, by compatriots. Each looked after only his own interests and not those of his neighbor . . . . The internees deplored that there was little solidarity among them. The most striking manifestation of this seemed to be the frequent discussions which opposed some to others, in particular French and foreign Jews. The French Jews reproached the foreigners for being the cause of their misfortunes, and the latter complained about France. Perhaps it is necessary to lay the responsibility at the door of the French Jews, many of whom came to the camp saying that they were superior Jews and that they would be released before the others. But one must recognize that their bitterness was justified, particularly when they were war veterans who had performed their duty for their country and who could not understand how they could be treated differently than their fellow citizens . . . . [122] The French and foreign Jews interned at the camp formed two hostile groups: the French Jews affirmed that their being there was the fault of the foreigners and they hoped for a special treatment by the authorities which never in fact came. The French Jews believed that they would be freed soon and they did not want to be seen in total solidarity with the foreigners . . . . The French Jew believed that it was because of the former that he was in the camp. He spoke of the foreign Jew with disdain . . . . Their deception brought even more bitterness when they saw that the Germans made no distinction between Jews and Jews . . . The foreign Jews in turn reproached the

---

121. Archives of the *Centre de Documentation Juive Contemporaine* (Paris), DLVI–99, quoted in Rajsfus, p. 69.

122. *Centre de Documentation Juive Contemporaine* archives, CCXIII–85, quoted in Rajsfus, p. 67.

French Jews for the attitude of France. This led to interminable discussions that ended in tumult and dispute . . . . [123]

Even more serious than the quarrels, the discussions, the arguments and the violence between French and foreign Jews was the discrimination against the latter carried out, not only by the guards, but also by the Jewish organizations and individuals put in charge of the camp by the SS, all of whom were French Jews who looked out for their fellows at the expense of the foreigners, following a policy promoted by the *Commissariat Général aux Questions Juives* in order to keep the prisoners divided by setting up classes of favorites and privileged groups.[124]

In both occupied and Vichy France, Jewish access to the professions was increasingly restricted. Jews were limited to no more than three percent of secondary and university students and to two percent of physicians, attorneys, architects, pharmacists, surgeons and dentists, considerably less than that which they had occupied previously. At the same time the *Institut d'Étude des Questions Juives* (Institute to Study Jewish Questions) was established in Paris to direct and promote pseudo-scientific research on Jews and the 'Jewish Question', and it began to publish anti-Semitic propaganda in the monthly *Le Cahier Juive* as well as in films and other forms of public dissemination.[125] Starting on 5 September 1941, it opened the first of a series of anti-Semitic exhibitions in Paris.[126]

On 21 November 1941, the *Union Général des Israélites de France* was established by the Vichy government in place of all other Jewish organizations, which were dissolved and their property confiscated, to serve as its principal instrument to organize and control the French Jews who remained in both occupied and unoccupied France,[127] all of whom were required to be affiliated with it. As it turned out, however, this organization served not only to facilitate German and French control over Jews but also

---

123. *Centre de Documentation Juive Contemporaine* archives, CCXIII–106, quoted in Rajsfus, pp. 67–68.

124. Rajsfus, pp. 72–75, 226–227; Michael R. Marrus, 'Jewish Leaders and the Holocaust', *French Historical Studies* XV (1987), pp. 316–331, however, denies the charge that French Jews sacrificed foreign Jews to save their own lives, while admitting that some wealthy members of French Jewry did act in this manner to save themselves, their families and their properties.

125. Published in the *Journal Officiel* of 11 June 1942.

126. Klarsfeld, *1941*, pp. 67, 72.

127. Law no. 5047 of 29 November 1941, in the *Journal Officiel,* 1 and 2 December 1941. LJSO, pp. 147–150.

to provide assistance to those who, deprived of most occupations, were falling into increasing poverty and despair.[128]

In the middle of July 1942, mass arrests and deportations of Jews in both zones of France began. Those who were allowed to remain in their homes were subjected to all sorts of restrictions.[129] Jews could not have telephones or radios in their homes.[130] They were prohibited from using bicycles on the public streets of Paris.[131] They could not leave their homes between 8 p.m. and 6 a.m. or change their places of residence without permission,[132] and they were forbidden to attend cinemas or other public entertainments or enter stores frequented by non-Jews.[133] When they did walk outside their homes, they had to affix yellow stars with six points in a prominent place on their clothing with the word '*Juif*' attached in large black letters.[134] Jews who violated these and other restrictions of this sort were subjected to severe punishment, usually immediate dispatch to the Drancy camp, and from there to Auschwitz. Arrests were made summarily and arbitrarily, often on the streets with no warning, and without any notification to their relatives or friends or, in the case of Jewish Turks, to the Turkish consulate as to why they were arrested or where they were sent.

In many ways the officials of the Vichy government as well as the French population throughout the country were even more severe against the Jews than were the Nazis,[135] unlike in neighboring Holland and

---

128. Klarsfeld, *1941*, p. 82.

129. There are many accounts of the persecution of France's Jews. One of the most comprehensive is that of Jacques Adler, *The Jews of Paris and the Final Solution* (New York and Oxford, 1987). See also David Diamant, *Les Juifs dans la Résistance française, 1940–1944* (Paris, 1971); and Michael R. Marrus and Robert O. Paxton, *Vichy et les Juifs* (Paris, 1981).

130. Turkish Consulate-General (Paris) to Turkish Embassy to Paris (Vichy) no. 460, 2 September 1941. Archives of Turkish Consulate-General (Paris).

131. Turkish Consulate-General (Paris) to Turkish Embassy (Berlin) no. 1942/282, 22/23 May 1942. Archives of Turkish Consulate-General.

132. Turkish Consulate-General (Paris) to Turkish Embassy (Berlin) no. 101, 28 February 1942. Archives of Turkish Consulate-General (Paris).

133. LJSO, p. 162.

134. Regulation of 29 May 1942.

135. For example see the report by Georg Ebert, head of the West European section of the Foreign Policy Office of the Nazi Party (*Aussenpolitische Amt der NSDAP*), to Alfred Rosenberg (16 September 1938), on the situation in France, where the pro-Nazi groups were rapidly gaining ground and the French were introducing measures against the Jewish emigrées as well as against all those who opposed this policy. J. Billig, *Alfred Rosenberg dans l'action idéologique, politique et administrataive du Reich hitlérien: Inventaire commenté de la collection*

Belgium, whose political, religious and business leaders as well as the mass of the people took an active and public role in supporting civil rights for Jews despite Nazi pressure to the contrary.[136]

In seeking explanations for the French collapse in the face of the German blitzkrieg, the Vichy government found the Jews convenient scapegoats. The process began shortly after the Nazi occupation with the law of 7 October 1940 which abolished the full French citizenship given to Algerian Jews by the law of 24 October 1870.[137] The first *Statute des Juifs*, enacted by the Vichy government on 3 October 1940,[138] essentially revoked the Edict of Nantes, which had provided French Jews with full citizenship during the course of the French Revolution.[139] The law's stated purpose was to 'defend the French organism from the microbe that was leading it towards mortal anemia.' It went on to state that it was unacceptable that 'followers of a minority cult (i.e. the Jews) could exercise an influence in countries of Christian civilization.' Jews were prohibited from holding public positions such as Chief of State, member of the government, the Council of State, courts on all levels, most ministries, particularly those of Foreign Affairs and Interior, governors general and other colonial officials, teachers in public and most private schools, military officers, the national corps of mines and bridges, officials of companies having any business with the government, inspectors of finances and all elected offices. Exceptions were, however, allowed for veterans of World War I and the first year of World

---

de documents conserves au Centre de Documentation Juive Contemporaine provenant des Archives du Reichsleiter et Ministre A. Rosenberg (Paris, 1963), no. 569, p. 180.

136. Compare Shlomo Kles, 'Resistance and fighting in Belgium during the Holocaust', (in Hebrew), *Zion* XLVII (1982), pp. 463–482; Michael R. Marrus and Robert O. Paxton, *Vichy et les Juifs* (Paris, Calmann-Lévy, 1981), and *Vichy France and the Jews* (New York, Basic Books, 1981); Michael Ryan, 'Responses of the Churches in the Netherlands to the Nazi Occupation', in Michael Ryan and Pieter de Jong, eds, *Human Responses to the Holocaust: Perpetrators and Victims, Bystanders and Resisters* (New York: Edwin Mellen Pr., 1981), pp. 121–143.

137. LJSO, pp. 31–32: *Statut des Juis d'Algerie;* M. Ansky, *Les Juifs d'Algérie du décret Crémieux à La Liberation* (Paris, 1950), and M. Abutbol, *Les Juifs d'Afrique du Nord sous Vichy* (Paris, 1983).

138. Published in the *Journal Officiel* of 18 October 1940, so this is often mistakenly given as the date of the law. Serge Klarsfeld, *Le Statut des Juifs de Vichy: Documentation* (Association Les Fils et Filles des Déportés Juifs de France, Paris, 1990); LJSO, pp. 19–21, 49–53.

139. This decree was anulled by General Giraud on 14 March 1943, and by General Charles DeGaulle on 20 October 1943.

War II and holders of the Legion of Honor, thus enabling eminent professors like Louis Halphen and Marc Bloch to continue to teach for a time.[140] Jews were not allowed in media such as journalism, the theater, radio or the cinema without special permission.[141] Jews were not removed from industry, agriculture and commercial enterprises in unoccupied France, however, until the issuance of supplementary laws on 2 June, 22 July and 17 November 1941, promulgated on the pretext that it was necessary to take such action in order to avoid direct German intervention to 'Aryanize' Jewish enterprises in the unoccupied part of the country.[142] On 15 October 1941, the Ministry of the Interior of unoccupied France created the *Police aux Questions Juives* for the purpose of enforcing its orders and decrees.[143]

The Vichy government's definition of a Jew imitated that of the Germans in order to avoid differences and conflicts between the two zones, but it made it even more severe in its Second Ordinance regarding 'Measures Against the Jews' of 18 October 1940, defining as Jews those who not only currently but formerly followed the Jewish religion as well as those who had more than two Jewish grandparents, and adding a clause that a woman having only two Jewish grandparents was still considered to be a Jew if she married one.[144] This can be compared with a declaration in 1991 by Ovadia Joseph, Sephardic Chief Rabbi of Israel, that for Russian emigrants to be considered as Jewish, they had not merely to provide documentary proof that their mothers were Jewish, but that their family was Jewish over four generations.[145]

Supplementary laws banned Jews from the additional professions of banker, money changer, stock or property agent, commissionnaire or concessionaire of games, and editor, administrator or writer of newspapers, except those of a strictly scientific or religious nature. On 2 November 1941, Jews were prohibited from acquiring commercial property without special authorization.

On 28 October 1941, the Vichy government decreed that all foreign Jews should be interned in special camps or assigned residences by the préfects of police in the districts where they lived, starting a process in which, during the next three years, some 70,000 Jews, almost all immigrants

---

140. LJSO, pp. 60–61.
141. LJSO, pp. 159–161.
142. Published in the *Journal Officiel* (Paris) on 14 June 1941.
143. Klarsfeld, *1941*, p. 80.
144. LJSO, pp. 23–25.
145. *Deutsche Presse–Agentur*, 27 June 1991.

to France, passed through Drancy on their way to the East, of whom almost 67,000 never returned.[146]

During the summer of 1942, moreover, all foreign male Jews aged 18 to 55 who had taken refuge in France after January 1933 and who did not have regular jobs were subjected to forced labor in special labor battalions, with the ultimate purpose of concentrating them so that they could be quickly sent to Drancy and then on to the extermination camps in the East as soon as the relevant decisions were made in Berlin.[147]

In all of this, not only the French police and other authorities, but also the mass of the French Christians in both occupied and unoccupied France, and the *colons*, though not the Muslims, in French North Africa,[148] acted with a severity against Jews which even the Germans did not equal. They accepted the convenient theory developed by the Vichy government that the decadence which had led to the French collapse was the fault of the Jews.[149] The bombing and burning of the major Parisian synagogues on 3 October 1941 was met with very little public protest.[150] While the French protested in later years that their anti-Jewish actions were forced by the German occupiers, even during the last year of the war, when Germany was hardly in a position to force the French to act, the latter kept the anti-Jewish laws and actions in force long after they were compelled to do so, even for some time after the war was over and the Nazis had left.[151]

---

146. LJSO, p. 22.

147. Report of Turkish Consulate-General (Marseilles) to Turkish Embassy to Paris (Vichy) no. 6127/679, 22 December 1942, in the Archives of the Turkish Embassy (Paris). Klarsfeld, *1941*, p. 81. Turkish Consulate-General (Paris) to Turkish Embassy to Paris (Vichy) no. 489, 4 September 1941. Archives of Turkish Consulate-General (Paris).

148. Michel Abitbol, *The Jews of North Africa during the Second World War* (Wayne State University Press, Detroit, Michigan, 1989); M. Ansky, *Les Juifs d'Algérie du Décret Crémieux à la libération* (Paris, 1950); Itzhak Abrahami, 'The Jewish communities of Tunisia during the Nazi Conquest' (in Hebrew), *Pe'amim*, no. 28 (1986), pp. 107–125; Michel Abitbol, 'The Jews of Algeria, Tunisia and Morocco, 1940–1943', *Pe'amim* no. 28 (1986), pp. 79–106..

149. The situation of Jews in France, and the hostility toward them of most Frenchmen as well as of the Vichy government, is described in considerable detail in the French-language report of the Jewish underground leader Marc Jarblum, dated 31 August 1943, in the Menachem Bader collection, Moreshet Archives (Israel), file D.1.64.

150. Klarsfeld, *1941*, pp. 76–77.

151. Rajsfus, *Drancy*, p. 227. Joseph Billig, *Le Commissariat Général aux questions juives, 1941–1944* (Centre de Documentation Juive contemporaine, Paris, 1960); François-Georges Dreyfus, *Histoire de Vichy* (Paris, Perrin, 1990), p. 302; André Kaspi, Serge Klarsfeld and Georges Wellers, *La France et le Question Juive* (Paris, Messinger, 1981); Henri Marrus and Robert Paxton, *Vichy et les Juifs* (Paris, Calmann-Levy, 1981); Richard Cohen, *The Burden*

Only the Jews living in southeastern France, in the area of Alpes-Maritimes centered in Nice, the Basses-Alpes, the Hautes-Alpes, Savoy and part of Isère, particularly Grenoble, got along reasonably well and were relatively secure for some time because of its occupation by Italy starting in November 1942, with the Italian soldiers of the IVth Army in many cases protecting the Jews there from the French police as well as the Germans, as they did in Croatia, the Macedonian coast, Greece and Macedonia during 1942 and 1943.[152]

After the fall of Mussolini on 25 July 1943 and the surrender to the Allies of the subsequent Italian government led by Marshall Badoglio, however, the Italian forces in all these areas were replaced by German troops, and the situation of the Jews there rapidly deteriorated as a result. Many of the Jews in southern France accompanied the Italian army back to Italy, but the subsequent German occupation of northern Italy following the collapse of the Italian government left their position there worse than it had been before, though German preoccupation with defending their positions

---

of Conscience: French Jewish Leadership during the Holocaust (Indiana University Press, Bloomington, Indiana, 1987).

152. Susan Zuccotti, *The Italians and the Holocaust: Persecution, Rescue, and Survival.* (New York, Basic Books, 1987); J. Bessis, *La Méditerranée fasciste: L'Italie mussolinienne et la Tunisie* (Paris, Karthala, 1981). It is interesting to note, however, that whereas the Italians were relatively protective in France and Italy, they persecuted the Jews of Libya and Tunisia during their military actions in North Africa in World War II, sending them to concentration camps after 1942. See Esther Aran, *Yalkut Moreshet* (Israel) XXXIII(1982) pp. 153–156; and Michel Abitbol, 'The Jews of Algeria, Tunisia and Morocco, 1940–1943' (in Hebrew), *Pe'amim* no. 28 (1986), pp. 79–106. On the Italian efforts to protect Greece's Jews from the Germans, see Lucillo Merci, Joseph Rochlitz and Menachem Shelach, 'Excerpts from the Salonika Diary of Lucillo Merci (February-August 1943)', *Yad Vashem Studies*, VIII (1987), pp. 293–323; Rainer Eckert, 'Die Verfolgung der Griechischen Juden im Deutschen Okkupationsgebiet Saloniki-Agais vom April 1941 bis zum Abschluss der Deportationen im August 1943', *Bulletin des Arbeitskreises 'Zweiter Weltkrieg'*, (East Germany), 1986 (1–4), pp. 41–69; Daniel Carpi, 'Nuovi Documenti per la Storia dell'Olocausto in Grecia: L'Atteggiamento Degli Italiani (1941–1943)', Michael, *On the History of the Jews in the Diaspora*, VII (1981), pp. 119–200; and Daniel Carpi, 'The Italian diplomat Luca Pietromarchi on his activities for the Jews of Croatia and Greece' (in Hebrew), *Yalkut Moreshet* no. 33 (1982), pp. 145–152. The Jews of northern Greece and Macedonia were, however, persecuted with particular brutality in the areas occupied by the Bulgarian army, which treated them in this manner to get German permission to annex those territories and to spare the Jews of Bulgaria. See Hans-Joachim Hoppe, 'Bulgarian Nationalities Policy in Occupied Thrace and Aegean Macedonia', *Nationalities Papers*, XIV/1–2 (1986), pp. 89–100.

against the Allied advance from the south moderated the persecution somewhat. In Greece, on the other hand, after German troops replaced the Italians in 1942, over two-thirds of the 70,000 Jews remaining in the country following a century of persecution at the hands of the Greeks were exterminated, including almost all of the 56,500 Jews of Salonica, with only a few Turkish and Italian citizens exempted, a situation which was the result, not only of Nazi brutality, but also of local cooperation with, or at least passive acceptance of, what the Germans were doing.[153]

ISSUANCE OF TURKISH PASSPORTS AND CERTIFICATES OF CITIZENSHIP TO JEWISH TURKS WHO HAD LOST THEIR CITIZENSHIP

It was against this background that Turkish diplomats stationed throughout Nazi-occupied western Europe did all they could, both at an official level and even more behind the scenes, and often at risk to their own lives, to protect those Jews who were Turkish citizens, and even those Jewish Turks who had forsaken their Turkish citizenship for what had seemed at the time the greater advantages of citizenship of one of the countries of western Europe, and who as a result were now in great mortal danger. Ambassador Namık Kemal Yolga, then a very young Vice Consul serving at the Turkish Consulate-General in Paris, but subsequently Secretary General of the Turkish Foreign Office, relates that caring for Jewish Turks and protecting them from Nazi persecution came to occupy most of his time as well as that of his colleagues:

> The German persecutions of Jews in occupied France did not begin immediately following the occupation, but by the middle of 1941, protection of our fellow countrymen of Jewish origin was our most important and pressing task. The actions of the Consulate-General in this respect were not just a matter of obeying our Constitution, which made no distinction among our fellow citizens based on religion or anything else–there is no such prejudice in our national character. That is, the anti-Semitism

---

153. Daniel Carpi, 'The Jews of Greece in the Holocaust period (1941–43) and the behavior of the Italian occupation authorities' (in Hebrew), *Yalkut Moreshet*, no. 31 (1981), pp. 7–38; Rae Dalven, *The Jews of Ioannina* (Philadelphia, Pa., 1990), pp. 38–47.

which can be seen in many countries in various degrees has never existed in Turkey at any time in history. To the contrary, Jewish Turks have never been mistreated by the state; they have lived amidst their fellow citizens of Turkey with friendship and love. Thus it was natural from all points of view that the Consulate-General's task of protecting Turkish citizens should be applied to Jewish Turks as it was to Turks of other religions.[154]

Most important of all the services provided was that of certifying the Turkish citizenship of Jews who would otherwise have been subjected to the full force of the anti-Jewish laws then being introduced in both occupied and unoccupied France. Many Jewish Turks had married non-Turkish spouses. Some had become French citizens, as had their children. A good number had for all practical purposes forgotten their Turkish heritage and had neglected to maintain their Turkish citizenship by registering. Even many of those who had registered had failed to keep the Turkish consulates informed of their current addresses. The closure of many Turkish consulates in Europe after the war started, moreover, made it extremely difficult for those who wished to retain or regain their Turkish citizenship to do so.[155] They soon found that in the light of the anti-Jewish measures being introduced it was essential to their survival for them to gain access to the Turkish consulates, however difficult that might be. For those who had abandoned their Turkish citizenship, moreover, they concluded that it was far more beneficial for them to be citizens of neutral Turkey than of the country to which they had subsequently given their loyalty, and they began to appeal by the thousands to have that citizenship restored.[156]

The Turkish government was at first rather reluctant to do so. Not only many government officials, but also many Turkish citizens began to wonder

---

154. Letter from Ambassador Namık Kemal Yolga to Stanford J. Shaw, 5 July 1991, translated by Stanford J. Shaw. For the full text see Appendix 3.

155. Turkish consulates-general were closed at Antwerp in Belgium, and at most locations in France other than Paris and Marseilles (later moved to Grenoble); also at Pireas and Salonica in Greece and throughout Bulgaria. The consulates at Rhodes and Marseilles (Grenoble) remained open because Turkey threatened to close the German consulate at Izmir if they were closed.

156. The dossiers regarding these appeals, and the subsequent decisions of the government in Ankara, are to be found carefully preserved in the Archives of the Turkish Consulate in Paris. Detailed study of these records is still needed, but cursory examination by the author indicated that a majority of the appeals to restore Turkish citizenship were granted, sometimes as a result of intervention by relatives or friends still citizens of Turkey.

why Turkey should risk a Nazi invasion in order to help people who had deserted the country during the years that the Republic was being created. In the light of appeals from the leaders of Turkish Jewry[157] as well as from Zionist leaders in the United States and Great Britain,[158] however, the Turkish government changed its position in early 1942, and sent out orders for such applications to be referred to Ankara for rapid consideration. In the meantime, Turkish consular officials throughout Europe placed those who had lost their citizenship because of failure to register, regardless of whether or not they had appealed for restoration, in a special category of *gayri muntazem vatandaşlar*, or 'irregular' citizens, who were given official consular protection against persecution until the bureaucratic procedures required for full restoration of their citizenship could be carried out[159] When necessary, moreover, Turkish consuls often issued passports and 'Certificates of Citizenship' (*vatandaşlık ilmühaberi*), in advance of final authorization from Ankara, to those of the 'irregular' Jewish Turks who were in imminent danger of deportation to almost certain death in the East as well as those suffering particularly badly from the anti-Jewish restrictions imposed both by the Vichy government and the German occupation authorities in northern France.[160]

---

157. See for example the letter to Turkish President Ismet İnönü from Yakar, no. 45 dated 15 October 1942, and support for this request from the Turkish Ambassador to Paris (Vichy) to the Turkish Ministry of Foreign Affairs, no. 1697–1067–6127, 29 December 1942, both in the archives of the Turkish Embassy (Paris).

158. Isaac Weissman (Lisbon) to Chaim Weizman, President of the Jewish Agency, London, 21 December 1943. Central Zionist Archives L 15, 128 II; Archives of the American Joint Distribution Committee (New York); Laurence Steinhardt papers, Library of Congress, Washington, D.C.

159. Turkish Ministry of Foreign Affairs (Ankara) to Turkish Embassy to Paris (Vichy) no. 6250/277, 13 April 1942, Archives of the Turkish Embassy (Paris); Report of Turkish Consulate-General (Paris) to Turkish Foreign Ministry, no. 17/9, on properties of *gayri muntazem* Jewish Turks in France, 13 January 1942, Archives of Turkish Consulate-General (Paris).

160. Consul-General (Marseilles) Bedi'i Arbel to Turkish Ambassador to Paris (Vichy) no. 39/4, 13 January 1943; Turkish Consul at Marseilles Fuad Carım to Turkish Embassy at Paris (Vichy), no. 591.104, 20 December 1943, Archives of Turkish Consulate-General (Marseilles) and Turkish Foreign Ministry (Ankara). Also Paris Embassy (Vichy) to Turkish Consulate-General (Marseilles), no. 1337/6127, 30 December 1943, Archives of the Turkish Embassy (Paris), and Turkish Foreign Ministry (Ankara). The Honorary Turkish Consul-General in Lyon, A. Routier, was especially active in issuing Certificates of Citizenship and passports to Jewish Turks living in France who had lost their Turkish citizenship due to failure to register for long periods of time because of their assumption of French citizenship. See

Ambassador Namık Kemal Yolga describes the situation at the Turkish Consulate-General in Paris during the Holocaust:

A matter which took up a great deal of our time was the situation of our 'irregular' fellow citizens, the term which we applied to those who were unable to secure the Certificates of Citizenship which we provided to those Turkish citizens who regularly registered at the Consulate-General while living for long periods of time in France. The area of France which the Paris Consulate-General was responsible for included the immediate area of Paris and vicinity, where most of the Turks in France were located. When the occupation authorities began persecuting Jews in France, the 'irregular' Turkish citizens stormed into the Consulate-General, at first crowding into the Chancery on the second floor, then filling the staircases which led up from the entrance hall, with the latecomers backing onto the sidewalk along Boulevard Haussmann, as can be seen in the photographs. Initially I would stand on the staircase landings, later on a chair at the building entrance, giving them information about the procedures that they had to follow and asking them to bring all the documents they could find which verified their Turkish citizenship. I remember that on a few occasions the only documents some of them could bring were receipts for taxes paid in Ottoman times. We then gave them documents of attestation, which stated that they had applied to the Consulate-General to regularize their citizenship situation and that these requests had been sent to Ankara. They were able to use these documents like Certificates of Citizenship which, I believe, were accepted for

---

report to the Turkish Ministry of Foreign Affairs on the activities of the Honorary Turkish Consul-General in Lyon, Archives of the Turkish Embassy (Paris) Dossier 6127, no. 638 26 November 1942); and miscellaneous other documents and reports in the same file. See also in Archives of the Turkish Embassy (Paris), Turkish Ambassador to Paris (Vichy) to Honorary Consul–General in Lyon Monsieur A. Routier, no. 1378, Vichy 20 October 1942, and no. 687/49, 19 December 1942; Fuad Carim, Turkish Consul (Marseilles) to Turkish Ambassador to Paris (Vichy), Grenoble no. 250/53, 3 June 1944.

registration with the police. This was our normal procedure for our 'irregular' fellow citizens. [161]

Ambassador Necdet Kent, who served as Vice Consul at the Turkish Consulate-General at Marseilles and Grenoble from 1941 to 1944, also relates his own experiences in assisting Jewish Turks in unoccupied France to prove or regularize their Turkish citizenship:

At that time there were two kinds of Jewish Turks in France. The first group consisted of Jews who at the end of World War I left Turkey with the French occupying forces and settled in France. Many of these no longer had Turkish passports, or if they still possessed them, they had expired. Many of them had no documents other than Birth Certificates issued by the Ottoman administration before the establishment of the Turkish Republic. They were considered to be 'without nationality' (*tabiyetsiz*) by the Turkish consulates.

Since the French administration was very liberal on such matters before World War II, it did nothing about this situation, and therefore these people did not bother to apply to the Turkish consulate to regularize their situation. The second group of Jewish Turks consisted of those who had left Turkey with valid passports but who for various reasons, particularly because of the outbreak of the war, could not return home; they were considered 'regular' (*régulier*) Turkish citizens.

When Nazi Germany occupied northern France, many Jewish Turks, like others as well, fled to unoccupied Vichy France, and therefore entered the district to which our consulate was assigned. The French referred to all those who came from the north as *repliés*, or 'people who had retreated.' Matters continued reasonably for some time after this exodus.

But when the Nazis occupied southern France, then things got much worse. Their first act was to load all the Jews they could capture into baggage cars and send them off to Germany. In response to complaints about this from Turkish citizens, we acted. If the status of the Turkish Jew applying for assistance to the ˙Consulate was 'regular', a Certificate of Citizenship document was

161. Namık Kemal Yolga to Stanford J. Shaw, 5 July 1991, translated by Stanford J. Shaw. See Appendix 3 for the complete statement.

immediately given to him. In addition, a statement of his Turkish citizenship and that his place of business was under the protection of Turkey was affixed in a prominent place which could be seen at the front of the establishment.

At first, the Nazis left this sort of Turkish citizen in peace. Even for those Jewish Turks whose status was not regular, after they filled out an application (*beyanname*) to regularize their status, they were given a document which stated that it was known that they were Turkish citizens and that procedures had been started to provide them with the necessary documents. By this method we saved many people from the Nazis.

However with the passage of time, and with changes in the district Gestapo chiefs, the attacks by the Nazis increased. During that time we had to go to Gestapo headquarters as many as three or four times daily in order to rescue our Jewish fellow citizens who had been arrested and detained. And just as bad, the Italians, who up to then had treated the Jews in their zone reasonably well, now began to emulate the Germans. One day I spent close to two hours arguing with the Italian Consul trying to get him to abandon his inhuman actions. I was somewhat successful with the Italians.[162]

While no official orders from Ankara requiring Turkish diplomats to specifically protect Jewish Turks being harassed or persecuted in Nazi-occupied Europe have been found to date, allusions to such orders in the correspondence, along with instructions issued to provide protection to all Turkish citizens regardless of religion, indicate that they were given by the Turkish Ministry of Foreign Affairs on several occasions during the war, and that in any case such actions were most certainly included in the established functions of all diplomats, that is to protect their own citizens regardless of religion. [163]

Relations between Jewish Turks and Muslims in France had remained excellent through the 1930s, as they had been in the Ottoman Empire, so at

---

162. Statement by retired Ambassador Necdet Kent to Quincentennial Foundation, Istanbul. Translated by Stanford J. Shaw. See Appendix 4 for the complete statement.

163. See, for example, Turkish Consul-General (Paris) to Turkish Ambassador to Paris (Vichy) no. 448, 3 October 1940 and no. 462, 4 October 1940; Turkish Consul-General (Paris) to Turkish Ministry of Foreign Affairs (Ankara) no. 475/136, 15 October 1940, and others in archives of Turkish Consulate-General (Paris).

times also the staff of the Muslim mosque in Paris provided Jewish Turks who had lost their Turkish citizenship with documents certifying that they were in fact Muslims, enabling many to escape from the Nazis.[164]

According to Ambassador Yolga, personal friendships were often established between the Jewish Turks and Consular officials:

> Our relations with our Jewish fellow citizens at that time were not just official, they also were personal. For example, our Consul-General, the late Cevdet Dülger, who was a bachelor and therefore gave great importance to being with other people, met almost every day with eight to ten friends, of whom three were leaders of our community of Jewish Turks, namely L. Fresco, S. Kohen, and R. Vidal, who had a carpet shop at the south corner of Saint Augustin square–I remember him with great affection. Dülger's successor as Consul-General, Fikret Şefik Özdoğancı, maintained the same friendships. [165]

Like Britain, its Commonwealth, and the United States, however, Turkey was quite restrictive in admitting for residence non-Turkish Jews except for those who came with particular professional skills such as the scientists and academicians who had been admitted in large numbers since the early 1930s.[166] This restriction was extended to those refugees who, after failing to secure a Turkish entry visa, secured citizenship in a third country, particularly those of South America which sold their papers, and then asked for a visa on the basis of their new citizenship.[167]

164. Archives of the French Ministry of Foreign Affairs (Quai d'Orsay, Paris), *Vichy-Europe-Serie Guerre 1939–1945, Vichy, Europe-Serie C 139, Question Juive*, 3 Septembre 1940-14 Septembre 1944, fol. 11. Le Directeur politique adjoint-Ministère des Affaires Etrangères (Quai d'Orsay) to Minister of Foreign Affairs, Vichy, 24 September 1940.

165. See Appendix 4.

166. Michael Blakeney, 'Australia and the Jewish Refugees from Central Europe: Government Policy, 1933–1939,' *Leo Baeck Institute Year Book* (Great Britain) XXIX (1984), pp. 103–134.

167. Turkish Ministry of Foreign Affairs, Consular and Multilegal Bureau instruction to all Embassies and Consulates, no. 22858/14, 26 February 1942. Turkish Ambassador to Paris (Vichy) to Turkish Consul-General (Marseilles) no. 6250/384, 21 March 1942, in Archives of the Turkish Embassy (Paris), dossier 164/6280, 19–3–42.

TURKISH DIPLOMATIC INTERVENTION TO PREVENT THE APPLICATION OF ANTI-JEWISH LAWS TO JEWISH TURKS IN FRANCE

The Turkish government was kept fully informed about the mounting horror of the Holocaust in France by a series of exhaustive reports submitted by its ambassadors in Vichy as well as by its consuls in Paris, Marseilles (Grenoble) and Lyon. Similar reports arrived regularly in Ankara from its diplomatic missions in Berlin, Vienna, the Hague and Prague.

The main problem facing Turkish diplomats in Europe, however, was finding out when persecutions or deportations of Jewish Turks were taking place, and to whom complaints and appeals should be made. Even for those Jews who retained their Turkish citizenship by registering annually, failure to keep in contact with the Turkish embassy or consulates often left the Turkish diplomats without any knowledge of what they were experiencing: when they were attacked or arrested, sent off to concentration camps, (and then to which camps), and when they were deported to the East. Information usually came from relatives, friends and at times landlords or business associates, but occasionally it came from the victims themselves when they were allowed to write from their places of imprisonment.

Such correspondence led the way to Turkish consular action to secure the release of Albert Gattegno and his wife Lily, who after their arrest on 4 August 1942 were released late the same month, only to be arrested again on 8 December 1942, released once again on 20 January 1943, and sent back to Turkey a year later as a result of the intervention of the Turkish Consulate-General in Paris.

THE ALBERT AND LILY GATTEGNO FILE

a. ALBERT GATTEGNO INFORMS TURKISH CONSULATE-GENERAL (PARIS) THAT HE AND WIFE WERE ARRESTED BY GERMANS ON 6 AUGUST 1942 AND SENT TO DRANCY PRISON CAMP. Albert Gattegno, Registration no. 15243, block 5, staircase 22, room 19, Drancy camp, to Turkish Consulate-General, 170 Boulevard Haussmann, Paris, 6 August 1942 (postmarked 7 August 1942). Archives of Turkish Embassy (Paris).

Drancy, 6 August 1942

Mr. Consul-General,

I have the honor to bring to your attention that on Tuesday 4 August at 8:00 in the morning two French inspectors came to my house and took my wife Lily Gattegno to Tourelles and me to Drancy. We do not know the reason for which we have been arrested. I wish you to know that having two children at young ages, I would appreciate it if you would do what is necessary with the competent authorities to secure our liberation. With my thanks in anticipation, please, Mr. Consul-General, receive my most sincere greetings.

(**signed**) Albert Gattegno

Turkish citizen, Certificate of Nationality no. 614 T.P.

Register no. 15243, block 5, staircase 22, room 19, Camp at Drancy

b. TURKISH CONSULATE-GENERAL INFORMS GERMAN EMBASSY (PARIS) THAT ALBERT AND LILY GATTEGNO ARE TURKISH CITIZENS AND ASKS FOR THEIR RELEASE. Turkish Consulate-General (Paris) to German Embassy (Paris) no. 32F/614T.P., Paris, 6 August 1942. Archives of Turkish Embassy (Paris).

Republic of Turkey, Consulate-General

Paris, 6 August 1942 no. 32F

To the Embassy of Germany,

The Consulate-General of Turkey presents its compliments to the Embassy of Germany and has the honor of bringing to its attention that it has just been informed that two of its citizens of Jewish religion, Mr. Albert Gattegno and his wife Lily, who bear Certificate of Nationality no. 614 TP, renewed under no. 521 on 6 December 1941, have been arrested Tuesday morning 4 August 1942 at their home, 49 Boulevard Gouvion Saint-Cyr, Paris XVIIème According to information obtained from the Préfecture of Police, Mr. Gattegno has been sent to the Internment Camp at Drancy and Madame Lily Gattegno has been sent to the Camp at Tourelles.

This Consulate-General would be grateful to the Embassy of Germany if it would intervene with the competent authorities to obtain the liberation of Mr. and Mrs. Gattegno if no crime has been recorded against them. The Consulate-General of Turkey thanks in advance the Embassy of Germany for the trouble that it will take and takes advantage of the occasion to reiterate to it the assurances of its very high consideration.

Paris, 6 August 1942

c. TURKISH CONSULATE-GENERAL INFORMS TOURELLES CONCENTRATION CAMP COMMANDER THAT LILY GATTEGNO IS TURKISH CITIZEN AND THAT STEPS ARE BEING TAKEN TO SECURE HER RELEASE. Turkish Consulate-General (Paris) to Director of the Internment Camp at Tourelles (Paris), no. 39F/614TP, 11 August 1942. Archives of the Turkish Consulate (Paris).

Republic of Turkey, Consulate-General at Paris
11 August 1942, no. 39F/614TP

The Director, Internment Camp at Tourelles, Paris

Mr. Director,

I have the honor of bringing to your attention that Madame Lily Gattegno, who it appears has just been interned at the Camp at Tourelles, placed under your direction, is a Turkish citizen, included in the Certificate of Nationality delivered to her husband, no. 614 T.P., renewed under no. 521 on 6 December 1941. I have undertaken the démarches with the competent authorities to secure the liberation of this citizen if no crime is attributed against her. Please accept, Mr. Director, the assurance of my special consideration.

(**signed**) The Consul

d. GERMAN EMBASSY INFORMS TURKISH CONSULATE THAT IT IS CONTACTING THE COMPETENT AUTHORITIES IN CASE OF ALBERT AND LILY GATTEGNO. German Embassy (Paris) to Turkish Consulate-General (Paris), no. 1801/42, 12 August 1942. Archives of the Turkish Embassy (Paris).

German Embassy, Paris
No. 1801/42, Paris, 12 August 1942

The German Embassy acknowledges receipt of the note of 6 August 1942 no. 32F regarding the arrest of Turkish citizens Albert and Lily Gattegno. It is getting into contact with the responsible authorities and will provide further information.

Consular minute: received 18 August 1942.
Résumé: Acknowledgment of reception . . . .The Embassy of Germany has gotten into contact immediately with the competent authority. It will communicate the result to us.

e. ALBERT AND LILY GATTEGNO INFORM TURKISH CONSULATE-GENERAL THAT THEY AGAIN HAVE BEEN ARRESTED AND PLACED IN DRANCY CONCENTRATION CAMP. Albert and Lily Gattegno, Drancy, 9 December 1942. Archives of Turkish Embassy (Paris), registration no. F 642. (see Document 1, above)

Drancy, 9 December 1942,

Mr. Consul-General of Turkey,
I permit myself to write to inform you that since yesterday morning, 8 December, my wife and I were arrested, at our home at 49 Boulevard Gouvion Saint-Cyr. After a time at the Commissariat at the Etoile, then at the Depot, we were taken about 6:00 a.m. again to the Camp at Drancy. We have not undergone any interrogation, and we are completely ignorant of the reasons for our arrest. As we left our apartment, the inspector himself affixed seals to it. I would be very grateful to you, Mr. Consul, if you would do what is necessary to secure our liberation and to prevent the seizure of our furniture. My wife and I know that your good will and firm intervention will secure our freedom once again. Despite the misfortune which has touched us, both of us keep our morale high. We ask in advance for excuse for all the bother that we cause you, and in the hope of receiving a comforting word from you, please receive, Mr. Consul-General, the expression of our high consideration as well as our special greetings.

(**signed**) Albert Gattegno
Lily Gattegno, no. 614 TP
Address here: Gattegno Albert, Block 5, Staircase 22, room 17, registration no. 17767. **Consular minute**: received 12 December 1942

Document 1. Albert Gattegno asks Turkish Consulate-General to secure his release and that of his wife after they are arrested a second time.

f. GERMAN EMBASSY INFORMS TURKISH CONSULATE-GENERAL THAT GERMANS WILL FREE THE GATTEGNOS IF IT RECEIVES DOCUMENTARY PROOF OF THEIR TURKISH NATIONALITY, AND THEIR ARREST WAS NOT DUE TO VIOLATION OF LAWS. German Embassy (Paris) to Turkish Consulate-General no. 1801/42, 10 December 1942. Archives of Turkish Embassy (Paris).

German Embassy, Paris
no. 1901/42, 10 December 1942

To Turkish Consulate-General, Paris,

The German Embassy is honored to answer the note of 6 August 1942 no. 32F by stating that the Préfect of Police responsible for the arrest of Albert and Lily Gattegno is ready to release them if documentary proof of their Turkish Citizenship is produced so long as this arrest was not motivated by a violation of the law. Further information can be secured from the German Embassy.

Consular minute: received 14 December 1942 N. Yolga, F 632. The competent German authorities have advised the Préfecture of Police to release the Gattegnos if they can furnish documents attesting to their Turkish nationality and if their arrest is not motivated by an infraction of the laws. 17 December 1942. Namık Kemal Yolga.

g. TURKISH CONSULATE-GENERAL INFORMS GERMAN EMBASSY THAT GATTEGNOS ARE TURKISH CITIZENS IN GOOD STANDING AND ASKS FOR THEIR RELEASE. Turkish Consulate-General (Paris) to German Embassy, 78 Rue de Lille, Paris VIIème, Paris, 10 December 1942, no. F 622. Archives of the Turkish Consulate (Paris).

Republic of Turkey, Turkish Consulate-General, Paris
10 December 1942, no. F 622

To the Embassy of Germany
78, Rue de Lille, Paris VIIème

The Consulate-General of Turkey in Paris presents its compliments to the Embassy of Germany and has the honor of bringing to its attention the following:

Madame Lily and Monsieur Albert Gattegno are Turkish citizens bearing Certificate of Nationality no. 614 TP, renewed under numbers 627 and 628 on 24 November 1942, valid until 24 November 1943. They were arrested once again in the morning of 8 December at their home at 49 Boulevard Gouvion St. Cyr at Paris XVII. These Turkish citizens who were the object of a letter of 6 August 1942 no. 32 from this Consulate had been released on the intervention of the Estimable Embassy of Germany shortly after that date. This Consulate-General asks the Embassy of Germany to have the goodness to intervene with the competent authorities to obtain the definitive liberation of Monsieur and Madame Gattegno.

The Consulate-General of Turkey thanks in advance the Embassy of Germany for the trouble that it will take in this regard, and takes advantage of this occasion to repeat to it the assurances of its high consideration.

(**signed**) Consul-General

h. TURKISH CONSULATE-GENERAL INFORMS PARIS PRÉFECTURE OF POLICE THAT GATTEGNOS ARE TURKISH CITIZENS AND THAT IT IS APPLYING TO GERMAN AUTHORITIES FOR THEIR RELEASE, AND ASKS THAT SEALS BE REMOVED FROM THEIR APARTMENT. Turkish Consulate-General (Paris) to Préfecture of Police (Paris) no. F 625, 12 December 1942. Archives of the Turkish Embassy (Paris).

Republic of Turkey, Turkish Consulate-General, Paris, 12 December 1942, F 625

Préfecture of Police, Paris

The Consulate-General of Turkey presents its compliments to the Préfecture of Police of Paris and has the honor to bring to its attention that seals were placed on the home of Mr. and Madame Gattegno, regular Turkish citizens, who live at 49, Boulevard Gouvion St. Cyr at Paris XVII, when they were arrested on 8 December at their home.

I have undertaken démarches with the competent authorities to secure the release of Mr. and Madame Gattegno.

They are of Turkish nationality, so I ask you to be so good as to give the necessary instructions so that the seals which were placed on the apartment of the above-named are removed.

The Consulate-General of Turkey thanks in advance the Préfecture of Police of Paris for the trouble that it will take in this regard, and takes advantage of this occasion to reiterate to it assurances of its high consideration.

(**signed**) The Consul-General

i. TURKISH CONSULATE-GENERAL INFORMS DRANCY CAMP COMMANDER THAT GATTEGNOS ARE TURKISH CITIZENS AND THAT IT HAS APPLIED FOR THEIR RELEASE. Turkish Consul-General (Paris) to Commander of Drancy Internment Camp no. F 626, 12 December 1942. Archives of Turkish Embassy (Paris).

Mr. Director, Drancy Internment Camp, Seine
Mr. Director,
I have the honor to bring to your attention that Mr. Albert and Madame Lily Gattegno, Turkish citizens regularly registered at our Consulate-General, and interned in the Drancy camp during last August and then released following the intervention of our Consulate, have again been arrested and brought to the camp which is under your direction. I have once again undertaken démarches with the competent authorities to secure the liberation of these Turkish citizens. In bringing this to your attention, I ask you, Mr. Director, to accept the assurance of my special sentiments. (**signed**) The Consul

j. TURKISH CONSULATE-GENERAL REMINDS GERMAN EMBASSY OF ITS AGREEMENT TO INTERVENE TO SECURE RELEASE OF GATTEGNOS FROM DRANCY CAMP. Turkish Consulate-General (Paris) to German Embassy (Paris), no. F 632, 17 December 1942. Archives of Turkish Consulate (Paris)

Republic of Turkey, Turkish Consulate-General, Paris
17 December 1942, no. F 632

The Consulate-General of Turkey presents its compliments to the Embassy of Germany and has the honor of bringing to its attention the fact that Mr. and Madame Gattegno, Turkish citizens, who were the object of its letter of 10 December, reference 1801/42, are still interned at the Camp at Drancy.

This Consulate-General thanks in advance the estimable Embassy of Germany for its obliging intervention to secure the liberation of the above-named, and takes advantage of this occasion to reiterate to it the assurances of its high consideration.
(**signed**), The Consul-General

k. TURKISH CONSULATE-GENERAL INFORMS ALBERT GATTEGNO THAT IT HAS INTERVENED WITH GERMAN AUTHORITIES TO SECURE HIS RELEASE AND THAT OF HIS WIFE. Turkish Consulate-General (Paris) to Albert Gattegno (Drancy), no. F 642, 17 December 1942. Archives of Turkish Consulate (Paris).

Republic of Turkey, Turkish Consulate-General, Paris
17 December 1942, no. F 642,

Mr. Albert Gattegno
Block 5, Staircase 22, Room 17, Registration no. 17767
Drancy Internment Camp (Seine)
Sir,

In response to your letter of 9 December, I can inform you that I have undertaken démarches with the competent authorities to secure your liberation and that of your wife as well as for your apartment and your furniture.

I ask you, Sir, to accept my special greetings.

(**signed**) The Consul. **Consular minute**: they have been freed

l. FRENCH PRÉFECTURE OF POLICE INFORMS TURKISH CONSULATE-GENERAL THAT IT IS CONSULTING THE *COMMISSAIRE GENERAL AUX QUESTIONS JUIVES* REGARDING ITS REQUEST THAT THE SEALS BE REMOVED FROM THE GATTEGNO APARTMENT. TURKISH CONSULATE NOTES THAT IN MEANTIME GATTEGNOS REMOVED THE SEALS THEMSELVES WHEN THEY WERE FREED. Pefecture of Police, Paris, to Turkish Consulate-General (Paris), 26 January 1943 no. 625. Archives of Turkish Embassy (Paris).

Préfecture of Police, Office of the Préfect
Paris, 26 January 1943, no. 625D

Mr. Consul-General of Turkey in Paris
Mr. Consul-General,

In response to your letter of 12 December last concerning the seals placed on the apartment situated at 49, Boulevard Gouvion Saint-Cyr at Paris and occupied by the Turkish Jewish citizens Cottegno (*sic*), I have the honor to inform you that I immediately consulted the *Commissaire Général aux Questions Juives.* I will not fail to inform you of his answer. Please accept, Mr. Consul-General, the assurance of my high consideration.

(**signed**), for the Préfect of Police, Directeur of his Office
Consular minute: received 27 January 1943. The seals were removed by themselves when they were freed.

m. GERMAN EMBASSY (PARIS) INFORMS TURKISH CONSULATE-GENERAL (PARIS) THAT ALBERT AND LILY GATTEGNO WERE FREED FROM DRANCY CAMP ON 20 JANUARY 1943. German Embassy (Paris) to Turkish Consulate-General (Paris), 2 March 1943 no. 1801/42. Archives of Turkish Embassy (Paris).

German Embassy, Paris
no. 1801/42, Paris, 2 March 1943

To the Turkish Consulate-General, Paris

The German Embassy is honored to state in reply to your note of 17 December 1942 no. 632 that the Turkish citizens Albert and Lily Gattegno were released from the Camp at Drancy on 20 January 1942.

German seal: Embassy of Germany, Paris
Consular minute: Received 4 March 1943 no. F 1147
Resumé: Reply to our letter of 17 December 1942 no. F 632
Albert and Lili Gattegno were released on 20 January 1943
File in dossier, 5 March 1943, Namık Kemal Yolga

n. FRENCH PRÉFECTURE OF POLICE INFORMS TURKISH CONSULATE-GENERAL THAT SEALS WERE PUT ON GATTEGNO APARTMENT CONFORMING TO DECISIONS OF GERMAN AUTHORITIES, AND THAT THEREFORE NOTHING CAN BE DONE ABOUT IT. TURKISH CONSULATE NOTES THAT THE GATTEGNOS REMOVED THE SEALS THEMSELVES WHEN THEY WERE FREED. Préfecture of Police (Paris) to Turkish Consulate-General (Paris), no. 11332D, Paris, 19 October 1943. Archives of Turkish Embassy, Paris.

Préfecture of Police, Office of the Préfect
Paris, 19 October 1943

Mr. Consul-General of Turkey in Paris

In response to your letter F 625 of 12 December 1942, and following my note of 26 January 1943, I have the honor of informing you that the measures taken relative to the home of your citizens Mr. and Madame Gattegno, who live at 48, Boulevard Gauvion Saint Cyr in Paris, were applied in conformity with the decisions of the German authorities. As a result, I express my regrets at not being able to give you satisfaction, and ask you to accept, Mr. Consul-General, the assurance of my high consideration.

For the Préfect of Police, Director of his Office (**signed**)

Consular minute: received 20 October 1943, Namık Kemal Yolga. The seals were removed by themselves when they were freed

o. ALBERT GATTEGNO ASKS TURKISH CONSULATE-GENERAL FOR A LETTER FOR THE ADMINISTRATOR OF HIS APARTMENT SO THAT HE CAN AUTHORIZE GATTEGNO TO SELL HIS FURNITURE AND HOUSE BEFORE LEAVING FOR TURKEY. Albert Gattegno to Turkish Consulate-General, Paris, 20 January 1944. Archives of Turkish Embassy, Paris.

A. Gattegno, 20 Rue N.-D. de Recouvrance, Paris 2^é
Crayons A.W. Faber,
Fournitures pour Coiffeurs, Coputellerie Fine
Paris, 20 January 1944

Consulate-General of Turkey in Paris
Mr. Consul-General,

Having requested repatriation, I solicit by this letter your Esteemed Benevolence for a letter from our Consulate-General for the administrator of the building of my home, 49 Boulevard Gouvion Saint Cyr, Paris XVII, so that he can authorize me to dispose of my furnitures, goods and house with full right. With my thanks in anticipation, please accept, Mr. Consul-General, my greetings.

(**signed**) A. Gattegno 614 TP

Home located at 49, Boulevard Gouvion Saint Cyr, Paris 17ᵉ

Administrator of the Building: Cabinet Jean Lecasble, 15 Rue de Tocqueville, Paris

p. TURKISH CONSUL-GENERAL (PARIS) INFORMS ALBERT GATTEGNO THAT AS A TURKISH CITIZEN HE IS FREE TO DISPOSE OF HIS GOODS AS HE WISHES. Turkish Consul-General to Mr. Gattegno, 49 Boulevard Gouvion St. Cyr, Paris XVII, 21 January 1944, no. F 3262/614 TP

Republic of Turkey, Turkish Consulate-General, Paris
21 January 1944, no. F 3262/614 TP

Sir,

In response to your letter of 20 January, I can inform you that as a properly registered Turkish citizen, protected by this Consulate-General, and about to return to Turkey very soon, you are free to dispose of your properties as you wish, and either sell them or rent them as you wish.

Please accept, Sir, my special greetings.

(**signed**) The Consul-General

Diplomatic action to protect Jewish Turks in occupied and unoccupied France was initially carried out under the general direction of the Turkish Embassy to France, located at first at Paris but subsequently moved to Vichy when the government led by Marshall Petain was established there early in 1941. From then until July 1943, Turkey's legation at Vichy, officially referred to as the Paris Embassy, was directed by Ambassador Behiç Erkin, who was succeeded by Ali Şevket Berker (September 1943–December 1944), and former Foreign Minister Numan Menemencioğlu (November 1944–1956).

Actual contact with German and French officials on behalf of Turkish citizens was handled for the most part, however, by the Turkish consulates located at Paris, Lyon, and Marseilles, the latter transferred to Grenoble after the extension of the Nazi occupation to the Mediterranean in 1942. The Paris Consulate-General was led when the war began by Cevdet Dülger

(August 1939–April 1942), then for a time by Acting Consul-General Namık Kemal Yolga (April–July 1942), who remained as Vice-Consul after Fikret Şefik Özdoğancı came from Ankara as Consul-General (July 1942–May 1945), while that at Marseilles and Grenoble was led by Bedi'i Arbel (April 1940–June 1943) and Fuad Carım (June 1943–May 1945), assisted by Vice-Consul Necdet Kent who served from 1941 until 1944, all of whom subsequently had distinguished careers in the Foreign Service of the Turkish Republic.

In the face of intense German pressure, and often at the risk of their own lives, these able diplomats led the way in protecting Jewish Turks, though because the Turkish Embassy at Vichy could not communicate regularly or securely with the Turkish consulate or the German authorities in Paris regarding the mistreatment of Jews in occupied France, most of this work was carried on by the Paris Consulate under the orders of the Turkish Embassy in Berlin, not only because communications between Paris and Berlin were far more regular than those between Paris and Vichy but also because of the latter's more direct access to the centers of German power.[168]

Turkish diplomats and consuls in Nazi-occupied countries protected resident Jewish Turks whenever they could, though the closure of many Turkish consulates in Europe made it extremely difficult for Jewish Turks to find Turkish diplomats who could act to protect them, leaving them to face Nazi persecution without assistance.

'Based on the fact that Turkish Constitutional Law makes no distinction among its citizens according to the religion to which they belong',[169] and Turkey's insistence on the '. . . inadmissibility of

---

168. Turkish Embassy to Paris (Vichy) to Turkish Ministry of Foreign Affairs (Ankara) no. 1195/768/6127, Vichy, 1 September 1942. Archives of the Turkish Embassy (Paris).

169. See, for example, Consulate-General of Turkey (Paris) to the German Embassy (Paris), no. 605, 28 December 1940, reacting to the German law of 12 November 1940 which ordered the seizure of all Jewish-owned businesses and domiciles in France, requesting the Nazis to restore the properties of Jewish Turks 'based on the fact that Constitution of the Turkish Reublic makes no distinction among its citizens regardless of the religion to which they belong . . , and the resulting German concessions for Jewish Turks, as stated in German Embassy (Paris) to Turkish Consulate-General (Paris), no. 1334, 28 February 1941, and no. R 425/41 of 4 October 1941, in the archives of the Turkish Embassy (Paris) and the Turkish Foreign ministry (Ankara). Also Consulate-General of Turkey (Paris) to Prefecture de la Sarthe/le Mans, 10 January 1941, intervening in the case of Monsieur Sarfati, 47 Rue de Normandie, Le Mans, demanding and securing the return of his property; and letter from Turkish Consul-General (Paris) to Monsieur Naville, Swiss Consulate (representing Turkish

discrimination between Turkish subjects of different religions resident in France. . . ,[170] the Turkish diplomats and consuls in France regularly intervened with German occupation authorities and French governmental and local officials to release those Jewish Turks who had been interned in concentration camps, subjected to forced labor or restrictive and discriminatory anti-Jewish laws and regulations of all sorts, or whose houses, apartments or shops had been confiscated or sealed in accordance with the provisions of the anti-Jewish laws imposed by the occupying commanders.[171]

A warning regarding Nazi discriminatory policies was sent on 16 June 1941 to the Turkish Embassy in Vichy by the Turkish Consul-General in Marseilles, Minister Bedi'i Arbel, that Turkish citizens in France were threatened with being sent to concentration camps if they did not register themselves and their property. [172] In reply, on 31 July 1941 the Turkish Ambassador to Paris (Vichy) made a formal inquiry to the French Ministry of Foreign Affairs (Vichy) relaying the Turkish government's concern regarding the extent to which the *Statut des Juifs* and other anti-Jewish laws enacted the previous month were intended to apply to Jewish Turks established in France in the light of Turkey's refusal to make a distinction between its citizens of different religions(Document 2):

> The Embassy of Turkey has the honor of informing the Ministry of Foreign Affairs that its Government, having been informed of the text of law no. 2,333 of 2 June 1941 which, under menace of penal sanctions, orders the inscription of Jews on a special register along with a declaration which they must make regarding their properties, feels that the measures which it dictates are also

---

interests in occupied France at that time), 6 September 1944, asking for the release of the siezed property of thirty nine Jewish Turks in various parts of France.

170. *L'Ambassade regrette, toutefois, de ne pas pouvoir changer son point de vue exprimé a diverses reprises concernant l'inadmissibilité d'une discrimination entre sujets turcs de differentes confessions résident en France* . . . .Turkish Ambassador to Paris (Vichy) to French Ministry of Foreign Affairs, no. 124–6127, Vichy, 23 January 1943. Archives of the Turkish Embassy (Paris).

171. Turkish Consulate-General (Paris) to Turkish Embassy to Paris (Vichy) no. 193, 12 May 1941. Archives of Turkish Consulate-General (Paris).

172. Consul-General (Marseilles) Bedi'i Arbel to Turkish Ambassador to Paris (Vichy), no. 280/50, 16 June 1941. Archives of the Turkish Embassy (Paris), dossier 288.6127, 20–VI–41.

applicable to Turkish citizens of Jewish origin established in France.

Turkey itself establishes no discrimination among its citizens according to race, religion or anything else and therefore feels unease regarding such discrimination imposed by the French government on those of its citizens who are established in France, so that the Turkish government can only reserve entirely its rights in what concerns those of the latter who are of the Jewish race.[173]

Vichy, le 31 Juillet 1941

L'Ambassade de Turquie a l'honneur d'informer le Ministère des Affaires Etrangères que son Gouvernement ayant eu connaissance du texte de la loi N° 2.333 du 2 Juin 1941 qui, prévoit sous menace de sanctions pénales l'inscription des juifs sur un registre spécial ainsi qu'une déclaration à faire par eux de leurs biens, estime qu'il lui semble ressortir du texte de cette loi que les mesures dont il s'agit sont également applicables aux ressortissants turcs d'origine juive établis en France.

Or, la Turquie n'établissant elle-même aucune discrimination entre ses ressortissants d'ordre racial, religieux ou autre, conçoit malaisément qu'une pareille discrimination soit faite par le Gouvernement français à l'égard de ceux de ses ressortissants établis en France et le Gouvernement turc ne peut que réserver entièrement ses droits en ce qui concerne ceux d'entre ces derniers qui sont de race juive.

L'Ambassade de Turquie en portant ce qui précède à la connaissance du Ministère des Affaires Etrangères saisit cette occasion de lui réitérer les assurances de sa haute considération.

Ministère des Affaires Etrangères
VICHY

Document 2. Turkey protests against anti-Jewish measures applied to Jewish Turks

---

173. Turkish Embassy to Paris (Vichy) to French Ministry of Foreign Affairs (Vichy), no. 924.6127, 31 July 1941. Archives of the Turkish Embassy (Paris), dossier 6127 no. 339 H.T. 13/11–8–41.

The French Ministry of Foreign Affairs answered on 8 August 1941, claiming that Turkish and other foreign Jews, by establishing themselves in France, implicitly accepted all its laws:

> . . . The Ministry has the honor of informing the (Turkish) Embassy that by establishing themselves in France, the individuals in question have implicitly agreed to submit themselves to the legislation of the country in which they wish to be guests. This principle has sufficient force that the measures regarding people of the Hebrew race apply to all Jews regardless, both those who are of French allegiance as well as those who are nationals of foreign countries (Document 3).[174]

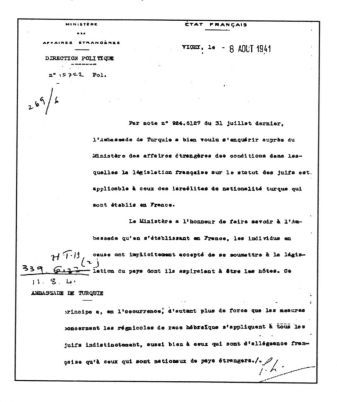

Document 3. France insists that foreign citizens in residence accept French laws, including anti-Jewish laws, and that Jewish Turks are treated equally with other Jews

174. French Ministry of Foreign Affairs (Vichy) to Turkish Embassy (Vichy) no. 15722, Vichy, 8 August 1941. Archives of the Turkish Embassy (Paris), no. 269/6 339 H.T. 13, received 11 August 1941. Dossier 6127/296/6.

The United States Embassy advised its citizens in France to accept this argument on the grounds that it did not discriminate among Jews:[175]

> Embassy of the United States of America
> Paris, 17 October 1940
>
> To the Consul-General of the Republic of Turkey
> My Dear Colleague,
> Please excuse me for having delayed so much in answering your letter of 2 October relative to the German regulation that requires the registration of persons belonging to the Jewish religion. For the moment, I answer to American citizens who inquire at the Embassy, that the latter, given the fact that they have voluntarily placed themselves under the laws and regulations in force in the occupied territory of France, can take initiative regarding them only in the case when a discrimination is established. According to what I understand the regulation in question establishes no distinction, and applies to all persons of Jewish religion resident in occupied territory. If you have an indication showing a contrary opinion, I would be very much obliged if you would let me know it.
> Please accept, My dear Colleague, the assurance of my very special consideration.
> **(signed)** Maynard B. Barnes, First Secretary of the Embassy[176]

Turkey, on the other hand continued to object to the application of anti-Jewish laws to Jewish Turks in France on the grounds that such actions violated the treaties signed between Turkey and France according which the nationals of Turkey were to enjoy the same civil rights in France that French citizens enjoyed in Turkey,[177] and also discriminated among Turkish citizens of different religions, protesting whenever Jewish Turks were subjected to the anti-Jewish laws:

---

175. Archives of the Turkish Embassy (Paris), file 6127.

176. Archives of the Turkish Embassy (Paris), file 6127.

177. Turkish Consulate-General (Paris) to Turkish Embassy to Paris (Vichy), 13 October 1941. Archives of the Turkish Embassy (Paris), dossier 6127. *L'étranger jouira en France des mêmes droits civils que ceux qui sont ou seront accordés aux Français par les traitüs de la nation a laquelle cet étranger appartiendra....*

of different religions, protesting whenever Jewish Turks were subjected to the anti-Jewish laws:

> While it is natural enough for foreigners to accept the laws of a country in which they live, in accordance with the strenuously expressed view of the French Foreign Minister that a foreigner who has settled in a country can be assumed to have accepted the attachment of his state and future to that country's laws, your answer must be that we reserve our rights in regard to a law which discriminates among Turkish citizens .... [178]

In fulfillment of instructions from Ankara, the Turkish Embassy to Paris (Vichy) continued its refusal to recognize the application of all anti-Jewish laws to Jewish Turks:

> The Embassy of Turkey has not been remiss in submitting to its Government the content of the verbal note of 8 August 1941 (no. 15722 POL) of the Ministry of Foreign Affairs relative to the situation of Jews of Turkish nationality in France. It has as a result been informed once again regarding the attitude and doctrine of the Turkish government on this subject: the latter, while not contesting the principle of the necessity for foreigners to obey the legislation of the country in which they are guests, maintains that it cannot accept discrimination among Turkish citizens residing abroad, and it therefore confirms all the reserves that the Embassy formulated in its note of 31 July 1941 no. 914/6127, notably in what concerns the acquired rights of its citizens.[179]

In early October 1942, Pierre Laval declared that France would not allow any interference by foreign governments in its internal affairs and that the anti-Jewish laws would apply to all Jews regardless of religion.[180] In

---

178. Turkish Embassy to Paris (Vichy) to French Foreign Office, 9 September 1941. Archives of the Turkish Embassy (Paris).

179. Turkish Embassy to Paris (Vichy) to French Ministry of Foreign Affairs, no. 1427/6127, Vichy, 22 December 1941. Archives of the Turkish Embassy (Paris).

180. Turkish Consul-General (Marseilles) Ambassador Bedi'i Arbel to Turkish Ambassador to Paris (Vichy) no. 523/93, 6 October 1942, and Turkish Ambassador to Paris (Vichy) to Turkish Consul-General (Marseilles), Vichy, no. 1364–6127, Vichy, 15 October 1942. Archives of the Turkish Embassy (Paris).

response, the Turkish Embassy to Paris (Vichy) again on 25 January 1943 repeated its stand to the French Ministry of Foreign Affairs that it could not accept discrimination among Turkish citizens resident in France on the basis of their race or religion:

> The Embassy regrets . . . that it is unable to change its point of view, expressed on numerous occasions, concerning the inadmissibility of discrimination among Turkish subjects of different religious confessions resident in France.
>
> This point of view appears to it entirely reinforced by the fact related in a notice sent on 31 December 1942 to the Ministry by the Counselor of this Embassy that as a result of the intervention of the Italian authorities, the Jews of that nationality are exempted from all discriminatory measures and by the fact more recently brought to its attention that the Portuguese consular authorities also have obtained from the préfectorial authorities of the Mediterranean coast exemption for the Jews of Portuguese nationality from the obligation to have the word Jew affixed to their identity and food card.
>
> Under these conditions, this Embassy can only continue to express all its reserves regarding the application of the measures which are envisaged to Jewish Turks . . . .[181]

The Turkish Consul-General in Marseilles, Bedi'i Arbel, repeatedly advised Jewish Turks not to obey the Vichy government's regulations requiring them to have their religious affiliation stamped in their residence and food papers on the grounds that this might well subject them to more serious persecution in future: [182]

Republic of Turkey, Consulate-General, Marseilles,
13 January 1941

Summary: Concerning the situation of Turkish citizens of Turkey
no. 39/4

---

181. Turkish Embassy to Paris (Vichy) to the French Ministry of Foreign Affairs (Vichy), 25 January 1943. Archives of the Turkish Embassy (Paris), dossier 6127.

182. Turkish Consulate-General (Marseilles) to Turkish Embassy to Paris (Vichy), no. 39/4, 13 January 1943; Turkish Embassy to Paris (Vichy) to Turkish Ministry of Foreign Affairs (Ankara) no. 6127/84, 4 February 1943, in Archives of Turkish Embassy (Paris), file 13–6127.

To the Embassy:

As is well known, Jews have been ordered to have the Jewish seal applied to their food and residence documents, with the threat of various punishments for violation. There is no entry whatsoever as to the religion of those who bear passports or certificates of citizenship issued by the Republic of Turkey. Nor is there any indication of their religion in the residence papers issued by the French. For this reason, those who are required to carry out this directive will have both their persons and their property subjected to all sorts of pursuits. In addition, it is not clear what will happen to those to whose papers this seal is applied when they are examined in the streets. Experience has shown us that they may well be put into a difficult situation. According to information coming from those who have returned here from the occupied zones, the regulation that Jewish Turks wear yellow stars on their breasts was only the start, and led the way to the application of the Jewish seal to their residence and food papers. According to investigations made here, the Italians have excused their Jews from such regulations. Among the neutral countries, the Consulate of Portugal has advised its Jewish citizens not to obey the orders in this respect. This Consulate has therefore given the same advice, and has recommended to Jews who are subjected to penalties as a result to apply to the Consulate, which will act in accordance with orders issued by higher authorities.

With my deepest respects,

(**signed**) Minister Bedi'i Arbel, 13 January 1943 no. 30-6127

At the same time as advice was given to Jewish Turks not to cooperate with officials attempting to impose anti-Jewish restrictions, Arbel along with the Turkish consular authorities in Paris, actively negotiated, in accordance with instructions from Ankara,[183] to exempt Jewish Turks from the anti-

---

183. See, for example, Turkish Minister of Foreign Affairs to Turkish Ambassador to Paris (Vichy) no. 18361/216, 12 December 1941, stating that '. . . while it is natural enough for a foreigner who has settled in a country to be considered as having attached his position and future to its laws, has been stated forcefully by the French Foreign Ministry, we must maintain our rights in relation to the mentioned laws which discriminate among Turkish citizens. . . .' Also Turkish Ambassador to Paris (Vichy) to Turkish Ministry of Foreign Affairs (Ankara), no. 476–6127, 10 January 1942. Archives of the Turkish Embassy (Paris).

Jewish laws which were being introduced in both occupied and unoccupied France.[184] Requests to this effect were made to the appropriate authorities by letter, telephone call, and personal contacts. In occupied France, contact was maintained not only with the regular French officials, particularly with the préfects of police and local mayors, but also with the German occupation officials, including the military commanders, the SS, the Gestapo and Concentration Camp commanders. Communications regarding those sent to concentration camps, including details as to the citizenship of the Jewish Turks involved and their registration with one of the two Turkish consulates in France, were usually sent individually to the German Ambassador in Paris, Otto Abetz,[185] and to the Commander of the Camp in which the Jewish Turks were imprisoned.

In the case of seizure or sealing of Jewish private property, protests and requests for exemptions for Jewish Turks and unsealing of their property were sent to both the French police and German authorities where the property was located, as well as to Ambassador Abetz, Adolph Eichmann's representative in Paris, head of the German security police in occupied France, SS Captain *Obersturmführer* Heinz Röthke, at 82, avenue Foch in Paris, to the *Dienstelle Westen*, at 54 avenue d'Iena, and/or to a certain Dr. Schmitt, head of the German Information Bureau in Paris, whose offices were located at 11 Rue de Saussieres, Paris, VIIIème.[186]

If no response was received within a month, or if appeals came for immediate action from the persons involved or from interested relatives or friends in France and Turkey, the communications were repeated even more

---

184. Turkish Consulate-General (Paris) to Turkish Embassy to Paris (Vichy) no. 82, 3 March 1941; no. 193, 12 May 1941; no. 218, 15 May 1941; no. 265, 4 June 1941; no. 353, 16 July 1941; no. 449, 20 August 1941; no. 451, 20 August 1941; Turkish Consulate-General (Paris) to German Embassy (Paris) no. 492, 5 September 1941, no. 493, 6 September 1941; Turkish Consulate-General (Paris) to Turkish Embassy (Berlin), no. 534, 2 October 1941, no. 536, 6 October 1941, no. 543, 6 October 1941, no. 544, 7 October 1941, no. 545, 8 October 1941, no. 546, 9 October 1941, no. 646, 11 December 1941, no. 687, 23 December 1941; no. Turkish Consulate-General (Paris) to Turkish Foreign Ministry (Ankara) no. 604/167, 21 November 1941; in Archives of Turkish Consulate-General (Paris).

185. On Abetz's role as German Ambassador in occupied Paris, see Jean Tournox, *Le royaume d'Otto* (Paris, 1982); Otto Abetz, *Histoire d'une politique franco-allemande, 1930-1950* (Paris, 1953); and Otto Abetz, *D'Une Prison* (Paris, 1950).

186. For example Turkish Consulate-General (Paris) to Monsieur le Docteur Schmitt, 11 rue des Saussaies, Paris VIIIème, no. F 2101, 12 July 1943. Archives of Turkish Embassy (Paris) and Turkish Foreign Ministry (Ankara), regarding the arrest of Turkish citizens Menahem and Samuel Hatem.

frequently and were supplemented by personal contacts, including at times visits to the camps themselves in order to deliver the necessary Certificates of Citizenship and Passports to the Jewish Turks in question.[187]

The Turkish requests usually took the following form:

Consulate-General of Turkey, Paris, no. 605
The Consulate-General of Turkey at Paris, basing itself on the fact that the Turkish Constitutional Law makes no distinction between its citizens because of their religion, has the honor of asking the Embassy of Germany to give instructions to the competent department that the decision that has begun to affect certain merchants of Turkish nationality, because of the regulation of 18 October 1940, be reconsidered (Document 4).

Document 4. Turkey protests application of anti-Jewish laws to Jewish Turks since its Constitution makes no distinction among citizens of different religions

---

187. Namık Kemal Yolga, Vice Consul in Paris from 1943 to 1945, told the author in an interview on 2 May 1991, as well as in his written statement presented in Appendix 3, that at times he not only went to the camp at Drancy but also to the German trains preparing to take Jews to Auschwitz for extermination in order to deliver personally papers to Jewish Turks, at times rescuing them from the deportation trains heading for the East at the very last minute.

Sometimes the French authorities would simply respond that they could do nothing because the measures in question had been carried out by the German occupation authorities, or by French officials at German insistence, and that application would have to be made directly to the latter, as was the case with the sealed apartment of the Gattegnos. [188]

When the German authorities proceeded to arrest Jewish Turks along with other foreign Jews in a series of raids throughout France in late December, 1940, the Turkish Embassy and consulates strongly protested in a series of notes.[189]

One of these concerned the arrest on the streets of Jewish Turks in Marseilles:[190]

Turkish Embassy, Vichy, 3 January 1943, no. 175–6127

To the Ministry of Foreign Affairs,

The Embassy of Turkey has the honor of bringing to the attention of the Ministry of Foreign Affairs a report which has just been sent by the Consulate-General of Turkey at Marseilles that in the course of an operation carried out recently in the Old Port, several Turkish citizens were also thrown out of their homes and interned in concentration camps.

This concerns the persons whose names and addresses are given in the attached list.

The Embassy would be grateful if the Ministry would intervene to assure the liberation of these persons as well as other Turkish subjects who are in the same situation . . . .

(**signed**) Behiç Erkin, Turkish Ambassador

---

188. See page 77 of this volume.

189. See Turkish Consul-General (Paris) to Turkish Ambassador to Paris (Vichy), no. 272/6127, 15 May 1941, Archives of the Turkish Embassy (Paris); Turkish Consulate-General (Paris) to German Embassy no. F451, 21 August 1941, concerning 16 arrested Jewish Turks; Turkish Consulate-General (Paris) to German Embassy no. F 492, 5 September 1941, reminding the German Embassy of its earlier protest; Turkish Consulate-General (Paris) to German Consulate-General (Paris) no. F 520, 25 September 1941.

190. Turkish Embassy at Paris (Vichy) to French Foreign Ministry (Vichy), 3 February 1943. no. 175.–6127, Archives of Turkish Embassy (Paris) and Turkish Foreign Ministry (Ankara).

List of Interned persons:

Name and Prenames   Place and Date of Birth   Address

Mlle Ester Kamhi, Istanbul, 1921, 3 Rue Nationale.MARSEILLES
Mlle Sol Kamhi, Istanbul, 1922, 3 Rue Nationale, MARSEILLES
Mme Mathilda Benadava, Izmir, 1909, Hotel Atlantic, MARSEILLES
Mr. Isak Avimelah, Istanbul, 1885, 44 Rue Thubaneau, MARSEILLES
Mr. Yeshua Avimelah, Ist., 1919, 44 Rue Thubaneau MARSEILLES
Mme Rachel Hasit, Istanbul, 1880, 4 Rue Mazagran, MARSEILLES
Mr. Lazar Hasit, Istanbul, 1922, 4 Rue Mazagran, MARSEILLES
Mme Kadın Avimelah, Ist., 1892, 44 Rue Thubaneau MARSEILLES
Mr. Ilya Arditti, Istanbul, 1920, 13 Rue d'Aubagne, MARSEILLES

As a result of continued Turkish protests, German ambassador Otto Abetz indicated that his government was willing to make exceptions for Jewish Turks:

German Embassy, Paris, no. 1334, to Turkish Consulate-General, Paris, 28 February 1941.

The German Embassy has the honor to inform the Turkish Consulate-General regarding its verbal note of 28 December 1940 no. 605 as follows:

The steps against Jews that were ordered by the Military Commander in France were developed together with the French state and were issued as part of an effort to organize and meet public security and other requirements. The authorities do not allow exceptions, and the steps apply to all people who are residents of France without consideration as to their nationality and regardless of the application of other laws.

The German Embassy is, however, willing, within the framework of the regulations, to support isolated cases requested by the Turkish Consulate-General regarding individual cases involving Jewish enterprises if they involve persons of Turkish nationality.[191]

---

191. Enclosed in Turkish Consul-General (Paris) Cevdet Dülger to Turkish Ambassador (Paris) no. 16–6127, 3 March 1941. Archives of the Turkish Embassy (Paris).

While Jewish Turks continued to be arrested along with other Jews despite these assurances, by May of the same year the Turkish Consul-General in Paris, Cevdet Dülger, was able to report that those who were Turkish citizens were being quickly released by the Germans, with apologies that their arrest had been the result of what they preferred to call mistakes:

REPUBLIC OF TURKEY, CONSULATE-GENERAL
Paris, 15 May 1941

To His Excellency the Ambassador,
Turkish Embassy to Paris (Vichy)
Yesterday about four thousand foreign Jews were gathered together by French authorities and sent to concentration camps. Most of these were citizens of occupied countries like Poland, Czechoslovakia and Austria. While some Jews who are Turkish citizens were also arrested, as a result of our intervention by telephone with the Préfect of Police, they said that it was a mistake, and that these would be released immediately.
I offer my most sincere regards.
The Consul-General,
(**signed**) Cevdet Dülger[192]

The mass arrests of Jews continued, however, in both the German and Vichy government zones, and while Turkish protests often were able to secure the release of their citizens, the responses were increasingly unhelpful as the war stretched on. Thus the local French police responded to complaints concerning arrests of Jews in Marseilles on the nights of 23 and 24 January 1943, that though the persons in question had been arrested only for questioning, they had, indeed, been transported to the concentration camp of Compiègne in the German Occupation zone:

State of France, Regional Préfecture of Marseilles, Intendant of Police
No. 896 POL, Marseilles, 9 February 1943
The Regional Préfect to the Consul-General of Turkey

---

192. Turkish Consul-General Cevdet Dülger to Turkish Embassy to Paris (Vichy), 15 May 1941. Archives of the Turkish Embassy (Paris).

REF: The Arrest of Turkish Subjects

REPLY: to your letters no. 58/12 of 25 January 1943, and no. 63/14 of 28 January 1943.

To the Consulate of Turkey,

Mr. Consul-General,

In response to your letters cited in the reference, I have the honor of informing you that it is true that a certain number of foreigners of all nationalities were apprehended in their homes during the nights of 22 to 23 and 23 to 24 January 1943. These foreigners were to be the object of a full examination, and for that reason were kept at the Prison of Beaumettes. Before these screening operations began, it was decided that they should be transferred to a center in the occupied zone so that the judicial records in Paris could be examined more easily. It is for that reason that a train of French and foreign citizens was sent during the morning of 24 January to the Camp at Compiègne where these persons are now located under the guard of the French and German police. I have sent to this Commission officials of my office. The case of your citizens will be pointed out to them. I will share with you the results of my inquiries . . . .

The Regional Préfecture, Intendant of Police

(**signed**) M. de Porzie. [193]

Soon after the initial orders were issued on 4 September 1942 requiring all foreign Jews who had entered France after December 1933 and who were currently without employment to register with the police so that they could be grouped into forced labor battalions of foreign workers,[194] the Turkish Embassy to Paris (Vichy) complained to the French Foreign Ministry, which replied that the measures had been taken because of pressure from the

193. Prefecture Régionale de Marseille. Intendant de Police to Turkish Consulate-General no. 296 POL, 9 February 1943. Archives of Turkish Embassy (Paris) and Turkish Foreign Ministry (Ankara).

194. Turkish Embassy to Paris (Vichy) to French Ministry of Foreign Affairs (Vichy) no. 1395, 20 October 1942. Archives of the Turkish Embassy (Paris). Filed on 16 June 1941, no. 272/6127.

German occupation authorities, and that the French government could therefore do nothing about them. [195]

Turkish Ambassador Behiç Erkin immediately protested to the French authorities:

> . . . foreign Jews of Turkish nationality enjoy . . . regular consular protection and are therefore exempted from incorporation (into work gangs of unemployed foreign Jews in France), whether or not they have employment and means of existence . . . . The Turkish Embassy cannot but view this measure as a grave attack on the most elementary interests and rights of Turkish citizens residing in France, and it is in direct contradiction with the assurances that the Ministry of Foreign Affairs gave it in its notes of last 26 October . . . . The Embassy . . . asks the Ministry of Foreign Affairs, in view of the urgency of the matter, to intervene with the competent authorities as rapidly as possible so that Turkish citizens will be exempted from the arbitrary action with which they are now threatened.[196]

He went on to report to Ankara on 15 December 1942:

> I have wired the French Foreign Ministry by telegram asking that Turkish Jewish subjects not be included in the decision recently published in the newspapers by the Préfecture of Marseilles that all foreign Jews who entered France since December 1933 and who are without work or in need be gathered in foreign worker groups. In the meantime the French police chief has instructed Jewish Turks who have asked for information from the Préfecture and from the Consulate that they should register themselves at the assembly offices in order to prevent more serious action to be taken against them. I am attaching samples of the letters which

---

195. Turkish Embassy (Paris/Vichy) to Turkish Foreign Ministry, no. 1667–1054–6127, no date, but probably 15 December 1942. (Turkish Foreign Ministry Archives, Ankara and Archives of Turkish Embassy, Paris).

196. Turkish Embassy to Paris (Vichy) to French Foreign Ministry, no. 1611–6127, 17 December 1942; also Turkish Embassy to Paris (Vichy) to Turkish Foreign Ministry (Ankara) no. 1667–1054–6127, and Turkish Embassy to Paris (Vichy) to Turkish Consulate-General (Marseilles), 15 December 1942. Archives of the Turkish Embassy (Paris), file 1620–1011–6127.

the Marseilles Consulate-General sent to the Provincial office and which the Embassy sent to the French Foreign Ministry. The answers will immediately be communicated to the Foreign Ministry.

The Counselor of the Turkish Embassy discussed the matter with M. Lagarde, who said that the measure was taken due to the insistence of the Germans. It is very probable that the French will not dare to secure any exemptions from carrying out this regulation. It is most likely therefore that we will receive a negative answer to our request. We ask therefore for instructions as to what we should do in that case.[197]

Erkin instructed his Consul-General in Marseilles to continue insisting on the rights of all Turkish citizens:[198]

Jewish citizens whose papers are in order cannot be subjected to forced labor, and if such situations arise it is natural that we should provide them with protection. The préfects of police should be reminded of the relevant instructions, and it is necessary to intervene with the competent authorities when necessary.[199]

When local authorities ignored the exemption and continued to impress Jewish Turks for local road labor projects, the Turkish Embassy to Paris (Vichy) protested to the French Foreign Ministry (Vichy),[200] and was assured by the latter that:

197. Turkish Embassy (Paris/Vichy) to Turkish Foreign Ministry, no. 1667–1054–6127. no date, but probably 15 December 1942 (Turkish Foreign Ministry Archives, Ankara and Archives of Turkish Embassy, Paris).

198. Turkish Consulate-General (Marseilles) to Turkish Embassy to Paris (Vichy) no. 686/128 (File 368–6127), Marseilles, 19 December 1942, and no. 6127/679, 22 December 1942, in Archives of Turkish Embassy (Paris).

199. Turkish Ambassador to Paris (Vichy) to Turkish Consul-General (Marseilles) no. 44–17, 27 January 1944. Archives of the Turkish Embassy (Paris) no. 27/I/44 17/169.

200. Turkish Embassy to Paris (Vichy) to French Foreign Ministry no. 1395, 20 October 1942. Archives of the Turkish Embassy (Paris).

Instructions have just been received that foreign workers enjoying consular protection cannot be included on labor lists without their agreement.[201]

The Turkish Consul-General in Marseilles, Bedi'i Arbel, then appealed directly to the local authorities who were attempting to carry out the order:[202]

> Consulate-General of Turkey, Marseilles
> 17 December 1942, no. 649/80
>
> Mr. Préfect,
> I have the honor of enclosing a copy of a letter that I have had to send to the Regional Préfect of Bouches-du-Rhone regarding a decree published in the newspapers on the subject of obligatory work to which all Jews are to be subjected regardless of their nationality. I am counting on your usual accommodation to apply a special regime to Jews who are Turkish citizens until an agreement is reached between our two governments. I have charged Mr. Necdet Kent, Vice Consul, to bring this communication to you personally and to discuss this matter with you. I hope that you will give him a favorable reply. As this matter is quite serious, I hope that he will be able to secure satisfactory results after having discussed the subject with you . . . .
> (**signed**) Bedi'i Arbel
> To Mr. Préfect of the Alpes-Maritimes, Nice

The Turkish Consulate at Marseilles was subsequently informed by its Préfect that Jewish Turks were being exempted from the labor regulations until he could receive further instructions from the Vichy government:

> State of France,
> Préfecture of Alpes-Maritimes, 4th Division, 2nd Bureau,
> no. I.G. REF 47240 4/2, Nice, 19 December 1942,

---

201. French Ministry of Foreign Affairs, *Unions Internationales*, no. 3491, Vichy, 26 October 1942. Archives of the Turkish Embassy (Paris) no. 567/27 X 1942.

202. Bedi'i Arbel, Turkish Consul-General (Marseilles) to Monsieur le Préfet des Alpes–Maritimes (Nice), Marseilles, no. 649/80, 17 December 1942. Archives of the Turkish Embassy (Paris) and Turkish Foreign Ministry (Ankara).

Dear Consul-General,

In response to your letter of 17 December of this year, and following the interview I have had with your Vice Consul M. Kent, I have the honor of informing you that I have contacted the Chief of Government regarding the case of the Jews who are Turkish citizens in relation to the measures to incorporate into Companies of Foreign Workers all foreign Jews who lack resources or who are indigent. While awaiting instructions from my government, I have ordered the suspension of these measures in regard to your citizens . . . .

(**signed**) The Préfect [203]

Turkey also successfully protected Jewish Turks in both zones from regulations requiring them to join other Jews in leaving certain border areas as well as being concentrated in ghettos and to insert the word Jew on their identity papers as well as their clothing.[204]

Whenever the Turkish diplomats noticed that Jewish Turks were being treated less favorably than those of other neutral countries, it immediately protested to the French and German authorities, securing rapid rectifications of the situations in question.[205]

The question of exemptions from the anti-Jewish laws in France for Jews of Turkey and other neutral countries was strenuously debated among

---

203. Prefect du Alpes Maritimes, 4é Division, 2d bureau, no. I.G., ref. no. 47240 4/2, to Turkish Consul-General (marseilles), Nice, 19 December 1942. Archives of Turkish Embassy (Paris) and Turkish Foreign Ministry (Ankara).

204. Turkish Embassy to Paris (Vichy) to Turkish Foreign Ministry no. 1667–1054–6127, no date, but probably 15 December 1942. Also Turkish Consul-General (Marseilles) Bedi'i Arbel to Monsieur le Préfet des Alpes–Maritimes (Nice) no. 649/80, 17 December 1942, and the response, exempting Jewish Turks from local labor regulations, Préfet du Alpes Maritimes, 4é Division, 2d bureau, no. I.G., ref. no. 47240 4/2 to Turkish Consul-General (Marseilles), Nice, 19 December 1942, in Turkish Foreign Ministry Archives (Ankara) and Archives of Turkish Embassy (Paris). Turkish Embassy to Paris (Vichy) to Turkish Consulate-General (Marseilles) no. 132–6127, 26 January 1943, no. 146-6127, 28 January 1943 and no. 24–6127, 9 January 1943; Turkish Embassy (Vichy) to Turkish Foreign Ministry (Ankara) no. 214–114–6127, Vichy, 8 February 1943; Turkish Consul-General (Marseilles), Namık Kemal Yolga to Turkish Ambassador to Paris (Vichy) no. 1876/43, Paris, 17 February 1943, in Archives of the Turkish Embassy (Paris), file 491–6127.

205. See, for example, Marseilles Vice Consul Namık Kemal Yolga to Paris Consulate-General, 26 July 1943, and Paris Consul-General Fikret Şefik Özdoğancı to Turkish Embassy to Paris (Vichy) no. 2937/62/6127, 24 December 1943, in Archives of Turkish Embassy (Paris).

German officials in Paris and Berlin with German Ambassador Abetz strongly supporting the desire of Himmler and Eichmann to end the exemptions :

> In connection with my written report of 7 September regarding the use of the Star of David, according to recent investigations there are in Paris alone the following number of Jews with foreign nationality who until now have not been required to wear the Star of David: 500 Italian Jews, 3790 Rumanian Jews, 1570 Hungarian Jews, 3046 Jewish Turks, 1416 Greek Jews, and a certain number of Spanish and Bulgarian Jews.
>
> It is reported that they behave in an arrogant way, and as a result there are considerable technical difficulties in carrying out the steps against Jews . . . .
>
> I ask you to make clear, as rapidly as possible, whether because of the recently published laws against Bulgarian Jews, they should from now onwards also be identified with the Star of David and sent to the concentration camps.
>   ABETZ.[206]

Again on 24 September, Abetz urged Berlin to pressure the neutral countries to apply the anti-Jewish laws to their own Jews:

> Excluding the Italians, who have in the occupied territories about 500 Jews, the following are causing special difficulties: The Turks with 3046 Jews, Spain with 285 Jews, the Greeks with 1416 Jews, the Hungarians with 1537 Jews, and Switzerland with 139 Jews. We are asking these governments, through the German representatives in their capitals, to prepare laws concerning Jews, or if there are valid laws already, to comply with them. . .
> ABETZ[207]

---

206. Berlin, *Auswärtiges Amt*/Ministry of Foreign Affairs, no. D III-774. My gratitude to Mr. Serge Klarsfeld, of Paris, France, for supplying me with a copy of this document from the Archives of the German Ministry of Foreign Affairs in Bonn.

207. Berlin, *Auswärtiges Amt*/ Ministry of Foreign Affairs no. D III–810, 21 September 1942. My gratitude to Mr. Serge Klarsfeld for supplying me with a copy of this document from the Archives of the German Ministry of Foreign Affairs in Bonn.

Even after the Final Solution was put into effect, however, the German Embassy in Paris continued to regularly advise the Turkish Consulate-General in Paris that it would release from concentration camps in France the Turkish citizens on whose behalf it was intervening if guarantees were given that these persons would immediately be repatriated to Turkey (Document 5):

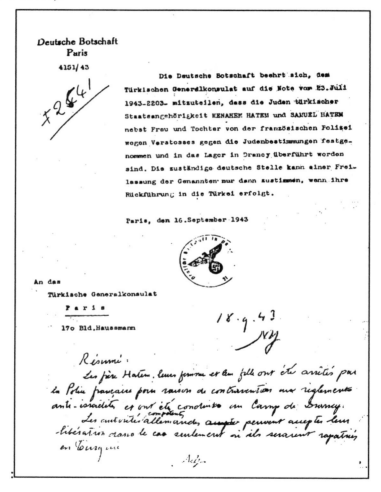

Document 5. Germans will release Jewish Turks from Concentration Camps in France if they are immediately repatriated to Turkey

At the same time that it granted exemptions and rectifications for Turkish citizens, however, the French Foreign Ministry at Vichy advised the Turkish Embassy that it could not secure the release of Jewish Turks who had committed what it, or the Germans, considered to be crimes, as for example in the case of Mr. Israel Avidor, who had been imprisoned since September 1942 at the Concentration Camp at Vernet (Ariège) even though he had been given permission by both the Turkish and French governments to be repatriated to Turkey:

> Vichy, 24 August 1942
> State of France, Ministry of Foreign Affairs
> Unions Internationales IC 12 no. 2896
>
> To the Embassy of Turkey, Vichy
> The Ministry of Foreign Affairs presents its compliments to the Embassy of Turkey and has the honor of informing it, regarding its note of last 29 May, that it has transmitted to the competent authorities the request of Mr. Israel Avidor asking that he be placed in a supervised residence.
> The Ministry of the Interior has just made it known that to its great regret it is not possible to presently envisage the liberation of the person in question because of his activity in communist circles and relations with individuals who are suspect from the national point of view.[208]

TURKISH INTERVENTION TO SECURE THE UNSEALING OF THE PARIS APARTMENTS OF JEWISH TURKS

When apartments or houses of Jewish Turks were confiscated and sealed by the Nazis or the French, the Turkish consulates went through lengthy procedures to get them unsealed and returned to those who owned or rented them. When the owners were themselves absent, either due to flight to southern France or elsewhere or to incarceration in concentration camps until the consulates could get them out, the keys to the unsealed apartments were turned over to Turkish administrators who cared for them until the owners returned. Similar efforts were made to secure the return of furniture, money, or even wine cellars that were confiscated when the apartments were

---

208. Archives of the Turkish Embassy (Paris), file 6127/462, 26 August 1942.

initially sealed, but in this the Turkish consulates were much less successful since the Germans usually insisted that the movable properties in question could no longer be traced.

Where apartments or shops were sealed while their owners or renters remained free, they were able to notify the Turkish consulates on their own, as for example in the cases of Vitali Benbassa, a Parisian dentist, who had fled to Nice soon after the Germans had arrived in Paris, and Eleonore Fresco, who had left her Paris apartment behind when she fled to Lyon. Examination of the documents in their files, which remain in the archives at the Turkish Embassy in Paris, gives an idea of the procedures that were followed:

THE VITALI BENBASSA FILE

Turkish citizen, no. 707 T.F. practicing dentistry in Paris at 89 Rue Lafayette
Fled to refuge in Nice and registered with Marseilles Consulate 6 January 1943
Property in Paris sealed by *Dienstelle Westen* on 20 February 1943
Property unsealed on 20 August 1943

a. TURKISH CONSULATE-GENERAL CERTIFIES THAT DENTIST VITALI BENBASSA IS TURKISH CITIZEN PROPERLY REGISTERED AT PARIS CONSULATE. Turkish Consulate-General, Paris, 23 October 1940. Archives of Turkish Embassy (Paris) and Turkish Foreign Ministry (Ankara).

Republic of Turkey
Paris Consulate General
No. 707 T.F.
Paris, 23 October 1940

The Consulate-General of Turkey at Paris certifies that Mr. Benbassa, occupying the apartment situated on the 2nd floor of the house located at 89 Rue Lafayette in Paris in order to exercise there the profession of dentist, is a Turkish citizen and inscribed as such on the registers of this Consulate under no. 707 T.F.

b. TURKISH CONSULATE INFORMED THAT GERMANS HAVE SEALED VITALI BENBASSA APARTMENT IN PARIS AND REMOVED HIS WINE CELLAR. M. Pinto, 30 Rue Pixéricourt, Paris XX to Turkish Consulate-General (Paris), 8 March 1943. Turkish registration no. F 1193. Archives of Turkish Embassy (Paris) and Turkish Foreign Ministry (Ankara) Paris 8 March 1943.

> Paris, 8 March 1943
> Mr. Consul-General of the Republic of Turkey, Paris
> Mr. Consul,
> Following my visit today, I have the honor of informing you by this letter that I have just learned that the apartment belonging to Turkish citizen Vitali Benbassa, the dentist, and located at 89 Rue Lafayette, Paris IX, was sealed on 20 February 1943 by the occupying authorities, *Dienstelle Westen, Abschnitt Gross-Paris,* Telephone Passy 85-42, while the contents of the wine seller were taken. Given that Mr. Benbassa is a Turkish citizen, regularly inscribed in your registers, and is presently in southern France, where he has been notified, and so that he will not suffer great losses caused by the removal of all his goods contained in the apartment, and considering that he is under the august protection of your grand authority, I ask you to have the goodness to intervene with all urgency with the competent authorities in order to spare his furniture the same fate as his wine cellar. In all expectations, and with all my recognition, I ask you to accept, Mr. Consul-General, the assurance of my most special consideration.
> **(signed)** Pinto
> **Consular minutes:** Pinto, 30 Rue Pixéricourt, Paris XX.
> F 1193. Mlle Bousquet 9-3-43, NY

c. TURKISH CONSUL-GENERAL (MARSEILLES) BEDI'I ARBEL CERTIFIES THAT VITALI HAYIM BENBASSA IS DULY REGISTERED TURKISH CITIZEN. Bedi'i Arbel, Orta Elçi, Turkish Consulate-General (Marseilles) to Consulate-General (Paris) no. 136/10, 11 March 1943. Archives of Turkish Embassy (Paris) and Turkish Foreign Ministry (Ankara).

> Consulate-General of Turkey
> Marseilles, 11 March 1943, no. 136/10
>
> To the Consulate-General at Paris,

I am sending you the original of a letter dated 11 March 1943 from Vitali Hayim Benbassa, who has Certificate of Citizenship no. 675/3935 dated 24 December 1940, which he obtained from higher authorities, and who is registered at our Consulate-General under no. 2747/5/4, dated 6 January 1943, and who now is resident in Nice. As can be understood from what he has written, his apartment in Paris has been occupied by the German authorities, and he asks that efforts be made to secure its evacuation.

With my deepest respects,
(**signed**) Bedi'i Arbel, Minister

Consular minute: Registration no. 178, date 19 March 1943. Mademoiselle Bousquet, 22 March 1943, Namık Yolga

d. VITALI HAYIM BENBASSA WRITES TURKISH CONSULATE (MARSEILLES) FROM NICE ASKING IT TO ARRANGE LIFTING OF SEALS FROM HIS PARIS APARTMENT. Hayim (Vitali) Benbassa, 172 bis Avenue de la Californie, Nice, to Turkish Consulate-General (Paris), 11 March 1943. Archives of Turkish Embassy (Paris) and Turkish Foreign Ministry (Ankara).

Nice, 13 March 1943

Mr. Consul-General of the Turkish Republic at Marseilles
Dear Mr. Consul,
I have the honor of informing you by the present letter that I have just received a letter from Paris which informs me that the occupying authorities: *Dienstelle Westen Abschnitt Gross-Paris,* telephone Passy 85.42 have sealed the apartment that I occupy on 89 Rue Lafayette in Paris on 20 February 1943, while removing the contents of my wine cellar. Since I am now located in southern France, and in order to avoid the great prejudice that the removal of all my goods in that apartment would cause me, being a Turkish citizen and regularly inscribed in your registers, the Paris Consulate has asked for an urgent communication from you to know if I am still regularly registered with your administration. Considering that I am under your protection and your great authority, I ask you to have the goodness to intervene with all

urgency with the competent authorities to spare my furniture the same fate as my wine seller. In view of the urgency, and the fact that I cannot travel since I am a foreigner, I have asked Madame Sidi to communicate this to you while awaiting the reception of my letter.

In this situation, and with all my gratitude, I ask you to accept, Mr. Consul-General, the assurance of my most estimable consideration.

Benbassa Hayim (Vitali), 172 bis Avenue de la Californie, Nice
Consular minute: V.O. 24-12-1942

e. HAYIM BENBASSA WRITES TURKISH CONSULATE (PARIS) ASKING REMOVAL OF SEALS FROM HIS PARIS APARTMENT. Hayim Benbassa, Nice, to Turkish Consulate-General (Paris), 16 March 1943. Archives of Turkish Embassy (Paris) and Turkish Foreign Ministry (Ankara).

Nice, 16 March 1943

Mr. Consul-General of the Turkish Republic in Paris
Mr. Consul,
I have just learned by a letter from Paris that my apartment that I occupy at 89 Rue Lafayette in Paris has been put under seals by the occupying authorities on 20 February 1943, while the contents of my wine cellar were removed. In view of the urgency, and the fact that I am ill in the south, without being able to travel, I have written to the Consulate at Marseilles, with which I am properly registered, so that his office will do what is necessary in Paris. On the other part, being always properly registered with your administration, and having my rights as a Turkish citizen, I ask you to intervene with the proper authorities in order to secure the unsealing of my apartment and to avoid any further removal of my property.
(signed) Hayim Benbassa

f. TURKISH CONSULATE-GENERAL (PARIS) ASKS GERMAN EMBASSY TO ARRANGE REMOVAL OF SEALS FROM PARIS APARTMENT OF VITALI HAYIM BENBASSA. Turkish Consulate-

General (Paris) to German Embassy (Paris) no. F 1198, 24 March 1943.
Archives of Turkish Embassy (Paris) and Turkish Foreign Ministry
(Ankara).

> Republic of Turkey, Paris Consulate-General
> 24 March 1943 no. F 1198

> To the Embassy of Germany,
> The Consulate-General of Turkey at Paris presents its
> compliments to the Embassy of Germany and has the honor of
> bringing to its attention the following:
> Mr. Vitali Hayim Benbassa is a Turkish citizen holding
> Certificate of Nationality no. 707 TP, registered at present at the
> Consulate-General of Turkey at Marseilles since 6 January 1943
> under no. 2747/5/4, living at 89 Rue Lafayette in Paris and
> presently located in southern France.
> Seals were put on the apartment of the aforementioned by
> the *Dienstelle Westen Abschnitt Gross-Paris* on 20 February 1943,
> and the contents of his wine cellar were removed.
> Since he is a Turkish citizen properly registered with the
> Turkish consulate, the Consulate-General of Turkey asks the
> Estimable Embassy of Germany to have the goodness to intervene
> as a matter of urgency with the occupying authorities so that the
> seals placed on the apartment in question are removed, that the
> contents of his wine cellar which were taken are restituted, and
> that the apartment of this Turkish citizen be left intact with its
> furniture installed there. This Consulate-General thanks in
> advance the Embassy of Germany for its obliging intervention to
> this effect, and seizes this occasion to reiterate to it the assurances
> of its high consideration.
> Paris, 24 March 1943
> (signed) Consul-General

g. ATTORNEY P. PINTO ASKS TURKISH CONSULATE-
GENERAL FOR CERTIFICATE SHOWING THAT APARTMENT OF
BENBASSA HAIM BELONGS TO TURKISH CITIZEN. P. Pinto to
Turkish Consulate-General (Paris), Paris, 27 March 1943. Archives of
Turkish Embassy (Paris) and Turkish Foreign Ministry (Ankara).

Mr. Consul-General of Turkey at Paris
Mr. Consul,

I have the honor to inform you by the present letter that, with powers granted me by Mr. Benbassa Hayim to pursue his affairs, I ask you to have the goodness to send me the necessary certificate to certify that his apartment situated at 89 Rue Lafayette in Paris belongs to a Turkish citizen. The copy of the lease and the last rental payment have been deposited with you. Please accept, Mr. Consul-General, the assurance of my high consideration.

(**signed**) P. Pinto, 27 March 1943

h. GERMAN EMBASSY INFORMS TURKISH CONSULATE-GENERAL THAT IT HAS CONTACTED AUTHORITIES REGARDING SEALS ON HAYIM BENBASSA APARTMENT AND WILL PROVIDE FURTHER INFORMATION WHEN AVAILABLE. German Embassy (Paris) to Turkish Consulate-General (Paris), Nr. 583/43 (Turkish Consular registration no. F 1500), Paris, 3 April 1943. Archives of Turkish Embassy (Paris) and Turkish Foreign Ministry (Ankara).

German Embassy, Paris, Prot.Er. 583/43

To the Turkish Consulate-General, Paris

The German Embassy wishes to acknowledge receipt of the note no. F 1193 of 24 March 1943. It is in contact with the relevant authorities, and will provide further information when it is received. Paris, 3 April 1943

i. TURKISH CONSULATE-GENERAL INFORMS M. PINTO THAT SEALS HAVE BEEN REMOVED FROM PARIS APARTMENT OF HAYIM BENBASSA. Turkish Consulate-General (Paris) to M. Pinto, 30, Rue Pixéricourt, Paris XXème, no. F 2205, 23 July 1945. Archives of Turkish Embassy (Paris) and Turkish Foreign Ministry (Ankara).

Republic of Turkey, Paris Consulate-General, no. F 2205
Mr. Pinto
30 Rue Pixéricourt, Paris XX
Sir,

Following a communication from the Embassy of Germany, I can inform you that the seals which had been placed on the apartment of Mr. Hayim Benbassa have been removed.

Please accept, Sir, my special greetings.

(**signed**) The Consul, Paris, 23 July 1943

j. PINTO INFORMS TURKISH CONSULATE THAT THOUGH GERMAN EMBASSY WROTE THAT SEALS HAD BEEN REMOVED FROM BENBASSA APARTMENT IN PARIS, THEY HAD IN FACT REMAINED. SUBSEQUENT NOTE STATES THAT TURKISH ADMINISTRATOR RECEP ZERMAN ATTENDED ACTUAL LIFTING OF SEALS ON 20 AUGUST 1943. S. Pinto, 30 Rue Pixéricourt, Paris XX to Turkish Consulate-General (Paris), 13 August 1943. Turkish registration no. F 2205. Archives of Turkish Embassy (Paris) and Turkish Foreign Ministry (Ankara).

Paris, 13 August 1943

To the Consulate-General of the Turkish Republic,

170 Boulevard Haussmann in Paris

Mr. Consul-General,

I have the honor of acknowledging receipt of your letter of 23 July 1943 no. F 2205 in which you informed me that as a result of a communication from the Embassy of Germany the seals which were placed on the apartment of Mr. Hayim Benbassa were removed.

I went to the apartment yesterday, and to my great regret, I learned that contrary to this communication, the seals remained. It is most likely a matter of a delay in execution or a mistake, and I ask you to do what is necessary.

In all expectation, I present you, Mr. Consul-General, the assurance of my highest consideration.

(**signed**) S. Pinto

Address: S. Pinto, 39 Rue Pixéricourt, Paris XX

Consular minute: Dossier of 16 August 1943. Namık Yolga. Mademoiselle Guicheau, Notify the Embassy of Germany, 16 August 1943. Mr. Zerman attended the removal of the seals, and the keys have been deposited at the consulate, 20 August 1943.

THE ELEONORE FRESCO FILE

Turkish citizen; certificate of nationality no. 870 TP, renewed at Marseilles on 16 March 1943 under number 2756/434/96, valid until 16 March 1944.

Wife of Philon D. Fresco, owner of Paris apartment, now living at 21, Rue de la Poste, c/o Mr. Albert Passy, Lyon-Villeurbanne.

Paris home: Villa Dancourt no. 1, Paris XVIIIème sealed by Germans.

Apartment unsealed on 9 July 1943 by agent Recep Zerman and German officials, keys turned over to Turkish Consulate-General.

a. ELEONORE FRESCO ASKS TURKISH CONSULATE TO SECURE REMOVAL OF SEALS TO HER APARTMENT IN PARIS. Eleonore Fresco, 21 Rue de la Poste, c/o Mr. Albert Passy, Lyon-Villeurbanne, to Turkish Consul-General (Paris), Lyon, 10 May 1943. Archives of Turkish Embassy (Paris) and Turkish Foreign Ministry (Ankara.)

Lyon, 10 May 1943
To Mr. Consul-General of Turkey at Paris,
Mr. Consul,

I have just been advised that the German authorities have just seized my furniture and placed seals on the door of my apartment located at 1 Villa Dancourt, Paris VIII, because I am a Jew. The concièrge of the building told them that I have Turkish nationality and am properly registered with the Consulate, but it had no effect. After making an inventory of my furniture, etc., and placing the seals, the German officers declared to the concièrge that they would return in a few days to remove everything.

I am a Turkish citizen, registered with you since my arrival in France in 1930, like my husband and my two children. In fear of finding myself in default according to the law, I have not ceased to register myself and to renew my Nationality Card for 1943 at the Turkish Consulate of Marseilles under no. 2757/434/96, dated 16 March 1943.

I ask you, in consequence, to be good enough to protect my legitimate interests and to protest against this arbitrary act. I left in my apartment my valuable furniture, precious paintings, lingerie, books, and the like, which today represent for me a small fortune. Please request, as a matter of urgency, the removal of the seals, because experience has shown previously that the German authorities have the habit of presenting one with a *fait accompli* before the arrival of a protest or legitimate claim. I have paid the rent of my apartment regularly, and if I have not returned from here to Paris with my family, this is only because it is forbidden for foreigners, particularly Jews, to enter the occupied zone.

In the hope that you will be good enough to do what is necessary as a matter of urgency, before it is too late, I ask you to accept, Mr. Consul, the assurance of my estimable consideration

(signed) Eleonore Fresco

Eleonore Fresco, wife of Philon D. Fresco, proprietor of the apartment, address: 21 Rue de la Poste, c/o Mr. Albert Passy, Lyon-Villeurbanne

Consular minute: 870 T.P. 13/5/943 R

b. TURKISH CONSULATE-GENERAL (PARIS) ASKS GERMAN EMBASSY (PARIS) TO SECURE REMOVAL OF SEALS FROM APARTMENT OF ELEONORE FRESCO. Turkish Consulate-General (Paris) to German Embassy (Paris) no. F 1754, 17 May 1943. Archives of Turkish Embassy (Paris) and Turkish Foreign Ministry (Paris).

Republic of Turkey, Paris Consulate-General
17 May 1943 no. F 1754

To the Embassy of Germany, 78, Rue de Lille, Paris VII

The Consulate-General of Turkey at Paris presents its compliments to the Embassy of Germany and has the honor of bringing what follows to its attention:

Madame Eleonore Fresco, Turkish citizen bearing Certificate of Nationality no. 870 TP, renewed at Marseilles on 16 March 1943 under no. 2756/434/96 and valid until 16 March 1944, at present living at Lyon, and who has her house at Paris VIII, 1 Villa Dancourt, has informed us that the occupying authorities have just placed seals on her apartment.

Since she is a Turkish citizen regularly registered, the Consulate-General of Turkey asks the Embassy of Germany to be good enough to intervene with the competent occupying authorities so that the seals placed on the apartment of Madame Eleonore Fresco be removed.

This Consulate-General thanks in advance the Estimable Embassy for the trouble that it will take in this regard, and seizes this occasion to reiterate to it the assurances of its high consideration.

(**signed**) Consul-General, Paris, 17 May 1943

c. ELEONORE FRESCO INFORMS TURKISH CONSULATE-GENERAL (PARIS) THAT SEALS STILL REMAIN ON HER PARIS APARTMENT. Eleonore Fresco, Allevard les Bains, France, to Turkish Consulate-General (Paris), 31 May 1943. Turkish registration no. F 1902. Archives of Turkish Embassy (Paris) and Turkish Foreign Ministry (Ankara).

Allevard les Bains, 31 May 1943

To Mr. Consul-General of Turkey, Paris
Mr. Consul,
I have the honor of informing you that despite your protest, the occupation authorities have not yet removed the seals placed by them on my apartment, situated at 1 Villa Danecourt, Paris XVIII.

I ask you, by the present letter, to be good enough to renew your protest, with even more energy, against this act, which is contrary to international conventions as well as those signed between Germany and Turkey. In thanking you in advance, I ask you to accept, Mr. Consul, the assurance of my estimable consideration.

(**signed**) E. Fresco
Eleonore Fresco

Consular minutes: Turkish citizen registered at Marseilles under no. 2756/434/96 of 16 March 1943'. 'F 1902 5/6/943

d. GERMAN AUTHORITIES INDICATE THEY ARE READY TO REMOVE SEALS FROM APARTMENT OF ELEONORE FRESCO IN PARIS. ASKS TURKISH CONSULATE TO NAME OFFICIAL TO GO WITH THEIR OFFICIALS TO BREAK SEAL AND REOPEN APARTMENT. Abschnittsleiter, Dienstelle Westen, Abschnitt Gross-Paris to Turkish Consulate-General, 170 Boulevard Haussmann, Paris, no. DW

5130/F. 650/Dre./Dr., 9 June 1943. Archives of the Turkish Embassy (Paris) and Turkish Foreign Ministry (Ankara).

> Dienstelle Westen, Abschnitt Gross-Paris
> DW 5130/F. 650/Dre./Dr., O.U.
> 9 June 1943

> To the Turkish Consulate-General, 170 Boulevard Haussmann, Paris
> Subject: Dwelling of Eleonore Fresco
> 1, Villa Dancourt, Paris

> In answer to your letter of 17 May 1943 in regard to the above-named matter, I can inform you that I am ready to unseal the dwelling. I ask you to appoint an official to go with our officials to break the seal and open the apartment.
> **(signed)** Abschnittsleiter (Sectional Director)

Consular minute: N. Yolga . B. Recep 14/6/943

e. RECEP ZERMAN TAKES OVER AS ADMINISTRATOR OF ELEONORE FRESCO APARTMENT IN PARIS. WENT WITH GERMAN OFFICIALS TO THE APARTMENT ON 9 JULY 1943, BROKE SEAL, FOUND EVERYTHING IN ORDER, LOCKED APARTMENT AND TURNED KEYS OVER TO NAMIK KEMAL YOLGA OF TURKISH CONSULATE. Recep Zerman to Turkish Consulate-General (Paris), 16 July 1943. Archives of Turkish Embassy (Paris).

> Paris, 16 July 1943
> To the Paris Consulate-General,
> I went with the German authorities on 9 July 1943 to the dwelling at 1 Villa Dancourt in Paris of Eleonore Fresco, a Turkish citizen regularly registered at our Marseilles Consulate-General, on which the German authorities had placed a seal. We found that the seal which had been placed on the front door had not been broken. We took the keys to the apartment from the concièrge, broke the seal and went inside. All the furniture in the rooms remained in order. The windows were closed from inside.

We all went outside together and locked the door. I took the keys with me and delivered them to the Vice Consul at the Consulate-General, Namık Kemal Yolga. This is all that happened.

(**signed**) Recep Zerman, Clerk

f. TURKISH CONSULATE-GENERAL INFORMS ELEONORE FRESCO THAT SEALS HAVE BEEN REMOVED FROM HER PARIS APARTMENT AND KEYS ARE AT CONSULATE. ASKS TO WHOM THEY SHOULD BE GIVEN. Namık Kemal Yolga, Acting Consul-General at Turkish Consulate-General (Paris) to Madame Eleonore Fresco, no. F 1306, 3 August 1943. Archives of Turkish Embassy (Paris) and Turkish Foreign Ministry (Ankara).

Consulate-General of Turkey
170 Boulevard Haussmann, Paris VIII
3 August 1943, no. F 1306

Madame Eleonore Fresco,
c/o Mr. Albert Passy,
21 Rue de la Poste
Lyon Villeurbanne (Rhone)
Madame,

Following your letter of 10 May, and after communications made with the competent authorities, I can inform you that the seals have been removed from your apartment situated at 1 Villa Dancourt in Paris XVIII, and that the keys are in the possession of this Consulate-General. I therefore ask you to be good enough to name a person to whom we can give the keys.

Please accept, madame, my estimable greetings.

(**signed**) N. Yolga Acting Consul

TURKISH INTERVENTION AGAINST SEQUESTRATION OF THE BUSINESSES OF JEWISH TURKS IN FRANCE

The basic regulations concerning sequestration of Jewish property in occupied France were issued on 12 November 1940 by German Military Administrator Otto von Stülpnagel:

Paris, 12 November 1940
The Military Commander in France, Department of Administration, Economic Branch, AZ: Wi I 615/40

Instructions for Provisional Administrators of Jewish enterprises:

The Provisional Administrators of Jewish enterprises above all have the duty to eliminate valid permits for Jews to enter the French economy.

So that the normal course of the French economy will not be interrupted, so that French and German customers can be taken care of, and so that no employee will have to lose his job, these enterprises at first must continue to operate. But the Provisional Administrator should pay attention to making sure that no Jew, neither the owner, if a single person, or an official of the company, like an administrative adviser or a company manager, in the case of a legal body, will have any real authority. So long as it is possible to retain the impression that it is needed for the operation of the company, Jews still will be allowed to withdraw sums of money, but this should be allowed in an emergency only, and this should not create the erroneous impression that the Jews are acting under the protection of the Provisional Administrators to prolong the existence of their businesses.

Jewish employees should be dismissed as soon as the businesses can be carried out without them. The Provisional Administrators should remember first of all that they are only temporarily in charge, and that final arrangements will be put in force as soon as possible.

Operation of the businesses without any participation of Jews can be accomplished in three ways:

(1) The Jews can decide to transfer or sell their rights to a non-Jew. This kind of arrangement is useful if no time is lost while it is carried out. Special attention should be given by the Provisional Administrators to making certain that the purchaser is entirely independent of Jewish influence. If there is any suspicion that they are in fact straw men who by a secondary agreement, or in a different way, will enable the Jew to return to the business later, this sort of arrangement should not be considered. When an agreement is achieved, it should be reported to the authorized Ministry, while suspicious contracts should be declared null and void.

(2) The Jews may not wish to sell their rights, as may be the case most often. In such a situation, the Provisional Administrator should sell the business to a non Jewish buyer either as a whole or in parts, as he is authorized to do in his order of appointment. He must still bring the contract for the approval of the Military Commander. This will be the normal manner of regularizing the company in the quickest possible way. In the case of branches where there are strong economic motivations, their sale to a competitor may be considered.

(3) Some of the businesses in question may not be economically viable or required in the French economy. Such enterprises should be liquidated by selling the inventory of goods, in whole or in parts, as soon as possible. New goods should not be purchased as the businesses in question should be locked up immediately after the clearance sale.

If the enterprise is not needed, then it should be reported to the Military Commander in France for approval, prior to the beginning of the sale of its stock, as a whole or in parts, or the sale of the enterprise as a whole. Four weeks after this step is taken, the Provisional Administrator must report how far negotiations have proceeded and what steps have been taken to bring their mission to an end. Commissioners who are not able to rapidly complete their missions will be called home.

The Provisional Administrators are not responsible for those who were previously the owners of the businesses in question, but only for the businesses put under their authority. Investigations will be made by both the German and French side as to the successes of the Provisional Administrators in disposing of the businesses put under their care.

Military Commander Stülpnagel.

gez. Thomas Kriegsverw, Secretary.[209]

It was not long before unoccupied France followed the German example with even more brutality and vehemence. Within a short time, then, throughout the country, whether under direct German or French rule, Jewish-operated businesses, shops and factories were assigned to French administrators, with the profits being sequestered by the state. As a result, the Turkish consulates general in Paris and Marseilles soon were receiving hundreds of requests from Jewish Turks for protection from such actions, as for example from Elie Merdjan, of Béziers:

La Maison du Bas
Elie Merjean
2, Rue de la République, Béziers
17 June 1942

Mr. Ambassador of the Turkish Republic, Vichy
Mr. Ambassador

I the undersigned Merdjan Elie, citizen of the Turkish Republic who entered France 16 May 1931, address myself to Your Excellency, representative of the Turkish Republic, to defend my interests which have been damaged as a result of the laws and measures decreed by the Commissariat on Jewish Questions. In effect, despite my nationality and my regular contacts with my consulate at Marseilles, my shop was given an Administrator since 27 December 1941. Since that day my money and my merchandise, and even worse my personal villa where I live with my family, have been sealed. I must attract your attention to the fact that yesterday, Tuesday 16 June 1942, my Administrator warned me verbally that he had received orders to liquidate my business by selling it before a notary of auctions, and that he would come today to evaluate my personal home, for what purpose I do not know.

---

209. Archives of the Turkish Embassy (Paris) and the Turkish Foreign Ministry (Ankara), dossier 6127.

Mr. Ambassador. I am the father of a family, born in the heart of Anatolia at the city of Manisa of a family which has been Turkish for many generations, and where I wish to remain. All my ancestors have always served our country, the last being my father who fought in the 1914–1918 war, and I myself participated in the rescue of my country at the time of the Greek invasion despite my young age in 1921.

Our Republic does not make any difference regarding race or religion, and it is for that reason that I make an urgent appeal to you, Mr. Ambassador, to intervene with authorities concerned with this matter in order to stop these measures in time. I have never had anyone reproach me in all my eleven years in France. I have carried out my trade with loyalty and honesty and my conduct has been exemplary . . . .

Sequestered Jewish properties were initially turned over to the same French administrators who handled the properties of non Turkish Jews.[210] On 18 March 1942 the French government in Vichy initially attempted to get the Turkish authorities to accept an arrangement by which Turkish administrators could be appointed, but only as 'observers' of the actions taken by the French administrators (Document 6):[211]

By its note of 22 January 1942, the Embassy of Turkey wished to attract the attention of the Ministry of Foreign Affairs to Mr. Ali Arslan and Mr. David Kohen, who are of Turkish nationality, regarding the properties for which the *Commissariat Général aux Questions Juives* has designated provisional administrators. The Embassy of Turkey requested that the administrators be chosen among persons of Turkish nationality. In response to this request, the Ministry of Foreign Affairs has the honor to inform the Embassy of Turkey that the *Commissariat Général aux Questions Juives* does not find it possible to appoint,

210. For example, Turkish Embassy to Paris (Vichy) to Turkish Consulate-General (Marseilles), no. 1604–6007, Vichy, 15 December 1942, as addition to no. 998/6127 of 4 August 1942; and Turkish Ambassador to Paris (Vichy) to Turkish Ministry of Foreign Affairs no. 1620–1011–6120, addition to no. 1202/773/6127 of 4 September 1942.

211. French Ministry of Foreign Affairs (Vichy) to Turkish Embassy to Paris (Vichy), no. 1037, 18 March 1942. Turkish Embassy to Paris (Vichy) to French Foreign Ministry (Vichy) no. 403/6127, 4 April 1942. Archives of the Turkish Embassy (Paris), dossier 6127.

for properties of foreign Jews, administrators of the same nationality.

On the other hand, wishing to give as much satisfaction as possible to the request of the Embassy of Turkey, it would voluntarily accept that beside the provisional French administrator, an observer of Turkish nationality designated by the Embassy of Turkey be charged with seeing to the safeguarding of the interests of his compatriots.

Under these conditions, the Ministry of Foreign Affairs would be very grateful to the Embassy of Turkey to be so good as to confirm that Mr. M. Muhtar and Mr. Kandemir can fulfill the functions of observers with the provisional administrators of the properties of Mr. Ali Arslan and Mr. David Kohen.

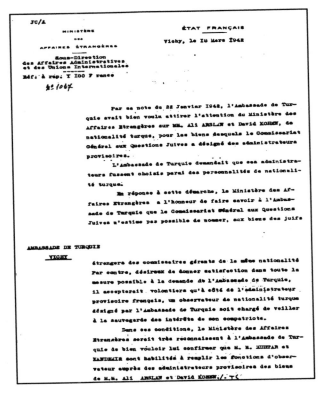

Document 6. France proposes that Turkish administrators of sequestered properties of Jewish Turks act as observers of acts of French administrators

Turkey absolutely opposed such a plan, maintaining that the property of all Turkish citizens, whether in or out of Turkey, was part of the national wealth, and could not be taken over by non-Turks:

> This attitude of the *Commissariat Général aux Questions Juives* surprises the Embassy since Monsieur René Gazagne, Director of the *Statut du Personnel* at the aforementioned *Commissariat Général*, declared to the First Secretary of the Embassy in the course of a conversation with him on this subject that provisional Turkish administrators would be appointed for the Jews of this nationality and on the basis of this agreement of principle, the Embassy has already sent to the *Commissariat Général* its list of candidates. The nomination of provisional Turkish administrators for the properties of Jews of this nationality, which the Embassy had requested, while maintaining the reserve in principle of its government on the entire question of applying to its citizens the French laws and regulations regarding Jews, constitutes in its eyes the most normal possible solution to the exceptional situation in question—by the fact that it restores the administration of the interests of Turks of Jewish race into the hands of persons of the same nationality–and the best measure to assure the minimum of guarantee in favor of the parties, while awaiting a definitive solution conforming to international rules and customs . . . . [212]

The Turkish government was determined that these properties be kept in Turkish hands and that they be administered for the benefit and profit of their original Jewish owners. Ankara's orders on this point were clear:

> If in future the German or French authorities require that these Jewish institutions to which these administrators have been assigned be administered in accordance with the needs of the French economy or that they be closed or sold to Aryans at low prices, our administrators must arrange for this to be done with the least damage and loss to the original owners.[213]

---

212. Archives of the Turkish Embassy (Paris), file 6127.

213. Assistant Minister of Foreign Affairs (Ankara) to Turkish Ambassador to Paris (Vichy), no. 31994/104, 8 August 1942. Archives of the Turkish Embassy (Paris).

Starting in November 1940, therefore, the Turkish consuls in Paris regularly insisted that Turkish businessmen replace French administrators of the stores, shops and apartments of Jewish Turks living in France,[214] though they agreed that these should be appointed by the French Commissioner for Jewish affairs from lists of candidates that it would supply, and that they be subjected to its directives.[215] They insisted on this point of view with equal vigor in their dealings with the Vichy government:

There is one very important point . . . which the response of the (French) Ministry does not sufficiently explain. It concerns the Embassy's insistence on the fact that in cases where Turkish citizens of Jewish religion established until now in France who possess enterprises which they have directed, and which now must be liquidated because of the impossibility of their carrying on the trades and professions to which Jews have been forbidden in France, forcing them to leave French territory, the product of these liquidations, after deduction of costs to carry out this operation, must be delivered to them in foreign currency. The Embassy added that these sums, the product of the work of Turkish citizens, appears to it to comprise, in a way and under a certain point of view, part of the patrimony of Turkey, so that nothing should be allowed to prevent these citizens from taking it with when returning to their own country after long years of activity . . . . The Embassy feels that the total of the product of the liquidation must be given to them and that this payment must be made in exportable foreign currency. The Embassy wishes to join this question with the more general matter of Jewish Turks having left France, or wishing to leave in view of a situation in which they are no longer allowed to work. It is of the opinion that Turkish citizens affected by the racial measures dictated by the French laws of 2 June, 22 July and 17 November 1942, and who have no alternative other than to leave France, should be able to secure the transfer abroad, and particularly to Turkey, of all their belongings. It can be that the French government, by the edict of these measures, wanted to defend the interests of the French

---

214. Turkish Consulate-General (Paris) to Turkish Embassy to Paris (Vichy) no. 673, 27 December 1940. Archives of the Turkish Embassy (Paris).

215. Turkish Consulate-General (Paris) to Turkish Embassy to Paris (Vichy) no. 82, 3 March 1941, Archives of Turkish Consulate-General (Paris).

collectivity, but the Embassy cannot believe that if these measures will end more or less necessarily in the departure of the individuals effected, the result would force them to leave their belongings in France, the operation thus being carried out at the expense of the Turkish collectivity charged with caring for its citizens and meeting their needs. The Embassy believes then, that the only possible equity can be achieved if Turkish citizens affected by these decisions be allowed to export all their belongings . . . . [216]

To this end, soon after the Germans began seizing the property of Jews, in addition to insisting on the full transferability of the assets of Jewish Turks to Turkey, the Turkish Foreign Ministry ordered the Paris consulate to accept deposits of the valuables of Jewish Turks to remove them from the possibility of seizure, and this was done throughout the remainder of the war.[217]

The Turkish position that fixed or moveable properties in France belonging to Turkish citizens had to be considered part of the Turkish national wealth, not subject to French laws applying to French Jews, was finally accepted both by the Vichy government and the German authorities, an interesting reversal of the old Capitulations rights which had enabled Europeans resident in the Ottoman Empire, and their local protégés, to avoid subjection to Ottoman laws.[218] Turkey thus secured French agreement that the property of Jewish Turks in France should be administered by Turkish citizens for the benefit of the original Jewish owners with the profits deposited in their names at the *Caisse des Dépots et Consignations,* from which the owner could draw with the permission of the Commissioner; that when necessary, the Turkish administrators could liquidate these properties at market prices, and that if the original owners were repatriated to Turkey, they would be allowed to transfer their assets by securing their equivalents in

---

216. Turkish Embassy to Paris (Vichy) to French Foreign Ministry (Vichy), 23 February 1943. Archives of the Turkish Embassy (Paris), dossier 6127.

217. Turkish Ambassador to Paris (Vichy) to the Turkish Consulate-General (Paris), 7 January 1941. Archives of the Turkish Embassy (Paris). For a list of the deposits of Jewish Turks left with the Turkish Consulate-General in Paris until April, 1944, see Appendix 6.

218. Turkish Ambassador to Paris (Vichy) to French Ministry of Foreign Affairs (Vichy) no. 822/6127, 5 July 1942, summarizing a conversation on the same day between the Turkish Ambassador Behiç Erkin and the French Chief of Government M. Laval. Archives of the Turkish Embassy (Paris).

blocked French credits in Turkey,[219] except for ten percent left deposited in a special account in France.[220]

On 3 August 1942 the Turkish Ambassador to Paris (Vichy) was able to inform his Consul-General in Marseilles (Grenoble) that the sale of the business of Elie Merdjan had been stopped and a Turkish administrator appointed, with the business in fact continuing to be operated by its original owner.[221] Jewish Turks in France, thus, while not able to operate or use their businesses or property officially, were in this way enabled to operate them in fact and to draw advances from their own money, while those who returned to Turkey were able to secure their assets from blocked French funds deposited at the Turkish National Bank in Ankara. Namik Kemal Yolga relates what happened:

> Our Consulate-General also had to provide protection on the economic side. The occupation forces attempted to 'Aryanize', that is to confiscate and place in the hands of non-Jewish Frenchmen, the shops and other economic establishments belonging to Jews. Our Consulate-General was able, however, to secure the appointment of other Turkish citizens as administrators (*gérant*) of the places of business belonging to Jewish Turks, with the selections in fact being made by me. And this was only a matter of form. In fact the businesses were thus not 'Aryanized', and they continued to be managed by their original Jewish owners. [222]

---

219. French Ministry of Finance (Vichy) to Turkish Embassy to Paris (Vichy), no. 268/6127, 19 February 1943. Archives of the Turkish Embassy (Paris).

220. For example, Turkish Consul-General (Paris) to M. Paul Aspord, French government-appointed Administrator (Paris), 10 September 1942, stating Turkish intention to take over administration of the business of the Turkish citizen Emmanuel Hadjes, 26 rue Cadet, Paris; and Turkish Consul-General to German Military Adminbistrator in France, 19 avenue Kléber (Paris), 13 October 1942, arranging to take over administration of the business of Turkish citizen M. Menahem. Turkish Embassy (Paris) to Turkish Consulat General (Marseilles), Vichy, no. 1604–6007, 15 December 1942, as addition to communication no. 998/6127 of 4 August 1942; and Turkish Embassy to Paris (Vichy) to Turkish Ministry of Foreign Affairs no. 1620–1011–6127, as addition to communication no. 1202/773/6127 of 4 September 1942, both in archives of Turkish Embassy (Paris), and Turkish Foreign Ministry (Ankara).

221. Turkish Ambassador to Paris (Vichy) to Turkish Consul-General (Marseilles) F1000–6127, 3 August 1942. Archives of the Turkish Embassy, Paris, file 6127.

222. See Appendix 3.

When the French or German authorities were notified that certain properties were owned by Jewish Turks, then, rather than sequestering them for administration by French businessmen, they would ask the Turkish Consulate-General to nominate a Turkish administrator:[223]

Marcel Brunaud, 6, Rue Felix Ziem, Paris XVIII
Ref: Aff Alcabes, no. 61,477

Monsieur le Consul de Turquie
170 Boulevard Haussmann, Paris
Mr. Consul-General

I have the honor of informing you that by the decision of the Commissariat General for Jewish Questions, I have been named Provisional Administrator of a bonneterie shop belonging to Monsieur Alcabes, 35 Rue St-Sébastien, Paris. Despite the lack of information and the absence of Monsieur Alcabes, who is imprisoned in the Camp at Drancy, I have just learned that he is of Turkish origin.

Under these conditions, I wish to ask you, if you judge it necessary, to name a Provisional Turkish administrator, and I will be happy to get into contact with him to transmit to him the small amount of documentation that I possess. In awaiting an answer, please accept the expression of my very special sentiments.
Consular minute: 588 TP reg no. 56, 28 February 1942.

---

223. As, for example Turkish Embassy to French Ministry of Foreign Affairs no. 6127/403, 4 April 1942, and French Ministry of Foreign Affairs to Turkish Embassy, Vichy, 31 July 1940, in Archives of French Ministry of Foreign Affairs, Quai d'Orsay, dossier Y 100 France no. 2697, asking the Turkish Embassy to provide it with a list of the confiscated properties which belonged to Jewish Turks, so that the *Commissariat Général aux Questions Juives* could decide on individual cases. It was specified, however, that this could be done only in unoccupied France, since similar cases in occupied France could be decided only by the German military authorities and attempted to certify the Turkish administrators only as observers of the actions of the French administrators. Turkish Embassy (Vichy) to French Ministry of Foreign Affairs (Vichy) no. 1201, 4 September 1942, in which the Turkish government insisted that France live up to its treaty obligations with Turkey by allowing the substitution of Turkish for French administrators of the property of Jewish Turks, a claim which was subsequently accepted.

The Turkish Consulate-General responded:

Turkish Consulate-General, Paris
10 September 1942

To M. Marcel Brunaud, 6 Rue Felix Ziem, Paris 8ème

In response to your letter of 20 August 1942, reference Affaire Alcabes No. 61477, I wish to inform you that this Consulate-General will immediately undertake the necessary efforts to nominate a Turkish administrator for the firm of Monsieur Alcabes, a Turkish citizen who is regularly registered at this Consulate-General.

Please accept my special greetings.

The Consul-General (**signed**)

P.S. Monsieur Alcabes is not imprisoned at Drancy, but is now at his home.[224]

In unoccupied France the Vichy government was much slower to accept such arrangements, continuing to insist that the properties of Jewish Turks be operated by French administrators, and largely for the financial benefit of its own treasury. It was in fact only on 31 July 1942 that the French Ministry of Foreign Affairs finally notified the Turkish Embassy that it had abandoned its claim that the Turkish administrators were only 'observers' and ' . . . had agreed to the naming of Turkish administrators to care for the goods and properties belonging to Jewish Turks', asking the Turkish Embassy to indicate the names of a number of Turkish businessmen who could act as administrators for the property of Jewish Turks, from whom the *Commissariat Général aux Questions Juives* would chose the administrator for each property.[225] But it continued to insist that:

> . . . these foreign administrators of the property of foreign Jews would have to follow strictly the instructions of the French government, and for that reason proceed to the liquidation of the

---

224. Archives of the Turkish Consulate-General (Paris).

225. French Ministry of Foreign Affairs, Department of International Unions, Vichy, 31 July 1942 to Turkish Embassy, Vichy. no. 2697. Turkish Embassy to Paris (Vichy) to French Ministry of Foreign Affairs (Vichy) no. 1201/6127, 4 September 1942; and Turkish Ministry of Foreign Affairs (Ankara) to Turkish Embassy to Paris (Vichy) no. 31999/109, 8 August 1942. Archives of the Turkish Embassy (Paris), dossier 6127.

Jewish properties in France, which by consequence meant that these foreign administrators would, in fact, be no more than 'liquidators', receiving instructions and making accounts not to their respective Consul-Generals, but only to the French government.[226]

The Turkish consulates, however, refused to accept this interpretation, and by observing Turkish rather than French laws in such cases, the Turkish administrators effectively applied a *fait accompli* in Turkey's favor which the French, in the end, did nothing to prevent.

TURKISH INTERVENTION TO PROTECT JEWS FROM DEPORTATION TO THE EAST

Starting on 24 August 1942 the German occupation forces began deporting to the Polish death camps Jewish men and women over eighteen years of age who had come from Poland, Czechoslovakia, Germany, Austria and Russia during the previous two decades, sending them first to the Drancy camp near Paris or to the camps at Compiègne or Vernet and then, usually within a month, onward to the East for rapid extermination. Jewish Turks often were caught up in the mass sweeps and arrests and sent off to the East despite their protestations that, as Turkish citizens, they were supposed to be exempt from such treatment. Only when their protests were supported by the active intervention of the Turkish consulates were they saved.

During the first two years of the occupation, the French and German authorities accepted the consulates' certification of Turkish citizenship without question, normally replying that they would release the Jews in question if their Turkish citizenship was documented and assurances were supplied that they would be repatriated to Turkey.[227] Starting in November, 1942, however, the Germans began to investigate the Turkish 'certificates of citizenship' and passports more vigorously and to immediately send away for extermination any Jews whose Turkish citizenship had lapsed or was in

---

226. Turkish Consul-General (Marseilles) to Turkish Embassy to Paris (Vichy), no. 387/61, 10 August 1943.

227. Turkish Ministry of Foreign Affairs (Ankara) to Turkish Embassy (Vichy), no. 277/6250, 13 April 1942; no. 567/3491/6127, 26 October 1942; no. 597/3459/46/6127, 25 September 1942; no. 19/101/6127, 13 January 1943;. Archives of the Turkish Embassy (Paris);

question to avoid protests from the Turkish representatives when the latter found out what had happened to persons whom they continued to declare to be Turkish citizens. During the winter of 1942–1943, moreover, the Vichy government began to cooperate actively with this German policy by moving to extradite to the East some 10,000 Jewish Turks living in southern France whose Turkish citizenship had lapsed because of failure to register during the previous five years. When reports of this reached Isaac Weissman, head of the Jewish Agency office in Lisbon, he wired his predecessor there, Chaim Barlas, who had become director of the Agency's office in Istanbul,[228] asking him to secure Turkish pressure on the Vichy government to rescind this decision and allow Jewish Turks to remain in unoccupied France whether or not they had retained their Turkish citizenship:

I BEG TO CONFIRM MY CABLE OF YESTERDAY, STATING: BARLAS INTERVENED TURKISH GOVERNMENT FOLLOWING MATTER THOUSANDS JEWISH TURKS LIVING FRANCE HAVE BEEN CONTESTED THEIR TURKISH NATIONALITY AS RESULT TURKISH LAW ABOUT 1935 SIMILAR TO POLISH 1938 GERMANS CONSIDER THEM NOW AS APATRIDES AND THOUSANDS HAVE ALREADY BEEN ARRESTED CONCENTRATION CAMPS THEIR DEPORTATION IMMINENT STOP THESE JEWS ARE TURKISH CITIZENS FOR GENERATIONS BORN ISTANBUL SMYRNA MANY AMONG THEM TURKISH WAR VETERANS STOP BARLAS INTERVENTION NAME HUMANITY THAT TURKISH GOVERNMENT GRANTS THEM TURKISH NATIONALITY FOR SAVING THESE UNFORTUNATES FROM DISASTER STOP JUST RECEIVED CABLE BARLAS 18/12 STATING CABLE MY BEHALF WISE WEIZMAN DESIRABLE TAKE UP MATTER WITH TURKISH AMBASSADORS ASKING THEIR INTERVENTION STOP SUGGEST ALSO WISE CABLING HIS AMBASSADOR HERE FULLSTOP CABLED MYSELF 13/12 TARTAKOWER SUGGESTING DÉMARCHES TURKISH AMBASSADOR WASHINGTON ASKING INSTRUCT EASTERMAN INTERVENE ALSO TURKISH AMBASSADOR LONDON STOP IF EASTERMAN NOT YET INTERVENED WONDER IF COORDINATED INTERVENTION PREFERABLE– ISAAC WEISSMAN.[229]

---

228. On the Jewish Agency operations in Istanbul under Barlas's leadership, see p. 257 of this volume and *passim* .

229. 21 December 1943. Central Zionist Archives L 15, 128 II. Laurence Steinhardt archives, Library of Congress, Washington, D.C.

Barlas went to Ankara and, along with American Ambassador to Turkey from 1942 until 1945, Laurence Steinhardt, appealed to the Turkish Foreign Minister Numan Menemencioğlu, who vigorously protested to both the German and Vichy governments, stating that even those Jews who had lost their Turkish citizenship because of failure to register under the 1935 law remained in fact 'irregular citizens' (*gayri muntazem vatandaş*) of Turkey, entitled to its protection, and thus legally exempt from the anti-Jewish laws, and threatening to withdraw the Turkish ambassador to Paris (Vichy) if they were harmed. As a result, the Vichy government relented in order to retain its good relations with Turkey, and the Jews in question remained safe, at least for a time, in unoccupied France. By this act, Menemencioğlu in essence provided Turkey's protection to those Jews who had lost their Turkish citizenship as well as to those who had retained it, saving them from almost certain death.

Steinhardt, who during his previous diplomatic service as Ambassador to the Soviet Union (1939–1942), had opposed American assistance to Jewish refugees from Stalin's iniquities but had experienced a change of heart soon after coming to Turkey,[230] subsequently wrote Barlas, praising Menemencioğlu's action:

> American Embassy,
> Ankara, February 9, 1944
>
> Mr. Ch. Barlas
> Ankara Palace Hotel, Ankara
> My dear Mr. Barlas,
> I am indebted to you for your kind letter of February 8th, and in acknowledging your generous expressions can only say that it has been a great satisfaction to me personally to have been in a position to have intervened with at least some degree of success on behalf of former Turkish citizens in France of Jewish origin.
> As I explained to you yesterday, while the Vichy government has as yet given no commitment to the Turkish Government, there is every evidence that the intervention of the Turkish authorities has caused the Vichy authorities to at least postpone if not altogether abandon their apparent intention to exile these unfortunates to almost certain death by turning them over to the

---

230. Henry L. Finegold, *The Politics of Rescue* (New York, 1970), pp. 285–287.

Nazi authorities. Should you have any reason to believe in the future that the Vichy authorities may succumb to Nazi pressure, I hope you will call the same to my attention immediately so that I may request the Turkish authorities to renew their protest.

I am also indebted to you for the figures set forth in your letter, which are encouraging in the increase shown in the movement in 1943 over 1942. I hope that our joint efforts this year will be successful in still further increasing the movement. I anticipate Mr. Hirschmann's[231] arrival in Ankara next week. As soon as he arrives, I think it would be desirable for us to go over the entire situation with him with a view to seeing what further steps can be taken to rescue Jewish refugees from the Balkans.

With kind personal regards,

Sincerely yours,

(**signed**) Laurence G. Steinhardt [232]

During the Second *Yad Vashem International Historical Conference on Rescue Attempts during the Holocaust,* held in Jerusalem 8–11 April 1974, these statements were confirmed by one of the participants in the work of the Jewish Agency in Geneva during the war,[233] Dr. Chaim Pazner, who stated:

In December 1943, Chaim Barlas notified me from Istanbul that he had received a cable from Isaac Weismann, the representative of the World Jewish Congress in Lisbon, that approximately ten thousand Jews who were Turkish citizens, but had been living in France for years and had neglected to register and renew their Turkish citizenship with the Turkish representation in France, were in danger of being deported to the death camps. Weismann requested that Barlas contact the competent Turkish authorities and attempt to save the above mentioned Jews. Upon receiving the telegram, Barlas immediately turned to the Turkish Foreign

231. Bloomingdale Department Store (New York City) executive Ira Hirschmann, who went to Turkey in 1944 as representative of the American War Refugee Board. See p. 293 of this volume and *passim.*

232. Laurence Steinhardt, United States Ambassador (Ankara) to Charles Barlas, Ankara Palace Hotel, Ankara, 9 February 1944, quoted in Charles Barlas, *Ha Atsala iyimei a seci* (Tel Aviv, 1975), supplement 8.

233. See page 256 of this volume.

Ministry in Ankara, submitted a detailed memorandum on the subject, and requested urgent action by the Turkish Legation in Paris. Upon being notified of the above, I promptly contacted Marc Jarblum, who was working in Geneva at the time, since the case involved Jews who lived in France. Jarblum immediately contacted his co-workers in France. We later received word from Istanbul and Paris that, with the exception of several score, these ten thousand Jews were saved from extermination.[234]

Even the German Ambassador to Turkey throughout the war, Franz von Papen, confirmed what Menemencioğlu had done, though attempting to leave the impression that the rescue effort had originated with him:

I learnt through one of the German emigré professors that the Secretary of the Jewish Agency had asked me to intervene in the matter of the threatened deportation to camps in Poland of 10,000 Jews living in Southern France. Most of them were former Turkish citizens of Levantine origin. I promised my help and discussed the matter with M. Menemencioğlu. There was no legal basis to warrant any official action on his part, but he authorized me to inform Hitler that the deportation of these former Turkish citizens would cause a sensation in Turkey and endanger friendly relations between the two countries. This démarche succeeded in quashing the whole affair.[235]

Without Turkey's intervention, thus, these Jews living in unoccupied France would most certainly have been deported.[236]

The Turkish Foreign Ministry also sent out a general order instructing its consulates throughout France to restore the citizenship of all Jewish Turks who could supply proper proof and to act on their own authority,

---

234. *Rescue Attempts during the Holocaust: Proceedings of the Second Yad Vashem International Historical Conference, Jerusalem, 8-11 April 1974* (Jerusalem, Yad Vashem, 1977), p. 649.

235. Franz von Papen, *Memoirs* (London, 1952), p. 522.

236. This action in regard to Jewish Turks in Vichy territory who had lost their Turkish citizenship contradicts the assertions in Christopher Browning, *The Final Solution and the German Foreign Office* (New York and London, 1978), p. 155, based entirely on the self-serving statements of German Foreign Office officials, that Turkey was not interested in those Jews who had lost their Turkish citizenship, and that it made no objection to their deportation from occupied France to Auschwitz in January 1943. See also p. 151 of this volume.

without authorization from Ankara, in questionable or emergency cases.[237] As a result, in the years that followed until the end of thc war the Turkish consulates provided former as well as current Jewish Turks with 'Certificates of Citizenship', (*Vatandaşlık Ilmühaberi*) which usually protected them:

Document 7. Turkish Certificate of Citizenship

Sometimes, however, the German authorities ignored the Turkish requests, which the consulates then repeated again and again before action usually was taken. When the German responses did come, they usually indicated a willingness to accede to the Turkish request on an individual basis. [238] The Turkish consulate was almost constantly corresponding with the German Embassy in Paris concerning Jewish Turks who had been wrongly sent to Drancy and other concentration camps along with French

237. Reported by the American Jewish Joint Distribution Committee's Istanbul representative R. Resnik to its Lisbon agent Schwartz on 25 April 1944, on the basis of a conversation carried on the previous day with the American Ambassador in Ankara, Laurence Steinhardt. General Zionist Archives (Jerusalem), L15, p. 213.

238. German Embassy (Paris) to Turkish Consulate-General (Paris), no. R 425/41, 4 October 1941. Archives of the Turkish Embassy (Paris) and Turkish Foreign Ministry (Ankara).

and other Jews:[239] Letters to the German Embassy were usually supplemented by messages to the responsible SS 'Jewish expert' (*Judenreferat*) in Paris, who in 1942 and 1943 was 'Storm Troop Chief' (*Obersturmführer*) Captain Heinz Röthke, Director of Service IV of the Gestapo in France, in overall charge of all the concentration camps in Occupied France as well as of the deportations then in progress to the East:

Republic of Turkey.
Paris Consulate-General,
17 January 1944, no. F 3207

To Captain Röthke,
83, avenue Foch, Paris V
My Dear Captain,

(1). As it was agreed during our last meeting, I ask you to find attached a list of Jews who are of Turkish nationality, arrested in the free zone and then taken to the internment camp of Drancy. Not having the dossiers of these persons in the Paris Consulate, we do not have the possibility of judging their nationality status. So we have asked the Consulate-General of Turkey at Marseilles (now at Grenoble) which of these are registered at that Consulate-General. Naturally we will hasten to communicate to you the names of the interned Jews who are indicated to us by our Consulate-General at Marseilles as being regular Turkish citizens.

(2). I profit from this occasion to call your attention to the following questions and ask for your assistance to solve them. Among the Turkish citizens who have been interned and whose liberation was previously asked for from the German Embassy and who are included on the list given to Mr. Klingenfuss, some have not yet been freed to the present day. This involves Madame Mari Barzilay and her daughter Ester,[240] who are in a warehouse at Quai de la Gare, Madame Matilda Benadava and Mr. Mordohay, son of Iliya, who are said to be at the camp at Compiègne, Mordohay Algazi, Salvator Gambas, Refka Grasyan,

---

239. Namık Kemal Yolga to Captain Heinz Röthke, F 3207, 17 January 1944. Archives of the Turkish Embassy (Paris), file 6127.

240. The Turkish consular file on the Barzilais can be found on p. 173 and *passim* of this volume.

Perle Kavariyero, Merkado Leon, Mazalto Leon, Refka Mitrani, Salamon Kamhi, and Alegra Modai, who are supposed to be at the Camp of Drancy. I ask you to do what is necessary to free these Turkish citizens as soon as possible for repatriation.

(3). The German Police authorities have just arrested and taken to the Camp at Drancy a number of regular Turkish citizens. You will find their names on the attached list no. 2. I ask you to give the necessary instructions for their release.

(4). I ask you to find on list no. 3 the names of some Turkish citizens whose apartments have been sealed. These persons, who were just freed from the Camp at Drancy, had not told us that their homes had been sealed. It is for this reason that their names were not on the list that I gave you the other day. I ask you to give the orders so that the seals are removed as soon as the persons involved present themselves at your office.

(5). The Commander of the Camp at Drancy has retained different Certificates of Nationality, Identity Cards and Turkish papers that he took from our citizens. I would be obliged if you would ask him to return these documents to us as soon as possible as soon as the Consulate-General can make the necessary arrangements for their repatriation. With my thanks for your obliging intervention to this effect, I ask you to believe, my dear Captain, in the assurance of my most special sentiments,

(**signed**) Namık Kemal Yolga, Vice Consul[241]

List no. 1: List of Jews who are of Turkish Nationality and regarding whom the Consulate-General has asked for information from the Turkish Consulate-General at Marseilles:

Eskenazi, Eliya (Nice)
Eskenazi, Esak (Lyon)
Madem, Mordo (Marseilles)
Avimelek, Isak (Marseilles)
Avimelek, Kadun (Marseilles)
Marko, Bohor (Marseilles)
Levi, Ester (Marseilles)
Levi, Sara (Marseilles)
Levi, Vida (Marseilles)

241. Namık Kemal Yolga, Turkish Consul-General (Paris) to Captain Heinz Röthke, no. F 3207, 17 January 1944. Archives of the Turkish Embassy (Paris).

Levi, Nesim (Marseilles)
Behar, Aron (Clermont-Ferrand)
Setil, Rashel (Marseilles)
Shalom, David (Nice)
Shalom, Deyzi (Nice)
Bendor, Matilda (Marseilles)

List no. 2: Names of Turkish citizens who have just been arrested and who are not on the list presented by Mr. Yolga. All living at 23 Arcenaux Lacombe at Biarritz

Sherez, Nesim	616TP	Istanbul 1902
Sherez, Ester	616TP	Istanbul, 1896
Sherez, Sara	616TP	Istanbul, 1925
Sherez, Nelly	616TP	Biarritz, 1932
Sherez, Suzan	616TP	Biarritz, 1939

List no. 3: Sealed apartments not on the list presented by Mr. Yolga:
Aelion, 140 bis Rue Lecourbe
Krespi, 40 bis avenue Diderot St. Maur
Kohen, 104 Quai de Jemmapes
Kastoriano, 22 Rue Baudin
Sherez, 23 Arceaux Lacombe Biarritz

List no. 4: Names of Turkish citizens whose papers have been retained by the commander of the Camp at Drancy:

Kamhi, Ester
Kamhi, Sol
Salis, Kalo
Salis, Refka
Levi, Samuel
Levi, Vida

By such means the Turkish diplomatic and consular authorities were reasonably successful in convincing the Germans and French to release many Jewish Turks imprisoned in the concentration camps set up in France, at Compiègne and Drancy in particular. As was the case with other problems, correspondence was followed up by personal appeals to the

German and French police and SS authorities as well as to the German Ambassador in Paris, Otto Abetz.

At times the Turkish diplomats personally delivered passports, certificates of Turkish nationality, and other relevant documents to the Concentration Camp commanders themselves, or to the Gestapo officials commanding the trains taking Jews to Auschwitz for extermination.[242]

Ambassador Necdet Kent relates one such experience while he served as Turkish Vice Consul at Marseilles (Grenoble), when he boarded such a train and rescued 80 Jewish Turks being sent to the East for extermination:

> One evening, a Turkish Jew from Izmir named Sidi Iscan, who worked at the Consulate as clerk and translator, (he has also passed away, may God give him rest) came to my house in a state of considerable excitement. He told me that the Germans had gathered up about eighty Jews and had taken them to the railroad station with the intention of loading them onto animal wagons for shipment to Germany. He could hardly hold back his tears. Without stopping to express my grief, I immediately tried to calm him and then took the fastest vehicle available to the Saint Charles railroad station in Marseilles. The scene there was unbelievable. I came to animal wagons filled with sobbing and groaning people. Sorrow and anger drove everything else from my mind. The most striking memory I have of that night is a sign I saw on one of the wagons, a phrase which I cannot erase from my mind: 'Enough fodder for twenty large animals or five hundred people should be loaded on this wagon'. Within each wagon there were as many as eighty people piled on top of one another. When the Gestapo officer in charge of the train station heard that I was there, he came to me and in a very cross manner asked me what I was looking for. With as much courtesy as I could force myself to summon, I told him that these people were Turkish citizens, that their arrest had been a mistake, and that it should be remedied at once by their release. The Gestapo officer said that he was carrying out his orders, and that these people were not Turks but just Jews. Seeing that I would get nowhere by making threats which could not be implemented if my requests were not carried out at once, I returned to Sidi Iscan and said, 'Come on, lets

---

242. Testimony of Namık Kemal Yolga, Turkish Vice Consul in Paris in 1943–1944, to Stanford J. Shaw on 3 May 1991.

board the train ourselves', and pushing aside the German soldier who tried to block my way, I boarded one of the wagons with Sidi Iscan beside me. This time it was the turn of the Gestapo officer to cry and even plead. I couldn't listen to anything he said, and amidst the crying glances of the Gestapo officer, the train began to move.

Since it was a long time ago, I cannot remember too well, but I remember that the train came to a stop when we came either to Arles or Nimes. A number of German officers climbed onto the car and immediately came to my side. I received them very coldly and did not even greet them. They told me that there had been a mistake, the train had left after I had boarded, the persons responsible would be punished, as soon as I left the train I could return to Marseilles with a car that would be assigned to me. I told them that it was not a mistake, that more than eighty Turkish citizens had been loaded onto this animal wagon because they were Jews, that as a citizen of a nation as well as the representative of a government which felt that religious beliefs could not cause such treatment, there could be no question of my leaving them alone, and that was why I was there. The officers said they would correct whatever mistakes had been made and asked if all those in the wagon were Turkish citizens.

All the people around me, women, men, and children, stood petrified while they watched this game being played for their lives. In the face of my refusal to compromise, and as a result of an order received by the Nazi officers, we all descended from the train. After a time the Germans left us alone. I will never forget what followed. The people who had been saved threw their arms around our necks and shook our hands, with expressions of gratitude in their eyes. After sending them all on their way to their homes, without even glancing at the Mercedes-Benz which the Nazis had provided for us, Sidi Iscan and I rented an automobile which ran on wood and returned to Marseilles.

I have rarely experienced in my life the internal peace which I felt as I entered my bed towards morning of that day. I have received letters from time to time over the years from many of my fellow travelers on the short train ride of that day. Today who knows how many of them are still in good health and how many have left us. I remember them all affectionately, even those who may no longer remember me . . . . [243]

Ambassador Namık Kemal Yolga, then Turkish Vice Consul in Paris, also interceded with German railroad officials to remove Jewish Turks from trains preparing to carry them from Drancy to Auschwitz.[244] There is some information that Turkish diplomats intervened in a similar way to secure the release of Jewish Turks imprisoned at the camp at Bergen-Belsen,[245] though the destruction of the Turkish Embassy in Berlin during the last days of the war makes it impossible to document these activities with the same precision as those mentioned in the archives of the Turkish Embassy and Consulate in Paris.

Such efforts were not always successful, however. On some occasions, as soon as the Germans learned that one or another of the Jewish inmates at Drancy or elsewhere was a Turkish citizen and that the Turkish government was intervening on their behalf, it quickly shipped them off to Auschwitz.

While most of those who were deported to the East never came back, a few survived and were liberated by the Russian army when it occupied Poland. One of these was Madame Rachel Mizrahi, who early in 1945 wrote the Turkish Consulate-General in Paris, to the great satisfaction of its diplomats and staff, that she had survived, and asking that her husband and children be notified if they could be found:

> Auschwitz (Upper Silesia), Poland
> 26 February 1945
>
> TO: Mr. Consul-General of Turkey, 170 Boulevard Haussmann, Paris, France
> FROM: Madame Rachel Mizrahi, A. 5568, Bloc 13, Auschwitz, Upper Silesia, Poland
>
> Mr. Consul-General,
> After nine months of captivity, I have just been freed by the Russians, who now are assuring our subsistence at Auschwitz in a

---

243. Statement of retired Ambassador Necdet Kent to the Quincentennial Foundation, Istanbul, translated by Stanford J. Shaw. The complete translated statement can be found in Appendix 4.

244. See Appendix 3.

245. Testimony no. O 3/766 in the Yad Vashem Central Archives (Tel Aviv).

perfect manner. I would appreciate it if you would give this news to my children, Jacques, Joseph, André, and Albert Mizrahi, at Institution Bouthelly, 28 Rue Grande Monthlery (Seine et Oise).

In particular, I ask you also to give me the result of the démarches undertaken to secure the liberation of my husband, a Turkish subject:

Name: Mizrahi

Prename: Issak   Aged 49 years

Address: 23, Boulevard Richard Lenoir, Paris

Arrested on 27 March 1944 at the office of Monsieur Bruniot, 76, Boulevard Haussmann, Paris.

He had his dossier at the Turkish Consulate-General because of his intended departure to Turkey with the four children.

In hoping that you will give me a rapid answer, please accept, Mr. Consul-General, my thanks in anticipation and my special salutations.

(signed) Mizrahi Rachel.[246]

REPATRIATION OF JEWISH TURKS TO TURKEY

Following the Nazi occupation of northern France in the summer of 1940 and the country's division between occupied and unoccupied zones, civilian travel outside the country without special permission was forbidden except for diplomats and members of the military on official business. French Jews were therefore unable to flee impending doom at the hands of the Nazis,[247] though during the remaining months of 1940 as well as most of 1941 and 1942 many did manage to slip into unoccupied France and across the Pyrennees into Spain,[248] and from there into Italy, where the authorities were notably easier on Jews than were the Germans. Travel from Italy

---

246. Archives of the Turkish Embassy (Paris), file 6127.

247. See the report of Turkish Consul-General (Marseilles) Bedi'i Arbel, no. 593/109, 18 November 1942, and the resulting protest of the Turkish Embassy to Paris (Vichy) to the French Foreign Ministry (Vichy), no. 1532/6127, of 24 November 1942,

248. Chaim U. Lipschitz and Ira Axelrod, *Franco, Spain, the Jews, and the Holocaust* (New York, Ktav, 1984).

onward to Turkey was difficult, however, particularly through the Nazi-created independent republic of Croatia as well as through Serbia due to the disinclination of their authorities to provide the necessary visas, preferring that the Jews remain in France where they would be more exposed to liquidation, and also due to Nazi efforts to prohibit the emigration of Jews from France so they could be more easily arrested.[249]

The Honorary Turkish Consul in Lyon, A. Routier, who for some time provided false certificates of Turkish citizenship to non-Turkish Jews wishing to escape from the Nazis, thus reported to the Turkish Ambassador to Paris (Vichy) on 3 October 1942:

> I have the honor to bring Your Excellency's attention to the case of several Turkish Jewish families who want to return to Turkey. The Consulate-General at Marseilles has given them (Turkish) passports and (French) exit visas and has told them that it will secure the visas necessary for them to cross foreign countries. They obtained the Italian visa easily and rapidly, but on condition that they could also obtain a Croatian visa. The Turkish Consul-General at Marseilles has written to the Turkish Consulate in Milan to get in touch with the Consulate of Croatia, but nothing has been accomplished. These people waited six months for permission to return, so they decided finally to ask for the visas directly from the Croatian Consulate at Zürich. The latter had them fill out the enclosed questionnaire. I telephoned this information to their Consulate at Zürich to find out if it was because they were Jewish that transit had not yet been granted. The Croatian Consulate responded that in fact no Jew has been admitted to transit that country. But if the (Turkish) Embassy or Consulate were to intervene, it is possible that the Croatian government will give such a visa . . . . [250]

---

249. Ted Morgan, *An Uncertain Hour: The French, the Germans, the Jews, the Barbie Trial, and the City of Lyon, 1940–1945* (New York, Morrow, 1990). See also Paris Consul-General to Vienna Consul-General, 24 May 1944, in Archives of Paris Embassy, File 1207, stating that when the train left Paris on 23 May 1944 at 7.25 p.m. with 47 Turkish refugees it had a collective German visa for all, but that the Bulgarian consulate in Paris had refused to provide them with a transit visa, and asking the Turkish Consulate-General in Vienna to intervene with its Bulgarian counterpart to secure the necessary visa so they could pass on to Istanbul.

250. Archives of the Turkish Embassy (Paris), no. 1532-6127, Vichy, 24 November 1941. Archives of the Turkish Embassy (Paris), file 6127.

The Turkish Consul-General at Marseilles, Minister Bedi'i Arbel, also described the difficulties involved:[251]

> Republic of Turkey Consulate-General
> Marseilles, 22 April 1942, No. 230-58
>
> To the Embassy,
> As is well-known, there are two routes to go to Turkey, via the north and via the south. Visas are secured from the Germans for the northern road. But two attempts have shown that such applications usually are rejected. The Italians do not use race for those who apply for permits for the southern route, but those who chose it must pass through Serbia. It is necessary to wait at the border for one or two weeks to secure permission from the German military authorities for this route, and then such applications are sometimes rejected, according to information from our Milan consulate. Inquiries here at the German Consulate confirm this. Under these conditions, it is improbable that Jewish citizens of Turkey wishing to return to the homeland can do so. Some of those wishing to return home will have to do their military service as a condition of their return. For such persons, their obligation is written on their nationality papers. But for such persons, their failure to return because of the difficulties described above will subject them to severe penalties such as the loss of citizenship because of their inability to perform their military duties. In view of this, it is necessary for us to make a special effort with the Germans to make it possible for them to return to Turkey, or, alternately, to indicate on their citizenship papers that their return has not been possible, so that they will not lose their citizenship. I ask for instructions.
> (**signed**) Bedi'i Arbel, Consul-General. File no. 270/6127

Since foreigners were in any case forbidden to leave France, the Turkish Embassy at Vichy had to ask for the assistance of the authorities in securing exit visas for Jewish Turks wishing to return to Turkey:

---

251. Bedi'i Arbel, Consulate-General (Marseilles) to Ambassador (Paris) no. 230–58, Marseilles, 22 April 1942. Archives of Turkish Embassy (Paris).

no. 1532-6127, Vichy, 24 November 1942.

The Embassy of Turkey presents its compliments to the Ministry of Foreign Affairs and has the honor of informing it that, according to information sent by the Turkish Consulate-General in Marseilles, the competent French authorities have been refusing exit visas to Turkish citizens desiring to return to Turkey, on the basis of an order given them by the Ministry of the Interior. Such a measure can have grave consequences for those involved, and greatly complicates the task of that Consulate. The Embassy cannot conceive of the legality of such a measure and believes that an error of interpretation has occurred. It asks the Ministry of Foreign Affairs therefore to study this problem as a matter of urgency . . . . [252]

The French responded that all persons in France were prohibited from leaving at that time, not just Jewish Turks, so that the measure was therefore not discriminatory:

> LV/SF.-State of France, Ministry of Foreign Affairs,
> Service for Foreigners, Vichy, 4 December 1942.
> To the Embassy of Turkey (Vichy),

In note no. 1532, dated 24 November last, the Embassy of Turkey wished to bring the attention of the Ministry of Foreign Affairs to the situation of Turkish citizens desiring to return to Turkey who are unable to secure the necessary exit visas from the Préfectorial authorities.

The Ministry has the honor of informing the Embassy that because of the closure of its frontiers, entry and exit from French territory is, until a new order is issued, prohibited to French as well as foreign citizens. Of course this measure does not apply to Turkish nationals with diplomatic passports.[253]

---

252. Turkish Embassy to Paris (Vichy) to French Ministry of Foreign Affairs (Vichy). Archives of the Turkish Embassy (Paris), file 6127.

253. French Ministry of Foreign Affairs (Vichy) to Turkish Embassy to Paris (Vichy), 4 December 1942. Archives of the Turkish Embassy (Paris), no. 651–6127, 8–XII–1942. Turkey's immediate response to this communication was to start issuing a few diplomatic passports to Jewish Turks in the most immediate danger of deportation to the East. See

Despite the desire of the Turkish authorities to facilitate the passage of Jewish Turks back to Turkey, then, as a result of problems such as these, thousands of Jews remained in southern France, either under the rule of Vichy or that of the Italians.[254] The former increasingly imitated, and at times exceeded, Nazi persecution against the Jews, but just as was often the case in Italy itself, the Italian occupation authorities were notably reluctant to carry out Nazi directives either to restrict, arrest or to deport the Jews in their district, much to the unhappiness and annoyance of Eichmann and his colleagues in Berlin.[255] The Italians at times even compelled the Vichy government to release Turkish and other foreign Jews arrested by the French police in the Italian zone for deportation to Paris and Auschwitz. At one point Eichmann's agents in Paris were complaining that 'The best of harmony prevails between the Italian troops and the Jewish population . . . . The Italians live in the homes of the Jews. The Jews invite them out and pay for them . . . . ' [256] The Jews who could, therefore, attempted to wait out the war in the Italian zone, particularly at Nice, and also in Tunisia, where thousands congregated well into 1943, until the collapse of the Italian war effort and their replacement by the Germans created a new surge of persecution during 1944 against which there was little escape.[257]

Even though both foreign and French Jews were prohibited from leaving France, a good number of Jewish Turks managed to secure

---

Turkish Consulate-General (Paris) to Turkish Foreign Ministry (Ankara), no. 6742, 4 January 1943. Archives of the Turkish Embassy (Paris), file 6127.

254. Turkish Embassy to Paris (Vichy) to Turkish Consul-General to Marseilles (Grenoble) no. 1594–6127, 9 December 1942; Turkish Consulate-General (Paris) to French Ministry of Foreign Affairs (Vichy), no. 1702–6127, 30 December 1942. Turkish Consulate-General (Marseilles) to Turkish Embassy to Paris (Vichy) no. 1704–6127, 31 December 1942: Archives of the Turkish Embassy (Paris). Klarsfeld, *Vichy-Auschwitz* I, 314.

255. John Bierman, 'How Italy Protected the Jews in the Occupied South of France, 1942–1943', Ivo Herzer, *et al.*, eds, *The Italian Refuge* (Washington, D.C., 1989), pp. 218–227. Leon Poliakov and Jacques Sabille, *Jews under the Italian Occupation* (Paris, 1955). Serge Klarsfeld, *Vichy-Auschwitz: Le rôle de Vichy dans la solution finale de la question juive en France, 1943–1944* (2 vols, Paris, 1985), and Susan Zuccotti, *The Italians and the Holocaust: Persecution, Rescue, Survival* (New York, 1987).

256. Poliakov and Sabille, p. 52. Klarsfeld, *Vichy-Auschwitz*, p. 219. Bierman, p. 220.

257. Zanvel Diamant, 'Jewish Refugees on the French Riviera', *Yivo Annual of Jewish Social Science VIII* (1953), pp. 264–280; Daniel Carpi, 'The Italian Government and the Jews of Tunisia in World War II (June 1940–May 1943)', (in Hebrew), *Zion* LII (1987), pp. 57–106; Michael Mazor, 'Les Juifs dans la clandestinité sous l'occupation italienne en France', *Le Monde Juif* XXVII/59 (July–September 1970), pp. 276–287.

permission to return to Turkey on an individual basis starting late in 1941 after the Turkish Ambassador to Paris (Vichy) had been alerted to the increasing persecution by the Consul-General in Paris at the time, Cevdet Dülger:

> As Your Excellency already knows, the measures and pressure taken in the occupied zone against both French and foreign Jews, which began with the placing of the word 'Jew' on their identity cards and shops, have increased. Recently they have insisted that Jews report to the French authorities every week, and they have begun to arrest Jews on the pretext that they are Communists, and for other pretexts as well. Since our citizens who are of this race are being subjected to the same persecutions, they have begun to apply to our consulate to secure their return to Turkey. I urge that the matter be referred to higher authority so that it can be settled between states.[258]

The process of securing, on an individual basis, passports from the Turkish consulates, and then visas from the Vichy government as well as transit visas from the countries through which they had to pass, created such a monumental task for the Turkish consulates that their officials regularly approached the Germans as well as the Vichy government with the proposal that Jewish Turks be given permission to return in groups if at all possible, for the most part through Italy since the Balkan states were unalterably opposed to saving any Jews from extinction in the Nazi death camps.[259]

---

258. Turkish Consul-General (Paris) Cevdet Dülger to Turkish Ambassador to Paris (Vichy), 29 September 1941. Archives of the Turkish Embassy (Paris). The matter was referred to the Ministry of Foreign Affairs (Ankara) by the Ambassador in file no. 1091–705–6127 on 7 October 1941.

259. Turkish Consulate-General (Paris) to German Embassy (Paris) no. 1942/135, 27 March 1942. Turkish Consulate-General; (Paris) to Turkish Embassy (Berlin) no. 1942/214, 8 May 1942. Turkish Consulate-General (Paris) to Turkish Embassy (Rome), no. 1942/436, 27 June 1942; Albert Haim (Toulouse) to Turkish Ambassador to Paris (Vichy) Behiç Erkin, 26 December 1942; Turkish Consul-General (Marseilles) Ambassador Bedi'i Arbel to Turkish Ambassador to Paris (Vichy) no. 689/130, 21 December 1942; Turkish Consulate-General (Marseilles) to Turkish Embassy to Paris (Vichy) no. 1704–6127, 31 December 1942. Archives of Turkish Consulate-General (Paris). The Turkish Ambassador to Paris (Vichy) advised Joseph Kaputo, then in flight at the Hotel des Pyrénnées at Eaux-Bonnes on the Mediterranean coast , in a letter dated 8 January 1943 (File number 21–6127, Archives of the Turkish Embassy, Paris), that: 'While this consulate will be happy to assist you in securing a

Already in early December the Turkish Consulate-General forwarded the applications of approximately one hundred Jewish Turks for visas to enable them to pass through German occupied territory on their way back to Turkey.[260] On 30 December 1942, Bedi'i Arbel (Marseilles) wrote to his Ambassador in Vichy describing the situation and asking for instructions:

> As a result of fear due to the recent increase of persecutions, (Turkish) citizens of Jewish race are applying to the Consulate in order to return to Turkey. The Italians are giving them visas without difficulty. But it is extremely difficult for the necessary applications to be made to various authorities involved one by one. It would be much easier to unite the individual applications by sending those who wish to go in caravans. Conversations will be held on this subject with the Italians here. It also will be necessary to discuss the matter at least once with the Bulgarian Consulate there. On the other hand it also will be necessary to ask the Capitol for exemptions from the restrictions on exit visas by the French. It will be necessary to get the Ministry of the Interior to smooth over the problems in order both to secure the necessary exemptions from these restrictions and also to unite the necessary applications. If it is possible for them to return by caravan, the Consulate-General is thinking of communicating this information for applications to concerned citizens via advertisements in newspapers in Marseilles, Nice and Lyon.
>
> With my deepest respects, I request instructions be issued to enlighten me regarding the procedure to be followed.[261]

At that time, Ankara continued to prefer to handle repatriation on an individual basis, so while the idea was forwarded to Turkey for study, instructions were issued for Turkish consulates to provide assistance to Jews

---

visa from the French Foreign Ministry, I have heard that in recent days some of our citizens through their own efforts have succeeded in securing exit visas and leaving France through Italy . . . . '

260. Turkish Consulate-General (Paris) to German Embassy (Paris), 29 January 1943, no. F 916/1, Archives of Turkish Embassy (Paris).

261. Bedi'i Arbel, Minister (*Orta Elçi*) to Turkish Embassy to Paris (Vichy), no. 705–136, Vichy, 30 December 1942. Archives of Turkish Foreign Ministry (Ankara) and Turkish Embassy (Paris).

wishing to return to Turkey only when visas could not be secured through normal channels, or when men of military age indicated their willingness to perform their military service on their return:[262]

> 7 January 1943
> To the Consulate-General in Marseilles
> This is an answer to your note 705/136 of 30 December 1942. I see drawbacks to some points in sending Jewish citizens of Turkey back to Turkey in caravans. Some may have been able to secure through their own efforts the French exit visas and the necessary visas from the Bulgarian Consulate, as was previously ordered. It would seem more appropriate that they should pursue the matter with the assistance of the Consulate-General only if they have difficulty in these applications.
> (**signed**) The Paris Ambassador.
> **Consular minute:** Received 7–1–43. [263]

As restrictions imposed on Jews of all nationalities became worse, however, the French Foreign Ministry admitted to the Turkish Embassy that it could not resist German demands for harsher treatment of Jews, and suggested that the only way for Jewish Turks to avoid subjection to the anti-Jewish measures would be for them to be repatriated to Turkey, in the process of which it would be happy to cooperate with the Turkish authorities if permission could be secured from the German occupation authorities:

---

262. Turkish Consul-General (Marseilles) Ambassador Bedi'i Arbel to Turkish Ambassador to Paris (Vichy) no. 705–136, 30 December 1942; Turkish Ambassador to Paris (Vichy) to Turkish Consul-General (Marseilles) no. 13–6127, 7 January 1942. Archives of Turkish Embassy (Paris) and Turkish Foreign Ministry (Ankara). Turkish Consulate-General (Paris) to Turkish Embassy (Berlin) no. 1942/214, 8 May 1942; Turkish Consulate-General (Paris) to German Consulate-General (Paris) no. 1942/802, 10 September 1942; Turkish Consul-General (Marseilles) Ambassador Bedi'i Arbel to Turkish Ambassador to Paris (Vichy), no. 39/4, 13 January 1943. Archives of the Turkish Embassy (Paris), no. 30–6127, 19 January 1943. In particular Turkish Consulate-General (Paris) to Turkish Embassy (Berlin) no. 1942/90/6, 3 February 1943. Archives of Turkish Consulate-General (Paris). See also: Turkish Foreign Ministry (Ankara), Consular section to Turkish Ambassador to Paris (Vichy) no. 314–6127, 17 June 1942, authorizing the immediate return of all Turkish male citizens willing to perform their military service in accordance with Turkish law.

263. Turkish Ambassador to Paris (Vichy), 7 January 1943, to Consul-General in Marseilles, no. 13–6127. Archives of the Turkish Embassy (Paris)

State of France, Ministry of Foreign Affairs
Department of International Unions,
Vichy, 13 January 1943
Reference: 'Unions', no. 101

The Embassy of Turkey wrote the Ministry of Foreign Affairs asking for information regarding the measures taken recently regarding Jewish Turks resident in France. In response to this request, the Ministry of Foreign Affairs has the honor of informing the Embassy of Turkey that the measures relative to foreign Jews are as follows:

(1). Assignment of Jews to certain designated residential areas. (Law no. 979, 9 November 1942).

(2). Obligation to have the word 'Jew' entered on identity papers and food ration cards (Law no. 1077 of 11 December 1942).

(3). Resettlement toward interior provinces of Jews recently installed in frontier provinces.[264]

These first measures are police measures that apply also to French Jews. So it is not possible to provide special dispensation. However execution of the measure proposed in paragraph 3 is now suspended. On the other hand, the French government has decided to incorporate in the groups of foreign workers unmarried Jews who entered France since January 1, 1933.

To avoid the application of these measures to Turkish citizens, the Ministry of Foreign Affairs would be disposed to look favorably on the return of the interested parties to their countries of origin. In a general way, the Ministry of Foreign Affairs would be happy to examine with the Embassy of Turkey the conditions necessary to secure repatriation of Jewish Turks desiring to avoid the measures being applied to foreign Jews.

---

264. '*Pour éviter que des ressortissants turcs ne soient soumis à cette mesure, le Ministère des Affaires Etrangères serait disposé à envisager favorablement le retour des intéressés dans leurs pays d'origine. D'une façon général, le Ministère des Affaires Etrangères serait heureux d'examiner avec l'Ambassade de Turquie les conditions dans lesquelles porrait s'effectuer le rapatriement des israélites turcs désireux d'éviter les mesures auxquelles sont actuellement soumis les israélites étrangers. . . .*' French Foreign Ministry (Vichy) to Turkish Embassy (Vichy) no. 101, 13 January 1943. Archives of the Turkish Embassy (Paris), no. 19–6127, 15 January 1943.

As a result, in May 1943 the Turkish Ministry of Foreign Affairs finally gave its consuls-general throughout Europe authority to act according to their own discretion and, without securing individual permission from Ankara, to give passports to Jewish Turks to return to Turkey, individually or in groups, and even when their citizenship papers were not entirely in order in cases where failure to act might cost the applicants their lives.[265] It was therefore with official governmental authorization that the Turkish diplomats thereafter regularly intervened with the French and German authorities in the difficult task of securing exit visas for Jewish Turks.[266] Even when the French continued to state that their borders were closed to the travel of civilians of all nationalities, except those with diplomatic passports,[267] the Turkish Embassy and consulates insisted that their nationals had the right to travel regardless.

Turkish citizens wishing to return to Turkey applied directly to the Turkish embassy or consulates, which placed advertisements in local papers to make certain that everyone eligible knew of the possibility of repatriation. If the applicants were men of military age, they had to promise to perform their military service following their return, which they rarely did in fact:

Turkish Embassy to Paris,
Vichy, 7 July 1943, no. 834-6127

To the Consul-General at Marseilles

---

265. Ministry of Foreign Affairs (Ankara) to Turkish Embassy to Paris (Vichy) no. 6127/256, 9 May 1943; Ministry of Foreign Affairs (Ankara) to Turkish Embassy to Paris (Vichy) no. 6127/291, 31 May 1943, approving list of Jewish Turks to whom visas had been given by the Embassy in fulfillment of the 9 May order; Turkish Consulate-General (Marseilles) to Turkish Embassy to Paris (Vichy), no. 6127/294, 2 June 1943, listing Jews to whom visas had been given to return to Turkey to enable them to perform their military service. Turkish Consulate-General (Paris) to Turkish Embassy to Paris (Vichy) no. 6127/591, 22 November 1943, in archives of Turkish Embassy (Paris). Turkish Ministry of Foreign Affairs Instruction (*Tahrirat*) no. 591/104, 20 December 1943; Turkish Ambassador to Paris (Vichy) to Turkish Consul-General (Marseilles) no. 1337/6127, 30 December 1943; Turkish Consul-General (Paris) to Turkish Consulate-General (Marseilles), no. 77/29 urgent, 26 January 1944. Archives of the Turkish Embassy (Paris).

266. *Aide-Memoire au sujet du transfert au Turquie des avoirs des ressortissants Turcs de race juive qui ne peuvent plus exercer en France aucune activité commerciale ou industrielle en raison de la législation d'exception que les Autorités Françaises prétendent leur appliquer,* Vichy, 3 February 1943. Archives of the Turkish Embassy (Paris).

267. Ministère des Affaires Etrangères, Services des Etrangers, Vichy, 4 December 1942. Archives of Turkish Embassy (Paris).

An instruction recently received from the Ministry of Foreign Affairs stated that for fifty-one of our Jewish citizens whose citizenship situation is in order and who wish to fulfill their military service and for others whose citizenship situation is also in order and who wish to go to other countries, passports may be issued without further authorization ask you therefore to act in accordance with this instruction.[268]

Many of those who applied attempted to emphasize the value of their particular services to the Turkish nation, as for example in the application of Dario Feldshtayn:[269]

Lyon, 14 January 1944

To the Consulate-General of the Republic of Turkey in Paris,
  Mr. Chief Consul,

I am a Turkish citizen, born in Istanbul in 1903, and after fulfilling my military service in Istanbul I worked as a chemist in a very important leather factory in Istanbul.

It is necessary to establish in our Turkish homeland manufacturing systems of leather factories like the modern systems in the great factories in Europe, and to create leather manufacture in our country with the same beautiful leather that has been manufactured in recent years in Europe, by bringing foreign experts and using them in our country.

In addition to the assistance given by our Republic government to establish such manufacturing, in 1939 I went to France to learn leather chemistry in order to benefit my country. I studied for four years in the School of Chemical Industry in Lyon and in the French School of Tannery. I finished first in my class, secured the degree of Engineer, and while I asked to return home, I unfortunately was unable to do so because of the current situation.

---

268. Paris Embassy (Vichy) to Consulate-General (Marseilles), Vichy, 7 July 1943, no. 834–6127. Archives of French Embassy (Paris), and Turkish Foreign Ministry.
    269. Dario Feldshtayn to Turkish Consul–General (Paris), Lyon, 14 January 1944. Archives of the Turkish Embassy (Paris) and Turkish Foreign Ministry (Ankara).

There is no doubt that because of the crisis in the world, our nation is short of many basic materials, and I am very desirous of enabling our country of benefiting from the new methods that I have learned. I have learned that you are arranging to send our Jewish countrymen to our country in caravans.

I am now resident in Lyon, possess my certificate of citizenship, birth certificate, and military documents, also my chemistry diploma. The passport by which I came from Istanbul is with the Consulate-General of Marseilles. It is not possible to go from here to Istanbul. If it would be possible to send me to Istanbul with a caravan sent from Paris, I would be very grateful, and our nation could benefit greatly from the education which I have had in Europe. I hope that you will answer this letter at once, and expectantly waiting an answer I present my respects, Sir.
(signed) **D. Feldshtayn.**

Dario Feldshtayn, Poste Restante R.P., Lyon (Rhone)

The Turkish authorities first ascertained whether the applicant's citizenship was in order and duly registered at the proper consulate:

Turkish Republic Paris Consulate-General, Paris, 21 January 1944

Subject: regarding Daryo Feldshtayn
no. 79/21, Urgent

To the Consulate-General of Marseilles,

An individual named Daryo Feldshtayn in Lyon has sent a letter to our Consulate-General staying that he came to France in 1939 to study leather chemistry, that he has finished his studies, and that he now wishes to return to our country to work as a leather chemist, that since he cannot return to Turkey from the south, he asks to join a caravan that will leave Paris. I ask that you check the veracity of this individual who states he has his birth certificate, military papers, and certificate of citizenship and that he is properly registered with higher authorities, to see whether or not he is a regular citizen, and if his papers are in order to check whether or not high authorities find it suitable for him to return to Turkey.

Initialed: Consul-General

Consulate-General of the Turkish Republic, Marseilles, 25 January 1944

To the Paris Consulate-General,

This is an answer to your letter no. 79/21 of 21 January 1944.The situation of Dario Feldshtayn, son of Leon, born in Istanbul in 1903, is entirely regular, and he is a Turkish citizen. There is no reason who he should not be included in a caravan.

Marseilles Consul-General

(**signed**) Fuad Carım

Turkish consulate note: received 27 January; registration no. 104

Lists of those whose papers were in order were turned over to the French Ministry of Foreign Affairs, which now issued group visas for their departure from France.[270] While as many as one thousand Jewish Turks were sent to Turkey by ship from southern France through the Mediterranean during 1943 and 1944, because of the danger involved many went by the train caravans which left only from Paris. Those living in unoccupied France, therefore, had to return to Paris to join the caravans to which they had been assigned, but on occasion those in difficulty with the French or German authorities in occupied France were arrested and deported before they could reach the Turkish consular authorities, causing the latter to complain on several occasions, though with little result.[271]

The Turkish government initially authorized each person to draw up to 3,000 French francs, or the equivalent in dollars, either from their French or Turkish bank accounts, to pay for their railroad tickets as well as for food and other expenses along the way back to Turkey.[272] When this was found to be insufficient, the sum was raised to ten thousand francs per person.[273]

---

270. See, for example, Turkish Embassy to Paris (Vichy) to French Foreign Ministry (Vichy) no. 591/104, 20 December 1943, and Turkish Embassy to Paris (Vichy) to Turkish Consulate-General (Marseilles) no. 1337/6127, 30 December 1943, in Archives of the Turkish Embassy (Paris).

271. Turkish Consulate-General to German Embassy, no. 501/21, 22 February 1944. Archives of the Turkish Embassy (Paris), file 6127.

272. Turkish Consul-General (Paris) Fikret Şefik Özdoğancı to Turkish Embassy to Paris (Vichy) no. 80/5, 21 January 1944. Archives of the Turkish Embassy (Paris) no. 25/13/169.

273. Turkish Ambassador to Paris (Vichy) to Turkish Consulate-General (Paris) no. 45/18, 27 January 1944. Archives of the Turkish Embassy (Paris) no. 27/18/170.

Some of the Jewish Turks thus leaving France deposited the remainder of their assets with the Turkish consulate in Paris for subsequent refund in Turkish liras back in Turkey.[274] Though many of those repatriated had just been released from Concentration Camps and were still in imminent danger of their lives, quite a number of them brought with them substantial amounts of personal belongings including jewelry, furniture, crystal lamps, beds, fur coats and the like, filling baggage cars as well as compartments with their goods. [275]

There are indications that at least three train caravans carrying Jewish Turks back to Turkey were organized by the Turkish Consulate-General in Paris and sent during the spring and summer of 1943, including one on 15 March 1943,[276] but these seem to have been composed for the most part of some two hundred men of military age whose citizenship was in order and who had indicated willingness to perform their military service in return for permission to return home.[277] On at least one occasion, in June 1943, the

---

274. See Appendix 6 for a list of the deposits made to the Turkish Consulate-General in Paris up to April 1944.

275. See, for example, the list of belongings sent back to Turkey in 1944 by Menahem Hatem, who had just been released from the Drancy Concentration Camp after one year of internment. They included his own suits, overcoats, underware and shoes, his wife's robes, lingerie, stocks, wool coats, fur wraps and coats, bed clothing, two Oriental rugs, bedding, mattresses, a suite of furniture, including three crystal lamps, and a substantial amount of personal jewelry. Menahem Hatem to Turkish Consulate-General (Paris), 5 February 1944. Archives of Turkish Embassy (Paris) and Turkish Foreign Ministry (Ankara).

276. A. Menassé to Turkish Consul-General (Paris), no. F 1204, 3 March 1943. Archives of Turkish Embassy (Paris) and Turkish Foreign Ministry (Ankara): Namık Kemal Yolga, for Turkish Consul-General (Paris), to *Commissariat Général aux Questions Juives*, Paris, 12 March 1943, no. F 1212. Archives of Turkish Embassy (Paris), '*Ayant appris qu'un deuxième convoi de rapatriement de nos compatriots est en voie de formation, je vous serai infinement obligé si vous voudrez bien nous noter pour le troisième convoi et vous en remerciè vivement*' Also Turkish Consulate-General (Paris) to Turkish Embassy (Berlin) no. 1942/102/8, 8 February 1943, no. 1943/367/18, 16 March 1943. Turkish Consulate-General (Paris) to Turkish Embassy to Paris (Vichy) no. 1943/207/2, 20 March 1943. Archives of Turkish Consulate-General (Paris). Turkish Ambassador to Paris (Vichy) to Turkish Consul-General (Marseilles) no. 44–17, 27 January 1944, in Archives of Turkish Embassy (Paris) no. 27/I/44 17/169.

277. Turkish Consulate-General (Marseilles) to Turkish Embassy to Paris (Vichy) no. 6127/55, 2 February 1943; Turkish Consulate-General (Marseilles) to Turkish Embassy to Paris (Vichy), no. 6127309, 12 June 1943, Archives of the Turkish Embassy (Paris). Turkish Consulate-General (Paris) to Turkish Embassy (Berlin) no. 1943/383/19, 23 April 1943; Turkish Ambassador to Paris (Vichy) to Turkish Consul-General (Marseilles) no. 676–6127, 31 May 1943; Turkish Consul-General (Marseilles) Fuad Carım, to Turkish Ambassador to

Turkish Consulate-General purchased *Wagon Lit* tickets for fifteen Jewish businessmen and their families who were being sent back to Turkey.[278] Repatriation of Jewish Turks *en masse*, however, had to await the result of negotiations between Turkish and German diplomats which went on through the latter months of 1943.

As German persecution of Jews in France became increasingly severe, the Ankara government had ordered its consulates to authorize group repatriation, as we have seen, but for this to be carried out, permission still was needed from the German occupation authorities as well as from those of the countries through which the train caravans had to pass. And while the Germans had initially encouraged Jewish immigration from their territory, the Final Solution policies had led the authorities to prohibit such departures. Germany now was determined that all the territories under its control should be made *Judenfrei* as soon as possible by sending Jewish citizens of the occupied countries off to the death camps for extermination. This 'solution' could not, however, easily be imposed on citizens of countries with which it still found it convenient to be on reasonably friendly terms. On 12 September 1942, therefore the Germans had authorized the Vichy government, French officials, and neutral representatives in occupied and unoccupied France, Holland and Belgium, including those from Italy, Turkey, Switzerland, Spain, Portugal, Denmark, Sweden, Finland, Hungary and Rumania, to evacuate their Jewish citizens, with a deadline set at 31 January 1943, after which all Jews remaining would be subject to the same anti-Jewish regulations regardless of nationality:

> It is suggested that it be announced to the Hungarian and Turkish governments, as well as to the Italians, that because of military reasons all the Jews in the western occupied territories will have to accept subjection to the steps that have been taken against other Jews. The Hungarian and Turkish governments should for reasons of courtesy be allowed to remove Jews of their nationality

---

Paris (Vichy) no. 407-78, 4 June 1943 ; Turkish Consul-General (Marseilles) to Turkish Ambassador to Paris (Vichy) no. 413–81, 12 June 1943; Turkish Consul-General (Paris) Fikret Şefik Özdoğancı to Turkish Ambassador to Paris (Vichy), no. 1140/25, 3 July 1943: archives of the Turkish Embassy (Paris) file no. 676–6127.

278. Direction-General des Wagons Lits, 40 rue de l'Arcade, Paris, to Turkish Consulate-General (Paris) no. 1956, 16 June 1943. Archives of the Turkish Consulate-General (Paris).

from the occupied territories in the West until 1 January 1943. After that date exceptions will no longer be possible . . . . Berlin, 19 September 1942

      (signed) LUTHER[279]

The Turkish Consulate-General in Paris immediately sent the German Consulate-General the applications of one hundred Jewish Turks wishing to return to Turkey, and these were granted on 20 February 1943.[280] Reports from Jews who were evacuated by train at this time indicate that Jews also were sent by train through the facilities of the Turkish consuls in Brussels and the Hague, but no documentary or statistical evidence regarding this has yet been uncovered. By March, the embassies of Italy and Turkey as well as the legations of Hungary and Bulgaria had indicated their willingness to organize such repatriation of their nationals, mostly Jews.

The original deadline imposed by the Germans for this evacuation was extended to 31 March 1943, but as a result of the requests of Spain, Italy, and Turkey the deadline was extended again and again throughout the year due to difficulties in organizing the evacuation, not the least among which, insofar as Turkey was concerned, was the reluctance of Croatia, Rumania, Serbia, and Bulgaria to grant the necessary transit visas, even after Germany had indicated its willingness to allow Jewish Turks to leave.[281] While Turkey initially indicated that, in accordance with its own laws, it could repatriate only those Jews who remained Turkish citizens, and not those who had allowed their citizenship to lapse because of their acquisition of French and other citizenship and their consequent failure to register within a five-year

279. Document no. NG–5123. Office of the Chief Consul for War Crimes. My gratitude to Mr. Serge Klarsfeld, of Paris, France, for providing me with a copy of this document. A general discussion of the German policy in this respect, directed by the extremely anti-Semitic Foreign Office official Martin Luther, based on German Foreign Office archives, can be found in Christopher R. Browning, *The Final Solution and the German Foreign Office: A Study of Referat D III of Abteilung Deutschland 1940–43* (New York and London, Holmes and Meier, 1978), pp. 102–108.

280. Turkish Consulate-General (Paris) to German Embassy (Paris), 29 January 1943, no. F 916/1, Archives of Turkish Embassy (Paris); Turkish Consulate-General (Paris) to German Embassy (Paris), no. F 1052, 20 February 1943. Archives of Turkish Embassy (Paris).

281. Turkish Vice Consul (Paris) to Consulate of Hungary (Paris) no. 1943/2227, 27 July 1943, to Rumanian Consulate (Paris) no. 1943/2238, 27 July 1943, to Bulgarian Consulate (Paris) no. 1943/2229, 27 July 1943, and to French Ministry of Foreign Affairs (Vichy) no. 2240, 27 July 1943, Archives of the Turkish Consulate-General (Paris).

period,[282] ultimately when the crunch came, as we have seen, Turkey protected these as well by placing them in the category of 'irregular citizens' (*gayri muntazem vatandaş*), issuing them with 'Certificates of Citizenship' on that basis, and pressuring both the Germans and the Vichy government to exclude them from the anti-Jewish laws as well as from deportation to Germany, resulting in an order to that effect secured by Wilhelm Melchers, of the Near East Desk in the Political Division of the German Foreign Office. [283]

From the start, the Vichy government had indicated that it would not accept or enforce deadlines imposed by the Germans on evacuations of Jews from its territory. Pierre Laval himself had protested against the order due to the effect it would have on French enterprises using slave Jewish labor,[284] but the Germans extended the deadline for occupied France only with great reluctance due to the insistence of many Nazi leaders in Berlin, particularly Adolph Eichmann, that all Jews be removed from Greater Germany in one way or another, whether citizens of neutral countries or not.

On 5 July 1943, Adolf Eichmann pressured the German Foreign Office to stimulate the neutral countries to immediate action:

> We do not consider it worthwhile to wait any longer or to meet these governments halfway. According to the present status of the final solution, there are now in the Reich area only those Jews who are partners in a Jewish-German mixed marriage and a few Jews of foreign nationality.[285]

Eichmann insisted that only one more deadline be allowed, 3 August 1943, but the German Foreign Office in fact extended it to October for all the neutral countries, and in addition Italy, although soon afterwards the latter was compelled to deport all its Jews immediately following its

282. Browning, *Final Solution*, pp. 155–156.

283. Testimony of Ambassador Namık Kemal Yolga, Turkish Consul in Paris during World War II, to the author on 25 April 1991.

284. President Laval (Vichy) to M. de Brinon (*liaison* to the German occupation authorities), 25 October 1943, in Archives of the French Ministry of Foreign Affairs, Quai d'Orsay (Paris), *Guerre 1939–1945, Vichy, Europe serie C 140*, fol. 191.

285. Adolph Eichmann to German Foreign Office, 5 July 1943, German Foreign Office Archives NG-2652–E, quoted in Raul Hilberg, *The Destruction of the European Jews* (New York, and London, 1985), II, 447.

surrender in September 1943 and occupation by both the Allies and the Germans.

Eichmann also instructed the German Foreign Ministry :

> . . . we ask that you put aside any possible scruples in the interest of finally solving the Jewish Problem, since in this matter the Reich has met the foreign governments halfway in the most generous manner.[286]

By October 1943 the Germans had reached agreements to allow Hungary, Italy, Switzerland, Spain, Portugal, Denmark, Sweden and Finland to evacuate their Jews despite the efforts of the Gestapo leaders in Paris and Berlin to scuttle the entire program and to deport Jews to the East regardless of their nationality.[287] An agreement with Turkey followed once the Germans had pressured the intervening countries to allow the Jewish Turks to pass through their territory, but because of the difficulties involved, Turkey asked for another postponement, to December 1943, which was granted by the German Foreign Office only with reluctance, and with considerable unhappiness expressed by Eichmann and his associates.[288]

After a series of negotiations between 4–15 November 1943 at the request of the Turkish Embassy the Germans finally authorized the Turkish government to send Jewish Turks back to Turkey by groups in train caravans.[289]

---

286. *ibid.*

287. French Ministry of Foreign Affairs, *Unions Internationales* Y–100/J no. 5693, Vichy, 9 November 1943, fol. 203–4; *Avis aux Israelites Roumains,* Vichy, 12 November 1943, fol. 205; Pierre Lavale to M.l de Brison, 13 November 1943, fol. 206; General Oberg to Pierre Laval via Brinon, no. 236, 8 November 1943, fol. 200–202, no. 249, 18 November 1943, fol. 207–208; Archives of French Ministry of Foreign Affairs (Paris), *Guerre, 1939–1945, Vichy, Europe serie C, 140.* Aside from Turkey, Spain was most active among neutral countries in seeking to protect its Jewish nationals resident in Nazi-occupied countries. Spain also offered little resistance to Jews escaping across its borders from France. See, for example, Haim Avni, 'Spanish Nationals in Greece and their Fate during the Holocaust', *Yad Vashem Studies on the European Jewish Catastrophe and Resistance,* VIII (1970), pp. 31–68.

288. Oberg to Pierre Laval via Brinon, no. 249, 18 November 1943, in Archives of Ministère des Affaires Etrangères (Quai d'Orsay), Paris, *Guerre 1939–1945, Vichy: Europe serie C, vol. 140,* fol. 207–208. Adolph Eichmann to German Foreign Office, 15 November 1942. German Foreign Office Archives, NG–2652–L, quoted in Hilberg, *Destruction of the European Jews* II, 447.

289. Ministère des Affaires Etrangères (Vichy), *Unions Internationales,* Y–100/J no. 5693, Vichy, 9 November 1943. Note for the Secretary General of the French Foreign Ministry. In Archives of the *Ministère des Affaires Etrangères* (Quai d'Orsay), *Guerre 1939–*

The Turkish consulates at Paris and Grenoble immediately began to organize their nationals, many of whom had applied for repatriation as individuals during the previous year, with advertisements placed in the leading local newspapers urging Jewish Turks to register for repatriation and reminding them of the deadline as well as the probable consequences if they failed to leave:[290]

> Republic of Turkey, Paris Consulate-General
> Paris, 26 January 1944 no. 77/29

> Summary: Regarding the return to Turkey of Jews in the free zone
> Urgent. For individual eyes only
> To the Consulate-General at Marseilles
> Answer to communication no. 16/11 of 18 January 1944
> About a year ago when the German authorities first proposed the return to their own country of the Jews of Turkey and of other neutral countries living in the occupied zone, the instructions which we received from the Foreign Ministry in response was that visas permitting the return of these Jews to Turkey should not be requested or granted for groups, but rather on an individual basis. Because of these instructions, while the Jews of all the other neutral countries and of Germany's allies have left France, our fellow countrymen have not been able to return to Turkey. However in recent months the German government has given special importance to this matter, and has stated that if the Jewish Turks have not left France by 31 January 1944, they will be treated like German Jews.
> Recently however as a result of efforts made in both Berlin and Ankara, instructions have been communicated to our Consulate-General through the embassies at Berlin and Paris as well as from Ankara that visas for return to Turkey can be given if

---

1945, Vichy, Europe serie C, vol. 140, fol. 203–204. German Embassy (Paris) to Turkish Consulate-General (Paris), no. 2534/XI/43, 15 November 1943. Archives of Turkish Embassy (Paris) and Turkish Ministry of Foreign Affairs (Ankara).

290. Turkish Ambassador to Paris (Vichy) to Turkish Consul-General (Paris) no. 21/9, 18 January 1944; Turkish Consul-General (Paris) to Turkish Consul-General (Marseilles) no. 35/11, 15 January 1944. Archives of the Turkish Embassy (Paris).

requested by Jews who are 'in order' Turkish citizens. In view of this, I propose that the problem of whether or not Jews in the free zone should or should not join the caravans which we are sending from Paris should be handled in the following manner:

Our government has not stated essentially that our Jewish fellow countrymen in France should return to Turkey all at once. Permission has been given at this time for visas to be given to them because of the consideration that most likely their total number will not be large. However the German government warning that all must leave by the end of 31 January refers to the Jews of the German occupied zone. Though the free zone has been partially occupied by German forces, the Germans have stated that there will be no change in the status of Jews there, so for the moment we don't have to worry about the Jewish Turks there. For this reason there is no need for them be returned immediately to Turkey. However, if approval is given for the circumstances mentioned below, decisions can be made for them on an individual basis.

(1). If there are among the Jewish youths living in the free zone those who have not yet been returned to Turkey by higher authorities in Ankara because they have failed to perform their military obligations and therefore have had visa problems, advantage should be taken of the present situation and they can be sent from Paris.

(2). If Jews in the occupied zone have decided, or find it necessary, to return to Turkey, we can facilitate their return together with close relatives like mothers, fathers, and siblings who are still children if we are convinced of the necessity of doing so.

(3). We can accept the return to Turkey of those whose return would be of use to the nation, like Dario Feldshtayn, mentioned in my letter no. 79–21 of 21 January 1944.

(4). Jewish Turks arrested in the free zone and sent to concentration camps in our district are being freed at this time by the German authorities on condition that they return to Turkey. Naturally such people are asking our Consulate-General for permission to return. For this reason, we feel it is essential that their departure from Paris be assured . . . .

Sometimes Jews were arrested and sent to concentration camps for relatively minor offenses, as in the case of Menahem Hatem, his wife Lisa, his brother Samuel, and his wife Rosa, who fell victim to the Nazi regulation forbidding Jews from having telephones or radios in their houses, causing their arrest at dispatch to Drancy and the sealing of their apartment:

THE MENAHEM HATEM FILE

Menahem Hatem, wife Lisa Hatem, Turkish Certificate of Nationality 1874 TP
Samuel Hatem, wife Rosa Hatem, Turkish Certificate of Nationality 1435 TP
Menahem Hatem residence: 25 Rue Boissière, Paris XVI
Arrested 9 July 1943, sent to Drancy Concentration Camp.
Freed: 15 January 1944
Repatriated to Turkey: 4 February 1944

a. MENAHEM HATEM ASKS TURKISH CONSULATE-GENERAL FOR ATTESTATION THAT HIS PARIS APARTMENT IS TURKISH PROPERTY SO IT WILL NOT BE SEALED BY AUTHORITIES. Menahem Hatem, 25, Rue Boissière, Paris XVIème, to Turkish Consulate, 8 February 1943. Archives of Turkish Embassy (Paris) and Turkish Foreign Ministry (Ankara).

> M. Hatem, 25, Rue Boissière, Paris XVI
> 1435 TP; 18-76 TP, Paris, 8 February 1943

> To the Turkish Consulate at Paris
> Mr. Consul-General,
> I have the honor of soliciting your assistance in providing a certificate that our apartment at 25 Rue Boissière is a Turkish property. I would be very obliged if you would provide me with this attestation in all urgency, since we will be repatriated tomorrow. With my thanks in anticipation, please, Mr. Consul-General, accept the assurance of my perfect consideration.
> **(signed)** N. Hatem
> **Consular minute:** 1874 TP attestation delivered with tariff 13 8/2/1943-initialed

b. MENAHEM HATEM AND SAMUEL HATEM AND THEIR FAMILIES ARE ARRESTED IN PARIS ON 9 JULY 1943 Cited in

Consulate-General letter of 12 July 1943. Date cited in Turkish Consul-General letter to German Embassy of 23 July 1943.

c. TURKISH CONSULATE-GENERAL COMPLAINS TO DR. SCHMITT ABOUT ARREST OF MENAHEM HATEM AND SAMUEL HATEM AND THEIR FAMILIES ALTHOUGH THEY ARE TURKISH CITIZENS. Turkish Consulate-General (Paris) to Monsieur le Docteur Schmitt, 11 Rue des Saussaires, Paris VIIIème, no. F 2101, 12 July 1943. Archives of Turkish Embassy (Paris) and Turkish Foreign Ministry (Ankara).

Consulate-General of Turkey
Paris, 12 July 1943, no. F 2101

Dr. Schmitt
11 Rue des Saussaires, Paris VIIIème
Dear Dr. Schmitt,

On the subject of the arrest of Messrs Menahem Hatem and Samuel Hatem and their families, I have the honor of bringing to your attention that these people are Turkish citizens holding respectively Certificates of Nationality no. 1874 TP, renewed on 26 September 1942 under number 423/424 and valid until 26 September 1943, and 1435 TP, renewed on 5 January 1943 under number 5/6 and good until 5 January 1944. These Turkish citizens have not committed any crime which would justify their internment at the Camp of Drancy, so I ask you to order their release. They are on the list of persons who have asked for their repatriation, and their request has been submitted to the competent Turkish government department. They will be repatriated as soon as the answer of that department has reached this Consulate-General.

In thanking you in advance for the trouble you are willing to take in this matter, I ask you to accept. *Monsieur le Docteur*, the assurance of my very special consideration.

(signed) Fikret Şefik Özdoğancı, the Consul-General

d. TURKISH CONSUL-GENERAL INFORMS COMMANDER OF DRANCY INTERNMENT CAMP THAT MR. AND MRS. MENAHEM HATEM AND SAMUEL HATEM ARE TURKISH CITIZENS, AND

THAT HE HAS ASKED GERMAN AUTHORITIES FOR THEIR RELEASE. Turkish Consul-General (Paris) to Commander of Drancy Internment Camp, no. F 2198, 22 July 1943. Archives of Turkish Embassy (Paris) and Turkish Foreign Ministry (Ankara).

Republic of Turkey, Consulate-General in Paris
22 July 1943, no. F 2198

Commander of the Internment Camp at Drancy (Seine)
Dear Mr. Commander,

I have the honor of bringing to your attention that Mr. and Mrs. Menahem Hatem, as well as Mr. and Mrs. Samuel Hatem, who have been interned in the camp placed under your estimable direction, are Turkish citizens bearing respectively Certificate of Nationality no. 1874 TP, renewed on 26 September 1942 under no. 423/424 and valid until 26 September 1943, and Certificate of Nationality no. 1435 TP, renewed on 5 January 1943 under the no. 5/6 and valid until 5 January 1944.

I have already made requests with the competent authorities to secure their liberation.

Please accept, Mr. Commander, the assurance of my very special consideration

(**signed**) Fikret Şefik Özdoğancı,
The Consul-General

e. TURKISH CONSULATE-GENERAL WRITES GERMAN EMBASSY ABOUT THE CASE OF MENAHEM AND SAMUEL HATEM. Turkish Consulate-General (Paris) to German Embassy (Paris) no. F 2203, 23 July 1943. Archives of Turkish Embassy (Paris) and Turkish Foreign Ministry (Ankara).

Republic of Turkey, Consulate-General at Paris
23 July 1943, no. F 2203

German Embassy, Paris
The Consulate-General of Turkey at Paris presents its compliments to the Embassy of Germany and has the honor of bringing to its attention the following:

On Wednesday 9 July 1943, Mr. Menahem Hatem, a Turkish citizen, was arrested when he was on Boulevard Bonne-Nouvelle. The police who arrested him then brought him to his house, at 25 Rue Boissière, where they arrested his wife, his brother Samuel Hatem, and the wife and daughter of the latter. All of these were in their home and had committed no crime. Nonetheless the police officers took all these Turkish citizens to the Police Station at Rue du Bouquet de Longchamp, and despite the various démarches of this Consulate-General with the police authorities, brought them to the Internment Camp at Drancy.

The Service IV B of the occupying police authorities and Dr. Schmitt promised their freedom and gave the order to this effect to the French police authorities. Later, however, the Services of Dr. Schmitt, based on the report of the French police authorities, answered that these people had been arrested because they possessed a telephone in their house.

The Consulate-General of Turkey has always been of the opinion that so long as the treaties and conventions presently existing between Turkey and Germany and between Turkey and France remain in force, Turkish citizens of Jewish religion cannot be prevented from having a telephone in their house and using it. In addition, if Jews of whatever nationality did not have the right to have a telephone, and as a result of this the telephone of the Hatem family had to be removed, it would be the competent service of the Telephone Administration that would carry this out. In fact, the people in question did not have a telephone in their house, but rather in their business establishment, which has been Aryanized and is being managed by an administrator.

The Estimable Embassy should be convinced that this situation does not constitute a crime justifying the interment of these five Turkish citizens. The Consulate-General of Turkey asks as a result that the Embassy of Germany have the goodness to intervene with the competent authorities so that Mr. and Mrs. Menahem Hatem as well as Mr., Mrs., and Miss Samuel Hatem be freed and that the seals which were placed on their apartment be removed as a matter of urgency.

Mr. and Mrs. Menahem Hatem possess Certificate of Nationality no. 1874 TP, renewed on 26 September 1942 under number 423/424 and valid until 26 September 1943, and Mr., Mrs.

and Miss Samuel Hatem bear Certificate of Nationality no. 1435 TP, renewed on 5 January 1943 under no. 5/6 and valid until 5 January 1944.

This Consulate-General thanks in advance the Embassy of Germany for its obliging intervention in this matter, and takes this occasion to reiterate to it the assurances of its high consideration.

(**signed**) Fikret Şefik Özdoğancı, Consul-General

f. TURKISH CONSULATE ASKS DRANCY CAMP COMMANDER TO PROVIDE MENAHEM AND SAMUEL HATEM WITH FORMS TO BE FILLED OUT TO GET VISAS TO GO TO TURKEY. Turkish Consulate-General (Paris) to Drancy Camp Commander, no. F 2201, 24 July 1943. Archives of the Turkish Embassy (Paris) and Turkish Foreign Ministry (Ankara).

Republic of Turkey, Paris Consulate-General
24 July 1943 no. F 2201
The Commander of Internment Camp at Drancy (Seine)
Mr. Commander,

I ask you to find inclosed ten forms for requests for visas which should be filled out by Mr. and Mrs. Menahem Hatem, and Mr. Mrs. and Mademoiselle Samuel Hatem, all Turkish citizens who were arrested and interned in the camp placed under your high direction.

Would you please communicate these to them and inform them that they must fill out two copies for each individual and add to them two photographs each.

With my thanks in anticipation for the trouble that you take in this respect, I ask you to accept, Mr. Commander, the assurance of my very special consideration.

(**signed**) The Consul
Paris, 24 July 1943

g. GERMAN EMBASSY ACKNOWLEDGES RECEIPT OF TURKISH EMBASSY LETTER REGARDING MENAHEM AND SAMUEL HATEM AND RESERVES ITS RESPONSE. German Embassy, Paris, no. 3634/43 to Turkish Consulate-General, Paris, 28 July 1943. Archives of the Turkish Embassy (Paris) and Turkish Foreign Ministry (Ankara) no. F 2280.

German Embassy, Paris, 28 July 1943, no. 3634/43

The German Embassy acknowledges receipt of the note no. 2203 of 23 July 1943 regarding the Turkish citizens Menahem and Samuel Hatem. The German authorities are occupied with this matter, and the German Embassy will communicate further when it is appropriate.

h. N. HATEM ASKS THAT SEALS BE REMOVED FROM HATEM APARTMENT AT 25 RUE BOISSIÈRE IN PARIS. N. Hatem to Turkish Consulate-General (Paris), 19 August 1943. Archives of the Turkish Embassy (Paris) and Turkish Foreign Ministry (Ankara).

Paris, 19 August 1943

To Mr. Consul-General of Turkey in Paris

Dear Mr. Consul-General

I ask the favor of arranging to remove the seals from the apartment of the Hatem family, 25 Rue Boissière, 1st floor, Paris XVI, that were installed by the authorities on 9 July. With my thanks in anticipation,

I ask you to believe, Mr. Consul-General, in the assurance of my special consideration.

(signed) N. Hatem, 1435 TP

Consular minute: Mlle Bousquet

19-9-1943. N.Y. (Namık Kemal Yolga)

i. TURKISH CONSULATE-GENERAL ASKS GERMAN DIENSTELLE WESTEN TO REMOVE SEALS FROM APARTMENT OF MENAHEM HATEM IN PARIS. Turkish Consul-General to Dienstelle Westen, Fort d'Iena, Paris, 24 August 1943, no. F 2397. Archives of the Turkish Embassy (Paris) and Turkish Foreign Ministry (Ankara).

Republic of Turkey, Consulate-General at Paris

24 August 1943 no. F 2397

To the Dienstelle Westen, Fort of Iena, Paris

The Consulate-General of Turkey presents its compliments to the Dienstelle Westen and has the honor of bringing to its attention the following:

By a letter of 23 July reference F 2203, this Consulate-General informed the Embassy of Germany of the arrest of Mr. Menahem Hatem and Mr. Samuel Hatem and their families and their internment at the Camp of Drancy. By this letter the Consulate-General asked for the liberation of these people and the lifting of the seals placed on their apartment.

The Embassy of Germany by a letter of 28 July, reference 3634/4 Dr. GO/G, answered that it had asked the competent authorities about this matter and that it reserved its response. The seals in the meantime remain on the apartment of the Hatem family, 25 Rue Boissière, Paris XVI. Since this involves Turkish citizens whose citizenship is in order, the Consulate-General asks the Dienstelle Westen to be good enough to intervene with the competent service to have the seals removed from the Hatem apartment.

Mr. and Mrs. Menahem Hatem have Certificate of Nationality no. 1874 TP, renewed on 26 September 1942 under number 423/424 and valid until 26 September 1943, and Mr., Mrs. and Miss Samuel Hatem have Certificate of Nationality no. 1435 TP, renewed on 5 January 1943 under number 5/6 and valid until 5 January 1944. The Consulate-General of Turkey thanks in advance the Dienstelle Western for its obliging intervention in this matter, and takes advantage of the occasion to reiterate to it the assurances of its high consideration.

(**signed**) Namık Kemal Yolga for the Consul-General

j. GERMAN EMBASSY INFORMS TURKISH CONSULATE THAT THE HATEMS WERE ARRESTED BECAUSE THEY VIOLATED ANTI JEWISH REGULATIONS. THE GERMANS WILL FREE THEM ONLY IF THEY ARE REPATRIATED TO TURKEY. German Embassy (Paris) to Turkish Consulate-General (Paris) no. 4151/43, 16 September 1943. Turkish file no. F 2541. Archives of the Turkish Embassy (Paris) and the Turkish Foreign Ministry (Ankara).

German Embassy, Paris, 4151/43

The German Embassy is honored to answer the note of 23 July 1943 no. 203 of the Turkish Consulate-General, that the Jews who are Turkish citizens Menahem Hatem and Samuel Hatem and their wives and daughter were arrested by the French police and interned at the Drancy camp because of violation of the anti-Jewish laws. The aforementioned German authorities can agree to their release only if they are returned to Turkey.

Paris, 16 September 1943

Consular minute: Résumé: The brothers Hatem, their wives and daughter have been arrested by the French police because of contravention of the anti-Jewish laws, and have been taken to the Camp at Drancy. The German authorities can accept their liberation only in the case that they are repatriated to Turkey. Namık Kemal Yolga.

k. N. HATEM ASKS TURKISH CONSULATE TO CERTIFY THAT RENT ON HATEM APARTMENT IS PAID THROUGH APRIL 1945 AND THAT THE APARTMENT IS UNDER THE PROTECTION OF THE TURKISH CONSULATE. N. Hatem (Paris) to Consul-General of Turkey, Paris, 24 September 1943, no. F 2586. Archives of Turkish Embassy (Paris) and Turkish Foreign Ministry (Ankara).

Paris, 24 September 1943

Mr. Vice Consul, Consulate-General of Turkey
Dear Mr. Vice Consul,
I ask the favor of your renewing for me the attached attestation that I have just found at the door of our apartment. In addition, one of the Certificates of Nationality comes due very soon, on 26 September 1943, and I would be very obliged if you could specify that our rent is paid until April 1945, and that this apartment is under the protection of the Turkish consulate.[291]

(**signed**) N. Hatem

l. TURKISH CONSULATE REPEATS REQUEST THAT SEALS BE REMOVED FROM HATEM APARTMENT IN PARIS BECAUSE WATER IS LEAKING FROM IT INTO APARTMENT BELOW. Turkish Consulate-General (Paris) to Dienstelle Westen, 54, avenue d'Iéna, Paris XVIème, F 2586, 15 October 1943. Archives of Turkish Embassy (Paris) and Turkish Foreign Ministry (Ankara).

---

291. Remainder of letter missing.

Republic of Turkey, Consulate-General at Paris
15 October 1943, no. F 2586

To the Dienstelle Westen
54, Avenue d'Iéna, Paris XVIème,

The Consulate-General of Turkey in Paris presents its compliments to the Dienstelle Westen and has the honor to bring the following to its attention:

By a letter of 24 August, reference F 2397, this Consulate-General informed the Dienstelle Westen of the arrest of Messrs. Menahem and Samuel Hatem and their families and the placing of seals on their apartment at 25 Rue Boissière in Paris XVIème. This Consulate-General had asked the Dienstelle Westen to intervene with the competent service to have the seals removed.

The Consulate-General has not yet received an answer from the Dienstelle Westen, and it appears that the renters of the floor beneath the Hatem apartment are complaining of a flow of water coming from that apartment. This Consulate-General therefore asks the Dienstelle Western to have the goodness to have the seals removed as a matter of urgency so that the water pipes can be repaired.

The Consulate-General of Turkey thanks in advance the Dienstelle Westen for the trouble that it will take in this matter, and takes advantage of the occasion to reiterate the assurances of its high consideration.

(**signed**) The Consul-General

m. N. HATEM ASKS TURKISH CONSULATE TO AUTHORIZE SENDING OF A SUITCASE OF CLOTHING TO HATEM FAMILY IMPRISONED AT DRANCY CAMP. N. Hatem to Turkish Consulate-General, Paris, 28 October 1943. Archives of Turkish Embassy (Paris).

Paris, 28 October 1943

To the Consul-General of Turkey in Paris
Dear Mr. Consul

I ask the favor of your authorization for the sending of a box of warm clothing and food to my family Hatem. I would be very grateful if you would give me this favor. With my thanks in anticipation, I ask you to accept, Mr. Consul-General, the assurance of my perfect consideration.

    (signed) N. Hatem, 25 Rue Boissière, Paris

    Consular minute: He will take them . . . . 8 November 1943.

    n. N. HATEM ASKS TURKISH CONSULATE TO RENEW EFFORT TO SECURE FREEDOM OF HER FAMILY FROM DRANCY CAMP AND TO PROVIDE PASSPORTS TO THE FAMILY FOR A RETURN TO TURKEY. N. Hatem to Turkish Consulate (Paris), 9 November 1943, no. F 2862.

    Paris, 9 November 1943

    To Mr. Consul-General of Turkey, Paris

    Dear Mr. Consul-General

    I have the honor of asking for your help in reactivating the liberation of my relatives, that is the five members of the Hatem family who were interned at Drancy since 8 July last:

    My uncle, Mr. Menahem Michel Hatem, born in Turkey at Istanbul–Certificate of Nationality no. 1874 TP, who was arrested on 8 July 1943 in front of the newspaper *Le Matin*;

    My aunt, Madame Lisa Hatem (1874 TP), born in Turkey;

    My father: Mr. Samuel Oscar Hatem, Certificate of Nationality no. 1335 TP, born in Istanbul on 18 February 1882;

    My mother: Madame Sol Hatem (1435 TP), born in Turkey on September 1892

    My sister: Mlle Rosa Hatem (1435 TP), born in Istanbul 10 March 1930

    were arrested on 9 July at their home, 25 Rue Boissière Paris XVIème. My relatives are Turkish subjects 'in order' with the Consulate-General of Turkey. I would be very grateful if you would provide us with passports to facilitate our departure for our country. In expectation of your favorable reception of my request, and thanking you in advance, I ask you to believe, Mr. Consul-General, the assurance of my perfect consideration.

    (signed) N. Hatem

    o. TURKISH CONSULATE REPEATS REQUEST TO GERMAN EMBASSY TO REMOVE SEALS FROM HATEM APARTMENT IN PARIS. Consulate-General of Turkey (Paris) to German Embassy (Paris), no. F 2862, 23 November 1943. Archives of Turkish Embassy (Paris) and Turkish Ministry of Foreign Affairs (Ankara).

Republic of Turkey, Consulate-General of Turkey
Paris, 23 November 1943, no. F 2862

To the Embassy of Germany,
78, Rue de Lille, Paris XIIème,

The Consulate-General of Turkey at Paris presents its compliments to the Embassy of Germany and has the honor of bringing to its attention what follows:

By a letter of 23 July 1943 Ref. F 2203 this Consulate-General informed the Embassy of Germany of the arrest of Mr. Menahem Hatem, his wife, his brother Samuel Hatem, the wife and daughter of the latter, of their internment at the Camp at Drancy, and the placing of seals on their apartment at 25, Rue Boissière. This Consulate-General then twice sent the Dienstelle Westen, 54, Avenue d'Iena at Paris requests to remove the seals in order to prevent continued complaints by the neighbors beneath the Hatem apartment about a flow of water from that apartment. The Dienstelle Westen not having answered the letters addressed to it, this Consulate-General asks the Embassy of Germany to be good enough to intervene with the competent service so that the seals of this apartment, which belongs to Turkish citizens 'in order', are removed as a matter of urgency.

This Consulate-General thanks in advance the Embassy of Germany for the trouble that it will take in this regard, and takes advantage of this occasion to reiterate the assurances of its high consideration.

Paris, 23 November 1943

p. GERMAN EMBASSY INFORMS TURKISH CONSULATE-GENERAL THAT HATEM HOUSE WAS SEALED BY FRENCH POLICE, NOT BY GERMANS. TURKISH CONSULATE STATES THAT THEY HAVE BEEN FREED. German Embassy (Paris) to Turkish Consulate-General (Paris), no. B 6262/43, 11 January 1944. Archives of Turkish Embassy (Paris) and Turkish Foreign Ministry (Ankara) no. F 3188.

The German Embassy, Paris
No. B 6262/43
Paris, 11 January 1944

To the Turkish Consulate-General, Paris

The German Embassy has the honor to respond to the Turkish Consulate-General note of 23 November 1943 no. F 2862 regarding the situation of the dwelling of Menahem Hatem, that this dwelling was not sealed by the Dienstelle Westen. The dwelling bears the seals of the French Police.

Consular minute: N. Yolga, 15/1/ . . . freed!

q. MENAHEM HATEM WRITES TURKISH CONSULATE AFTER RELEASE FROM PRISON THAT THE ADMINISTRATOR OF HIS BUSINESS HAS THREATENED TO HAVE HIM RETURNED TO PRISON UNLESS HE PAYS MONEY. Menahem Hatem, 25 Rue Boissière, Paris to Turkish Consulate-General, 21 January 1944. no. F 3236.

Hatem Menahem
25 Rue Boissière, Paris
Paris, 21 January 1944

Mr. Consul-General of Turkey

I have the honor of asking you for protection regarding a difference that I have with my temporary Administrator, M. Giraux Fernard, 10 Rue Auber. This is what happened. When I was arrested I had in my safe about 125,000 francs, which I spent as needed. On my return my Administrator Mr. Fernand Giraux, 10 Rue Auber, demanded in a categorical manner the return of that sum, and this evening at about 6 p.m. he threatened me that he would immediately advise the Court of Jewish Affairs and the Gestapo, claiming that he would have me arrested immediately. It is useless to tell you, Mr. Consul, that after all that I endured, such a threat has put me in a state, and I ask you to do what is necessary to settle this affair as soon as possible. I am at this moment at the Consulate, and I am awaiting the opportunity to talk with you to give you more details verbally. Please accept, Mr. Consul, the expression of my most special sentiments.

(**signed**) M. Hatem

Consular minute: 21 January 1944. The question has been settled between him and his administrator. F 3236.

r. HATEMS IN ANTICIPATION OF BEING REPATRIATED TO TURKEY ON 4 FEBRUARY 1944 ASK LETTER FROM CONSUL AUTHORIZING THEM TO SELL OR RENT THEIR FURNITURE AND TO RENT OUT THE APARTMENT THAT THEY OCCUPY. S. Hatem to Consul-General (Paris), Paris, 27 January 1944. Archives of Turkish Embassy (Paris) and Turkish Foreign Ministry (Ankara).

> Paris, 27 January 1944
> Consulate-General of Turkey, Paris
>
> Mr. Consul-General,
> Before being repatriated on 4 February next, we want to ask you by the present note to be good enough to address us a letter authorizing us to sell or rent our furniture and to rent the apartment that we occupy in the building at 25 Rue Boissière, Paris XVIème.
> We thank you for this and ask you to accept, Mr. Consul-General, the expression of our perfect consideration.
> (**signed**) S. Hatem
> Hatem Menahem
> Hatem Samuel
> **Turkish consular note**: answer, 28 January 1944R

s. M. HATEM ASKS TURKISH CONSULATE FOR AUTHORIZATION TO TAKE FURNITURE, CLOTHING, AND HOUSEHOLD ARTICLES WITH HIM AND FAMILY ON TRAIN TO TURKEY. Menahem Hatem to Turkish Consulate-General (Paris), 5 February 1944. Archives of Turkish Embassy (Paris) and Turkish Foreign Ministry (Ankara).

> Paris, 5 February 1944
> To the Consulate-General of Turkey, Paris
> Mr. Consul-General,
> I have the honor of remitting to you herewith the list of objects that I will take with me to Istanbul, as a result of my repatriation to Turkey, objects that are in trunks and packages

being sent by baggage car, and suitcases that I will take in the compartment. I ask you to legalize this list so that I will not have any difficulties at the Customs.

I thank you for this and ask you to accept, Mr. Consul-General, the expression of my high consideration.

signed) M. Hatem

Consular minute: 1874 TP 9/2/1944

List of objects belonging to Mr. M. Hatem and transported to Istanbul, Turkey in trunks and boxes on the baggage car and in suitcases in the apartment:

Men's clothing—suits, overcoat, lingerie, shoes.

Woman's clothing: robes, lingerie, stockings, wool coats and fur wraps, fur coats, shoes, women's handbags, toilet articles, etc.

Bed clothing and mattresses.

2 Oriental rugs, bedding.

suite of furniture including three crystal lamps.

personal jewelry.

t. TURKISH CONSULATE-GENERAL INFORMS MENAHEM HATEM THAT AS A TURKISH CITIZEN RETURNING TO TURKEY HE IS FREE TO DISPOSE OF HIS BELONGINGS OR TAKE THEM ALONG AS HE WISHES. Turkish Consul-General (Paris) to Menahem Hatem, 25, Rue Boissière, Paris XVIème, F 8490, 14 February 1944. Archives of Turkish Embassy (Paris) and Turkish Foreign Ministry (Ankara).

Consulate-General of Turkey, Paris

14 February 1944, no. F 8490

To Mr. Hatem, 25 Rue Boissière, Paris XVIème,

In response to your letter of the 8th of this month, I can inform you that as a Turkish citizen returning imminently to Turkey, you are free to dispose of your possessions as you wish, to sell them or place them wherever you want.

Please, Sir, accept my greetings

(*signed*) Consul-General Fikret Şefik Özdoğancı

THE SAMUEL AND VIDA LEVI FILE

Samuel Levi
Wife Vida Levi
Arrested at Nice and sent to Compiègne (Oise) concentration camp
Sent to Drancy concentration camp in October 1943
Sent to Vittel internment camp in November 1943
Freed on 13 January 1944
Repatriated to Turkey on 9 February 1944

a. MARSEILLES TURKISH CONSUL-GENERAL FUAD CARIM INFORMS PARIS CONSULATE-GENERAL THAT SAMUEL LEVI AND WIFE VIDA WERE ARRESTED AT NICE AND SENT TO COMPIÈGNE CONCENTRATION CAMP, ASKS FOR NECESSARY STEPS TO GET THEM OUT. Turkish Consul-General (Marseilles) Fuad Carım, to Turkish Consulate-General (Paris), Marseilles, 27 September 1943. Archives of Turkish Embassy (Paris) and Turkish Foreign Ministry (Ankara).

> Republic of Turkey Consulate-General
> Marseilles, 27 September 1943
> To the Paris Consulate-General,
> We have received information that one of our 'in order' citizens, Samuel Levi and his wife Vida, who are registered at our Consulate no. 2522/504/III, dated 25 March 1943, were arrested at Nice and sent to the Compiègne concentration camp near Paris. I ask that you do what is necessary.
> (signed) Fuad Carım, Consul-General
> Consular minute: 2/10/1944 request for liberation
> Mlle Bousquet 5-10-43 NY (Namık Kemal Yolga)
> Paris Consulate registration no. 2154, Date 2-10-43

b. TURKISH CONSUL-GENERAL (PARIS) INFORMS COMPIÈGNE CAMP COMMANDER THAT INTERNEES SAMUEL AND VIDA LEVI ARE TURKISH CITIZENS AND THAT HE HAS ASKED AUTHORITIES FOR THEIR RELEASE. Turkish Consul-General (Paris) to Commander of Compiègne (Oise) Concentration Camp, 5 October 1943, no. F 2644. Archives of Turkish Embassy (Paris) and Turkish Foreign Ministry (Ankara).

> Consulate-General of Turkey, Paris

5 October 1943 no. F 2644

To Commander of Compiègne Concentration Camp (Oise)
Dear Mr. Commander,

I have the honor to bring to your attention that Mr. Samuel Levi and his wife Vida, citizens of Turkey and bearing Certificate of Nationality no. 2522/504/111 delivered on 25 March 1943, have just been arrested at Nice and brought to the Camp placed under your High Direction, where they are now interned. I have already made the necessary démarches with the competent authorities to secure their liberation.

Please be assured, Mr. Commander, of my most special consideration.

(signed) The Consul-General

c. TURKISH CONSUL-GENERAL (PARIS) INFORMS GERMAN EMBASSY (PARIS) THAT COMPIÈGNE INTERNEES SAMUEL AND VIDA LEVI ARE TURKISH CITIZENS AND ASKS THAT THEY BE RELEASED. Turkish Consul-General (Paris) Fikret Şefik Özdoğancı, to German Embassy, 75 Rue de Lille (Paris, VIIème), no. F 2641, 6 October 1943. Archives of Turkish Embassy (Paris) and Turkish Foreign Ministry (Ankara).

Republic of Turkey, Paris Consulate-General
Paris, 6 October 1943 no. F 2641

To the Embassy of Germany
78, Rue de Lille, Paris VIIème

The Consulate-General of Turkey at Paris presents its compliments to the Embassy of Germany and has the honor of bringing to its attention what follows:

Mr. Samuel Levi and his wife Vida, Turkish citizens bearing Certificate of Nationality no. 2522/504/111, delivered on 25 March 1943 by the Consulate-General of Turkey at Marseilles, were arrested at Nice and sent to the Internment Camp at Compiègne. Since these are 'in order' Turkish citizens, the Consulate-General of Turkey asks the Embassy of Germany to be good enough to intervene with the competent authorities to secure the liberation of Mr. Samuel and Madame Vida Levi so long as no crime has been attributed to them.

This Consulate-General thanks in advance the Embassy of Germany for its obliging intervention in this effect and takes advantage of the occasion to reiterate to it the assurances of its high consideration.

(**signed**) The Consul-General

d. GERMAN CONCENTRATION CAMP AUTHORITIES AT COMPIÈGNE INFORM TURKISH CONSULATE-GENERAL THAT SAMUEL AND VIDA LEVI ARE NOT KNOWN AT THAT CAMP. Frontstalag 122, Compiègne, to Turkish Consulate-General (Paris) no. F 2729, 13 October 1943. Archives of Turkish Embassy (Paris) and Turkish Foreign Ministry (Ankara).

Frontstalag 122 I c/S, Compiègne, 13 October 1943

To the Turkish Consulate-General, Paris
Your letter of 11 October 1943 was communicated to the competent authorities of the Security Police and the SD of the district of the Military Commander in France, on Avenue Foch in Paris, but they responded that Samuel and Vida Levy are not known at that camp.

(**signed**) The Commander
Consular minutes: 18/10/1943
camp commander 9 October 1943 Namık Yolga

e. TURKISH CONSULATE-GENERAL (PARIS) INFORMS DRANCY INTERMENT CAMP COMMANDER THAT SAMUEL AND VIDA LEVI ARE TURKISH CITIZENS AND THAT IT HAS ASKED GERMAN AUTHORITIES FOR THEIR RELEASE. Turkish Consul-General (Paris) to Commander of Drancy Internment Camp, Paris, 20 October 1943, no. F 2729. Archives of Turkish Embassy (Paris) and Turkish Foreign Ministry (Ankara).

Republic of Turkey, Consulate-General
Paris, 20 October 1943, no. F 2729

To Mr. Commander, Internment Camp at Drancy (Seine)

Mr. Commander,

I have the honor of bringing to your attention that Mr. Samuel Levi and his wife Vida, Turkish citizens bearing Certificate of Nationality no. 2522/504/11 delivered on 25 March 1943, were arrested at Nice and brought to the Camp placed under your High Direction, where they are now interned. I have already undertaken communications with the competent authorities to secure their release.

Please be assured, Mr. Commander, of my very special consideration.

(signed) Fikret Şefik Özdoğancı,
Consul-General

f. GERMANS INFORM TURKISH CONSULATE-GENERAL (PARIS) THAT SAMUEL LEVI IS INTERNED AT VITTEL INTERNMENT CAMP. *Der Befehlshaber der Sicherheitspolizei und des SD im Bereich des Militaerbefehlshabers Frankreich*, Paris, to Turkish Consulate-General, Paris, no. II pol 4 Ho/Pr, 15 November 1943. Turkish registration no. F2917, Archives of Turkish Embassy (Paris) and Turkish Foreign Ministry (Ankara).

Commander of the Security Police and of the SD in the district of the Military Commander Paris no. II pol 4 Ho/Pr, 15 November 1943

Ref: Samuel Levi
Response to: Letter no. 2644 of 5 October 1943
To the Consulate-General of Turkey, Paris
Levi is at the Internment Camp at Vittel
(signed) Commander of the S.A. Battalion
Consular minute: B. Yolga: 19/4/1944

Turkish Consular Translation: Levi for the moment is at the internment camp at Vittel. Namık Yolga, 22 November 1943.

g. TURKISH CONSULATE-GENERAL (PARIS) ASKS COMMANDER OF VITTEL (VOSGES) INTERNMENT CAMP TO RELEASE TURKISH CITIZENS SAMUEL AND VIDA LEVI, AND

THEY ARE RELEASED Turkish Consul-General (Paris) Fikret Şefik Özdoğancı, to Commander of Vittel (Vosges) Internment Camp, no. F 2917, 30 November 1943. Archives of Turkish Embassy (Paris) and Turkish Foreign Ministry (Ankara), 30 November 1943.

> Republic of Turkey, Paris Consulate-General
> 30 November 1943 no. 2917
>
> To Mr. Commander of the Internment Camp of Vittel (Vosges)
> Mr. Commander,
>
> I have the honor of bringing to your attention that Mr. Samuel Levi and his wife Vida, Turkish Citizens, bearing Certificate of Nationality no. 2522/504/111, delivered on 25 March 1943, have been arrested at Nice and brought to the camp placed under your direction, where they are now interned. I have already undertaken the communications necessary with the competent authorities to secure their release.
> Please accept, Mr. Commander, the assurance of my very special consideration.
> **(signed)** Fikret Şefik Özdoğancı Consul-General
> **Consular minutes:** 1556TP request for liberation
> freed 13 January, repatriated 9 February

THE ESTER BARZILAI FILE

Madame Marie Barzilay
Mademoiselle Ester Barzilay (daughter)
Arrested and taken to Drancy: 8 September 1943
Released: 6 March 1944
Repatriated to Turkey 29 March 1944

a. TURKISH CONSULATE-GENERAL (PARIS) NOTIFIED OF ARREST OF MARIE BARZILAY AND HER DAUGHTER ESTER BARZILAY BECAUSE THEY TRANSMITTED LETTER FROM PERSON INTERNED AT DRANCY TO HIS ATTORNEY. F. Brasilia, 6, Rue de Vintimille, Paris 9ème, to Turkish Consulate-General, 9 September

1943. Archives of Turkish Embassy (Paris) and Turkish Foreign Ministry (Ankara).

F. Barzilay, 6 Rue de Vintimille, Paris IXème
9 September 1943

Mr. Consul,

On Tuesday evening 8 September Madame Marie Barzilay and her daughter Ester were arrested at their home, 6 Rue de Vintimille, by the Germans. The reason which was given is as follows. Mr. Namer, who is now interned at the Camp at Drancy, is said to have written a letter to his administrator Arif Paşa and because he did not know the latter's address, sent the letter care of Mrs. Barzilay. These two persons have been placed among those scheduled for deportation to the East. I claim for them the protection of the Consulate of Turkey and ask you to make the necessary démarches to secure their liberation.

I ask you, Mr. Consul, to accept my special salutations.

(signed) F. Barzilay

Consular minute: 570 TP Certificate of Citizenship no. 95-96, dated 18 February 1943.

b. TURKISH CONSULATE-GENERAL INFORMS GERMAN EMBASSY THAT MARIE AND ESTER BARZILAY ARE TURKISH CITIZENS AND ASKS THEIR RELEASE FROM DRANCY CAMP. Turkish Consulate-General (Paris) to German Embassy (Paris) no. F 2486, 9 September 1943. Archives of Turkish Embassy (Paris) and Turkish Foreign Ministry (Ankara).

Republic of Turkey, Paris Consulate-General
9 September 1943, no. F 2486

To the Embassy of Germany
78, Rue de Lille, Paris VII

The Consulate-General of Turkey presents its compliments to the Embassy of Germany and has the honor to bring to its knowledge the following:

Mrs. Mari Barzilay and Miss Ester Barzilay, holders of Certificate of Nationality no. 570 TP renewed on 18 February

1943 under number 95/96 and valid until 18 February 1944, were arrested on 8 September at their home at 6 Rue de Vintimille in Paris, and sent to the internment camp at Drancy.

Since these are Turkish citizens who have committed no crime, the Consulate-General of Turkey asks the Embassy of Germany to be so good as to intervene as a matter of urgency with the competent authorities so that Madame and Mademoiselle Barzilay can be freed.

This Consulate-General thanks in advance the Embassy of Germany for its obliging intervention in this matter, and takes advantage of this occasion to reiterate to it assurances of its high consideration.

(**signed**) Namık Kemal Yolga

c. TURKISH CONSULATE-GENERAL (PARIS) INFORMS COMMANDER OF DRANCY INTERNMENT CAMP THAT MARIE AND ESTER BARZILAY ARE TURKISH CITIZENS AND THAT IT HAS ASKED FOR THEIR RELEASE. CONSULATE NOTES THAT THEY HAVE BEEN RELEASED AS A RESULT. Acting Turkish Consul-General (Paris), Namık Kemal Yolga, to Commander of Drancy Internment Camp, no. F 2487, 9 September 1943. Archives of Turkish Embassy (Paris) and Turkish Foreign Ministry (Ankara), 9 September 1943.

Republic of Turkey, Paris Consulate-General
9 September 1943 no. F 2487

To the Commander of the Internment Camp at Drancy
Mr. Commander,

I have the honor of bringing to your attention that Madame Marie and Mademoiselle Ester Barzilay, who have just been arrested and brought to the Camp placed under your High Direction, are Turkish citizens bearing Certificate of Nationality no. 570 TP, renewed on 18 February 1943 under no. 95/96 and valid until 18 February 1944. I have already undertaken the démarches with the competent authorities to secure their release.

Please accept, Mr. Commander, the assurance of my special consideration.

(**signed**) Namık Kemal Yolga, Acting Consul-General
Consular minute: freedom. 570TP. freed, repatriated.

d. ESTER BARZILAY ASKS TURKISH CONSULATE TO ARRANGE REPATRIATION TO TURKEY FOR HERSELF AND HER DAUGHTER. Ester Barzilay to Turkish Consulate-General (Paris), Nice, 6 March 1944. Archives of Turkish Consulate (Paris).

Nice, 6 March 1944

Consulate-General of the Republic of Turkey, Paris
Mr. Consul-General,

I am taking the liberty of sending you this letter to ask you for the favor of being included among the travelers of the convoy which is being formed at Paris for repatriation. I am at the same time going to the Grenoble consulate to reclaim my passport.

I ask you if you would have the good will to arrange for my passport to be turned over to me since we will have to leave Nice in a few days. It is very possible that we will be forced to go into a corner of France if it is not possible to return to my country. As soon as I receive my passport, I will go to Paris to profit from the convoy that you assign me to. In the expectation of receiving a favorable response, I thank you in advance for all you are doing for me, and ask you to accept my most sincere greetings.

(**signed**) E. Barzilay
Address: Madame Ester Barzilay, c/o Madame Sadoke
29 Boulevard de Tzarevitch, Nice
Consulate note: Passport F 3629.

e. ESTER BARZILAY INFORMS TURKISH CONSULATE-GENERAL (PARIS) THAT SHE HAS APPLIED TO TURKISH CONSULATE-GENERAL (GRENOBLE) FOR HER PASSPORT AND PERMISSION TO RETURN TO TURKEY. Ester Barzilay (Nice) to Turkish Consulate-General (Paris), 16 March 1944. Archives of Turkish Embassy (Paris).

Nice, 16 March 1944

The Consulate-General of Turkey, Paris
Mr. Consul-General,

I have the honor of transmitting to you herewith, following my request of last week, the telegraphic response that I have received from your Consulate-General at Grenoble that leaves my repatriation depending on your agreement. I add that in accordance with its instructions by letter of 10 March, I have given them my birth certificate and two photographs.

I hope thus to obtain my passport in the next few days, and ask you to immediately enter my name for repatriation since I am alone and ill and wish to join my parents who are about to leave for Paris and Istanbul.

With expression of my gratitude, I have the honor of presenting to you, Mr. Consul-General, assurances of my highest considerations.

(signed) E. Barzilay

Madame Ester Barzilay, c/o Madame Savok

29 Boulevard Tzarewitch.

Consular minute: F 3728, (received) 18 March 1944.

f. ESTER BARZILAY SENDS PHOTOGRAPHS TO TURKISH CONSULATE-GENERAL (PARIS), APPLYING FOR PASSPORT TO RETURN TO TURKEY. Ester Barzilay (Nice) to Turkish Consulate-General (Paris), Nice, 18 March 1944. Archives of Turkish Consulate (Paris).

Nice, 18 March 1944

Consulate-General of Turkey, Paris

Mr. Consul,

I have just received a telegram from Grenoble asking me for two photographs that you will find attached. I hope that you will reserve a place for me in the next convoy that is supposed to take place on the 28th of this month. In thanking you greatly for all your assistance, I ask you to accept. Mr. Consul, my most special greetings.

(signed) E. Barzilay

Consular minute: Mademoiselle Mousquet: Put her on the list as a matter of urgency. 21 March 1944. N.Y.

g. TURKISH CONSULATE-GENERAL (PARIS) INFORMS ESTER BARZILAY THAT SHE IS INCLUDED IN CARAVAN SENDING JEWISH TURKS TO PARIS LEAVING ON 29 MARCH 1944.

Turkish Consulate-General (Paris) to Ester Barzilay (Nice), Paris, 22 March 1944.

> Paris Consulate-General of Turkey
> 22 March 1944
>
> Urgent, by express mail
>
> Madame Ester Barzilay
> 29, Boulevard Tzarevitch
> Nice, Alpes Maritimes
>
> Madame,
> In response to your request, I can inform you that you have been included in the convoy that is supposed to leave on the 29th of this month. As a result, I ask you to come to Paris as soon as possible bringing your passport, since you have formalities to carry out with the Préfecture of Police.
> Please accept my greetings, Madame
> Paris, 22 March 1944.
> (**signed**) Consul-General. N(amık) Y(olga).
>
> **Consular minute:** She came and left with the caravan. 29 March 1944. N.Y.

THE ISAK BITRAN FILE

Wife: Sarah Bitran
Arrested near home: 1 October 1942, sent to Drancy Concentration Camp
Released from Drancy: 12 March 1943
Repatriated to Turkey with train convoy: 15 March 1943

a. TURKISH CONSULATE-GENERAL INFORMS SS CAPTAIN HEINZ RÖTHKE THAT ISAK BITRAN IS TURKISH CITIZEN AND ASKS FOR HIS RELEASE. Turkish Consulate-General (Paris) to Captain Heinz Röthke, 31 bis Avenue Foch, Paris, 2 October 1942 no. F 1331. Archives of Turkish Consulate (Paris).

Republic of Turkey, Consulate-General at Paris
2 October 1942 no. F 1331

Captain Röthke
31 bis Avenue Foch, Paris
Dear Captain Röthke,

The Consulate-General of Turkey at Paris has been informed that one of its Jewish citizens, Mr. Isak Bitran, holder of Passport no. 61 delivered by this Consulate-General on 20 May 1942, was arrested in Rue Sedaine, where he lives, when he was returning to his home. This Consulate-General has the honor to ask the competent German authorities to have the courtesy to free Mr. Isak Bitran if no crime has been attributed against him. The Consulate-General of Turkey thanks in advance the competent German authorities for the trouble which they are willing to take in this regard, and takes advantage of this opportunity to reiterate the assurances of its very high consideration.

(signed) Consul-General

b. TURKISH CONSULATE-GENERAL (PARIS) INFORMS DRANCY CAMP COMMANDER THAT HE HAS BEEN TOLD THAT TURKISH CITIZEN ISAK BITRAN WAS ARRESTED AND SENT TO DRANCY. ASKS IF BITRAN IS AT DRANCY SO THAT HE CAN REQUEST HIS RELEASE. Turkish Consulate-General (Paris) to Drancy Camp Commander no. F 134, 2 October 1942. Archives of Turkish Embassy (Paris).

Republic of Turkey, Consulate-General, Paris
2 October 1942, no. F 134

Mr. Director, Internment Camp at Drancy
Mr. Director,

This Consulate-General has been informed that one of its citizens, Mr. Isak Bitran, holder of passport no. 61, delivered by this Consulate-General on 20 May 1942, has been arrested by the German police of Paris and sent to Drancy for internment. I ask you to have the goodness to inform me if in fact this Turkish citizen is interned in the Internment Camp placed under your direction, so that I can undertake, without delay, the démarches with the occupying authorities in order to obtain the liberation of my citizen so long as no crime is imputed against him.

In the expectation of a prompt response, I ask you to accept, Mr. Director, the assurance of my very special consideration.

(**signed**) The Consul

c. TURKISH CONSULATE-GENERAL (PARIS) INFORMS GERMAN EMBASSY (PARIS) THAT ISAK BITRAN IS TURKISH CITIZEN AND ASKS HIS RELEASE FROM DRANCY. Turkish Consulate-General (Paris) to German Embassy (Paris) no. F 130, 5 October 1942. Archives of Turkish Embassy (Paris).

Republic of Turkey, Consulate-General, Paris
5 October 1942 no. F 130

German Embassy, Paris
The Consulate-General of Turkey presents its compliments to the Embassy of Germany and has the honor to bring to its attention that it has been informed that one of its citizens of Jewish religion, Mr. Isak Bitran, holder of passport no. 61, delivered by this Consulate-General on 20 May 1942, has been arrested in Rue Sedaine at 11:00 a.m. on 2 October by the German police and sent to Drancy. This Consulate-General would be grateful to the German Embassy if it would intervene with the competent authorities to secure the release of Mr. Isak Bitran if no crime has been attributed against him, This Consulate-General thanks in advance the Embassy of Germany for the trouble which will be willing to take in this matter and takes advantage of the occasion to reiterate the assurances of its very high consideration.

(**signed**) The Consul

d. SS CAPTAIN HEINZ RÖTHKE INFORMS TURKISH CONSULATE-GENERAL (PARIS) THAT ISAK BITRAN WAS ARRESTED ON 1 OCTOBER FOR PARTICIPATING IN ANTI-GERMAN ACTION AND SENT TO DRANCY CAMP, AND IT IS NOT INTENDED TO RELEASE HIM. Storm Troop Commander H. Röthke, *Der Befehlshaber der Sicherheitspolizei und des SD im Bereich des*

Militaerbefehlshabers in Frankreich, to Turkish Consulate-General (Paris) no. IV J SA 241 d, Paris, 3 October 1942. Archives of Turkish Embassy (Paris)

Commander of the Security Police and the SD
in the District of the Military Commander in France
Paris, 3 October 1942
IV J SA 241 d, Ah/Bir

To the Turkish Consulate-General, Paris
Subject: the Turkish Jew Isak Bitran, born 21 February 1904 at Istanbul, Turkey, dwelling at 83 Rue Sedaine, Paris
Reference: Letter of 2 October 1942 no. F 133
The Jew Isak Bitran was arrested on 1 October 1942 on account of anti-German activities and sent to the Jew Camp at Drancy. Releasing him is not intended. It is however possible that the Council for Jews, which is in charge of determining his guilt, might make an exception in a case involving one of your citizens.
(**signed**) H. Röthke,
SS-Chief Storm trooper

e. ISAK BITRAN'S WIFE SARAH DENIES HE WAS INVOLVED IN POLITICAL ACTION AND ASKS FOR HIS RELEASE SO THAT FAMILY CAN RETURN TO TURKEY. Sarah Bitran, 83 Rue Sedaine, Paris, to Turkish Consulate-General (Paris), 19 October 1942. Archives of Turkish Embassy (Paris).

83 Rue Sedaine, Paris
19 October 1942

Mr. Consul-General of Turkey at Paris
170 Boulevard Haussmann, Paris VIII
Your Excellency
Convinced that you take seriously the protection and defense of an innocent citizen, I have the honor of exposing to you the following:
My husband Bitran Isaac, father of two children, taken on the 1st of October of this year and at present interned at the camp

at Drancy, is the victim of a mistake, the proofs of which should be presented to the German authorities:

1. My husband took no part in the gathering that took place on Boulevard Voltaire and knew nothing about the incident.

2. He was taken by a simple and flagrant confusion while he was returning to his home on Rue Sedaine, where he lives.

3. He therefore committed no gesture or action which could be badly interpreted. He committed no crime and is entirely innocent.

4. He has known from the start, for seven months, the sufferings of the camp, by the privation of his wife and children, and is incapable of committing the least act of hostility.

5. He dreams only of returning to his country with his family which he asked for several months ago, and for which formalities are already in process.

In the name of sacred justice, and persuaded by your magnanimous sentiments of which you have already given proof by the audience that you gave me, and having no other means of defense than your high and benevolent authority, I ask you to be our faithful interpreter with the occupying authorities and repair this error by having him freed. In the expectation of your loyal and energetic intervention, please accept, Mr. Consul-General, the expression of sincere recognition of a mother of two children in tears, a heart torn apart, and in the greatest despair, as well as the assurance of my very special consideration.

(**signed**) his wife Sarah Bitran, 83 Rue Sedaine

f. TURKISH CONSULATE-GENERAL AGAIN ASKS GERMAN EMBASSY TO ARRANGE RELEASE OF ISAK BITRAN. Turkish Consulate-General (Paris) to German Embassy (Paris) no. F 476, 18 November 1942. Archives of Turkish Embassy (Paris).

Republic of Turkey, Consulate-General at Paris
18 November 1942

The Consulate-General of Turkey by its note of 2 October no. F 133, asked the Embassy of Germany to intervene with the competent authorities to secure the release of Mr. Isak Bitran, one of our citizens of Jewish religion, holder of passport no. 61

delivered by this Consulate on 20 May 1942, who was arrested on 2 October last by the German police and sent to the Internment Camp at Drancy, where he has remained since that time, if no crime has been found against him.

Not having received an answer to his note, the Consulate-General of Turkey permits itself to recall the case of Mr. Isak Bitran to the Estimable Embassy of Germany and to thank it in advance for the trouble that it will take in this respect.

This Consulate-General takes advantage of this occasion to reiterate to the German Embassy assurances of its high consideration.

(**signed**) The Consul-General

g. GERMAN EMBASSY INFORMS TURKISH CONSULATE-GENERAL THAT ISAK BITRAN WAS INTERNED BECAUSE OF HIS ANTI-GERMAN CONDUCT AND THAT THE SS AND THE *SURÉTÉ* POLICE HAVE NO INTENTION OF RELEASING HIM. German Embassy (Paris) to Turkish Consulate-General (Paris), 3 December 1942. Archives of the Turkish Embassy (Paris), F 561.

German Embassy, Paris
3 December 1942

To the Turkish Consulate-General, Paris

In response to the note of the Turkish Consulate-General of 19 November 1942, the Jew Isak Bitran, according to the information provided by the Commander of the Security Police and the SS to the German Embassy, was interned because of anti-German activity, and that they therefore have no intention of releasing him.

(**signed**)

Consular minute: Résumé: The Commissariat of Police of *Sureté* and the SS have informed the Embassy of Germany that the Jew Isak Bitran was interned because of his anti-German conduct and that they do not have the intention of releasing him. 3 December 1942. Namık Kemal Yolga.

h. ISAK BITRAN WRITES TURKISH CONSULATE-GENERAL (PARIS) FROM DRANCY CONCENTRATION CAMP ASKING IT TO INTERVENE TO SECURE HIS RELEASE. Isak Bitran (Drancy) to Turkish Consulate-General (Paris), 28 January 1943. Archives of Turkish Consulate-General (Paris).

Drancy, 28 January 1943

Mr. Consul-General

I have the honor to bring to your attention that I have been interned at the Drancy camp since my arrest on 3 September last.[292] I am convinced that if you are good enough to intervene again with the German authorities, it will be very useful.

I profit from this occasion to ask you to remit to my wife all documents which were deposited at the Consulate last 27 September.

I thank you in advance for everything that you will do for us, and in the expectation of hearing from you, I ask you to accept, Mr. Consul, the assurances of my perfect consideration.

(**signed**) Bitran T.P. 1030.

Consular minute: received 1 February 1943.

i. TURKISH CONSULATE-GENERAL (PARIS) ASKS GERMAN EMBASSY (PARIS) TO ARRANGE RELEASE OF ISAK BITRAN AND TO PROVIDE VISA FOR HIM AND OTHER TURKISH CITIZENS WISHING TO RETURN TO TURKEY. Turkish Consulate-General (Paris) to German Embassy (Paris), 29 January 1943, no. F 916/1, Archives of Turkish Embassy (Paris).

Republic of Turkey, Consulate-General at Paris
29 January 1943

The Embassy of Germany
78, Rue de Lille, Paris VIIème
The Consulate-General of Turkey at Paris presents its compliments to the Embassy of German and has the honor of bringing to its attention the following:

---

292. Bitran actually was arrested on 1 October 1942.

By a letter of 18 November 1942, reference F 476, this Consulate-General asked the German Embassy to be good enough to intervene with the competent authorities so that Mr. Isak Bitran, Turkish citizen, bearer of Passport no. 61 delivered 20 May 1942 and valid until 20 May 1943, and presently interned at the Drancy Camp, be freed. In addition, a request for a visa to enable Mr. Isak Bitran to return to Turkey was submitted for the approval of the German Consulate-General two months ago, along with the applications of about one hundred Turkish citizens.

The answer to the requests for visas probably will be communicated soon, and the Consulate-General of Turkey asks the Embassy of Germany to have the good will to intervene with the competent authorities to hasten the liberation of Mr. Isak Bitran so that this Turkish citizen can begin preparations to return to Turkey.

The Consulate-General of Turkey thanks in advance the Estimable Embassy of Germany for its obliging intervention in this matter, and seizes on this occasion to reiterate to it the assurances of its high consideration.

(**signed**) Consul-General, Paris,
29 January 1943

j. TURKISH CONSULATE-GENERAL (PARIS) INFORMS ISAK BITRAN THAT IT HAS APPLIED TO GERMANS TO SECURE HIS RELEASE AND THAT IT HAS PROVIDED MRS. BITRAN WITH CERTIFICATE SHOWING OWNERSHIP OF FAMILY AUTOMOBILE. Turkish Consulate-General (Paris) to Isak Bitran (Drancy), no. F 911, 17 February 1943. Archives of Turkish Embassy (Paris).

Republic of Turkey, Consulate-General of Turkey
170 Boulevard Haussmann, Paris VIII

Mr. Bitran, Registration no. 1077, Staircase 21, 4th floor
Camp at Drancy (Seine),
Sir,

In response to your card of 28 January, I can inform you that we have made the necessary démarches with the competent authorities to secure your release. In addition, a certificate specifying that the small Rosengart truck is your property as well as the papers of this automobile have been given to Mrs. Bitran.

Please accept, Sir, our special greetings.
(**signed**) The Consul
Consular minute: freed on 12 March

k. TURKISH CONSULATE-GENERAL (PARIS) REMINDS GERMAN EMBASSY OF ITS REQUEST TO FREE ISAK BITRAN AND HERMAN ROTHENBERG. ASKS THAT THEY BE FREED SINCE THEY HAVE BEEN GIVEN VISAS TO RETURN TO TURKEY ALONG WITH OTHER TURKISH CITIZENS. Turkish Consulate-General (Paris) to German Embassy (Paris) no. F 1058, 20 February 1943. Archives of Turkish Embassy (Paris).

Consulate-General of Turkey
Paris, 20 February 1943

Embassy of Germany
78, Rue de Lille, Paris XVIIème
The Consulate-General of Turkey at Paris presents its compliments to the German Embassy and has the honor of bringing to its attention that, among the Turkish citizens to whom transit visas have been given to return to Turkey, two Turkish citizens are still interned in the Drancy camp, Mr. Herman Rothenberg, registration no. 17723, and Mr. Isak Bitran, registration no. 1077. This Consulate-General asks the Estimable Embassy of Germany to have the goodwill to intervene urgently with the competent authorities so that Mr. Herman Rothenberg and Mr. Isak Bitran will be freed as soon as possible so they can prepare their departure, which will take place very shortly.

This Consulate-General thanks in advance the Embassy of Germany for its obliging intervention in this matter and seizes on this occasion to reiterate to it the assurances of its high consideration.
(**signed**) The Consul-General
Consular minute: freed on 12 March

l. TURKISH CONSULATE-GENERAL (PARIS) ASKS COMMISSARIAT GENERAL AUX QUESTIONS JUIVES FOR PERMISSION FOR ISAK BITRAN TO SELL HIS AUTOMOBILE BEFORE RETURNING TO TURKEY WITH GERMAN PERMISSION.

Turkish Consulate-General (Paris) to *Commissariat Général aux Questions Juives*, 2 place des Petits-Pères, Paris, 2ème, no. F 1212, 12 March 1943. Archives of Turkish Embassy (Paris).

> Republic of Turkey, Consulate-General of Turkey,
> Paris, 12 March 1943
> Commissariat Général aux Questions Juives
> 2, place des Petits-Pères, Paris 2ème
> Gentlemen,
> At the request of Mr. Isak Bitran, who lives at 83 Rue Sedaine at Paris XIème, I wish to inform you that this person, citizen of Turkey registered with our Consulate-General, has obtained a transit visa from the German authorities, and will be repatriated by a convoy leaving for Turkey on 15 March next.
> As a result, I ask you to be good enough to authorize Mr. Isak Bitran, owner of an automobile of the Rosengart make no. 2.113.424, registered under the number 3944 RM1, to sell his automobile to Mr. Akkawi, who lives at 36, Rue de Cléry in Paris. I ask you to accept, Gentlemen, my special greetings.
> Paris, 12 March 1943
> (**signed**) Namık Kemal Yolga for the Consul

m. GERMAN EMBASSY INFORMS TURKISH CONSULATE-GENERAL THAT ISAK BITRAN AND HERMAN ROTHENBERG WERE RELEASED FROM DRANCY CAMP ON 12 MARCH 1943. German Embassy (Paris) to Turkish Consulate-General (Paris) n.d. Archives of Turkish Embassy (Paris).

> German Embassy, Paris
>
> To the Turkish Consulate-General
> 170 Boulevard Haussmann, Paris
> The German Embassy, in response to the note of the Turkish Consulate-General no. 1052 of 20 February 1943, informs it that the release of the Turkish citizens of Jewish race Herman Rothenberg and Isak Bitran from the Drancy camp took place on 12 March 1943.
> Seal: German Embassy in Paris
> **Consular minute**s: received 16 March 1943. Namık Yolga

Résumé: H. Rothenberg and I. Bitran were released on 12 March 1941. 17 April 1943. Namık Yolga.

THE MAYER KOHEN FILE

Arrested for war profiteering, 23 October 1943 and sentenced to 6 months prison by 11ème Chambre correctionnelle

Apartment sealed by French police on 29 November 1943

20 May 1943: Germans say he will be released if immediately repatriated to Turkey.

1 January 1944: released from prison and turned over to German occupation authorities who sent him to Drancy camp.

13 January 1944: released from Drancy.

9 February 1944: leaves Paris in repatriation caravan at Gare de l'Est, 7 p.m.

a. FRENCH ATTORNEY WRITES TURKISH CONSULATE-GENERAL (PARIS) ABOUT SITUATION OF MAYER KOHEN. 8 September 1942. Text lacks. Mentioned in letter of 3 December 1942.

b. FRENCH ATTORNEY WRITES SECOND LETTER TO TURKISH CONSULATE-GENERAL ABOUT SITUATION OF MAYER KOHEN. ASKS TURKISH CONSULATE TO INTERVENE WITH FRENCH AUTHORITIES TO PREVENT HIS ARREST AFTER COMPLETION OF JAIL SENTENCE ORDERED BY FRENCH COURT FOR ILLEGALLY INCREASING PRICES. Biib(?) to Turkish Consulate (Paris), 3 December 1942. F 586. Archives of Turkish Embassy (Paris) and Turkish Foreign Ministry (Ankara).

38 Avenue Hoche, Paris, VIII
Telephone: Carnot 18-04
Paris, 3 December 1942

To the Consul of Turkey
170 Bd Haussmann in Paris
Mr. Consul,

I have already written you by letter dated 8 September last regarding the situation of Mr. Mayer Kohen, Turkish citizen, who lives at Paris, 104 Quai de Jemmapes. Mr. Kohen, who was indicted for illegal price raising with several other people, appeared on 23 October last before the 11th *Chambre du*

Tribunal, which sentenced him to six months in prison. Mr. Mayer Kohen appealed this decision, and soon will appear again before the court. In the meantime, the sentenced pronounced against him by the 11th *Chambre du Tribunal* is to expire at the start of the month of January 1943. He would be freed on that date if the German authorities had not asked that at the expiration of that sentence, Mr. Mayer Kohen and his co-conspirators be placed at their disposal because they are Jews. While it is true that two of the co-conspirators of Mr. Mayer Kohen are in violation of the law regarding Jews, it is not the same for Mr. Mayer Kohen who, being a Turkish subject, is not required to bear the Jewish star and is protected by his nationality.

I am, then, informing you very exactly regarding this situation so that you can henceforth intervene with the German authorities who, because of probable ignorance of his Turkish nationality, have asked that Mr. Mayer Kohen be put at their disposal after the completion of his sentence. It is necessary to act immediately so that all the necessary instructions be given by the competent German authorities to avoid Mr. Mayer's transfer to an internment center after he is freed. I am at your disposal to provide all necessary additional information, and thank you in advance for doing what is necessary in the interest of your citizen.

I ask you to accept, Mr. Consul, the homage of my sentiments of high consideration.

(**signed**) Biib.... Avocat a la Cour.

c. TURKISH CONSULATE ASKS GERMAN EMBASSY TO STOP GERMAN AUTHORITIES FROM ARRESTING MAYER KOHEN AFTER HIS RELEASE FROM FRENCH JAIL SINCE HE IS TURKISH CITIZEN. Turkish Consulate-General (Paris) to German Embassy (Paris), F 719, 7 January 1943. Archives of Turkish Embassy (Paris) and Turkish Foreign Ministry (Ankara).

Republic of Turkey
Paris Consulate-General
7 January 1943 no. F 719

To the German Embassy, Paris

The Consulate-General of Turkey at Paris presents its compliments to the Embassy of Germany and has the honor of bringing to its attention the following facts:

Turkish citizen Mr. Mayer Kohen, who holds Certificate of Nationality no. 1489 TP, renewed under no. 519 dated 20 October 1943 and valid until 29 October 1943, was arrested and condemned on 23 October last by the 11th *Chambre du Tribunal* to six months in prison for illegal price increases. The sentence pronounced against this Turkish citizen will expire on 1 January, but a communication from his Attorney informs us that the occupying authorities have asked the competent French officials to place him at their disposal when he leaves prison.

In view of the Turkish nationality of M. Mayer Kohen, this Consulate-General asks the Estimable Embassy of Germany to have the goodness to intervene with the competent authorities so that he, having served his sentence, is definitively freed and not sent to an internment camp.

The Consulate-General of Turkey asks the Embassy of Germany to find herewith attached a copy of the letter of the Attorney of Mr. Mayer Kohen, and takes advantage of this occasion to reiterate to it the assurances of its high consideration.

(**signed**) Fikret Şefik Özdoğancı, Consul-General

d. TURKISH CONSUL-GENERAL (PARIS) ASKS COMMANDER OF DRANCY INTERNMENT CAMP TO RELEASE MAYER KOHEN SINCE HE IS TURKISH CITIZEN. Turkish Consul-General (Paris) to Commander Internment Camp at Drancy (Seine), F 798, 12 January 1943. Archives of the Turkish Embassy (Paris) and Turkish Foreign Ministry (Ankara).

Republic of Turkey, Paris Consulate-General
Paris, 12 January 1943, no. F 798

To the Commander of the Drancy Internment Camp (Seine)
Mr. Commander,

I have the honor of bringing to your attention that Mr. Mayer Kohen, who appears to have been interned in the Camp at Drancy placed under your High Direction, is a Turkish citizen, holding Certificate of Nationality no. 1489 TP, renewed under no. 519 on 20 October 1942 and valid until 20 October 1943. I have already undertaken the applications with competent authorities to secure the liberation of my citizen.

Please accept, Mr. Director, the assurance of my very special consideration.

(**signed**) Fikret Şefik Özdoğancı, Consul-General

e. TURKISH CONSULATE ASKS GERMAN EMBASSY IN PARIS TO ARRANGE RELEASE OF MAYER COHEN FROM DRANCY CAMP SINCE HE IS TURKISH CITIZEN. Turkish Consul (Paris) to German Embassy (Paris), F 815, 15 January 1943. Archives of the Turkish Embassy (Paris) and Turkish Foreign Ministry (Ankara).

Republic of Turkey, Paris Consulate-General
15 January 1943 no. F 815

To the Embassy of Germany
78, Rue de Lille, Paris VIII

The Consulate-General of Turkey at Paris presents its compliments to the Embassy of Germany and has the honor of bringing to its attention the following:

Mr. Mayer Kohen, Turkish citizen, holder of Certificate of Nationality no. 1489 TP, renewed under no. 519 on 20 October 1942 and valid until 20 October 1943, the object of a letter of 7 January no. F 719 from this Consulate, is now at the Camp at Drancy where he is interned.

In view of the nationality of Mr. Mayer Kohen and the expiration of the sentence that he served due to condemnation by the French authorities, the Consulate-General of Turkey asks the Estimable Embassy of Germany to be good enough to intervene with the competent authorities to obtain the definitive freedom of Mr. Meyer.

The Consulate-General thanks in advance the Embassy of Germany for the trouble that it will take in this matter, and takes advantage of this occasion to reiterate to it the assurances of its high consideration.

(**signed**) Fikret Şefik Özdoğancı

f. TURKISH CONSUL-GENERAL IN PARIS WRITES MEYER KOHEN IN DRANCY CAMP FOR HIM TO FILL OUT REQUEST

FOR TURKISH VISA SO HE CAN BE RELEASED FROM THE CAMP AND SENT TO TURKEY. Turkish Consul (Paris) to Mayer Kohen, Registration no. 18254, Staircase no. 21, Chambre 4, Camp de Drancy, no. F 1216, 18 March 1943. Archives of Turkish Embassy (Paris)

> Consulate-General of Turkey
> 170, Boulevard Haussmann, Paris, VIII
> 18 March 1944, no. F 1216
>
> Mr. Mayer Kohen
> Registration no. 18254, Staircase 21, Room 4, Drancy Camp
>
> Sir,
> I can inform you that I have asked the Director of the Internment Camp to be good enough to give you two forms to request visas which you should fill out in the German language and return to us as quickly as possible so that we can do what is necessary to assure your trip to Turkey. Please accept, Sir, my special greetings.
> **(signed)** Consul-General
> Paris, 18 March 1944

g. MRS. KOHEN ASKS TURKISH CONSULATE-GENERAL TO ARRANGE FOR UNSEALING OF HER APARTMENT IN PARIS. Madame Cohen, 104 bis Quai de Jemmapes, Paris X, n.d. Archives of the Turkish Embassy (Paris) and Turkish Foreign Ministry (Ankara).

> To the Consulate-General of Turkey in Paris,
> Mr. Consul-General
> By this letter I have the honor of requesting that you send me a Certificate of Attestation to place on the door of my apartment where I live, 104 Quai de Jemmapes, Paris X. Please accept, Mr. Consul-General, the assurance of my very special consideration
> **(signed)** Madame Cohen, 104 Quai des Jemmapes, Paris, X
>
> P.S. I ask you also, Mr. Consul, to do for me what is necessary to secure removal of the seals that were put on my apartment on 29 November 1943.

Please accept, Sir, my most sincere gratitude.
(**signed**) Madame Cohen

Consular minute: 1489 TP. 20-10-1942 date and 519 S. certificate of nationality

h. MRS. MEYER COHEN INFORMS TURKISH CONSULATE THAT HER HUSBAND, STILL IN DRANCY CAMP, IS ILL AND NOT BEING WELL CARED FOR. Mrs. Cohen to Turkish Consul-General (Paris), 23 March 1943. Archives of Turkish Embassy (Paris) and Turkish Foreign Ministry (Ankara).

Paris, 23 March 1943

Mr. Consul-General,
The state of distress in which I find myself obliges me to ask for your good will so that I can expose the following facts to you:
My husband, Mr. Mayer Kohen, Turkish citizen, born at Edirne (Turkey) in 1903, has been interned for more than eight months and is now in the camp at Drancy. He has been stricken by acute eczema and the conditions in which he lives prevent him from caring for this illness.
The anguish of seeing my husband and the father of my child menaced by an illness forces me to ask for your protection and to ask you to intervene with the competent authorities to secure his liberation. I have no-one else to turn to other than you, and I hope that you will do all that is possible to avoid the ruin of an entire family. I thank you in advance, and ask you to accept, Mr. Consul-General, the expression of my profoundly respectful sentiments.
(**signed**) M. Cohen
Consular minutes: Namık Yolga 1489 T.P. 28/3/1943

i. LETTER TO TURKISH CONSULATE FROM MEYER KOHEN IN DRANCY CAMP. Mr. Mayer Kohen, Registration no. 18254, Drancy (Seine), no. F 1441, 27 March 1943. Archives of Turkish Embassy (Paris) and Turkish Foreign Ministry (Ankara).
Post Card stamped by: Drancy Internment Camp, Censorship department.

Mayer Kohen, Internment Camp at Drancy, Registration no. 18254,

> To Mr. Consul-General of Turkey at Paris
> 170 Boulevard Haussmann, Paris
> Mr. Consul,

I wish to inform you that I am in the infirmary of the Camp, suffering from acute eczema whose scabs have covered my ears, spread to my hands, and become worse every day due to lack of care or medication. I am obliged to do everything myself, which is very difficult for me. Would you please, Mr. Consul-General, do me the favor of having me transferred to a clinic or a hospital so that I can be cared for before my departure for Turkey. I ask you to do all that is possible . . . .

> **(signed)** Mayer Kohen

j. TURKISH CONSULATE ASKS GERMAN EMBASSY TO ARRANGE TO TRANSFER MAYER KOHEN TO ROTHSCHILD HOSPITAL IN PARIS SO THAT HE CAN BE TREATED PROPERLY. Turkish Consul (Paris) to German Embassy (Paris), no. F 1441, 16 April 1943. Archives of the Turkish Embassy (Paris) and Turkish Foreign Ministry (Ankara).

> Republic of Turkey, Paris Consulate-General
> 16 April 1943 no. F 1441

> To the German Embassy
> 78, Rue de Lille, Paris VII

The Consulate-General of Turkey in Paris presents its compliments to the Embassy of Germany and has the honor of bringing to its attention the following:

By a letter no., F 815 of 15 January 1943, this Consulate-General informed the Embassy of Germany of the internment in the Camp at Drancy of Mr. Mayer Kohen, Turkish citizen, and asked for his liberation. This Turkish citizen has informed us that he presently suffers from a very acute eczema and that he lacks care at the Drancy Camp. Mr. Mayer Kohen wishes to be transferred to the Rothschild Hospital where he can be given proper care. This person being of Turkish nationality, this

Consulate-General asks the Estimable Embassy of Germany to have the goodness to intervene with the competent authorities so that Mr. Mayer Kohen can be transferred to the Rothschild Hospital.

This Consulate-General of Turkey thanks in advance the Embassy of Germany for the trouble it will take in this regard, and takes advantage of this occasion to reiterate to it the assurances of its high consideration.

(**signed**) Fikret Şefik Özdoğancı, Consul-General

k. TURKISH CONSULATE ASKS GERMAN EMBASSY IN PARIS IF MEYER COHEN HAS BEEN TRANSFERRED TO DRANCY HOSPITAL. Turkish Consul-General (Paris) to German Embassy (Paris), no. F 1649, 4 May 1943. Archives of the Turkish Embassy (Paris) and Turkish Foreign Ministry (Ankara).

Republic of Turkey, Paris Consulate-General
4 May 1943 no. F 1649
To the Embassy of Germany
76, Rue de Lille, Paris VIII

The Consulate-General of Turkey in Paris presents its compliments to the Embassy of Germany and has the honor of asking it for the favor of letting it know whether something has been done regarding our note no. F 1441 of 16 April 1943 concerning Mr. Mayer Kohen, Turkish citizen, presently interned in the Camp at Drancy and now located in its infirmary.

This Consulate-General thanks in advance the Embassy of Germany for the trouble it will take in this respect and takes advantage of this occasion to reiterate to it the assurances of its high consideration.

(**signed**) Fikret Şefik Özdoğancı, Consul-General

l. GERMAN EMBASSY (PARIS) INFORMS TURKISH CONSULATE-GENERAL (PARIS) THAT MEYER COHEN WILL BE RELEASED IF HE IS IMMEDIATELY SENT TO TURKEY. RELEASED ON 13 JANUARY 1944, REPATRIATED ON 9 FEBRUARY 1944. German Embassy, Paris, to Turkish Consulate-General, Paris, no. 2173/43, 20 May 1943. Archives of the Turkish Embassy (Paris) and the Turkish Foreign Ministry (Ankara).

German Embassy, Paris
Paris, 20 May 1943
2173/43

To the Turkish Consulate-General,

The German Embassy is responding to notes of 16 April 1943 no. 441 and 4 May 1943 no. 1649 concerning the Turkish Citizen Cohen Mayer who, according to information from the responsible German officials and the French police, was convicted of unallowable price increases, Black Market trade and other violations, and for that reason was sent to the Camp at Drancy. His release can be arranged by the German officials only if the Turkish Consulate-General can give assurances in a positive fashion that Cohen Mayer will be immediately repatriated to Turkey.

German Embassy, Paris
2173/43

Consular minutes: received 22 May 1943 Namık Yolga. Freed on 13 January, to be repatriated on 9 February. He has left.

m. TURKISH CONSULATE INFORMS PARIS POLICE THAT MEYER COHEN IS AT ROTHSCHILD HOSPITAL IN PARIS AFTER RELEASE FROM DRANCY CAMP. ASKS THAT POLICE NOT BOTHER HIM SINCE HE IS ABOUT TO BE SENT BACK TO TURKEY. Turkish Consulate-General (Paris) to Préfecturate of Police (Paris), no. F 3207, 14 January 1944. Archives of the Turkish Embassy (Paris) and Turkish Foreign Ministry (Ankara).

Republic of Turkey, Paris Consulate-General
Paris, 14 January 1944 no. F 3207

To the Préfecture of Police, Paris

The Consulate-General of Turkey at Paris presents its compliments to the Préfecturate of Police and has the honor of bringing to its attention, in response to the letter of 31 December 1942 no. 141320 of the Service of Deportation, bearing the mention 'Order for expulsion', that Mr. Mayer Kohen is a Turkish Citizen bearing Certificate of Nationality no. 1489 TP.

Mr. Mayer Kohen is temporarily at the Rothschild Orphanage, having been freed from the Internment Camp at Drancy, and he is to be repatriated to Turkey by a convoy which will leave very short.

As a result, this Consulate-General asks the Préfecture of Police to order its services not to disturb Mr. Mayer Kohen during the time he remains at Paris before his departure.

This Consulate-General thanks in advance the Préfecture of Police for the trouble that it will take in this respect, and takes advantage of this occasion to reiterate to it the assurances of its high consideration.

(**signed**) Fikret Şefik Özdoğancı, Consul-General,
Paris, 14 January 1944

n. MEYER COHEN ASKS TURKISH CONSULATE FOR AUTHORIZATION TO SELL HIS PERSONAL BELONGINGS BEFORE RETURNING TO TURKEY. Meyer Cohen, 104 Quai Jummapes, Paris X to Turkish Consulate-General, n.d. (received 24 January 1944).

Cohen-Mayer
104 Quai Jemmapes, Paris X
25 January 1944
To Mr. Consul-General of Turkey at Paris

Mr. Consul-General,
Being on the list of those who will leave on the next convoy, I have the honor to request your authorization so as to be able to sell my furniture. In thanking you, please accept my respectful greetings.

(**signed**) M. Cohen
Consular minute: answer, 24 January 1944. 1489 TP.

o. TURKISH CONSULATE INFORMS MAYER COHEN THAT SINCE HE IS A TURKISH CITIZEN PROTECTED BY THE TURKISH CONSULATE-GENERAL HE IS FREE TO DISPOSE OF HIS PROPERTY AS HE WISHES SO LONG AS HE RETURNS TO TURKEY QUICKLY. Turkish Consulate-General to Monsieur Mayer

Kohen, no. F 3260, 25 January 1944. Archives of the Turkish Embassy
(Paris) and Turkish Foreign Ministry (Ankara).

> Republic of Turkey, Paris Consulate-General
> Paris, 25 January 1944 no. F 3260
> Monsieur Mayer Kohen
> 104, Quai de Jemmapes, Paris X
> Sir,
> In response to your letter of the 25th of this month, I can
> inform you that as a Turkish citizen 'in order', protected by the
> Consulate-General, you are free to dispose of your belongings as
> you wish, and to sell or deposit them wherever you want, since you
> will be returning to Turkey very shortly.
> Please, Sir, accept my special greetings.
> (**signed**) Fikret Şefik Özdoğancı,

p. MAYER KOHEN TO LEAVE PARIS FOR TURKEY IN TRAIN
CARAVAN LEAVING ON 9 FEBRUARY 1944. Turkish Consulate-
General (Paris) to Mayer Kohen, 8 February 1944. Archives of the Turkish
Embassy (Paris) and Turkish Foreign Ministry (Ankara).

> Republic of Turkey, Paris Consulate-General
> 8 February 1944
>
> Mr. Mayer Kohen
> 104 Quai de Jemmapes, Paris X
> Sir,
> The Consulate-General informs you that the departure of
> the convoy that you will join has been fixed for 9 February, that is
> tomorrow. We have learned that you have not yet presented
> yourself to Mitropa, 3 Place de l'Opera, to secure your tickets. We
> ask you, therefore, to go there in all urgency, and we expect to see
> you at the Gare de l'Est tomorrow Wednesday, at 7 PM.
> Please accept, Sir, my greetings
> (**signed**), 8 February 1944

As a result of the strenuous efforts of the Turkish Consulate-General
in Paris, 414 Jewish Turks, 11 Muslims and 2 Christians were returned to
Turkey by means of a regular bimonthly rotation of train caravans sent

between 2 February and 25 May 1944, in addition to approximately one thousand Jewish Turks sent by small boats from the coast of the French Riviera.[293] Additional train caravans carrying approximately twenty Jewish refugees on each trip went from Brussels.

Most seem to have left the *Gare du Nord* or the *Gare de l'Est* in Paris in the early evening, or from Brussels in the early afternoon, and passing through Austria and Hungary, went on to Istanbul via the original route of the Orient Express, that is via Budapest, Bucharest and Sofia. Passage usually was reserved in private compartments for each family on special *Wagon-Lit* sleeping cars, separate from the regular passenger cars, with the fares paid for by the refugees themselves or by their families in Turkey. Each train usually was accompanied by at least one member of the staffs of the Turkish consulates at Paris or Brussels. At every major stop it was met by local Turkish officials who acted to facilitate their onward journeys and to provide provisions and other necessities for the trip. At times, although visas invariably were obtained from Nazi officials in Paris or Brussels before each train departed, difficulties were raised as they passed through the Nazi Allied countries in Eastern Europe, particularly by Croatia, Serbia and Bulgaria, with the local Turkish consuls securing permission from the countries concerned only after applying considerable pressure, sometimes through the leading Nazis in Berlin.[294] As a result, when the trains reached the borders of such countries, they had to wait for hours while local visas were obtained and the customs officials examined the refugees and their baggages, often stealing almost everything before allowing the trains to go on to their next destination. At times the special cars carrying the refugees had to be detached so that the trains could go on without them, leaving them to wait several days before they could be re-attached to the next train bound

---

293. Reported by Fikret Şefik Özdoğancı, Turkish Consul-General in Paris, to Turkish Ambassador to Paris (Vichy), no. 827/43, 31 May 1944. Archives of Turkish Embassy (Paris) and Turkish Foreign Ministry (Ankara). Turkish Consul-General (Paris) to Turkish Consul-General (Marseilles) no. 77/29, Paris, 26 January 1944. Archives of Turkish Embassy (Paris) and Turkish Ministry of Foreign Affairs (Ankara).

294. Turkish Consulate-General (Paris) to Turkish Consulate-General (Vienna), no. 744/219, 24 May 1944. Archives of Turkish Embassy (Paris) and Turkish Foreign Ministry (Ankara), no. 17/93/179. See Hans–Joachim Hoppe, 'Bulgarian Nationalities Policy in Occupied Thrace and Aegean Macedonia', *Nationalities Papers*, XIV/1–2 (1986), pp. 89–100; Nissan Oren, 'The Bulgarian Exception: A Reassessment of the Salvation of the Jewish Community', *Yad Vashem Studies* VII (1968), pp. 83–106; and Hans–Joachim Hoppe, 'Germany, Bulgaria, Greece: their Relations and Bulgarian Policy in Occupied Greece', *Journal of the Hellenic Diaspora* XI/3 (1984), pp. 41–54.

for Istanbul. The trains were admitted without difficulty into Turkey, though the refugees usually were held in camps near the border for some time while their papers were checked. One or two caravans seem to have proceeded normally, taking two to three days for the journey, but the remainder seem to have taken a much longer time due to delays in securing visas and clearing customs at the various frontiers past which the trains had to go.

The caravans were sent during the final breakup of the Nazi Empire, however, with unsettled local conditions sometimes requiring last-minute shifts in schedules and routes. Those sent in April and May 1944, therefore, apparently went by alternate routes eastward around Hungary through Poland and Rumania, or southward through the postwar route of the Orient Express, via Croatia[295] and Yugoslavia on their way through Bulgaria to Istanbul.

Under such conditions of uncertainty, the Turkish Consul in Paris was so concerned about the situation that he refused to send the eighth caravan until news came of the safe arrival of the previous one in Istanbul:

> Republic of Turkey. Paris Consulate-General, 470/16
>
> Paris, 11.4.1944
>
> Summary: Whether or not the most recent Turkish citizen caravan has reached its destination safely
>
> To the Paris Embassy (Vichy) authorities
>
> The concerned German authorities have informed us that the most recent of the Jewish Turks' caravans which are returning to Turkey under conditions known by higher authorities, which left Paris on 28 March, was compelled to change its route because of current conditions in Hungary and follow a more northern route, passing through a city on the southern border of the 'General Government' of Poland, and going via Rumania and Bulgaria to Istanbul.
>
> While the Consulate-General suggested that the caravan pass through Croatia because of the possibility that a secure route could not be found in the northern part of Rumania due to war

---

295. Although the Croats persecuted Jews as well as Serbs severely during World War II, they were convinced by the Nazis to allow the caravans of Jewish Turks to pass through. Lazo M. Kostich, *The Holocaust in the Independent State of Croatia: An Account Based on German, Italian and the Other Sources* (Chicago, Liberty, 1981). Yeshayahu Jelinke, 'The liquidation of Serbs, Jews and Gypsies in the independent Croatian state,' '(in Hebrew), *Yalkut Moreshet* (Israel) , XXVI (1978), 61–70.

conditions, the Germans replied that this road also was not safe, and it stated that there was no doubt that the German authorities would arrange during the trip for the caravan to go via the most secure route. Under these conditions, I do not want to send out this month's caravan, already arranged, including Turkish citizens living in both the north and south zones, which most likely would be the last one, until I myself learn that the 29 March caravan has reached Turkey safely. I ask for permission to inquire by telegram of the governor of Istanbul whether or not the 29 March caravan led by Adil Aksioti has arrived safely in Turkey.

(signed) Fikret Şefik Özdoğancı, Consul-General.[296]

The refugees arrived in Istanbul at the Sirkeci Terminus of the Orient Express, located immediately below the Topkapı palace which for centuries had housed the mighty sultans of the Ottoman line. From there they returned to their homes throughout the city, or for those who had spent all their lives in France and had no homes in Turkey, housing and where necessary food and clothing, were provided by Istanbul's Jewish community through an organization of the Chief Rabbinate directed by Hayim Eliezer Kohen and Simon Brod, the latter a Jewish merchant from Istanbul, and bya the Jewish Agency office directed by Chaim Barlas.

Most of the latter were given lodgings at small hotels in the immediate vicinity of the Sirkeci railroad station, with care provided by the Sirkeci synagogue, immediately across from the railroad tracks, which had been constructed originally in the late nineteenth century to house the thousands of Jewish refugees flooding into Istanbul from the pogroms which began in Czarist Russia in 1881.

Almost all the refugees quickly found occupations and lived quite comfortably in Turkey throughout the war. Those who were of military age were conscripted into the Turkish army, in which they served with distinction beside their Muslim and Jewish brothers, though many experienced difficulties from the fact that since they had spent all or most of their lives in France or elsewhere in western Europe, they communicated in Turkish with

---

296. Turkish Consul-General (Paris) Fikret Şefik Özdoğancı to Turkish Embassy to Paris (Vichy) and Turkish Foreign Ministry, Paris, no. 470/16, 11 April 1944. Archives of Turkish Embassy (Paris) and Turkish Foreign Ministry (Ankara).

considerable difficulty. Problems such as these led many of them to return to France immediately following the conclusion of peace in 1945.[297]

On 11 May 1944 the German Embassy in Paris informed the Turkish Consulate-General that the 31 January 1944 deadline for repatriation of Jewish Turks had long since expired, that therefore, the eighth caravan of 1944, sent from Paris on 25 May 1944 would be the last, that all Jewish Turks remaining at the Drancy camp would be free to go, but that all Jewish Turks remaining in France afterwards would be subjected to the same treatment meted out to all other Jews by the Germans:

> Replying to the statement made by Mr. Fikret Şefik Özdoğancı, Consul-General of Turkey, to Doctor Klingenfuss, Counselor of the Legation, the Embassy of Germany has the honor of informing the Consulate-General of Turkey as follows:
>
> By its note of 15 November 1943, Number 2534/XI/43–1 the Embassy of Germany made known the conditions by which Jews who are Turkish citizens would be allowed to undertake their return trip to Turkey until 31 January 1944, although the limit originally set was fixed at 10 October (1943).
>
> Because of the objections presented by the Consulate-General of Turkey, it agreed to the request of the Consulate-General to prolong the deadline for repatriation by several weeks.
>
> The Embassy of Germany has noted that the Consulate-General of Turkey has taken measures so that one more convoy will leave on 16 May 1944 and a last one a few days later. After discussions with the Commander of the Security Police (*Befehlshaber de la Sichersheits-polizei*) and with the SD at the office of the Military Commander in France and in agreement with him, the Embassy of Germany can inform the Consulate-General that, in consideration of the alleged technical difficulties, the departure of these two convoys is authorized. The Jews still interned at Drancy will be freed for their repatriation under condition that they are added to one of these two caravans.
>
> The Embassy of Germany attracts the attention of the Consulate-General to the fact that once these two convoys have left—at the latest on 25 May 1944, Jewish citizens of Turkey will be subjected to all measures concerning Jews that are in force here,

---

297. Testimony to Stanford J. Shaw on 16 December 1991 by Hayim Eliezer Kohen, Director of Protocol at the Chief Rabbinate in Istanbul,

and that subsequent requests for liberation can no longer be taken into consideration in France.
    Paris, 11 May 1944.[298]

Özdoğancı then again wrote his Ambassador at Vichy that while caravans of Jewish Turks going to Turkey had been sent since early February, they had been suspended for a time because of worries over what had happened to the most recent caravan because of difficulties in Hungary and Rumania. In view of the German ultimatum, however, his fear that Jewish Turks remaining in France would be arrested, and the news that the last caravan had, indeed, arrived in Istanbul, the caravans would resume (Document 8):

Republic of Turkey, Paris Consulate-General
no. 644/33, Paris, 17 May 1944

Summary: regarding the return to Turkey of Jewish citizens of Turkey,

To the Paris Embassy, Vichy, Urgent
    As Your Excellency knows, those of our Jewish fellow citizens who have indicated their wish to return to Turkey have since the month of February been sent in caravans from Paris to Istanbul. However, since no news has been received for some time from the caravan which set out under difficult conditions on 29 March, the sending of a new caravan was postponed. In addition, since we had not received a satisfactory answer from German authorities to our numerous requests regarding the evacuation of our Jewish fellow citizens who are imprisoned in the camps, the organization of new caravans was prevented.
    However a few days ago, I learned that the 29 March caravan had reached Istanbul safely. I therefore called on Counselor Mr. Klingenfuss, who is the Jewish expert at the German Embassy and renewed our request to evacuate about thirty of our fellow citizens from the camps.
    Klingenfuss in response stated that the German military authorities and police already were complaining that the matter of

---

298. Archives of the Turkish Embassy (Paris), file 6127.

the evacuation to Turkey of Jewish Turks had not yet been completed and that he did not know whether or not the responsible German officials would permit the organization of another caravan. But the next day by telephone he informed me that permission would be granted for the dispatch of two more caravans, of which the latest would have to leave by the 25th of the month.

At the same time I received from the German embassy a note from the German officials confirming this decision. In the note, which is attached with its French translation, it is stated that, according to his standpoint, in summary, after 25 May 1944 Jewish Turks remaining in France will be subject to the same anti-Jewish measures as all other Jews, and that no further evacuations would be permitted for those remaining within France. Mr. Klingenfuss in our conversation added that after 25 May arrests of Jewish Turks would begin.

I have informed our citizens in contact with the Consulate-General of the contents of this new communication. The number of Jewish and other citizens who have for some time applied to return to Turkey have reached the number which will require the sending of two train cars, and two cars have been prepared to send them to Turkey on 23 and 25 May.

Please accept my deepest respects.

(signed) Fikret Şefik Özdoğancı, Consul-General.[299]

---

299. Turkish Consul-General (Paris) to Turkish Embassy in Paris (Vichy), no. 644/33, 17 May 1944 and to Turkish Embassy in Berlin. Archives of Turkish Embassy (Paris) and Turkish Foreign Ministry (Ankara), file 6127.

PARIS BAŞKONSOLOSLUĞU
644/33
Ek 2
acele

Paris 17.5.1944
Hulâsa:Musevi vatandaşların
memlekete avdetleri hakkında

Paris Büyük Elçiliğine
Vichy

Malûmu Devletleri oldugu üzere musevi vatandaşlardan memlekete avdet arzusunu izhar edenler Şubat ayından beri birer vagonluk kafile halinde Paris'den İstanbul'a sevkedilmekde idi.Ancak 29 Mart tarihinde müşkil şartlar içinde yola çıkan kafileden uzun zaman haber alınamadığından yeni bir kafile teşkili tehir edilmişdi. Diğer tarafdan kamplarda mevkuf musevi vatandaşların tahliyeleri hakkındaki mütevali taleblerimize alman makamlarınca müsaid bir cevap verilmemiş olması da yeni kafilenin teşkiline mani oluyordu. Bundan bir kaç gün evvel 29 Mart kafilesinin salimen İstanbul'a muvasalatı öğrenildiğinden alman sefaretinde yahudi işlerile uğraşan müsteşar Mösyö Klingenfus 'u ziyaret ederek toplama kamplarında bulunan 30 kadar vatandaşımızın tahliyesini istemişdim.

Bay Klingenfus cevaben türk musevilerinin memlekete iadeleri işinin hala bitirilmemiş olmasından alman askeri makamları ile polisinin şikâyette bulunduklarından bahisle yeni kafile teşkiline alakadâr alman makamlarınca müsaade edilip edilmeyeceğini bilmediğini söyledi ve ancak ertesi gün telefonla en sonuncusu ayın 25 inde hareket etmek üzere iki kafilenin sevkine müsaade olunacağını bildirdi. Ayni zamanda alman sefareti yukarda arzettiğim muhaveremiz üzerine alman makamlarınca alınan kararı bir nota ile teyid etti.

Bir örneği ile fransızca tercemesi ilişik maruz notada türk yehudileri meselesinin son aylarda geçirdiği safhaları,kendi noktai nazarlarına göre,hulâsa edildikden sonra bilhassa 25 Mayıs 1944 tarihinden sonra türk vatandaşı musevilerin yahudi aleyhdarı tedbirlere tâbi tutulacakları ve Fransa dahilinde tahliye taleblerinin nazarı itibare alınmayacağı bildirilmektedir.

Bay Klingenfus görüşmemizde 25 Mayısdan itibaren türk musevilerinin tevkifine başlanacağını da söylemiştir.

Alman sefaretinin bu yeni tebligini vatandaşlara Başkonsolosluğu asdırdığım bir yazı ile bildirdim. Bir müddetten beri memlekete dönmek için müracaatta bulunan yahudi ve diğer vatandaşların yekûnu iki vagla sevkedilmesi icâbedecek bir yeküna varmıştır. Bunları memlekete göndermek üzere 23 ve 25 Mayıs'da hareket edecek iki vagon hazırlatmıştır.

Document 8. Turkish Consulate-General (Paris) to send two final caravans of Jewish Turks to Turkey, after which those remaining will be subject to anti-Jewish laws in France.

The Turkish Consulate decided to send two final caravans, one on 23 May and one two days later, but subsequently decided that all those wishing to go before the deadline could be handled on the earlier train, the eighth sent in 1944, so the later one, the ninth, was canceled due to lack of applicants at the time.[300] Some Jewish Turks, however, remained at Drancy

300. German Embassy (Paris) to Turkish Consulate-General (Paris), no B 24 27/44, 11 May 1944, enclosed in Turkish Consul-General (Paris) to Turkish Embassy to Paris (Vichy) no. 644/33, 17 May 1944. Turkish Ambassador to Paris (Vichy) to Turkish Consul-General (Marseilles) no. 378/175, 27 May 1944. Turkish Consul-General (Marseilles) Fuad Carım to

even after the departure of the last caravan. At the end of May, the Turkish Consulate-General in Paris reported that there were thirty-one Jewish Turks left in the camp, but that the Germans said they were not there and had no information as to where they were.[301] The Turkish consuls in Paris continued to try to find the remaining Jewish Turks and to secure permission for subsequent caravans, but without success as far as can be ascertained.[302]

Following Turkey's entry into the war on the side of the Allies and the consequent break of relations with Germany and Vichy France, negotiations were carried on by the Swiss Consul-General in Paris Monsieur Naville, but as far as is known, no other caravans were sent, and few of the 304 Jewish Turks remaining at Drancy and elsewhere in occupied France survived thereafter, excluding the Karaites, who were successful in getting the Germans to agree with their argument that they were not Jews either racially or spiritually, and that the anti-Jewish laws should not be applied to them:

Turkish Embassy to Paris (Vichy) no. 231/44, 30 May 1944. Archives of the Turkish Embassy (Paris), no. 135/55; and of the Turkish Foreign Ministry (Ankara).

301. Consul-General (Paris) to Turkish Foreign Ministry (Ankara) no. 746/182, Paris, 19 June 1944. Archives of Turkish Embassy (Paris) and Turkish Foreign Ministry (Ankara) states that there were 31 Turkish citizens left in Paris, but a German Foreign Ministry note dated Berlin 6 June 1944 states that the Turkish Embassy in Vichy asked that one hundred Jewish Turks remaining in France be returned to Turkey (*Durchdruck als Konzept (R'Schrift 1B.) Ko. Auswärtiges Amt Inl. II L080 g*, Berlin 6 June 1944, and this is repeated in a letter from *Der Chef der Sicherheitspolizei und des SD*, IV A 4 b (I) a 2314/43 g(82), Berlin, Prinz Albrecht Strasse 8, 14 Juni 1944, to *Auswärtige Amt, z.Hd.v.Herrn Legationsrat von Thadden*, both supplied to me through the courtesy of Mr. Serge Klarsfeld of Paris. Whatever the number, the Germans continued to insist that none were left. However examination of the lists of prisoners provided by von Thadden shows that many of those transported to the East at that time and listed as of Italian, Spanish and Portuguese citizenship in the transportation lists had been born in the Ottoman Empire before the establishment of the Turkish Republic, and presumably had assumed the citizenship of the countries concerned in the meantime, leading to their extermination during the last years of the war.

302. Turkish Consul-General (Paris) Fikret Şefik Özdoğancı to Turkish Embassy to Paris (Vichy) no. 644/33, 17 May 1944; Turkish Embassy to Paris (Vichy) to French Ministry of Foreign Affairs (Vichy), no. 477/92, 17 July 1944. Turkish Consul-General (Paris) to Monsieur Naville, Swiss Consulate (Paris), 6 September 1944. Turkish Consulate-General (Paris) to Turkish Embassy (Berlin), no. 1086/22, 14 June 1944. Archives of the Turkish Embassy (Paris) and Turkish Foreign Ministry (Ankara).

Republic of Turkey, Paris Consulate-General
Paris, 31 May 1944 no. 874/41

Summary: regarding Jewish Turks who have remained in the occupied zone.

To the Paris Embassy (Vichy)
Response to note no. 391-182 of 29 May 1944

I communicated in my letter dated 12 April 1944 that in a list given to the German embassy I reported that 628 Jewish Turks remained in the district of our Consulate-General at the start of this year. Since recently one of those on the list, a woman, declared that she and her children were in fact Christian and that she would defend herself in a case being handled by the French and German authorities, responsibility lies with her. The list was reduced accordingly, and the matter was communicated to the German Embassy. In addition, thirteen Turkish citizens have stated that religiously they are Karaites, that racially they have no connection with Jews, and that in matters of religion there are very substantial differences between them and the Jews. The Karaites have informed us that the German institute which cares for matters of race has accepted this viewpoint, and has stated that the anti-Jewish laws will not be applied to them, so they have also asked us to remove their names also from the list which our Consulate-General gave to the German Embassy. Out of these thirteen who have produced documents from the French authorities recognizing them as members of the Paris Karaite community, eight have Turkish birth certificates which certify their religion as Karaite, and we have written the German Embassy asking that their names be removed from the list.

Regarding the remaining five, we have written the Population Census Department in Ankara, and we will act in accordance with their answer. In any case, by removing two Christians and eight Karaites, the total of 628 Jewish Turks was reduced to 618.

In the eight caravans sent to Turkey between the start of February and 23 May, 314 Jews from our service district returned to Turkey. Under these circumstances, it means that 304 Jewish Turks have remained. Out of this total, five are the remaining

Karaites, who are not subject to the anti-Jewish laws. Out the 304, moreover, 14 persons in three families who remained because of illnesses and other reasons are ready to form a new caravan.

Though our Chancery has informed the remaining 290 individuals in numerous communications of the declarations of the German authorities in their regard, they have not yet asked to leave. For this reason I assume that they have decided to remain in France for one reason or another and to save themselves by hiding if necessary. It is probable that a good number of the 290 have recently gone to the free zone. In addition it is likely that about 30 of those Turkish citizens who remained have been deported outside France.

Please accept my most sincere respects,

(**signed**) Fikret Şefik Özdoğancı, Consul-General

Consular minute: Foreign Affairs Ministry informed. Filed.[303]

Consul-General Fikret Şefik Özdoğancı informed his Ambassador to Paris (Vichy) regarding the train caravans sent during the first half of 1944:

Republic of Turkey Paris Consulate-General

Paris, 31 May 1944, no. 827/43

Regarding the return to Turkey of imprisoned Jewish Turks

To the Paris Embassy (Vichy) in response to order no. 163/360 dated 24 May 1944:

Recently the German authorities informed us that the dispatch of Jewish Turks back to Turkey would have to end on 25 May. It was decided, therefore, to send a second caravan on 25 May in addition to the one already arranged for 23 May. But

---

303. Turkish Consul-General (Paris) Fikret Şefik Özdoğancı to Turkish Embassy to Paris (Vichy) no. 874/31, 31 May 1944, reporting that there were 628 Jewish Turks registered at the Consulate as of April 1944. Of these, ten had stated that since they were Karaites, and therefore had no blood connection with Jews, and this claim had been accepted by the Germans. This left 618 Jews, of whom 314 had been sent in the caravans back to Turkey, leaving 304 in occupied France. Özdoganci also reported to the Turkish Foreign Ministry (no. 746/182, Paris, 19 June 1944. Archives of the Turkish Embassy (Paris) and Turkish Foreign Ministry (Ankara) that the German authorities could give no information on the fate of the Farhi family and thirty-one other Jewish Turks who were in the concentration camp at Drancy in June 1944, shortly after the last Turkish train caravan left for Istanbul. Presumably the latter were murdered by the Germans.

many of our Jewish fellow citizens in the southern zone who had requested permission to return to Turkey at the last minute for various reasons did not come, while most of those still imprisoned at Drancy were not released. Since therefore there was no-one left in the district of our Consulate-General wishing to return to Turkey, we were able to send only a single caravan of 47 people on 23 May, while the 25 May caravan was not sent.

According to the details in the attached statistical table, in the eight caravans that were sent starting in February of this year, including the 23 May caravan, there were in all 429 Turkish citizens, of whom one hundred came from the free zone and 414 from our zone, including 314 Jews, eleven Muslims, of whom five came from the south district and six from the north, and four Christians, of whom two came from the south and two from the north. While there are 304 Jewish Turks still registered with us, none of these has communicated their desire to return to Turkey. Our Consulate-General has for six months issued numerous communications regarding the intentions of the German authorities, but they still have not indicated a desire to return. Together with three persons who were not able to reach Paris in time for the 23 May caravan, there are for now twenty citizens in Paris ready to go, but since the 25 May caravan was canceled we are working to arrange another caravan.

Regarding the freeing of our citizens who are imprisoned in camps: As a result of efforts with the German Embassy which I communicated in my letter of 17 May 1944, twenty-two Jewish Turks who were imprisoned at the Drancy camp were freed, but in examining their papers it was discovered that only nine of them were regular 'in order' Turkish citizens and the remainder were not 'in order', but the latter also were released though we did not particularly do anything on their behalf. In accordance with instructions received from Ankara, we are continuing efforts with the German Embassy and the German police to secure the immediate release of an additional thirty one Jewish Turks, regarding whom we have sent numerous communications, so that they can be returned to Turkey at once with the last caravan, which is now being arranged. Both the Embassy and the police received this request in a positive manner and promised that they will be released shortly.

Turkey and the Holocaust

However, referring openly to the issue of Jewish citizens of Turkey who have already been deported (to the East), a subject which until now, because of it's sensitivity, was not the object of a clear attempt on our part, we were informed that a large number of these Turkish citizens had been deported despite our official and behind the scenes efforts, and it was suggested that our Berlin Embassy should attempt to learn their whereabouts and attempt to secure their return to France. If these efforts achieve success and the Turkish citizens still imprisoned in the camps are freed, they also will join those already waiting in forming a final group to be returned to Turkey. Please accept my deepest respects,

(**signed**) Fikret Şefik Özdoğancı, Consul-General[304]

		TRAIN CARAVANS OF TURKISH CITIZENS SENT FROM PARIS TO ISTANBUL BETWEEN 8 FEBRUARY AND 23 MAY 1944						
No.	Known Date	From Occupied France			From Unoccupied France			Totals
		Muslims	Christians	Jews	Muslims	Christians	Jews	
1	2/08/44			61				61
2	3/28/44			33			19	33
3	unknown	1		54			3	58
4	unknown	1		41			4	46
5	unknown			45			13	58
6	unknown			47	1		3	51
7	5/16/44	1		28	3		24	56
8	5/23/44	3	2	5	1		34	47
TOTAL		6	2	314	5		100	429

Most of the approximately 896 Jewish Turks remaining in southern France registered at the Marseilles (Grenoble) consulate[305] either went in

---

304. Turkish Consul-General in Paris Fikret Şefik Özdoğancı to Paris Turkish Embassy (Vichy), no. 827/43, 31 May 1944. Archives of the Turkish Embassy (Paris), and of the Turkish Foreign Ministry (Ankara). File number: K.T. 6/6/4, K. no. 155, T. no. 189

305. Consul-General Fuad Carım (Grenoble) to Turkish Embassy to Paris (Vichy) no. 246/49, 31 May 1944, in Archives of the Turkish Embassy (Paris) no. 151/168 and Turkish Foreign Ministry (Ankara), reported that 896 Jewish citizens of Turkey, both adults and children, were registered at his consulate at that time, and of these 374 had been given

1. The Staff of the Turkish Consulate-General in Paris at the celebration of Turkish Republic Holiday in 1943. *Left to right*: Germaine Guicheteau, Local Clerk Refik İleri, Consul-General Fikret Özdoğancı's daughter Mina (later Mina Türkmen); Consul-General Fikret Özdoğancı, his wife Nüzhet Hanım, Vice Consul Namık Kemal Yolga, Tcherna Frisch, Local Clerk Nerman Özdoğancı, niece of the Consul-General, Recep Zerman and Janine Bousquet.

2. The Staff of the Turkish Consulate-General in Paris on the occasion of the celebration of Turkish Republic Holiday (*Cumhuriyet Bayramı*) in 1941. *Left to right:* Chancellor Namık Kemal Yolga, Consul-General Dülger, and local clerks Guicheteau, Frisch, and Zerman.

3. and 4.   Jewish Turks standing in front of the Turkish Consulate-General in Paris in 1943 (*above*) and 1944 (*below*) to get passports and visas to enable them to return to Turkey.

5. (*above*) The Sirkeci Terminal railroad tracks of the Orient Express, where Jewish refugees coming from Europe arrived in Istanbul.

6. (*below*) The Sirkeci Terminal building in Istanbul.

7. (*above*) The Sirkeci Synagogue.
8. (*below*) Istanbul University main gate.

9. (*above*) The Haydarpaşa railroad station, terminus of the Anatolian and Syrian railway system used by Jews going by land to Palestine.

10. (*below*) The Haydarpaşa synagogue.

11. (*right*) Exterior of the Chief
     Rabbinate in Istanbul.

12. (*left*) The Tokatlian Hotel
     (Istanbul).

13. The Pera Palas Hotel (Istanbul), center of Jewish Agency operations to rescue East European Jews during World War II.

14. Bebek on the Bosporus where many Jewish refugees in Turkey lived during World War II.

small boats across the Mediterranean to North Africa, where they were often mistreated by the *colons*, slipped into Italy or Spain, or managed to hold out in France until the arrival of the Allied forces.[306]

Out of the approximately 70,000 Jews of all nationalities who were imprisoned at Drancy throughout the war, only some 3,000 were saved from extermination, and while some were also British, American and Spanish Jews,[307] by far the bulk of those who survived were Jewish Turks, who were saved directly as a result of the efforts of the Turkish government and, in particular, of its diplomats in France.[308]

Many of those who were rescued from the Nazis expressed their gratitude to the Turkish diplomats involved as well as to the Turkish government and people. One of the most striking of these was the message sent by Eleonore Fresco, whose Paris apartment had been unsealed as a result of the efforts of the Paris Consulate-General:[309]

---

passports. Of these, 74 male Jewish Turks had been given passports because of their request to return to Turkey to perform their military service, but only for of these had done so. He estimated that some of these who had received passports had left France without informing the consulate, leading to his conclusion that approximately seven hundred remained.

306. Turkish Consul-General (Paris) to Turkish Embassy to Paris (Vichy), no. 644/33, 17 May 1944, and to Turkish Embassy in Berlin. Turkish Consul-General to Marseilles (Grenoble) Fuad Carım to Turkish Embassy to Paris (Vichy) no. 231/44, 20 May 1944. Archives of the Turkish Embassy (paris) and the Turkish Foreign Ministry (Ankara).

307. Rajsfus, *Drancy*, pp. 17, 226.

308. Serge Klarsfeld, in his monumental *Mémorial de la Déportation des Juifs de France, 1942–1944* (Paris, 1983), published in English translation as *Memorial to the Jews Deported from France, 1942–1944* (New York, 1983), pp. xxxvi–xxxvii, counted 1,282 Jewish Turks as having been deported from Drancy to Auschwitz, out of a total of 67,693. This information repeated with minor changes in Gérard Silvain, *La Question Juive en Europe, 1933–1945* (Paris, 1985), p. 415, and Rajsfus, *Drancy*, p. 365. This number included 949 Jewish Turks whose citizenship was fully in order and 333 who were *gayri mumtaze*, with irregular status. However examination of Klarsfeld's tables, which list the Jews sent to the East with their places of birth and citizenship, demonstrates that this number included only those Jewish Turks who had retained their Turkish citizenship in regular or irregular status. There were also several thousand Jews born in the Ottoman Empire or Turkey who had abandoned their Turkish nationality and taken up French citiizenship and were counted as such.

309. Eleonore Fresco to Turkish Consul-General (Paris), F 2874, 16 August 1943. Archives of Turkish Consulate-General (Paris) and Turkish Foreign Ministry (Ankara).

310. Archives of the Turkish Embassy (Paris), 870 TP.

Mr. Consul,

Having learned from friends in Paris that thanks to your energetic intervention with the occupation authorities, the seals that they had attached on my apartment on 1 Villa Dancourt, 18th district, have been removed and that the keys are now deposited with you for my use, I wish to declare to you by this letter the expression of my most complete gratitude for the energy that you have applied to defend my interests. It pleases me moreover to recognize that during this unhappy war each time that a Turkish citizen properly registered in accordance with the laws of his country had recourse to the Paris Consulate for a just cause, he has always received from you and your colleagues the greatest possible paternal welcome and support, if I can express it in that way. This reflects the humane and liberal spirit which drives the eminent men who direct the Republic of Turkey .... [310]

Turkish intervention was not always successful however. In many cases, as soon as the Nazis learned that the Turkish authorities were about to apply for the release of one of their citizens, the latter were sent off to Germany before anything could be done, leading to recriminations that somehow the Turkish diplomats 'could have done more,' as if the fault was theirs' rather that of the Nazis. Two of the most tragic cases of this sort were those of Isak Kastoryano and Yuda Farhi and their families.

THE ISAK (ISAAC) KASTORYANO FILE

Isak (Izak, Isaac) Kastoryano (Kastoriyano)
Mother: Madame Vve Ventura Kastoryano
Arrested in southern France at Beziers Herault in April 1944 on way to Paris for repatriation caravan and sent to Drancy Concentration Camp; his Paris apartment and store sealed.
Deported to Germany.

a. ISAK KASTORYANO ASKS TURKISH AMBASSADOR (VICHY) TO REGISTER HIS RECENT MARRIAGE TO A FRENCH CITIZEN SO THAT SHE CAN BECOME TURKISH CITIZEN. ASKS HIM TO INTERVENE WITH FRENCH AUTHORITIES TO GET THEM A PASS TO TRAVEL TO MARSEILLES CONSULATE TO

COMPLETE FORMALITIES OF REGISTRATION AND APPLICATION TO RETURN TO TURKEY. Isaac Kastoryano, Saint Jean de Bruel (Aveyron), to Turkish Ambassador (Vichy), 10 March 1943.

> I. Kastoryano, c/o Madame Viata
> St. Jean du Bruel, Aveyron
> Saint Jean de Bruel, 10 March 1943

> To Mr. Ambassador of the Turkish Republic at Vichy
> Mr. Ambassador,
> Living for now at Saint Jean du Bruel (Aveyron) after having resided for ten years at Paris, I lived eighteen months at Bezière, from which I was sent away, and I wish to return to Turkey to bring an end to these peregrinations.
> Having married a women with French nationality, I wish to register my marriage at the Turkish consulate so that my wife will acquire Turkish nationality. The French authorities, however, have refused me a safe conduct pass as a foreigner to go to the consulate at Marseilles to carry out the necessary formalities for myself and my family. But to complete the formalities, my presence at the Consulate in person is necessary.
> Therefore, I would be very obliged to you, Mr. Ambassador, if you would be so good as to intervene with the French authorities so that I can obtain a safe-conduct to enable me to go to the Consulate at Marseilles to complete these formalities.
> In expectation of a favorable response, I ask you to accept, Mr. Ambassador, the assurance of my very high consideration.
> (**signed**) I. Kastoryano

> Turkish citizen registered at the Consulate at Marseilles
> Certificate of Nationality no. 968/463
> valid from 13 January 1943 until 13 January 1944
> **Consular minute:** 125-6127/15-3-1943

b. TURKISH EMBASSY ASKS MARSEILLES CONSULATE TO VALIDATE INFORMATION ABOUT REGISTRATION OF ISAK KASTORYANO. Turkish Embassy (Vichy) to Turkish Consulate-General (Marseilles), no. 352-6127, 17 March 1943. Archives of the Turkish Embassy (Paris) and Turkish Foreign Ministry (Ankara).

Embassy of the Republic of Turkey, Vichy, 17 March 1943, no. 352–6127

To the Marseilles Consulate-General,

I am enclosing the copy of a letter received from a person named Kastoryano Isaac who lives at an address in Saint Jean du Bruel. The aforementioned claims that he is a Turkish citizen, and states that he wishes to return to Turkey, and that he wants a safe-conduct so that he can proceed to your Consulate-General to carry out the necessary formalities. I ask you to ascertain whether or not the aforementioned is one of our citizens, and if this proves to be true to secure for him the necessary safe-conduct.

(**signed**) Paris Ambassador

c. GERMAN OFFICIALS IDENTIFY FOUR PROPERTIES BELONGING TO JEWISH TURKS, INCLUDING ONE BELONGING TO ISAK KASTORYANO, AND ASK TURKISH CONSULATE TO APPOINT TURKISH ADMINISTRATORS FOR THEM. *Der Militaerbefehlshaber in Frankreich*, 24 Avenue Klèber 24, Paris, to Turkish Consulate-General (Paris), no. Wi 1/1, 29 April 1943. Archives of Turkish Embassy (Paris) and Turkish Foreign Ministry (Ankara).

The Military Commander in France,
Paris, 29 April 1943, Avenue Klèber, 24
Telephone: Kle 6800/09
Bal 1850/59 Wi I/1

To the Turkish Consulate-General, Paris

The following properties belong to Jewish Turks:

Nathan Enterprises, 47 Rue Popincourt, Paris. Owed by the Jewess Rachel Nathan, widow of Behar

Kastoryano Enterprises, 83 Rue de Cléry, Paris. Owned by the Jew Isaac Kastoryano

Property at 7 Place Cardinal Marcier in Enghien-les-Bains. Owned by the Jewess Yahiel Rebecca, widow of Nahum.

Property at 16 Rue du Palais de Justice, Melun (S.et M.). Owned by the Jew Gargui Marco.

I ask for the nomination of an administrator for each.

(**signed**) Chief of Military Administration under orders

For the Military Commander

Consular minute B. Yolga 6/5/943 1221 TP.

They ask us to designate administrators for four houses belonging to Jewish Turks. 6-5-43. N.Y. (Namık Kemal Yolga)

d. TURKISH CONSULATE DRAFT OF LETTER NEVER SENT INFORMING GERMAN MILITARY COMMANDER IN FRANCE THAT OF THE FOUR NAMES PRESENTED IN 29 APRIL 1943 LETTER, ONLY ISAK KASTORYANO IS REGISTERED AS A TURKISH CITIZEN. Turkish Consulate-General (Paris) to Military Commander in France, Paris, 13 May 1943. Archives of Turkish Embassy (Paris).

Republic of Turkey, Paris Consulate-General, Paris, 13 May 1943

To the Military Commander in France

24, avenue Kléber, Paris XVI

The Consulate-General of Turkey at Paris presents its compliments to the Military Commander in France and has the honor of bringing to his attention, in response to his letter of 29 April reference Wi I/1, that:

Madame Rachel Nathan, living at 47 Rue Popincourt, Paris XI,
Madame Rebecca Yahielo, living at 7 place du Cardinal Mercier
    at Enghien-les-bains
Mr. Marco Gargui, living at 16, Rue to Palais de Justice at Melun
    (S.et M.):
are not inscribed on the registers of this Consulate-General as Turkish citizens,

And that Mr. Isaac Kastoryano, living at 83 Rue de Cléry in Paris is a Turkish citizen with Certificate of Nationality no. 1221 TP.

This Consulate-General takes this occasion to reiterate to the Military Commander in France the assurances of its high consideration.

(**signed**) Consul-General

Consular minutes: This draft was not sent

Marseilles 30-12-42 2639-968-463 Certificate of Nationality valid from 13/1/43 to 13/1/44.

e. TURKISH CONSULATE (PARIS) ASKS MARSEILLES CONSULATE ABOUT STATUS OF ISAK KASTORYANO. Turkish Consul-General (Paris) to Marseilles Consulate-General, 19 May 1943. Archives of Turkish Embassy (Paris) and Turkish Foreign Ministry (Ankara).

Republic of Turkey, Paris Consulate-General
19 May 1943.

To the Marseilles Consulate-General

I ask you for information as to whether or not Isak Kastoryano, born in Istanbul in 1905 as the son of Rafail and his wife Ventro, to whom passport no. 30 dated 6 March 1942 was given on the basis of a Nationality Certificate (*Vatandaşlık ilmühaberi*) no. 608/3784 dated 12 February 1940, has asked for a Certificate of Nationality or secured a new passport.

(**signed**) The Consul
Consular minutes: 1008-83 1221 T.P.

f. TURKISH CONSULATE (PARIS) INFORMS GERMAN MILITARY COMMANDER IN FRANCE THAT OF THE FOUR NAMES PRESENTED IN 29 APRIL 1943 LETTER, THREE ARE NOT TURKISH CITIZENS, ONLY ISAAC KASTORYANO IS REGISTERED AS A TURKISH CITIZEN.[311] Turkish Consulate-General to the Military Commander in France, 24 avenue Kléber, Paris XVI, 19 May 1943, no. F 1771. Archives of Turkish Embassy (Paris) and Turkish Foreign Ministry (Ankara).

Republic of Turkey, Paris Consulate-General
19 May 1943 no. F 1771

The Military Commander in France
24 Avenue Kléber, Paris

The Consulate-General of Turkey in Paris presents its compliments to the Military Commander in France and has the honor to bring to his attention, in response to his letter of 29 April reference Wi I/1, that

---

311. The others most likely had lost their Turkish citizenship due to failure to register within five years while living in France, by Turkish Law of 1935.

–Madame Rachel Nathan living at 47, Rue Popincourt, Paris, XI

–Madame Rebecca Yahiel, living at 7, place du Cardinal Mercier at Enghien les bains, and

–Monsieur Marco Gargui, living at 16, Rue du Palais de Justice at Melun (S. et M.),

are not inscribed on the rolls of this Consulate-General as Turkish citizens.

This Consulate-General takes this occasion to reiterate to the Military Commander in France the assurances of its high consideration.

Paris, 19 May 1943
(**signed**) Consul-General

g. TURKISH CONSULATE-GENERAL (PARIS) IN SEPARATE LETTER INFORMS GERMAN MILITARY COMMANDER IN FRANCE THAT ISAK KASTORYANO IS A TURKISH CITIZEN AND THAT HE WILL NAME A TURKISH ADMINISTRATOR FOR HIS BUSINESS.   Turkish   Consulate-General   (Paris)   to   Der Militaerbefehlshabers in Frankreich, 24, avenue Kléber, Paris XVI, no. F 1782, 22 May 1943. Archives of Turkish Embassy (Paris) and Turkish Foreign Ministry (Ankara).

Republic of Turkey, Paris Consulate-General
22 May 1943 no. F 1782

To the Military Commander in France
24 Avenue Kléber, Paris XVI

The Consulate-General of Turkey in Paris presents its compliments to the Military Commander in France and has the honor of bringing to his attention that, in response to his letter of 29 April reference Wi I/1, Mr. Isaac Kastoryano, living at 83 Rue de Cléry in Paris is a Turkish citizen registered at the Consulate-General of Turkey at Paris under the number 1221 TP until 1940, and that he now is in the unoccupied zone, where he must be registered at the Consulate of Turkey at Marseilles.

This Consulate-General is about to ask him to designate for us a Turkish administrator, and as soon as his answer arrives, we will inform the estimable Military Commander.

This Consulate-General takes this occasion to reiterate to the Military Commander in France the assurances of its high consideration.

(**signed**) Consul-General, Paris, 22 May 1941

h. GERMAN AUTHORITIES INFORM TURKISH CONSULATE THAT ONLY IT, AND NOT THE TURKISH JEW ISAK KASTORYANO, HAS THE RIGHT TO NAME A TURKISH ADMINISTRATOR FOR HIS BUSINESS. *Der Militaerbefehlshabers in Frankreich*, Paris, to Turkish Consulate-General (Paris) no. Wi I/1-10867/43, 27 May 1943. Archives of the Turkish Embassy (Paris) and Turkish Foreign Ministry (Ankara). Turkish registration no. F 1859.

The Military Commander in France, Economy Division
Wi I/1-10867/43
Paris, 27 May 1943, Avenue Kleber 24
Telephone: Kle 6800/09
        Bal 1850/59

To the Turkish Consulate-General, Paris

You have informed us that Mr. (Recep) Zerman has been appointed as the administrator for the Turkish Jew Isaac Kastoryano, Paris, at 82 Rue de Cléry. I must, however, observe, that only the Consulate-General and not the Jew has the right to chose an administrator. This is a legal precaution so that the property will not be subjected to the wishes and influence of the Jew. The administrator must be entirely independent of his influence.

(**signed**) Chief of Military Administration, for the Military commander

Consular minute: F 1859 31/5/943 R I have secured the letter of appointment. 14 October 1943 R. Zerman

i. TURKISH CONSULATE-GENERAL (MARSEILLES) INFORMS TURKISH CONSULATE-GENERAL (PARIS) THAT ISAK KASTORYANO IS REGISTERED IN MARSEILLES AS TURKISH

CITIZEN. Marseilles Turkish Consul-General Fuad Carım to Paris Consulate-General no. 411-77, 11 June 1943. Archives of Turkish Embassy (Paris) and Turkish Foreign Ministry (Ankara).

> Republic of Turkey Consulate-General
> Marseilles, 11 June 1943 no. 411-77
> Summary: Isak Kastoryano has been found to be registered
>
> To the Paris Consulate-General,
> Answer to letter of 19 May 1943 no. 1008/83
> It has been learned from examining the records that the aforementioned Isak Kastoryano secured Certificate of Nationality no. 2639/968/413 dated 30 December 1942 from our Consulate-General.
> I present my compliments
> (**signed**) Fuad Carım, Marseilles Consul-General
> **Consular minute:** 1221 T.P. 14/6/943
> no. 673, date 14 June 1943

j. ISAK KASTORYANO'S BROTHER JACQUES KASTORYANO INFORMS TURKISH CONSULATE-GENERAL (PARIS) THAT WHILE HIS BROTHER IS IN FREE ZONE HIS APARTMENT IN PARIS HAS BEEN SEALED BY GERMAN OCCUPYING AUTHORITIES. ASKS CONSULATE TO GET IT UNSEALED. TURKISH CONSULATE ASKS SS CAPTAIN RÖTHKE TO UNSEAL THE APARTMENT. Jacques Kastoryano, 151 Faubourg Poissonière, Paris IX, to Turkish Consulate-General (Paris), 13 January 1944. Turkish registration no. F 3189. Archives of Turkish Embassy (Paris) and Turkish Foreign Ministry (Ankara).

> Kastoryano Jacques
> 151, Faubourg Poissonière, Paris IX
> Paris, 13 January 1944
>
> Mr. Consul-General of Turkey
> 170 Boulevard Haussmann, Paris
> Mr. Consul-General

I have the honor of bringing to your attention that my brother, Mr. Kastoryano Isak, presently in the free zone, and having his apartment in Paris IX, 22 Rue Baudin, registered at your consulate under the number 1221 TP, passport no 30/186, has had his apartment put under seals by the occupying authorities.

In consequence, would you have the goodness to do what is necessary.

I ask you to believe, Mr. Ambassador, with my thanks, my very estimable sentiments.

(**signed**) Kastoryano

Consular minute B. Yolga 15/1/943 R removal of the seals has been asked of Mr. Röthke

k. TURKISH CONSULATE-GENERAL (PARIS) INFORMS GERMAN EMBASSY (PARIS) THAT ISAK KASTORYANO IS TURKISH CITIZEN NOW IN MARSEILLES AND ASKS THAT SEALS BE REMOVED FROM HIS APARTMENT IN PARIS. Turkish Consulate-General (Paris) to German Embassy, 78, Rue de Lille, Paris VIIème no. F 3373, 2 February 1944. Archives of Turkish Embassy (Paris) and Turkish Foreign Ministry (Ankara).

Republic of Turkey, Paris Consulate-General
2 February 1944 no. F 3373

Embassy of Germany
78 Rue de Lille, Paris VIIème

The Consulate-General of Turkey at Paris presents its compliments to the Embassy of Germany and has the honor of bringing to its attention the following:

This Consulate-General has just been informed that seals have been placed on the apartment of Mr. Isak Kastoryano, living at 22 Rue Baudin in Paris IXème. Mr. Isak Kastoryano is a Turkish citizen with title to Certificate of Nationality no. 2639-1221 TP, delivered on 30 December 1942 by the Consulate-General of Turkey at Marseilles, and he is now in the unoccupied zone. Since this involves the apartment of a Turkish citizen, this Consulate-General asks the Embassy of Germany to be good enough to intervene with the competent authorities so that the seals are removed.

This Consulate-General thanks in advance the Embassy of Germany for its obliging intervention to this effect, and seizes on this occasion to reiterate to it the assurances of its high consideration.

(**signed**) Consul-General
Paris, 2 February 1944

l. JACQUES KASTORYANO TELLS TURKISH CONSULATE-GENERAL THAT HE CANNOT PROVIDE COPY OF LEASE FOR ISAK KASTORYANO'S APARTMENT SINCE ADMINISTRATOR REFUSES TO GIVE HIM COPY. ASKS HIM TO ACT ANYWAY TO HAVE SEALS REMOVED. Jacques Kastoryano (Paris) to Turkish Consul-General (Paris), 7 February 1944. Archives of Turkish Embassy (Paris) and Turkish Ministry of Foreign Affairs (Ankara).

J. Kastoryano
151, Faubourg Poissonière, Paris
Paris, 7 February 1944

Mr. Consul-General of Turkey
170 Boulevard Haussmann, Paris
Mr. Consul-General,

Following the letter that I sent you regarding my brother, M. Kastoryano Isak, registered at your Consulate under no. 1221 TP, passport 30/186, on whose apartment at 22 Rue Baudin Paris IXème seals were placed, regarding what you asked me for, I regret to inform you that I cannot give you the lease regarding his rent, since he has it and he is presently in the southern zone. I asked for a duplicate from the administrator, but the latter refused to give it. When I came to the consulate recently, I did give you the receipts for rent, proving that he is the renter of the building at 22 Rue Baudin. As a result, I would be very grateful if you would do what is necessary. With my thanks, I ask you to believe, Mr. Consul-General, in my most estimable sentiments.

(**signed**) Kastoryano

Consular minute request to remove the seals in letter no.
F 337. The necessary has been carried out. February 1943.

m. ISAK KASTORYANO WRITES TURKISH CONSUL-GENERAL FROM DRANCY CAMP THAT HE WAS ARRESTED WHEN HE CAME TO PARIS TO JOIN REPATRIATION CARAVAN TO TURKEY. ASKS THAT HE BE SCHEDULED FOR NEXT CONVEY. Isak Kastoryano to Turkish Consul-General, 30 May 1944. Archives of Turkish Embassy (Paris) and Turkish Foreign Ministry (Ankara).

> Internment Camp at Drancy
> 30 May 1944

I am not in possession of a passport since, as it is stated on the interior sheet of each page, every Turkish citizen arriving in France is required within six months to present himself to the Consulate to have himself enrolled on the register and to receive in exchange for the passport a Certificate of Nationality. I am, therefore, in possession of Certificate of Nationality no. 2639, issued by the Consulate-General of Turkey at Marseilles dated 3 January 1942, and extended so that it is now valid until 13 January 1945. I also asked the Consulate for my repatriation, and I have in my possession a telegram advising me that the Consulate in Paris had agreed to my repatriation and that, before my departure, I should go to the Consulate at Grenoble to regain the passport issued to me for that reason. I was about to leave for Paris as soon as the date of the convey was fixed, and it was during that time that I was arrested and sent to the Internment Camp at Drancy.

I ask your help to secure reconsideration of my case, and as result of my Turkish nationality, to ask that laws regarding Turkish citizens be applied to me. I ask also permission to communicate with the Consulate-General of Turkey in Paris to again secure a place for my wife and child as well as myself in the next repatriation convoy.[312]

> **(signed)** Isak Kastoryano
> **Consular minute:** received at 12 noon, 30 May 1944

n. TURKISH CONSULATE-GENERAL WRITES CAPTAIN RÖTHKE ASKING THAT ISAK KASTORYANO BE RELEASED FROM DRANCY CAMP SINCE HE IS TURKISH CITIZEN

---

312. Author's note: the last train caravan allowed by the German occupation authorities left Paris on 25 May 1944.

SCHEDULED TO BE REPATRIATED TO TURKEY. Turkish Consul-General (Paris) to Captain Röthke, 140, Boulevard Haussmann, Paris 8ème, no. F 4259, 30 May 1944. Archives of Turkish Embassy (Paris) and Turkish Foreign Ministry (Ankara).

> Republic of Turkey
> Paris Consulate-General
> 30 May 1944 no. F 4259
>
> To Captain Röthke
> 140 Boulevard Haussmann, Paris VIII
> Dear Monsieur le Capitaine,
> I have the honor of bringing to your attention that Mr. Isak Kastoryano, who is presently interned at the Camp at Drancy, is a Turkish citizen holding Certificate of Nationality no. 2629, delivered by the Consulate-General of Turkey at Grenoble and valid until 23 January 1945. I as you, Monsieur le Capitaine, to be good enough to intervene as a matter of urgency with the competent authorities in order to avoid the deportation of Mr. Kastoryano, and to free him as soon as possible since he is to be repatriated to Turkey very shortly.
> In thanking you in advance for your amiable intervention, I ask you to accept, Monsieur le Capitaine, the assurance of my estimable consideration.
> **(signed)** The Consul-General

o. TURKISH CONSULATE-GENERAL WRITES DRANCY CAMP COMMANDER THAT INTERNEE ISAK KASTORYANO IS TURKISH CITIZEN AND ASKING THAT HE BE FREED SO HE CAN BE REPATRIATED TO TURKEY. Turkish Consulate-General (Paris) to Drancy Camp Commander no. F 4200, 30 May 1944. Archives of Turkish Embassy (Paris) and Turkish Foreign Ministry (Ankara).

> Republic of Turkey, Paris Consulate-General
> 30 May 1944, no. F 4200
>
> To The Commander, Internment Camp at Drancy (Seine)
> Mr. Commander,

I can inform you that Mr. Isak Kastoryano, who is now interned at the Drancy Camp, is a Turkish citizen, holding Certificate of Nationality no. 2629, issued by the Consulate-General of Turkey at Grenoble and valid until 23 January 1945.

I ask you to intervene with the competent service so that Mr. Isak Kastoryano is freed urgently so that he can be repatriated, which is scheduled to be carried out very shortly. In thanking you for your amiable intervention to this effect, I ask you to accept, Mr. Commander, my estimable greetings.

(**signed**) Consul-General , Paris, 30 May 1944

p. ADMINISTRATOR OF ISAK KASTORYANO PROPERTIES RECEP ZERMAN REPORTS THAT THE LATTER IS IMPRISONED AT DRANCY CAMP AND THAT SEALS HAVE NOT YET BEEN REMOVED FROM HIS APARTMENT IN PARIS. Recep Zerman to Turkish Consulate-General (Paris), 21 July 1944. Archives of Turkish Embassy (Paris) and Turkish Foreign Ministry (Ankara).

Paris, 21 July 1944

To the Republic of Turkey Paris Consulate-General,

I wish to present the following information regarding our fellow citizen Isak Kastoryano, who is registered in dossier no. 1221 TP at the Consulate-General and for whom I have been appointed administrator by higher authorities:

1. Isak Kastoryano was living in the southern district. I have heard that he was arrested near Beziers Herault and sent to the Drancy camp.

2. Isak Kastoryano's apartment in Paris at 22 Rue Baudin was sealed by the occupation authorities, but the letter written by higher authorities in February 1944 asking that the seals be removed has not yet been answered, and the apartment remains closed.

I ask for permission to do what is felt to be necessary to act regarding the two points mentioned above.

(**signed**) Recep Zerman, Local clerk

Paris, 21 July 1944

Consular minute: 28/7/944 R

q. TURKISH CONSULATE-GENERAL (PARIS) ASKS GERMAN EMBASSY (PARIS) TO SECURE LIBERATION OF TURKISH CITIZEN ISAK KASTORYANO SO HE CAN BE IMMEDIATELY REPATRIATED TO TURKEY. Turkish Consulate-General (Paris) to German Embassy (Paris), no. F 4620, 28 July 1944. Archives of Turkish Embassy (Paris) and Turkish Foreign Ministry (Ankara).

Republic of Turkey, Paris Consulate-General
28 July 1944, no. F 4620

To the Embassy of Germany
78 Rue de Lille, Paris VII

The Consulate-General of Turkey at Paris presents its compliments to the Embassy of Germany and has the honor of bringing to its attention that it has just been informed that Mr. Isak Kastoryano is now in the Camp at Drancy. Mr. Isak Kastoryano is a Turkish citizen, holding Certificate of Nationality no 2629 delivered by the Consulate-General of Turkey at Grenoble and valid until 23 January 1945. Given that this involves a Turkish citizen regularly inscribed at the Consulate, this Consulate-General asks the Embassy of Germany to be good enough to intervene with the competent authorities to secure the release of Mr. Isak Kastoryano as a matter of urgency so that he can be repatriated imminently.

The Consulate-General of Turkey thanks in advance the Embassy of Germany for its obliging intervention to this effect, and seizes on this occasion to reiterate to it the assurances of its high consideration.

(**signed**) Consul-General , Paris, 28 July 1944

r. TURKISH CONSULATE-GENERAL AGAIN ASKS COMMANDER OF DRANCY INTERMENT CAMP TO SECURE FREEDOM FOR ISAK KASTORYANO. Turkish Consulate-General (Paris) to Drancy Camp Commander, no. F 4621, Paris, 28 July 1944. Archives of Turkish Embassy (Paris) and Turkish Foreign Ministry (Ankara).

Republic of Turkey , Paris Consulate-General
Paris, 28 July 1944, no. F 4621

To Mr. Commander, Internment Camp at Drancy,

Mr. Commander,

I can inform you that Mr. Isak Kastoryano, who is at present interned at the Camp of Drancy, is a Turkish citizen, holding Certificate of Nationality no. 2629 delivered by the Consulate-General of Turkey at Grenoble and valid until 23 January 1945. I ask you to be good enough to intervene with the competent service so that Mr. Isak Kastoryano is liberated as a matter of urgency so that he can be repatriated imminently.

In thanking you for your amiable intervention to this effect, I ask you to accept, Mr. Commander, my estimable greetings.

(signed) Fikret Şefik Özdoğancı, Consul-General,

Paris, 28 July 1944

s. TURKISH CONSULATE-GENERAL (PARIS) ASKS GERMAN EMBASSY TO SECURE REMOVAL OF SEALS FROM APARTMENT OF ISAK KASTORYANO IN PARIS. Turkish Consulate-General (Paris) to German Embassy (Paris), no. F 8638, 1 August 1944. Archives of Turkish Embassy (Paris) and Turkish Foreign Ministry (Ankara).

Republic of Turkey, Paris Consulate-General

1 August 1944, no. F 8638

To the Embassy of Germany

78 Rue de Lille, Paris VII

The Consulate-General of Turkey in Paris presents its compliments to the Embassy of Germany and has the honor to bring to its attention the following:

By a letter dated 2 February 1944 reference F 3373, this Consulate-General informed the Embassy of Germany of the putting under seals of the apartment of Mr. Isak Kastoryano, 22 Rue Baudin in Paris IX, and asked for the removal of the seals. Until this day no authority has acted to do so.

Since this involves the apartment of a Turkish citizen, this Consulate-General asks the Embassy of Germany to be good enough to intervene with the competent authorities so that the seals are removed from the apartment of Mr. Isak Kastoryano. The Consulate-General of Turkey thanks in advance the Embassy of Germany for the trouble that it will take in this regard, and seizes on this occasion to reiterate its assurances of its high consideration.

(**signed**) Fikret Şefik Özdoğancı, Consul-General,
Paris, 1 August 1944

t. TURKISH CONSULATE-GENERAL (PARIS) ASKS DIENSTELLE WESTEN TO REMOVE SEALS FROM APARTMENT OF ISAK KASTORYANO IN PARIS. Turkish Consulate-General (Paris) to Dienstelle Westen, 54 avenue d'Iéna, Paris XVIème, no. F 4629, 1 August 1944. Archives of Turkish Embassy (Paris) and Turkish Foreign Ministry (Ankara).

Republic of Turkey, Paris Consulate-General
1 August 1944 no. F 4629

To the Dienstelle Westen
54 avenue d'Iéna, Paris XVI

The Consulate-General of Turkey in Paris presents its compliments to the Dienstelle Westen and has the honor to ask it to be good enough to proceed to the removal of the seals that have been placed since January 1944 on the apartment of Mr. Isak Kastoryano, Turkish citizen, at 22 Rue Baudin in Paris IXème.

This Consulate-General thanks in advance the Dienstelle Westen for the trouble that it will take in this regard, and seizes on this occasion to reiterate to it assurances of its estimable consideration.

(**signed**) Fikret Şefik Özdoğancı,
Consul-General
Paris, 1 August 1944

u. ISAK KASTORYANO'S MOTHER MADAME VVE. VENTURA KASTORYANO INFORMS TURKISH CONSULATE-GENERAL THAT HER SON, HIS WIFE AND FAMILY WERE DEPORTED TO GERMANY, THAT SHE IS TAKING OVER HIS BUSINESS, AND ASKS THAT ADMINISTRATION OF STORE BE TURNED OVER TO HER UNTIL RETURN OF HER SON AND FAMILY FROM CAPTIVITY. Madame Vve. Ventura Kastoryano, 151 Rue du Faubourg Poissonniere, Paris IXème, to Turkish Consul-General (Paris), Paris, 25 March 1945. Archives of Turkish Embassy (Paris) and Turkish Foreign Ministry (Ankara).

Paris, 25 March 1945
To Mr. Consul-General of Turkey in Paris
Excellency,

I have the honor to bring to your attention that Mr. Recep Zerman was named administrator for the period of the occupation of the store situated at 83 Rue de Cléry in Paris which belonged to my son Isak Kastoryano, who is of Turkish nationality. My son is at present deported in Germany with his wife and his child. Since I am presently engaged in re-assembling all his properties, I would be obliged if you would do what is necessary so that the administration of the shop of my son is confided in me until his return from captivity. I remain at your disposition for all information regarding this matter. I ask you, Your Excellency, to be good enough to accept the expression of my high consideration.

(signed) F. Eskenazi, for Madame V. Kastoryano
Madame Vve. Ventura Kastoryano
151 Rue du Faubourg Poissonière, Paris IXème
Consular minute: dossier 26/3/945 RS

v. TURKISH CONSULATE-GENERAL INFORMS ISAK KASTORYANO'S MOTHER VENTURA KASTORYANO THAT ADMINISTRATOR RECEP ZERMAN HAS BEEN INSTRUCTED TO TURN ADMINISTRATION OF HER SON'S STORE OVER TO HER. Turkish Consulate-General (Paris) to Madame Ventura Kastoryano, Paris, no. 5266, 29 March 1945. Archives of Turkish Embassy (Paris) and Turkish Foreign Ministry (Ankara).

Republic of Turkey, Paris Consulate-General
29 March 1945 no. 5266

Madame Ventura Kastoryano
151 Rue du Faubourg Poissonière, Paris IXème
Madame,

In response to your letter of the 25th of this month, I can inform you that Mr. Recep Zerman has received instructions to turn over to you the administration of the shop of your son, Mr. Isak Kastoryano, 83 Rue de Cléry in Paris. As a result, I ask you to get into direct contact with Mr. Zerman.

Please accept, Madame, my estimable greetings,
(**signed**) Fikret Şefik Özdoğancı, The Consul-General

THE YUDA (LEON) FARHI FILE

Yuda Lech Farhi, 69 Rue Macau, Bordeaux, France
Wife: Reyna/Regina Farhi (born Alfandary)
Daughter: Arlette Farhi
Father: Salamon Cemil Farhi, Beyoğlu, Minare Sokak no. 22, Istanbul
Arrested at Bordeaux, interned at Mérignac Concentration Camp: 21 December 1943
Transferred to Drancy Concentration Camp, 1 January 1944
Deported to Germany: 20 January 1944

a. YUDA FARHI ASKS TURKISH CONSULATE (PARIS) TO RETURN HIS UPDATED NATIONALITY CARD. CARD WAS SENT TO LOCAL PRÉFECTURE OF POLICE, BUT IT WAS RETURNED AFTER FARHI FAMILY WAS ARRESTED AND SENT TO MÉRIGNAC CONCENTRATION CAMP. Yuda Farhi, 69, Rue de Macau, Bordeaux, to Turkish Consulate-General (Paris), 17 December 1943. Archives of the Turkish Embassy (Paris).

Y. Farhi, 69, Rue de Macau, Bordeaux, Gironde
Bordeaux, 17 December 1943

The Consulate-General of Turkey
170, Boulevard Haussmann, Paris 8ème
Gentlemen

In my letter of 8 November last, I had the honor to send you my Turkish Nationality Card no. 2633 TP/85/9, issued by your Consulate-General, asking you to renew it for a year. To this day it has not yet been returned to me. Because of present circumstances, I must carry this Nationality Card at all times. I would therefore be particularly obliged if you would proceed with its renewal so that my citizenship will be in order.

Regarding the indication of my family name 'Farhi' on that nationality card, I have the honor of informing you that it is that name that is used on my Marriage Certificate no. 2885, which your Consulate-General delivered to me dated 1 August 1927, and it has been used on my various preceding nationality cards.

I would appreciate it if you do what is necessary to carry out the request in my letter of 8 November 1943. Please be assured, Gentlemen, of my most special consideration.

(**signed**) Leon Farhi.

Consular minutes: The certificate was sent to the Préfecture of the Gironde. Certificate returned

b. FARHI WRITES TURKISH CONSULATE (PARIS) FROM MÉRIGNAC CONCENTRATION CAMP ASKING THAT IT ARRANGE FOR HIS RELEASE AND THAT OF HIS FAMILY. Leon Farhi, Camp de Mérignac, to Turkish Consulate-General (Paris), 22 December 1943. (Archives of the Turkish Embassy, Paris).

Mérignac Camp (Gironde), 22 December 1943

Consulate-General of Turkey
170 Boulevard Haussmann, Paris VIIIème
Dear Mr. Consul-General,

I am writing you this letter from the Mérignac Concentration Camp near Bordeaux where I have been with my wife and my daughter, aged 11, since the 21st of this month. I do not know the reasons which have caused this measure regarding me and my family, since no authority has told me anything. In these conditions, I have the honor of asking you, Mr. Consul-General, to make the applications which are necessary in such circumstances in order to secure my freedom and that of my wife and daughter. I hope that you will take my case into serious consideration and that you will willingly do all that you can to enable us to avoid a prolonged stay in a concentration camp, since my young daughter in particular is not well.

My Certificate of Nationality was sent to you by me on 8 November last with the necessary renewal tax and photographs. I would appreciate your arranging to send me this document as soon as the annual renewal procedures are completed in your office. In addition, I have the honor of informing you that I would like to be repatriated to Turkey, with my wife and my daughter, as soon as possible. I would appreciate your sending me by return mail all information relative to repatriation, and the forms which must be filled out and signed to this effect.

I have great hopes, Mr. Consul-General, that your intervention with the German and French authorities will have a satisfactory result and that we will quickly be freed. I wish to convey to you my highest consideration.

> (signed) Leon Farhi
> Concentration Camp at Mérignac (Gironde)
> Former Address: 69 Rue de Macau, Bordeaux
> **Consular minute** 2633 TP 24/12/44 received Reg. no. F3086

c. TURKISH CONSULATE-GENERAL INFORMS GERMAN EMBASSY (PARIS) THAT FARHI FAMILY ARE TURKISH CITIZENS AND ASKS FOR THEIR RELEASE. Turkish Consulate-General (Paris) to German Embassy, 78, Rue de Lille, Paris VIIème,F 3091, Archives of Turkish Embassy (Paris), 23 December 1943.

> Republic of Turkey. Turkish Consulate-General, Paris
> 23 December 1943

German Embassy, 78, Rue de Lille, Paris, VIIème

The Consulate-General of Turkey at Paris presents its compliments to the German Embassy and has the honor of bringing to its knowledge the following:

This Consulate-General has just been informed that Mr. Yuda Farhi, his wife and their small daughter, have been arrested at their home at 69, Rue de Macau at Bordeaux, then interned, and their apartment put under seals.

These are Turkish citizens, properly registered, bearers of Certificate of Nationality no. 2633 TP, renewed on 3 December 1943 under no. 685 and good until 8 November 1944. This Consulate-General therefore asks the German Embassy to intervene with the competent authorities so that Mr. Farhi, his wife and their small daughter are released.

The Consulate-General of Turkish thanks the German Embassy in advance for its obliging intervention in this matter, and takes advantage of this occasion to reiterate to it assurances of its highest consideration.

(signed), The Consul-General

d. TURKISH CONSULATE (GENERAL) INFORMS PRÉFECTURE DE LA GIRONDE (BORDEAUX) THAT YUDA FARHI AND FAMILY ARE TURKISH CITIZENS, THAT APPLICATIONS ARE BEING MADE FOR THEIR RELEASE, AND THAT THEIR APARTMENT IN BORDEAUX SHOULD BE UNSEALED. Turkish Consulate-General (Paris) to Préfecture de la Gironde (Bordeaux), Paris, F3092, 23 December 1943. Archives of Turkish Embassy (Paris).

Republic of Turkey. Consulate-General at Paris,
23 December 1943

Préfecture de la Gironde, Bordeaux

The Consulate-General of Turkey at Paris presents its compliments to the Préfecture of the Gironde and has the honor of bringing to its attention the following:

This Consulate-General has been informed that Mr. Yuda Farhi, his wife and their small daughter, have been arrested by the police and their apartment has been sealed.

Their Turkish Certificate of Nationality no. 2633 TP was at this Consulate-General in order to extend its validity when they were arrested, and for that reason at that time they did not have in their possession Turkish papers showing their nationality. The Consulate-General of Turkey asks the Préfecture de la Gironde to deliver to Mr. and Mrs. Farhi their Nationality Certificate as well as the attached papers. Requests for their liberation have already been undertaken by this Consulate-General with the competent authorities.

In addition, since they are Turkish citizens regularly registered, bearers of Certificate of Nationality no. 2633 TP, renewed on 3 December 1943 under no. 685 and good until 8 November 1944, this Consulate-General asks the Préfecture of the Gironde to intervene with the competent authorities so that the seals are removed from the Farhi apartment.

This Consulate-General thanks in advance the Préfecture of the Gironde for its obliging intervention in this matter, and takes advantage of this occasion to reiterate to it assurances of its highest consideration.

(**signed**) The Consul-General

e. TURKISH CONSULATE-GENERAL INFORMS FRIEND OF FARHIS THAT EFFORTS ARE BEING MADE TO SECURE THEIR RELEASE. Turkish Consulate-General (Paris) to Madame Heraud, 69 Rue de Macau, Bordeaux, Paris, F 3096, 23 December 1943. Archives of Turkish Embassy (Paris).

Republic of Turkey. Consulate-General, Paris, 23 December 1943

Madame Heraud,
69 Rue de Macau, Bordeaux
Dear Madame,

In response to your letter of the 21st of this month, I can inform you that we have immediately undertaken the necessary démarches to secure the freedom of Mr. Farhi and his family and the removal of the seals that have been put on their apartment. I would appreciate it if you would keep me informed of anything you may be able to learn about them.

Please accept, Madame, my most special greetings.
(**signed**) The Consul-General

f. LEON FARHI AGAIN APPEALS TO TURKISH CONSULATE (PARIS) TO GET HIM AND FAMILY OUT OF CONCENTRATION CAMP, TO SECURE UNSEALING OF HIS APARTMENT IN BORDEAUX, AND RETURN OF FAMILY MONEY AND JEWELS CONFISCATED BY POLICE AT TIME OF ARREST. Leon Farhi, Mérignac (Gironde) to Turkish Consulate-General (Paris), 26 December 1943. Archives of Turkish Embassy (Paris).

Mérignac (Gironde), 26 December 1943

To Mr. Consul-General of Turkey at Paris
Mr. Consul-General,

I have the honor of confirming to you my letter of the 23rd of this month in which I informed you that I have been interned with my wife and daughter at the concentration camp at Mérignac near Bordeaux since the 22nd of this month. The reasons for this internment of me and my family has not been given to me yet, and

I am entirely in ignorance for the reasons for the measures that have been taken against us.

I wish also to bring to your attention today that seals have been put on the door of the apartment that I occupy at 69, Rue de Macau at Bordeaux, and that I cannot make use of the clothing, lingerie and other things that are there. In addition, the jewels belonging to my wife, which are family relics, have been taken recently by the Police as well as a portfolio which contained money, including 2,600 francs belonging to my daughter, which have been sequestered by the Police which came to arrest us on the 22nd of this month, at 4 o'clock on the morning, at our home in Bordeaux.

I leave it to you, Mr. Consul-General, to appreciate and judge these facts for what they are worth to give you an idea of the sad fate that has been reserved for us. I am married, and father of a little daughter 11 years old. I have never been involved in politics, and my legal record is perfect. I have a situation of a very moderate fortune, and I cannot bear this rude blow that has been struck against me without any reason, in jailing me, with my family, in a concentration camp, and by the seizure of family jewels of my wife that are worth more than 60,000 francs.

I place our sad fate in your hands and I have the honor to request that you:

1: Ask for the immediate lifting of the seals placed on my apartment at 69, Rue de Macau at Bordeaux, so that I can arrange to secure the warm covers and clothing which we have an urgent need to keep us from the rigorous cold which we experience in the concentration camp where we are now located.

2: To claim the restoration to me or my wife or to any authority that you designate of the jewels taken from my wife and the money of my daughter (2,600 francs), which they appropriated without reason;

3: to do all necessary with the competent German and French authorities to secure our prompt release.

I wish to raise an energetic protest against all the arbitrary acts that have been struck against us, and place all our hope in our government that you represent, for I know perfectly the sentiments of great protection and good will of which our leaders have given proof on many occasions regarding the Turkish Jewish minority.

I am a Turkish citizen perfectly in order, possessing the following documents:

Certificate of Nationality (now in course of renewal at your offices)

Certificate attesting to my military service in Turkey

Marriage documents delivered by your Consulate-General on 1 August 1927

Documents of birth of my wife and myself kept in your archives in Paris

I have the firm hope that you will be able to defend my cause and our material and moral interests. In the situation in which I find myself I have no-one except you, Mr. Consul-General, who can save me and secure my freedom. I express in advance my profound recognition and my greatest thanks and I ask you to believe, Mr. Consul-General, in the expression of my highest consideration and most devoted sentiments.

(**signed**) Leon Farhi

Consular minute: received 28 December 1943

g. LEON FARHI INFORMS TURKISH CONSUL-GENERAL THAT HE AND FAMILY HAVE BEEN TRANSFERRED TO DRANCY CONCENTRATION CAMP, AND HE AGAIN ASKS TURKISH CONSUL-GENERAL (PARIS) FOR ASSISTANCE. Leon Farhi, Drancy Concentration Camp, Paris, to Turkish Consul-General (Paris), 30 December 1943. Archives of Turkish Embassy (Paris).

30 December 1943

To Mr. Consul-General of Turkey at Paris

Dear Mr. Consul-General,

I have the honor to confirm to you my two letters that I sent to you from the Concentration Camp at Mérignac (Gironde). I hope that they have reached you and that you have taken into consideration the sad situation in which my wife, my daughter and I have found ourselves since the 21st of this month. Today the authorities carried out our transfer to the Concentration Camp at Drancy, near Paris, where we will be interned tomorrow. Other compatriots from Bordeaux have undergone the same experience.

We still do not know the real reasons for the measures of internment taken regarding Turkish citizens and which are effecting women, old people, and children. I fear that from Drancy we will be sent toward other camps outside the country, as has been done to many people resident in France who are of the Jewish religion. If a new transfer of this sort is imposed on my small family, it will be fatal for us. I plead with you, Mr. Consul-General, to have pity on us and save us. It is with tears in my eyes that I write you this letter from the train that is taking us toward our Drancy camp. My wife and my daughter are in the same convoy, and they are depressed with the idea of the miserable state which has been imposed on us. I beg you to protect us and to act rapidly before it is too late and we are sent abroad to endure even worse suffering.

I ask to be freed as soon as possible, with my wife and child, and to return to Turkey with the least possible delay. I have members of my family who still live in Turkey, and I have the natural desire of a father to place his wife and daughter outside the concentration camps. I put all my hopes in your hands, and I appeal to your generosity and your pity.

All my papers are in order as you know, and my Certificate of Nationality was sent to you on the 8th of last month, so that it could be renewed, with the sum of 240 francs tax as well as the necessary photographs.

I have in my possession my Marriage Certificate, issued by your Consulate-General on 1 August 1927 as well as my Certificate of Military Service, delivered by the Techirkie[313] military bureau in Istanbul.

We bear up in the hope that your intervention will secure our quick release, and hope we will have the fortune to return to Turkey.

We await with a comprehensible impatience the result of your interventions, and I hope you will accept, Mr. Consul-General, the assurance of my highest consideration and profound gratitude.

(**signed**) Leon Farhi).

L. Farhi, Drancy Concentration Camp (Seine et Oise)

---

313. This may have been the Teşvikiye district of Istanbul.

P.S. I should inform you, in addition, that seals were put on the door of my apartment the day of our arrest, and that the Police took possession of the jewels of my wife (value about 60,000 francs) and moneys of my daughter, about 2,600 francs, without giving us any receipt. I ask you to protest against this as well as against the enormous prejudice which we have experienced.

Your very devoted (**signed**) Leon Farhi.

Consular minute: received 3 January 1944 R

h. TURKISH CONSULATE-GENERAL (PARIS) INFORMS DRANCY CONCENTRATION CAMP COMMANDER THAT FARHI FAMILY ARE TURKISH CITIZENS AND THAT APPLICATION HAS BEEN MADE FOR THEIR RELEASE. Turkish Consulate-General (Paris) to Commander of the Internment Camp at Drancy, Paris, F 3105, 30 December 1943.

Republic of Turkey. Turkish Consulate-General, Paris
30 December 1943

Mr. Commander of the Internment Camp at Drancy (Seine)
Mr. Commander,

I have the honor of bringing to your knowledge that Mr. Yuda Farhi, his wife and their small daughter, who were arrested at Bordeaux and then interned at the Camp at Mérignac, have now been transferred to the Camp placed under your esteemed direction.

Mr. Yuda Farhi and his family bear Certificate of Nationality no. 2633 TP, renewed on 3 December 1943 under no. 685 and good until 8 November 1944.

I have already made the necessary applications with the competent authorities to secure their liberation.

Please accept, Mr. Commander, the assurance of my most special consideration.

(**signed**) The Consul-General

i. TURKISH CONSULATE-GENERAL (PARIS) ASKS GERMAN EMBASSY FOR RELEASE OF LEON FARHI AND FAMILY. Turkish

Consulate-General (Paris) to German Embassy (Paris), F 3454, 30 December 1943. Archives of Turkish Embassy (Paris).

> Republic of Turkey, Turkish Consulate-General, Paris
> 30 December 1943, F 3454

> The German Embassy, Paris
> The Consulate-General of Turkey at Paris presents its compliments to the German Embassy and has the honor of bringing to its knowledge the following:
> This Consulate-General informed the German Embassy on 23 December 1943 that Mr. Yuda Farhi, his wife and their small daughter were arrested at their home at 69, Rue de Macau at Bordeaux, then interned, and their apartment put under seals, but has not yet received an acknowledgment of this communication or of action taken as a result.
> Leon Farhi and his family are Turkish citizens, properly registered, bearers of Certificate of Nationality no. 2633 TP, renewed on 3 December 1943 under no. 685 and good until 8 November 1944. This Consulate-General therefore asks the German Embassy to intervene with the competent authorities so that Mr. Farhi, his wife and their small daughter are released. The Consulate-General of Turkish thanks the German Embassy in advance for its obliging intervention in this matter, and takes advantage of this occasion to reiterate to it assurances of its highest consideration.
> (**signed**) the Consul-General

j. PRÉFECT OF THE GIRONDE (BORDEAUX) INFORMS TURKISH CONSULATE-GENERAL (PARIS) THAT FARHI FAMILY HAS BEEN MOVED TO THE DRANCY CONCENTRATION CAMP. Secretary General of the Préfecture de la Gironde, Bordeaux, to Turkish Consulate-General (Paris), F 3160, 3 January 1944. Archives of Turkish embassy (Paris).

> State of France, Préfecture of the Gironde
> 1st Division, Bureau 3, Bordeaux, 3 January 1944
> Mr. Consul-General of Turkey, Paris
> Dear Mr. Consul-General

I have the honor of indicating reception of your letter of the 23rd December in which you called my attention to your citizens Mr. and Mrs. Yuda Farhi, who were the object of an internment measure. I immediately intervened with the competent authorities who informed me that Mr. and Mrs. Yuda Farhi and their daughter have been transferred to the Camp at Drancy (Seine).

I am informing you of this without delay to permit you to take the necessary actions that you consider useful. You will find enclosed the documents that you communicated to me.

Please accept, Mr. Consul-General, the assurance of my highest consideration.

(**signed**) The Secretary General, delegated by the Préfect.

Consular minute: received 10 January 1944. R.

k. ONE MONTH AFTER UNANSWERED LETTER TO GERMAN EMBASSY (PARIS), TURKISH CONSULATE ASKS SS CAPTAIN RÖTHKE TO INTERVENE TO SECURE RELEASE OF FARHI FAMILY. STATES UNHAPPINESS AT RUMORS THAT TURKISH CITIZENS ARE BEING DEPORTED TO THE EAST. ASKS HIS HELP IN SECURING THEIR RELEASE. Namık Kemal Yolga, for Turkish Consul-General (Paris) to SS Captain Heinz Röthke, Paris, no. F 3370, Paris, 3 February 1944. Archives of the Turkish Embassy (Paris).

Republic of Turkey, Turkish Consulate-General, Paris, 3 February 1944, no. F 3370

Monsieur le Capitain Röthke
Dear Captain,

We have informed you several times, sometimes by letters, sometimes by telephone, of the arrest of Turkish citizens living in Bordeaux, notably of Yuda Farhi, his wife Reyna, and their daughter, who live at 69 Rue Macau in Bordeaux. These Turkish citizens were arrested on 21 December, taken to the Camp at Mèrigny, and then to the Camp at Drancy.

Information has recently circulated regarding the deportation of Mr. Yuda Farhi and his family: that they are now at Metz in preparation for being sent further away.

We cannot quite believe it, but it appears that despite two letters no. F 3207 and 3304 of 17 and 28 January, as well as numerous telephone communications, regularly registered Turkish citizens are being deported, and we wish to inform you of these rumors.

In addition, by these two letters we asked you to arrange the liberation of Turkish citizens who had already been interned at Drancy, and who are supposed to be repatriated to Turkey very soon.

We ask you to intervene with all urgency so that Mr. Yuda Farhi and his family are not deported, but to the contrary, are freed.

Counting on your intervention to this effect, we ask you to accept. Mr. Captain, the assurance of our most special sentiments.

(**signed**) Namık Kemal Yolga, for the Consul-General

1. LEON FARHI'S FATHER IN ISTANBUL ASKS TURKISH GOVERNMENT TO HELP GET HIS SON OUT OF CONCENTRATION CAMP. Salamon Cemil Farhi to Turkish Ministry of Foreign Affairs, 26 February 1944. Archives of Turkish Embassy (Paris)
22 Minare Sokak, Beyoğlu, Istanbul
Former Cashier of the Turkish Tobacco Monopoly Salamon Cemil Farhi

To Ministry of Foreign Affairs
I am Salamon Cemil Farhi, a citizen of Turkey. Since I have learned that my son Leon Farhi, my daughter in law, and my granddaughter Arlet Farhi have been mistakenly sent to a concentration camp by the Germans in France, I venture to present the facts as follows to higher authorities:

My son Leon Farhi, his wife Rejin, and his daughter Arlet Farhi sent their Nationality Card (certificate of citizenship) which they carried to the Consulate-General of the Turkish Republic in Paris for its annual visa renewal on 9 November 1943. These documents were returned to Bordeaux by the Paris Consulate-General on 22 December 1943 with the renewal visa attached. However between these two dates these three members of a family were arrested by the German occupation authorities despite their statement that they were Turkish citizens on the pretext that they were not carrying their documents; and on 20 January 1944 they were sent from the Drancy Camp where they were incarcerated to an unknown destination. All the repeated interventions made to the German authorities by numerous applications and requests made to the Paris Consulate-General have not brought any results.

To this day I have received no news about the life or death of this family, whose whereabouts are unknown. I ask with all sincerity that efforts be made immediately with the Paris Consulate-General and the German authorities since these people have been treated in violation of the most basic elements of their rights, even though they were citizens of the Turkish Republic in possession of their regular Turkish passports. Since the matter is of utmost urgency, I ask that permission be given for immediate action.

26 February 1944
Address: Minare sokak 22 in Beyoğlu,
Former Tobacco Monopoly Cashier
(**signed**) Salamon Cemil Farhi

m. TURKISH EMBASSY TO PARIS (VICHY) SENDS SALAMON FARHI LETTER REGARDING LEON FARHI FAMILY TO TURKISH CONSULATE-GENERAL (PARIS) FOR ACTION. Turkish Embassy to Paris (Vichy) to Turkish Consulate-General (Paris) no. 154-63, Vichy, 3 March 1944. Archives of the Turkish Consulate (Paris).

Republic of Turkey, Embassy to Paris
Vichy, 3 March 1944

To the Consulate-General in Paris,
I present herewith a copy of the request sent in a letter to the Embassy regarding our fellow countryman Leon Farhi and his wife who have been imprisoned.
(**signed**): B. Uşakligil, Assistant to the Ambassador to Paris
Consular stamp: The Paris Consulate-General, received no. 383, 14 March 1944.

n. TURKISH CONSULATE-GENERAL (PARIS) REPORTS TO TURKISH EMBASSY TO PARIS (VICHY) REGARDING LEON FAMILY SITUATION. Turkish Consul-General (Paris) to Turkish

Embassy to Paris (Vichy), no. 383/10, 20 March 1944. Archives of Turkish Consulate (Paris).

> Republic of Turkey, Paris Consulate-General
> Paris, 20 March 1944, no. 383/10
> Regarding: the family of Yuda Leon Farhi,

To the Paris Embassy,
This is in response to your letter no. 154/63 of 3 March 1944.

We learned from a letter sent to our Consulate-General by those interested in the affair that Yuda Leon Farhi, one of our citizens registered at our Consulate-General, along with his wife and daughter, were arrested at Bordeaux and sent to the Mérignac Concentration Camp. Our Consulate-General immediately informed the Préfecturate of the Gironde that since they were regular Turkish citizens they should be released and their apartment unsealed. At the same time the same request was made to the German Embassy, in the same manner as to the Préfecturate of the Gironde.

In a letter sent by the Préfecturate of the Gironde to our Consulate-General, we were informed that Leon Farhi and his family had been sent to the Drancy Concentration Camp. On receiving this news we applied to the director of the Drancy Camp asking that the family be released. In reply to our letter the German Police Chief stated that the Farhi family was not at the Drancy camp. Since our Consulate-General has learned through private channels from concerned individuals that the family has in fact been sent to Germany despite our requests, we have written again on this matter to the responsible German Police Chief, but the list of arrested Turkish citizens sent to us by this official did not include the name of the Farhi family. Despite the efforts we have made to date, therefore, I fear that this family has been sent away. Despite this, I wish to assure you that our efforts in this regard will continue. Please accept my deepest best wishes,
(**signed**) Consul-General

o. SALAMON FARHI BROTHER MARCO FARHI (ISTANBUL) ASKS TURKISH EMBASSY (VICHY) TO ASSIST SEARCH FOR LEON FARHI AND FAMILY. Marco Farhi (Istanbul) to Turkish

Ambassador (Vichy), date unreadable. Archives of Turkish Embassy (Paris).

Your Excellency,

My elder brother Cemil Farhi, who wrote to Your Excellency on 15 January 1944, recently was able to go to Paris. During his stay there, he learned with anguish that his son, Mr. Leon Farhi, Turkish subject, along with his wife and daughter, were arrested at Bordeaux by the Germans in December while their Nationality Card was in Paris, and despite the efforts of your Consulate at Paris, they were deported on 20 January of this year. You can imagine, Your Excellency, with what anguish this aged and almost blind man of 77 years of age has returned to Istanbul. We permit ourselves to ask you, Your Excellency, to provide your useful intervention in order that this innocent and entirely in order family be freed as early as possible. I hope, Your Excellency, that just as you helped me during my stay in Ankara concerning the repatriation of my late daughter at Sofia, that you will do the same for my nephew and his family.

Thanking your in advance, please accept, Your Excellency, my most special respects.

(**signed**) M. Farhi.

p. TURKISH AMBASSADOR TO PARIS (VICHY) SENDS MARCO FARHI LETTER TO TURKISH CONSULATE-GENERAL (PARIS) FOR ACTION. Turkish Ambassador to Paris Şevki Berker (Vichy) to Turkish Consulate-General (Paris) no. 172-74, T.P. 2633, Vichy, 24 March 1944. Archives of Turkish Consulate (Paris) and Turkish Embassy (Paris).

Republic of Turkey, Embassy to Paris
no. 172-74, Vichy, 24 March 1944
Regarding Leon Farhi and his wife

To the Paris Consulate-General,

I am sending a copy of a letter received from Marco Farhi from Istanbul. I ask for information as to what the Consulate-General has done or not done regarding the aforementioned Leon Farhi and his wife.

(signed) Şevki Berker, Paris Ambassador
Consular minute: received 27 March 1944 N(amık) Y(olga), stamped: no. 419, 27 March 1944.

q. TURKISH FOREIGN MINISTRY TRANSMITS TO TURKISH CONSULATE-GENERAL (PARIS) REQUEST OF SALAMON FARHI REGARDING FATE OF SON LEON FARHI AND FAMILY. Assistant to the Foreign Minister R. Raymar to Paris Consulate-General no. 26247/69/2633 T.P., Ankara, 8 April 1944. Archives of Turkish Consulate (Paris).

Republic of Turkey, Ministry of Foreign Affairs
Department of Consulates and Mixed Law
General no. 26247, Special no. 69, Enclosure 1[314]

To the Paris Consulate-General,
I am attaching a copy of the petition sent to our Ministry by Salamon Cemil Farhi, who lives in Istanbul, asking for investigation of the fate of his son Leon Farhi, his wife Rejin and daughter Arlet, who he has learned was sent from the Drancy Concentration Camp near Paris to an unknown destination. I ask you for information as to whether their papers were in order or not, and for the result of the actions which you have taken regarding them.
(signed) R.A. Raymar, Assistant to the Foreign Minister
Consular minute: Received 18 May 1944 R. A. Consular stamp: Paris Consulate-General, no. 746, 18 May 1944.

r. TURKISH CONSULATE (PARIS) ASKS TURKISH EMBASSY (BERLIN) TO INTERVENE WITH GERMAN AUTHORITIES TO SECURE RELEASE OF LEON FARHI FAMILY AND 43 OTHER JEWISH TURKS IMPRISONED IN FRANCE FOR NO REASON DURING SPRING OF 1944. Turkish Consulate-General (Paris) to Turkish Embassy (Berlin) no. 1086/22, 14 June 1944. Archives of Turkish Consulate-General (Paris)

Republic of Turkey, Consulate-General (Paris)
no. 1086/22, 14 June 1944

---

314. The enclosure was not found in the Turkish Embassy Archives.

To the Ambassador in Berlin,

It has come to our attention that, despite our informing the German Ambassador, the French government, and the responsible German and French police authorities that Leon Farhi, his wife and daughter, are Turkish citizens who should be released immediately, that they have been deported to an unknown place and fate in Germany along with 43 other Jewish Turks who are properly registered as Turkish citizens with this Consulate.

I respectfully ask, therefore, that you intervene with the highest authorities of the German government to secure their release. With deepest respects,

(**signed**) Consul-General of Turkey (Paris)

s. TURKISH CONSULATE (PARIS) INFORMS TURKISH FOREIGN MINISTRY THAT GERMANS STATE WHEREABOUTS OF LEON FARHI FAMILY AND THIRTY ONE OTHER JEWISH TURKS DEPORTED TO GERMANY FROM FRANCE IS UNKNOWN AND THAT NO JEWS REMAIN IN THE DRANCY CAMP. Turkish Consul-General (Paris) to Foreign Ministry no. 746/182, Paris, 19 June 1944. Archives of the Turkish Consulate (Paris).

Republic of Turkey, Paris Consulate-General
no. 746/182, Paris, 19 June 1944
Regarding the Yuda Farhi and his family

This is a response to your letter no. 26247-69 of 8 April 1944. I am enclosing copies of two reports which I sent to our Paris and Berlin embassies on 8 May 1944 regarding the arrest and deportation by the Germans of Yuda (Leon) Farhi and his family, the subject of the petition presented to Higher Authorities of the state by Salamon Cemil Farhi in Istanbul. In the answer now received in response to our efforts with the German authorities in Paris asking that they investigate the location and secure the return of about thirty Jewish Turkish citizens who were arrested by the German police and after being kept in concentration camps for a time deported, they state that after the release of a few individuals remaining in the camp, there are no other Turkish citizens at the Drancy camp, and that there is no information on the present location of thirty one people on the list. Our Berlin Embassy, to whom I communicated this matter, is now making efforts with the German Foreign Ministry for the return to Turkey of the thirty one Turkish Jewish citizens who were deported from France.

I communicate this matter with my deepest respect.

(signed) The Consul-General

t. FARHI FAMILY COMPLAINS THAT TURKISH CONSULATE IN PARIS SHOULD HAVE DONE MORE TO RESCUE LEON FARHI AND FAMILY. Albert Sevi, 16, Avenue du Général Clavery, Paris, XVI France, to Turkish Ambassador (Vichy), 16 April 1945. Archives of Turkish Embassy (Paris).

Paris, 16 April 1945

To The Ambassador of the Turkish Republic to the Provisional Government of the French Republic

33, Rue de Villejust, Paris, XVI

Mr. Ambassador

As a result of the special broadcast relative to Jewish deportees on French Radio yesterday Sunday the 15th of April at 1:45 p.m., I have the honor to bring the following facts to your attention.

About 20 December 1943, I was advised by letter from Bordeaux that Mr. Leon Farhi, his wife Regina Farhi (my sister-in-law), born Alfandary, as well as their daughter Arlette Farhi, now aged 12 1/2 years, entirely in order with their Turkish nationality and inscribed on the registers of the Turkish Consulate in Paris, had been arrested by the German occupation authorities and sent to the concentration camp at Mérigny, 4 kilometers from Bordeaux. As soon as I received this letter, I hurried to Mr. Consul-General in order to ask him to intervene as a matter of urgency to secure their immediate liberation. Mr. Leon Farhi, as he was usually referred to in Bordeaux, had more than a month earlier sent to the Turkish Consulate in Paris his Turkish nationality cards to secure their renewal. I asked the Consul-General to return them as a matter of urgency in order to secure their release from the camp at Mérignac. Leon Farhi had asked for their return several time before his arrest, without ever having received them.

On 31 December 1943, about a dozen days after their arrest, the cards still had not reached them despite my pressing demands made daily to the Consul-General, and unhappily all three persons were interned at the Drancy camp. I presented myself again to the Consul to inform him that the three absent dear ones had arrived at Drancy, and to ask him to again do all that was necessary to secure their freedom. Through several secret letters sent from within the camp, with an emotion easy to understand, I learned that the Farhi family, because it was impossible to prove their Turkish nationality due to lack of their nationality cards, had been assigned to deportation. I went once again to the Consul to inform him of the great peril that the Farhi family was in, and to beg him to go himself in person to Drancy to snatch them from deportation, and perhaps from death. Consuls of other foreign countries have taken the initiative to make such démarches as I asked him to do, and have succeeded to freeing their defenseless citizens from the hands of the barbarous and cruel Germans, and I believe from this that had the same effort been made by the Turkish consul the Farhi family would be safe and sound today.

Unhappily, despite my numerous visits to the Turkish Consulate and the supplications of my wife who accompanied me, I learned that the Farhi family was deported on 20 January 1944, that is three weeks after their arrival at Drancy. I wish to remark respectfully to the Ambassador that he should have immediately used all his power as representative of the Turkish Republic, and even more of a country that was neutral at the time, that he should have asked for and energetically demanded, the liberation of citizens of the Turkish Republic in the briefest possible time, and in this way stop their deportation. I went again to the Consul to inform him of this bad news, but the only answer he gave me was to inform me that he had not been advised officially of this. I greatly regret that I must inform you of all these details, each of which has its importance but you will understand, Mr. Ambassador, that our heart and thoughts do not cease to be with our absent ones, of whom we have had no news since 20 January 1944, the day of their deportation. Several members of the Farhi family, both those in Paris and abroad, and for whom I am their interpreter, have charged me to write you to ask you respectfully to intervene, if possible by diplomatic means, and as rapidly as possible, with the Soviet and Polish authorities to seek out these three persons in case they have had the good fortune of being freed by the Allied armies. I still hope that these three persons will return in good health, for the unpardonable negligence of the Consul could have had very serious consequences, which I am sure you realize. I believe it is my duty to inform you that the father of Mr. Leon Farhi, Mr. Cemil Farhi, in Turkey since February 1944, was an official of the Turkish state for more than forty years, and as such as full right to your protection.

With the warm thanks of all the members of the family for all you might be able to undertake in the interest of our three dear absent ones, and in the expectation of receiving favorable news from you, I ask you, Mr. Ambassador, to accept the expression of my high consideration.

(signed) Albert Sevi
Albert Sevi,
16 Avenue du Général Clavery XVI.

u. TURKISH AMBASSADOR TO PARIS ASKS TURKISH CONSULATE (PARIS) FOR INFORMATION REGARDING TREATMENT OF LEON FARHI CASE, IN RESPONSE TO LETTER OF ALBERT SEVI. Ambassador Numan Menemencioğlu to Paris Consulate-General, no. 310, Paris, 11 May 1945. Archives of Turkish Embassy, Paris.

Republic of Turkey, Paris Embassy
no. 310, Paris, 11 May 1945

To the Paris Consulate-General
A copy of the letter sent to the Embassy regarding the situation of one of our fellow countrymen in France, Leon Farhi and his family, has been sent. I ask the Consulate-General to provide whatever information it has on this matter.

The Ambassador
(signed) N. Menemencioğlu
Consular notation: received 12 May 1945
Consular stamp: Paris Consulate no. 519, 12 May 1945.

v. TURKISH CONSULATE (PARIS) EXPLAINS ITS ACTIONS IN LEON FARHI CASE TO TURKISH EMBASSY (PARIS). Turkish Consul-General (Paris) to Turkish Ambassador (Paris) no. 519/43, 25 May 1945. Archives of the Turkish Embassy (Paris).

Republic of Turkey, Consulate-General of Turkey
Paris, 25 May 1945,
no. 519/43

To the Paris Embassy,
This is response to your letter no. 310 of 11 May 1945
Leon Farhi and his family were Turkish citizens who were properly registered at our Consulate-General. Investigation into the Farhi dossier reveals that the Consulate-General was informed by a letter from Mme Herend that Mr. Farhi, along with his wife and daughter, were arrested by the Germans on 21 December 1943. Immediately after receiving this letter, on 23 December 1943 in letters no. F 3091 and F 3092, the Consulate-General wrote the German Embassy in Paris and the Préfect of Gironde in Bordeaux informing them that the members of this family were Turkish citizens and asking that they be immediately released.

To the letter sent to the Préfecturate was attached the Certificate of Citizenship extended by the Consulate-General. When no answer was received from the German Embassy after a short time, the Consul-General at that time made secret personal contacts with that Embassy.

The Préfecturate of the Gironde answered that the family had been moved from the Mérignac camp to the Drancy camp. Again according to the information in the dossier, the necessary efforts were made with the proper authorities in this matter, informing them that this family was composed of Turkish citizens and asking that they be released, including a letter dated 30 December 1943 to the commander of the camp at Drancy.

According to the Consul-General at that time, the members of the Leon Farhi family were among forty three members of Turkish Jewish families that were arrested by the Germans at that time for no reason, that he made numerous secret efforts with the German police to secure their release, and that when positive results were not achieved, he informed our Berlin Embassy in a letter no. 1086/22 of 14 June 1944, asking it to intervene with the German government to secure their release. Since it was impossible to search the camps in Germany for our imprisoned Jewish fellow citizens after Turkey broke relations with Germany, this matter was carried out by the Swiss Embassy in Berlin, but despite their efforts no information has been secured to this date.

I communicate this information with my deepest respects.

(**signed**) Consul-General

TURKISH ASSISTANCE TO THE JEWS OF GREECE UNDER NAZI OCCUPATION

Detailed studies remain to be undertaken regarding the assistance given to Jewish Turks by Turkish diplomats in Germany as well as Nazi-occupied territory outside of France during the Second World War, though there are indications that Turkey was able to provide some help in Belgium, the Netherlands, Spain and Italy in particular. The recent researches of Yitzhak Kerem (Israel) have, however, together with accounts by the survivors, provided a good deal of information regarding the important role played by Turkish diplomats in saving Jews in Greece during the war.[315] Kerem points out that those of the Jewish Turks who had gone to Greece as part of the exchanges of population carried out in 1922 between Greece and Turkey following the Turkish War for Independence, but who had kept their Turkish citizenship throughout these years despite Greek pressure for them to defect, were assisted by the Turkish representatives in Athens and Salonica to retain their properties and lives once the Germans replaced the Italians in occupation of the country and began to carry out anti-Jewish measures starting in April 1941. Just as was the case in Paris, Lyon and Marseilles, moreover, so also in Athens and Salonica, staff members of the Turkish consulates in Greece certified the Turkish citizenship of Greek Jews who were in danger, and at times issued false citizenship and identity papers to rescue those who had lost their Turkish citizenship because of failure to register with the local Turkish consulates during the 1920s and 1930s.[316]

---

315. Yitzhak Kerem, 'Efforts to Rescue the Jews of Greece during the Second World War', (in Hebrew), *Pe'amim*, no. 27 (1986), pp. 77–109.

316. Kerem, p. 86.

Under the leadership of Solomon Berki, regular escapes were arranged by train through Nazi-held Western Thrace to Haydari, on foot to the towns of Demotica, Neah, Orestias and Sufli along the Turkish border, or to the village of Emorion, near the Maritza River, from which the refugees walked or swam across the border to safety in Turkey.[317]

While in most European countries occupied by the Nazis, including even Germany itself, many native Christian citizens generously assisted Jews to hide from their persecutors, and when possible to escape entirely, few Greeks helped their Jewish fellow citizens, with the sole exception of a handful in Athens, and most actively cooperated with the persecution and deportations.[318] Even the Greek partisans generally charged as much as five British sovereigns (thirty Palestinian pounds) for each Jew they helped in this manner, although those who fought alongside Jews against the German occupiers were sometimes more generous.[319] Other escapes were carried out by a coalition of Mossad agents based in Istanbul[320] and British intelligence officers from Egypt who cooperated with Greek partisans to ferry Jews in small boats across the Aegean via the island of Çeşme to Izmir, where they were cared for by the local Jewish community.[321] Most of these refugees were sent on to Palestine in small boats arranged by Mossad agents.

Contact between Jews in Greece and Izmir were organized by Beni Arkadi, a wealthy Izmir businessman, and Raphael Barki, who had earlier escaped from Greece to Izmir and who throughout 1943 and 1944 maintained contacts with his brother in Athens through the Greek

---

317. Kerem, pp. 86–87, 93; Kerem, 'The Glory of the Sephardic Community of Salonika and its Destruction in the Holocaust,' American Sephardi Federation Annual Convention, Chicago, Ill., 2-4 September 1990, 'The Jews of Greece and Salonika in the Holocaust,' B'nai Brith Hillel Foundation Lecture, University of Minnesota, 15 October 1991.

318. Kerem, p. 100; Rae Dalven, *The Jews of Ioannina* (Philadelphia, Pa., 1990), pp. 38–47.

319. Avneri, *Velos,* p. 356; Steven Bowman, 'Joseph Matsas and the Greek Resistance', *Journal of the Hellenic Diaspora* XVII (1991), pp. 49–53; Joseph Matsas, 'The Participation of the Greek Jews in the National Resistance, 1940-1945', ed. Steven Bowman, *Journal of the Hellenic Diaspora* XVII (1991), pp. 55–68; P.J. Vatikiotis, *Among Arabs and Jews: A Personal Experience, 1936–1990* (London, Weidenfeld and Nicolson, 1991); Rae Dalven, *The Jews of Ioannina* (Philadelphia, 1990), pp. 38–49.

320. See p. 268 .

321. Arieh Avneri, *From 'Velos' to 'Taurus', The First Jewish 'Illegal' Immigration to Mandatory Palestine, 1934-1944* (Tel Aviv, 1985), pp. 355–356.

partisans.[322] Among the Greek politicians who used this route for their own escape was George Papandreou, who went to Cairo to join the Greek government in exile, and who became Prime Minister of Greece following the war. It is estimated that approximately 859 Jews from Greece reached Izmir, and later Palestine, in this manner.Some of the refugees were occasionally sent back to Greece by local border guards because of the lack of papers or visas, but in most cases they were welcomed by the Turkish soldiers, who helped them cross to the Turkish side of the border, as related by a number of veterans of Turkey's Thracian border guards, including an officer in the Edirne district at the time, Emin Kural, father of the author's wife, Ezel Kural Shaw.[323]

Those Jewish families from Athens who could avoid the Nazi nets escaped to monasteries at Mount Athos from which small boats carried them to refuge in Turkey, though sometimes it took months of concealment before transportation could be arranged.[324] Ninety-one percent of the approximately 2,000 Jews living at Janina were deported and killed by the Germans, principally in 1944.[325] When the Jews of Kastoria, slightly south of the Albanian border on the Adriatic, were captured by the Germans and sent to Auschwitz following their replacement of the Italians early in 1944, only two families were freed, both because they were proven to be Turkish citizens through the vigorous intervention of the Turkish Embassy in Athens.[326] While the Bulgarian army occupying part of Greek Macedonia ruthlessly deported all the Jews living there into German hands for extermination at Auschwitz, the Bulgarians allowed Jewish Turks to live freely in their own country, and that it was for the most part the latter who subsequently fled across the border into Turkey and from there to Palestine.[327]

---

322. Avneri, *Velos*, p. 355.

323. His wife, Mrs. Seniha Kural, related that she was visited almost daily by Jewish women from Edirne. When asked why, she was told that they figured that so long as the Turkish officer kept his wife in Edirne, they reasoned that the Nazis would not come, and that they were reasonably safe, at least for the moment.

324. This information is based on Kerem's interviews in Athens with Moshe Dolinsky on 16 December 1985 and 23 February 1986 and with Moshe Nahmias on 19 January 1986, cited in Kerem, p. 100.

325. Dalven, *The Jews of Ioannina*, pp. 38–45.

326. Kerem, p. 102.

327. Kerem, pp. 95–96; Kerem,, 'The Bulgarian Deportation of the Jews of Macedonia, Pirot and Thrace,' 21st Annual Conference of the Association for Jewish Studies, Boston, Mass., 17–19 December 1989.

Turkish and Greek Jews alike were deported to the death camps from the island of Corfu,[328] but on the island of Rhodes, where Jews had prospered during three hundred ninety years of Ottoman rule until 1917 and under Italian occupation from then until 1943, Turkey's Consul, Selahattin Ülkümen, saved the Turkish citizens among the Jewish colony of some 2,000 after the Germans took over the island following Mussolini's removal from power and Italy's armistice with the Allies. On 19 July 1944 the Gestapo ordered all of the island's Jewish population to gather at its headquarters in order register for 'temporary transportation to a small island nearby', but in fact to send them to the gas chambers at Auschwitz. Ülkümen went to the German commanding officer, General Kleeman, reminded him that Turkey was neutral in the war, and asked him to release forty-two Jews, including not only those who were Turkish citizens but also their spouses and relatives, even though many of the latter were Italian and Greek citizens. Some time earlier Ülkümen had secured the release of thirty-nine Turkish and Greek boatmen who had been condemned to death for taking Italian soldiers to refuge in Turkey following the German occupation, but this time the commander at first refused, stating that under Nazi law all Jews were Jews and had to go to the concentration camps. Ülkümen responded by quoting his instructions received from Ankara, the same as those sent to Paris, that 'under Turkish law all citizens were equal. We didn't differentiate between citizens who were Jewish, Christian or Muslim'. He went on to inform Kleeman that 'I would advise my Government if he didn't release the Jewish Turks . . . it would cause an international incident. Then he agreed'.

The Jews protected by Ülkümen were released, though not until they were subjected to considerable additional harassment by the Nazi authorities. Ülkümen, however, continued to provide protection and moral support to those whom he had rescued and who remained on the island, all of whom were in mortal fear that they would also suffer the same fate since they still were required to report to the Gestapo daily and never knew whether or not they would be able to return to their homes. Soon afterwards, the Greek Jews on Rhodes, numbering 1,673 in all, were deported to Greece, and from there onward to extermination, with only one hundred and fifty one surviving the war. In retaliation for his assistance to Rhodes' Jews, immediately after Turkey joined the Allies and declared war on the Axis, German planes bombed the Turkish consulate, killing Ülkümen's pregnant wife Mihrinissa Hanım as well as two other employees

328. Pearl Liba Preschel, *The Jews of Corfu*, Unpublished Ph.D. dissertation, New York University, 1984.

and deported Ülkümen to Piraeus, on mainland Greece, where he spent the remainder of the war in confinement.

During the next six months the forty-two Jewish Turks remaining on Rhodes were subjected to almost constant harassment by the Gestapo, which often detained them for long periods of time, though it did not deport them as planned, presumably because of the disorder which spread throughout the Third Reich during the last days of the war. Finally early in January, 1945, when the German commander learned that representatives of the International Red Cross were about to visit Rhodes to look into the situation of its population, most likely to avoid the very damaging testimony as to their treatment which would have been given, he ordered the remaining Jews to go to Turkey, which they did the next day, in small boats across a stormy sea to safety at the port of Marmaris, a journey strangely symbolic of the exodus of the Sephardic Jews from Spain through the Mediterranean to welcome in Ottoman Turkey following their expulsion by the Inquisition in 1492. [329]

The head of the thirty-five person Jewish community that remained on Rhodes following the war, Maurice Sauriano, recently stated 'I am indebted to the Turkish Consul who made extraordinary efforts to save my life and those of my fellow countrymen'. As a result of the efforts of Quincentennial Foundation Vice President, historian Naim Güleryüz, who amassed the necessary testimony from those survivors who were still living, Ülkümen was honored by the Yad Vashem Foundation of Israel on 13 December 1989 as a 'righteous Gentile', one of those non Jews who risked their own lives to rescue Jews subjected to persecution and death by the Nazis, with his name being inscribed and a tree planted in his honor at the 'Path of the Righteous.'

---

329. These events are detailed in: Naim Güleryüz, 'Temmuz 1944–Rodos: Selahattin Ülkümen ve Matilde Turiel', *Şalom*, 25 April 1990; Naim Güleryüz, 'Türk Konsolosu'nin ölümünden döndürdüğü 42 Yahudi', *Yaşam* (monthly supplement to *Şalom*), August 1986, pp. 10–13; See also Rabbi Marc D. Angel, *The Jews of Rhodes: The History of a Sephardic Community* (New York, 1980), pp. 151–153; Joseph Nehama, *In Memoriam: Hommage aux Victimes Juives des Nazis en Grèce* (2 vols, Salonica, 1949) II, 74–76; Yossef Ben, *Greece in the Holocaust* (in Hebrew) (Tel Aviv, 1985), p. 62; Avram Galante, *Appendice à l'Histoire des Juifs de Rhodes* (Istanbul, 1948), pp. 38–40; Hizkia M. Franco, *Les Martyrs juifs de Rhodes et de Cos* (Elisabethville, Katanga, 1952); Rachel A. Bortnick, 'Rightous Gentile: Selahattin Ülkümen', *A.A.J.F.T. Newsletter*, September 1991, p. 6; Kerem, p. 105.

3

Istanbul Activities in Rescuing European Jews from the Nazis

In evaluating Turkey's role in rescuing European Jewry from the Holocaust, it is instructive to compare its position as a neutral country in relation to the Jewish Agency for Palestine and other such rescue organizations with those of neutral Switzerland and Rumania, whose situation and policies were quite different. Istanbul and Geneva were the leading cities of the most important neutral countries in Europe during World War II, a situation which enabled them to become the major rescue centers of the time. In the face of wartime pressures, however, each had to limit the rescue operations in different ways in accorance with their understanding of the dangers which might have to be faced if their neutrality was breached by these operations. Switzerland, never was under direct Nazi threat of invasion, so it was able to follow a policy of theoretical neutrality, enabling the Jewish Agency to operate with little restriction, though the Swiss did something that the Turks never did. They usually refused to accept Jewish refugees fleeing across the border from Germany if their passports had been marked 'Jew' by the Nazis. Rumania, on the other hand, in the light of its historic anti-Semitism, fully accepted and approved the Final Solution, and in response to British pressure to prevent Jews from leaving so they would not go to Palestine, imposed a prohibition on Jewish refugees passing through Rumanian ports and cooperated with Adolph Eichmann's agents in deporting its large Jewish population to the extermination camps until the impending Allied victory convinced it to alter its policy.[330]

Turkey, on the other hand, was compelled to be a neutral state in practice, since it was under immediate threat of Nazi invasion from Greece or across the Black Sea and through the Caucasus, initially by the Soviet

---

330. Ofer, *Escaping the Holocaust*, pp. 187–188.

Union and later by the invading German army. It also was being pressured by its British ally to prohibit all aid to Jewish refugees, and in fact not to admit them at all, even when Germany was allowing them to leave, because of Britain's fear that they would go on to Palestine. In response to these pressures and dangers, Turkey at times officially prohibited all activities by foreign rescue organizations such as the Jewish Agency, and closely watched the activities of all foreign groups operating in the country, but even at such times it in fact condoned and even assisted the rescue operations far more significantly than any other neutral country in Europe throughout the war.

Turkey was of unique importance to all those who wanted to help European Jews being subjected to increasing persecution by the Nazis. It was close to Nazi-occupied southeastern and eastern Europe. It was the locale of representatives not only of the western Allies but also of most of the European governments in exile. It was the key, moreover, to the only escape route left for Jewish refugees going from Europe to Palestine once the route previously used by the Jewish Agency's Geneva Office through France to Marseilles, and from there across the Mediterranean to Palestine, was closed as a result of the German occupation of France and Italy's entry into the war during the summer of 1940. Turkey consequently came to constitute a true 'Bridge to Palestine', a transit center that enabled Jews being persecuted in their own countries to go on to the Holy Land, both by land and sea, making possible the salvation of thousands who would otherwise have been exterminated.[331]

The Geneva office of the Jewish Agency, directed by Richard Lichtheim and Chaim Pazner, remained a center of Jewish efforts to help and rescue Jews in western Europe, but the Istanbul office became far more important and active as the war and the Holocaust progressed. Part of the reason for this was, simply, its location. It was far closer to Palestine than was Switzerland. Switzerland was surrounded by the Nazis on all sides, while Turkey had direct access by land to Europe on one side and to Iraq and Syria on the other, as well as to the Black Sea and across the Mediterranean, to Palestine. Moreover Switzerland in many ways shared Nazi hatred of the Jews, and in any case was determined not to compromise its neutrality by going out of its way to help them in any way. Turkey also did not wish to stimulate a Nazi attack, but much of its restrictive policies seem to have

---

331. Barlas, *ibid.*

been only for show, while it in fact assisted the Jewish Agency in a massive way to carry out its activities.[332]

Because of its strategic location and the willingness of its government to help, then, Istanbul replaced Geneva as the center of the Jewish Agency refugee operations just as Germany shifted from a policy of deporting Jews or encouraging their emigration, to one of extermination, the Final Solution. The 'Eretz Israel Delegation in Istanbul',[333] operating as agent of the Jerusalem Rescue Council (*Vaad ha-Hatzala*), previously established in Palestine by the Jewish Agency to assist European Jews being persecuted by the Nazis, was led from early December 1940 until 1945 by Chaim (Haim, Charles) Barlas, who had been head of the Jewish Agency Immigration Department in Jerusalem during the previous decade, and more recently director of its Geneva office.[334] Barlas also represented the Jewish Agency in Istanbul as head of its Immigration (*Aliyah*) Department and Palestine Office, and in addition acted as World Jewish Congress Representative in Turkey from 1941 to 1943.[335] Eliahu Eilat (Epstein), who had been appointed to direct the Istanbul office by the Jewish Agency's political department at a time when Istanbul still was considered of lesser importance than Geneva, now assisted Barlas along with Dr. Joseph Golden of the Palestine (*Eretz Israel*) Bureau's *Aliyah* department, who had been in Turkey since before the war, and Ruben Resnik, representative of the American Jewish Joint Distribution Committee, who maintained offices at the American Consulate in the Tepebaşı section of Istanbul, overlooking the Golden Horn.[336]

From headquarters divided between the Pera Palas and Continental hotels, also located at Tepebaşı, near the British and American embassies

---

332. This was the gist of Shertock's report to the Executive meeting of the Jewish Agency in Tel Aviv on 22 August 1943. Dina Porat, *Entangled Leadership*, p. 262.

333. J. Brand, *The Satan and the Soul* (in Hebrew) (Tel Aviv, 1960), 34; I. Wiesman, *Confronting the Mighty Evil* (in Hebrew) (Tel Aviv, 1968), 44–46; Shabtai Tevet, *David's Envy, III, The Burning Soil* (in Hebrew) (Jerusalem, 1987), 432; Eliahu Stern, 'The Contacts between the Delegation in Israel and Polish Jewry', *Yalkut Moreshet*, no. 39 (May 1985), p. 135

334. Barlas's own account of his role in establishing the Istanbul office of the Jewish Agency is in Barlas, *ibid.*, p. 102 and *passim*.

335. The mimeographed newsletters in Hebrew of *Vaad Hatzalah*, giving detailed reports on Nazi atrocities against Jews, particularly at the Sobibor death camp, are found in the Vad Vashem Central Archives (Jerusalem) for the years from 1940–1947.

336. The archives of this Istanbul mission and from the Rescue Center in Istanbul are among the Records of the *Histadrut* Executive (Tel Aviv), H–CL/37, box no. 666 (1943–1945).

and as far as possible from the German Embassy, whose agents established themselves at the Park Hotel, at the other end of Beyoğlu near the German Embassy located at Taksim Square, Barlas and his colleagues established branches at Ankara, Izmir and Edirne to carry out monumental the task of rescuing Jews persecuted throughout Europe, and particularly in Eastern Europe. The Istanbul office originally had been subordinate to that established by the Jewish Agency in Geneva in its task of getting information about what was happening to Jews in Nazi-occupied Europe as well as helping them with food and medicine, but as Sweden as well as Switzerland became isolated and unhelpful due to the developing Nazi power and consequent pressure starting early in 1942, Barlas's Istanbul office became increasingly important and in fact the center of all the Jewish Agency rescue operations in Europe. [337]

The first problem that Barlas faced involved thousands of Jews stranded in Lithuania and Rumania after the Mediterranean route was closed due to the German occupation of France and invasion of Yugoslavia and Greece, and also after the Final Solution was put into effect and further Jewish emigration from Hitler's Europe prohibited. Turkey until that point had itself forbidden the passage of refugees through the Black Sea to the Mediterranean and beyond and had greatly limited the activities of foreign agencies in its country, except those directly related to running religious and charity institutions such as hospitals and orphanages, in order to preserve its neutrality and forestall the possibility of a Nazi invasion following the collapse of Greece. Arriving in Istanbul in late August 1940, however, Barlas successfully moved to change this policy. He secured the assistance of Sami Gunzberg, a Hungarian Jew who had intervened in the 1930s to secure European financial assistance for Turkey's industrialization programs led by its President, Mustafa Kemal Atatürk, and who had also served as Atatürk's dentist before the latter's death in 1938. Through Gunzberg's good offices, he soon was in contact with leading officials of the government in Ankara, including Atatürk's successor as President, Ismet İnönü, who personally approved Turkey's cooperation in the rescue effort but insisted that its interest be kept quiet due to his fears of stimulating a German invasion.[338]

---

337. Porat, *Blue and Yellow*, pp. 116–120.

338. Chaim Weizmann to Sami Gunzberg, 20 August and 7 September 1940. Chaim Weizmann Archives (Jerusalem). Quoted in Michael J. Cohen, ed., *The Letters and Papers of Chaim Weizmann. Series A. Letters. XX (July 1940–January 1943)* (New Brunswick, N.J., 1974), p. 68.

As a result of this encouragement, on 9 October 1940 Barlas presented the Turkish government with an official memorandum describing the plight of European Jewry, and in particular that of Jewish refugees then scattered all over neighboring countries and being subjected to persecution, not only by the Nazis, but also by their local sympathizers. Recalling Turkish assistance to Jewish refugees from persecution over the centuries, he asked Turkey to abandon its previous restrictions on immigrants and instead to make special provisions for the passage of these refugees who were fleeing through southeastern Europe, and who had already received British permits to land in Palestine if they could only get there:

(1). The quota of immigration certificates for workers, students, etc. is assigned each semester by the Government of Palestine to the Jewish Agency for Palestine, which destines them in favor of Jewish immigrants. It is to the Jewish Agency for Palestine also that falls the task of financing the immigrants as well as the ability to establish them in Palestine.

(2). Immigration to Palestine, whatever may have been the difficulties that have had to be overcome since war broke out, will not continue unless it is pursued. The Jewish Agency for Palestine opened for this purpose, even before the declaration of war, a temporary bureau at Geneva to arrange for immigration to Palestine. Supported by the consulates of His Britannic Majesty in neutral countries, it has arranged the immigration of about 8,000 refugees from Germany, Lithuania, Rumania, etc. These immigrants were sent on their way, until the declaration of war, by Italy in compact groups through Trieste and Marseilles to Palestine.

(3). In June 1940, after the entry of Italy into the war, it became impossible for reasons that are very well known, to achieve transport by boat to Palestine across the Mediterranean. The sole possible route that remained was that by land across Turkey and Syria, with the immigrants using the Istanbul-Tripoli railroad, going on by car to Haifa.

(4). These immigrants are approved through the efforts of the Jewish Agency for Palestine, on the basis of certificates of immigration approved by the Government of Palestine. Each immigrant who possesses a certificate of immigration, receives the Palestine visa through a British Consulate, giving him the right of definitive establishment in the country. The transit visa for Syria is given on the basis of his entry visa for Palestine.

(5). The organization of immigration by this path unfortunately is blocked by the refusal of Turkish transit visas for Polish and former German Jewish immigrants. This problem hurts the Jewish refugees in the most difficult way after they have lived through the worst possible experiences and misery and seek by immigration their only means to regain their health and lives.

(6). The Jewish Agency for Palestine permits itself to submit in this way its request to the Government of the Republic of Turkey asking it to transmit instructions to its consulates in Bucharest, Belgrade, Geneva, Kaunas, Stockholm and Salonica, authorizing them to give Turkish transit visas to all those who have certificates of immigration and entry visas to Palestine, regardless of their passport.

(7). In order to assure in an indisputable manner the continuation of their trip on to Palestine, we propose the following procedure:

a) The transportation of immigrants will be carried out in groups by boat or train to Istanbul, continuing immediately without stop from Haydarpaşa by train for Syria.

b) Part of the immigrants will ultimately arrive by boat at Iskenderun (Alexandretta), going on without stop to Syria by car.

c) During the time the immigrants are on the train, they will be escorted by members of the Turkish police.

d) The Jewish Agency for Palestine is entirely ready to provide whatever financial bond is required, fixed by the Government of the Republic of Turkey, guaranteeing the immediate departure from Turkish soil of all the immigrants who will remain in Turkey only during the time necessary to carry out the formalities needed for the trip.

(8). The Jewish Agency for Palestine is happy to recall in these circumstances the extremely humanitarian treatment given by Turkey to the Jews over the centuries and expresses the hope that the Government of the Republic of Turkey will furnish the means, in these difficult times for the Jewish people, to give these immigrants the means to reach the goal of their travels, Palestine.[339]

In response to this appeal, and in the face of German demands that Turkey refuse to accept new Jewish emigrants from Germany, and even that it return all those who had already arrived, on 30 January 1941 the Turkish government promulgated the special Transit Law no. 2/15132 (*Transit Geçme Kararnamesi*), modeled on similar regulations in force in Great Britain, which permitted the settlement in Turkey of certain categories refugees being persecuted in their own countries, in imitation of the restrictions then imposed by Britain and the United States, and also allowed thousands more Jewish refugees to transit through Turkey on their way to Palestine and other places so long as they held valid visas to enter these countries after leaving Turkey:

Republic of Turkey, Prime Minister's Office
Department of Decisions (*Kararlar dairesi Müdürlüğü*)
no. 2/15132

DECISION (*Kararname*)
In cases where the measures taken concerning Jewish foreign subjects who are pressured in their own countries do not entirely meet today's situation, ordinance no. 2/9498 dated 29 August 1938 will be replaced by the application of the following measures, which were accepted at the meeting of the Council of Ministers on 30 January 1941 upon Ministry of Foreign Affairs request no. 98/33 dated 22 January 1941.

(1). The entry into and establishment in Turkey of Jewish individuals–whatever their religion is today–who are subjected to restrictions in regard to living and travel by the countries of which they are citizens, is forbidden. In the countries which subject their Jewish subjects to restrictions, the Consulates of Turkey to whom requests for visas are made will ask the persons concerned to show a certificate provided by the competent local authorities attesting that they are not among those Jews subjected to restrictions.

(2). The question of determining which governments subject their Jewish subjects to restrictions and of advising the relevant

---

339. Barlas, *ibid.*, pp. 222–223.

Turkish authorities of this, will be carried out by the Ministry of Foreign Affairs.

(3). For those whose employment is needed by the departments and institutions of Turkey or persons whose commercial or economic utility is recognized by the appropriate official authorities and whose entry into the country and regarding whom no barrier to their residence in this country is seen by the Ministry of the Interior, upon application mentioning the need and use of their residence, the Ministry of Foreign Affairs can apply to the Council of Ministers for special permission for entry visas for such persons. If Jews included in this clause wish to bring with them their mothers and fathers whom they care for, their male sons who have not yet reached their majority, and their unmarried daughters, they should make their request to the Ministry of Foreign Affairs, which is free to accept or refuse such requests. Specialists can stay in Turkey only for the duration of their employment. At the end of this period, if another decision has not been made by the Cabinet, neither their stay in Turkey nor that of their relatives mentioned in the preceding paragraph can be extended. If the work of persons permitted to enter the country because of their commercial or economic use requires them to continuously leave and re-enter Turkey, this will be arranged according to the decision taken by the Cabinet, which will determine the number of times that the persons concerned can enter Turkey during each period of six months and how many days they can remain their after each arrival.

(4). The prohibitions of this regulation do not apply to Jews of foreign citizenship who permanently resided in Turkey for a time before 29 August 1938. For the latter, those who leave temporarily for a period no longer than six months can obtain entry visas for their return certified by the consulates of Turkey.

(5). The prohibitions of this regulation concern Jews whose residence in Turkey is limited and who are subjected to restrictions in their own countries; on condition that:

(a) they possess entry visas for the country they are going to, or transit visas for the country through which they will pass after Turkey, or just an entry visa for the first country to which they will go after leaving Turkey;

(b) possess at the least tickets for transporting them across Turkish frontiers to foreign countries, the consulates of Turkey may give them transit visas without asking for permission. Those who secure visas for transit in this way must cross the frontiers of Turkey at the latest fifteen days before the final date of the visa of the first country which they will reach after leaving Turkey.

(6). For Jews subjected to restrictions, the Ministry of Foreign Affairs will determine the maximum number of transit visas which can be issued by each Consulate during each two week period. In case requests for transit visas would result in a situation taking on the aspect of a mass immigration, the consulates will inform the Ministry of Foreign Affairs of the situation. If it sees the need for it, it can increase proportionally the number of transit visas which it fixed previously. In this case, the consulates will give transit visas relating to the date of the visas held by the persons concerned for the first country that they will reach after leaving our territory.

(7). Consulates giving transit visas by this regulation will register them and draw up tables which they will post on the first and sixteenth day of each month to the Foreign Affairs Ministry.

(8). To arrange transit matters of persons subjected to this regulation regarding their stay in Turkey, and to make certain that they leave within fifteen days, there will be regular contacts between the Director of the Consular Section of the Ministry of Foreign Affairs and Ministry of Transportation. 31 January 1941.
President of the Republic Ismet Inönü
Prime Minister Dr. Refik Saydam
Minister of Finance F. Ağrali
Minister of Public Works Ali Fuad Cebesoy
Minister of Justice Fethi Okyar
Minister of Education Hasan Ali Yucel
Minister of National Defense S. Arıkan
Minister of the Interior Faik Öztrak
Minister of Foreign Affairs S. Saraçoğlu[340]

---

340. Text in Barlas, *ibid.*, pp. 228–233. Cohen, ed. *Chaim Weizmann*, XX, 68. Also Sami Gunzberg to Captain Whithall, British Passport officer in Istanbul, 23 January 1941, in Central Zionist Archives, A 169/2. 'Haim Barlas informed Weizmann on 20 February 1941 that the Turkish Government had published regulations giving transit rights through Turkey to all

The *Kararname* was put into effect by a law enacted by the Grand National Assembly on 12 February 1941 which authorized the Jewish Agency office in Istanbul to organize the passage of Jewish immigrants persecuted in their homelands via Turkey to Palestine.[341] Jewish victims of Nazi persecution anywhere in Europe were allowed to pass through Turkey either if they held visas to enter the country to which they would go immediately after leaving Turkey, or at least visas to the country that was their final destination, a major contribution to the Jews who had nowhere else to go. The Turkish Ministry of Finance was authorized to advance hard currency to Barlas and his associates to help them fund their operations and provide food, clothing and supplies to Jews suffering from persecution as well as to pay for their transportation, either for railroad tickets or to charter ships when necessary. Instructions were sent to Turkish consulates throughout Europe ordering them to issue transit visas to Jewish refugees on condition that they had in their possession entry visas or transit visas issued by other countries as well as transportation tickets which would enable them to leave Turkey.[342] It was this act by the Turkish government, more than anything else, that made it possible for the Jewish Agency and its associated organizations to save thousands of East European Jews from the Holocaust.

Chaim Barlas later confirmed this in his memoirs:

> One of the most important reasons for the success of the Jewish immigration to Palestine was the consent of the Turkish government, which even though subject to German influence and under danger of invasion by sea and land, enabled Jewish immigrants to pass through Turkey in accordance with the requests made by the Jewish Agency. The 'Transit Law' which was passed by the Turkish Cabinet on 12 February 1941, became the primary basis of this immigration movement.[343]

Jews guaranteed entry into country of final destination' (Cohen, *Weizmann*, p. 68n). Also Haim Weizmann to Lord Moyne, London, 24 February 1941, quoted in Cohen, ed. *Weizmann*, p. 113–114.

341. Barlas, *ibid.*, appendix documents 232 and 234.

342. Barlas, *ibid.*, pp. 24–25.

343. Barlas, *ibid.*, p. 174.

The Jewish Agency network supplied the refugees not only with British visas to Palestine, as authorized within the severe restrictions of the British White Paper of 1939, but also with passports issued by consuls of a number of Latin American countries as well as of neutral Portugal and Switzerland, documents which came to be known throughout Europe as 'protection certificates'.[344] The refugees were allowed to come to Istanbul in groups, and after staying for a time so that their passage could be arranged, to go on to Palestine by land or sea.[345] Arriving in Istanbul by the same route of the *Orient Express* taken by the Jewish Turks sent back from western Europe by train caravans arranged by the Turkish diplomats in Paris and Brussels,[346] or by boat through the Black Sea, they usually remained at the small hotels grouped around the Sirkeci Railroad terminus, and were accepted as temporary members of the Sirkeci synagogue built in the late nineteenth century opposite the station's railroad tracks to house Jewish refugees fleeing from the Russian pogroms, with their housing, food and clothing provided by local Jewish groups organized and directed by the Chief Rabbinate of Istanbul as well as by the Jewish Agency. As a result of constant British and German pressure, the Turkish government itself did not openly assist the refugees while they were in Turkey waiting for transportation or visas to go on to Palestine. However, it did nothing to stop local Jewish groups from providing assistance to the refugees, and it in fact provided them with facilities to secure hard currency, food, and other supplies as needed.

Many of those who already had official visas to enter Palestine were quickly transported from Sirkeci across the Sea of Marmara to Haydarpaşa, locale of the terminus of the Anatolian Railroad system. Just as was the case for those remaining at Sirkeci, assistance and temporary membership was provided for them by the local synagogue and its agencies, in this case by the famous Haydarpaşa synagogue, which had been built in the late nineteenth century to care for the refugees coming from Central Europe and Russia, against the violent opposition of the local Greek population, which had been overcome only by the personal intervention of Sultan Abdülhamid II, in gratitude for which the synagogue had been named after him *Hemdat*

---

344. Nathan Eck, 'The Rescue of Jews with the Aid of Passports and Citizenship Papers of Latin American States, *Yad Vashem Studies*, no. 1 (1957), 125–152.

345. Barlas, *ibid.*, p. 25.

346. See above, p. 210.

Israel.[347] There they remained until space could be found for them on the *Taurus Express*, which departed weekly for the long trip through the Taurus mountains into Syria and onward to Palestine.

Those refugees who did not have official permission to enter Palestine were sent through Turkey to the Mediterranean coast, particularly to the ports of Marmaris and Bodrum, from which they were sent 'illegally' on small boats to Palestine.[348] The Turkish government as well as private Turkish citizens, Jewish and non Jewish alike, provided fuel and food to these ships despite constant British objections, on the grounds that failure to do so would subject Turkey to even more international criticism if the ships were sunk or their passengers starved to death, since in such cases the British invariably tried to blame Turkey for the disasters.[349] As a result, 4,400 Jewish refugees passed through Turkey on their way to Palestine during 1941 alone, and even greater numbers in subsequent years, reaching a total of as many as an estimated 100,000 by the end of the war.[350]

Even after the Final Solution was put into effect, Germany allowed thousands of Jews to leave the countries under its control for Turkey and Palestine as the result of the *Exchange Plan* which was negotiated through the good offices of the International Red Cross representatives in Geneva and Ankara, according to which groups of German citizens who had been stranded at the start of the war in the British colonies, in particular in South Africa and Australia, were sent to Istanbul, where they were sent on by train to Germany in exchange for Jewish refugees coming mainly from Germany, Austria and France. It was these Jewish refugees, brought to Turkey on what came to be known as the *Istanbul Lists*, who were the first eye-witnesses to tell the outside world of the mounting Nazi atrocities against the Jews of central and western Europe once the Final Solution had been put fully into effect. Their stories were reported from Istanbul to America and elsewhere with the full cooperation and assistance of the Turkish government.[351]

In addition to these fortunate few, hundreds of other refugees without entry or transit visas or visas for them to go on to other countries were allowed to pass across the border into Turkey, often without any papers at

---

347. Shaw, *Jews of the Ottoman Empire*, pp. 204–205.

348. Ofer, *Escaping the Holocaust*, p. 164;; Avneri, *From 'Velos' to 'Taurus'*, p. 311.

349. Ofer, *Escaping the Holocaust*, p. 165-175; William Perl, *The Four-Front War: From the Holocaust to the Promised Land* (New York, Crown, 1979), pp. 215–262.

350. Yehuda Slutsky, *History of the Hagana, vol. III: From Resistance to War* (Tel Aviv, 1972), p. 171.

351. Barlas, *ibid.*, pp. 152–153.

all, and despite the *Kararname* and other regulations to the contrary, since there was nowhere else that they could go. Such refugees were allowed to remain in the country throughout the war, assisted by local Jewish self-help organizations, the Jewish Agency and other rescue groups working with it, as well as by the Turkish Red Crescent and, behind the scenes, agencies of the Turkish government.

Already in late 1940, the various *Kibbutz* pioneer organizations in Palestine had asked the directors of the Jewish Agency to create a representative office in Istanbul for them, in addition to that directed by Barlas, to establish contacts with and to assist members living in Nazi-occupied countries. Initially Barlas was able to convince the Jewish Agency directors in Palestine that such an operation would only duplicate his own efforts and create difficulties with the Turkish government, which had allowed his office to be established only with great reluctance due to its fear of a German invasion if its neutrality was violated.[352] Turkey had allowed Barlas to operate not only because of any proposed operations in Nazi-occupied Europe but also because his activities constituted a window into the Soviet Union, where thousands of Turks had long been oppressed under Russian rule and were seeking an opportunity to free themselves. Indeed, most of Barlas's successes in 1940 and 1941 came not from Nazi-occupied territory but, rather, from Lithuania, from which 2,000 Jewish refugees came through Turkey to Palestine, but this lane was closed with the German invasion of the Soviet Union starting in June 1941.

Once Barlas had secured Turkish permission and made the initial arrangements, however, and as Nazi pressure against European Jewry increased with enactment of the Final Solution in late December 1942, the pressure from the *kibbutzim* and other groups in Palestine increased. Already during the previous spring, Melekh Neustadt had come to Istanbul as representative of the *Histadrut* executive to consider whether it could be used as a base to contact and perhaps rescue *kibbutz* members and others suffering under the Nazi yoke. On his return he reported that Istanbul was not only the most convenient base for such an operation but it was in fact the only place from which the Jews of Eastern Europe could be observed and assisted. Neustadt recommended that the *Histadrut* set up a representative bureau in Istanbul to deal not merely with *Aliyah* immigration activities, as Barlas had been doing, but also with political questions, which had been handled by Epstein, and with actual rescue operations to save Jews

352. Dina Porat, *Entangled Leadership*, p. 218.

who were being threatened with imminent extermination by the Nazis.[353]
During a key meeting held at *Histadrut* headquarters in Jerusalem on 16
August 1942, Barlas continued to resist the proposal, citing the difficulties
that would be involved in coordinating overlapping operations as well as
keeping them secret, and promising instead to widen his own operations to
include rescue efforts as well as large scale correspondence to contact, not
only *kibbutz* members, but all Jews being persecuted by the Nazis
throughout Europe.

In the light of Barlas's objections, the *Histadrut* finally decided to send
to Istanbul Eliezer Leder, a member of 'The Rescue Committee for the
Deliverance and Assistance of Polish Jewry' to investigate the situation again
before any final action was taken. The other groups involved were, however,
unwilling to wait any longer, particularly now that the Final Solution was
becoming more and more evident; they wanted to have their own
representatives in Istanbul rather than relying on others to act on their
behalf. Barlas's office was therefore joined in Istanbul by agents of a number
of other Jewish organizations from Palestine devoted to rescuing European
Jewry from the horrors of the Holocaust.

As a result, by the end of 1943 there were present in Istanbul, in
addition to Barlas and his group, fourteen other Palestinian agents working
actively on behalf of European Jewry. Among them was a group that
organized 'illegal immigration' (*Aliyah Bet*) to Palestine, the *Mossad li-
Aliyah* (Organization for Immigration), created originally on 7 July 1939 by
the *Haganah* office based in Paris to rescue Jews from Nazi-occupied
Europe, which set up its own office in Istanbul under the direction first of
Zvi Yechi'eli (October 1941–November 1942), replaced after he went to
Cairo to train volunteers for being parachuted into Nazi Europe by Ze'ev
Shind and Tzvi Yekhieh, who arrived in February 1943.[354] Others included
Victor (Venya) Pomerantz, then a member of the *Kibbutz Ramat Rachel*,[355]
representing the Palestinian *ha-Kibbutz ha-Meuchad* (the United Kibbutz)
movement, who arrived in November, 1942, and Menahem Bader[356] of the

353. Dina Porat, *Entangled Leadership*, p. 218.

354. The background is given in Yehuda Slutsky, *History of the Hagana, vol. III, From
Resistance to War* (in Hebrew) (Tel Aviv, 1972), pp. 78–80.

355. Now Ze'ev Hadari, a Professor at Beersheba University

356. Ariel Horwitz, 'Menaham Bader's Mission in Istanbul and the Contacts of
Hashomer–Hatzair with European Jewry', (in Hebrew) *Yalkut Moreshet* no. 35 (April 1983),
pp. 152–202. Menachem Bader's papers are found in the Moreshet archives, located at Givet
Haviva, a seminary of the *Kibbutz Artzi* movement near Hadera, Israel. They contain detailed

ha-Kibbutz ha-Artzi (*Kibbutz Mizra'*), who also represented the *ha-Shomer ha-Tsa'ir* movement starting in January, 1943. Both immediately set to establishing contact with and assisting their members still in Europe.[357]

Between March and October 1943, they were joined by Theodore (Teddy) Kolleck, for many years subsequently mayor of Israeli Jerusalem, who was sent to Istanbul as representative of the Political Committee of the Jewish Agency, serving to create and operate the *Histadrut* Rescue and Relief Committee in Istanbul, which in many ways duplicated the efforts of Barlas in helping Jews throughout Eastern Europe with the financial assistance of the Zionist Organization.[358] In May of the same year Kalman Rosenblatt arrived as representative of the *ha-'Oved Hzioni* (Zionist worker) movement and the Alliance of General Zionists (*Brit ha-Ziyomin ha-Klaliyim*) and Moshe Auerbuch (Agami) joined the *Mossad Aliyah* operations. At times Yitzhak Gruenbaum, Chairman of the Jewish Agency Rescue Committee in Jerusalem, came to Istanbul to supervise and advise on their operations.[359]

In July and August 1943 they were joined by David Zimand, of the Zionist Youth movement (*Ha'noar ha-zioni*), who also represented the Alliance of Pioneering Organizations (*Brit ha-Irgumin ha-Chaduziyim*); Ya'akov Griffel, representing the Orthodox Movement *Agudat Israel*; Joseph Klarman, of the Palestinian Revisionists (Jabotinsky movement),[360] and Meir Tuval, of the Yugoslavian (*olim*) immigrants rescue committee. Ehud Avriel, who had been recruited to *Mossad* in 1942, came to Istanbul in August 1943 to represent the Jewish Agency Political Department in place

---

information on the activities of the Rescue Council delegation of the Jewish Agency operating in Istanbul as well as information on Nazi atrocities against Jews in Czechoslovakia, the Ukraine, and in particular Galizia. He discusses his operations in Turkey in some detail in Menahem Bader, *Sad Missions* (in Hebrew) (Tel Aviv, 1978), p. 42.

357. Dalia Ofer, *Escaping the Holocaust* (New York and Oxford, 1990), p. 211; Dina Porat, *Entangled Leadership*, p. 219.

358. Ofer, *Escaping the Holocaust*, pp. 43–44.

359. The Yitzhak Gruenbaum collection, located at the Moreshet Archives, Givat Haviva, Israel (no. C. 14), have considerable information regarding Turkish assistance to Jewish refugees as well as on the Jewish Agency operations in Istanbul, with some 43 testimonies refugees who arrived in Palestine via Turkey. (file C.14.7.24).

360. The activities of the Revisionists in .Turkey are described in detail by one of the participants in the activities sending Jewish refugees to Istanbul from Rumania, William R. Perl, *The Four-Front War: From the Holocaust to the Promised Land* (New York, Crown, 1979), particularly pp. 359–361.

of Teddy Kolleck.[361] Akiva Levinski, from *Kibbutz Ma'ayan Zvi*, representing the Youth *Aliyah* (*Aliyat ha-No'ar*), arrived in October 1943, followed by Yosef Vinner, of the Religious Labor movement (*ha-Poel ha-Mizrakhi*); Yitzhak Miterani, of the Bulgarian immigrants (*olim*) Rescue Committee; Abraham Tehomi and Yitzhak Zazevsky, of the *EZEL*, or *Irgun Zeva'i Le'umi*, the Jewish national military organization; as well as agents of other Palestinian Jewish organizations who joined the Yeshiva Aid Committee (*Vaad ha-Hatzala*) organized by the Orthodox Jews of America[362]and used the channels which Barlas had set up to not only assist Jews suffering from persecution, but also to help many of them escape through Turkey to Palestine.[363]

Of all these groups, only that led by Barlas was officially recognized by both the Turkish and British authorities as the semi-official representative of the Jewish Agency for Palestine. The others operated in Turkey illegally, under various disguises, usually as businessmen or journalists, using Barlas's experience and organization to carry out their unauthorized activities, to the extreme annoyance of the Turkish government, which knew exactly what they were doing, and which feared that such operations would provide the Nazis with the final pretext they needed to invade the country. Pomerantz thus operated as a buyer of Turkish lumber for shipment to Palestine. Teddy Kolleck was a hazelnut merchant and Menahem Bader a journalist. They constantly feared that the Turkish government would find out about their real work and expel them, but in fact the Turkish Ministry of the Interior allowed them to continue anyway despite constant German pressure to have them imprisoned or expelled.[364]

After a time, the Jewish Agency operation in Istanbul was divided into functional committees, which at least partially absorbed the other 'illegal' groups. The Joint Distribution Committee agents in Istanbul were Barlas and Resnik. The Rescue Committee was chaired by Barlas, with Menahem

---

361. Avneri, *From 'Velos' to 'Taurus'*, pp. 331–334.

362. Organized and led by Rabbi Eliezer Silver of the Union of Orthodox Rabbis in the United States. Its report on its activities directed from Istanbul during 1942 is found in the Moreshet Archives (Israel) D 1: 599. Documents relating to its activities in Istanbul are in the Ghetto Fighters Archives/*Beit Lohamei Haghettaot*, Z. 1063–1074.

363. Detailed reports on the activities of the Rescue Council based in Istanbul are found in the Menachem Bader collection, at the Moreshet Archives, Givat Haviva, Israel, particularly in files D.1.36–D.1.44.

364. Dalia Ofer, *Escaping the Holocaust* (New York and Oxford, 1990), pp. 211–212; Barry Rubin, *Istanbul Intrigues*, p. 209.

Bader as Secretary and Venya, Leder, Sina, Gripel and Klarsen as members, and with Resnik as American Joint Distribution Committee delegate. The Assistance and Rescue Committee was composed of Bader, Venya and Gripol. The Committee for Contacts with other Countries consisted of Leder, Venya and Klerman. The Committee for Gathering Information included Leder, Levinsky, Ehud and Venya; and the Advisory Committee for the Agency was chaired by Barlas, with Bader as Secretary and Shind as member.

Barlas himself continued to protest that there were too many Palestinian agents in Turkey and that the 'illegal' rescue operations, if uncovered by Turkish security, would endanger his 'legal' operations assisting Jews in Nazi-occupied Europe. As Teddy Kolleck later wrote of his relations with Chaim Barlas:

> We did not ease his way . . . . Barlas thought that legality was the most important issue, and we thought that the illegal acts were the essence and the legal ones only the cover for them.[365]

When Kolleck returned to Palestine later in 1943 he carried the message to the Rescue Committee in Tel Aviv and to the Jewish Labor Party (*Mapai*) that all these different individuals and groups were often working at cross purposes and wasting money which should have been used to help the suffering Jews in Europe, and, even worse, in the process they were exciting the suspicions of the Turkish Ministry of the Interior, which was already alarmed and worried since the British and Nazi representatives were constantly complaining about their activities. Kolleck concluded that four or five good people could do the work better than all those concentrated in Istanbul. Little was done, however to remedy this situation The representatives of the Bulgarian and Yugoslav immigrants (*olim*) to Palestine along with the Rumanian, Dutch, Hungarian and Greek representatives complained that most of the leading agents of the Yishuv in Istanbul were Ashkenazi Jews who discriminated against their people, the Sephardim, so that they had to send their agents as well to protect their interests. Kolleck and Gruenbaum replied that if any more people were sent and the delegation in Istanbul came to number as many as thirty people, Turkey would most certainly be forced to expel most or all of them as a

---

365. Teddy Kolleck, *One Jerusalem* (in Hebrew) (Tel Aviv, Maariv Bookshop, 1979), p. 154.

result of British and German pressure.[366] In August 1943, Moshe Cherokee (later Israeli Foreign Minister and Prime Minister Moshe Shertock) went to Istanbul to investigate the Palestinian delegation, returning with reports of disorder and constant arguments which were 'killing the soul of its activities'. Like Kolleck he recommended that the delegation be substantially reduced in numbers. He added that in view of the importance of its operations, a senior member of *Mapai* such as Golda Meir, or even David Ben Gurion or Yitzhak Ben Zvi, all later leaders of the new Israeli state, should be appointed to oversee its work and coordinate the various operations.

Early in 1944 Shaul Mei'rov (later Avigur), head of the *Mossad Aliyah Bet*, came to Istanbul to look at the situation. He concluded that the problems in Istanbul were only reflections of the internal political quarrels then going on among Jewish leaders in Palestine, and he criticized Barlas for his apparent inability to control the situation. Nothing could be done, however, and the confusion continued, at least until the spring of 1944 when the increase of rescue operations from Eastern Europe as well as the visit to Istanbul of Palestine Chief Rabbi Herzog in December 1943 and January 1944, finally helped to diffuse the quarrels and get the various members of the delegation to work together far more harmoniously than they had for some time.[367]

The Palestine delegation ultimately became too large for its original offices at the Pera Palas and the Continental Hotel, so its headquarters was moved to a private apartment building nearby, which became the 'Palestine Office', not only a center for its agents going to and from eastern Europe, but also for classes in Hebrew and other matters needed to prepare those refugees who had reached Istanbul with the information and knowledge needed for them to successfully reach and live in Palestine. After a time, these Palestinian representatives divided the delegation into two groups, one including the agents of the *Mossad* along with newly arriving agents of the Jewish Agency, and the other including Bader, Pomerantz and Schind, with their efforts coordinated, not without difficulty and many disputes, by Barlas.[368]

Together, however, Barlas's 'legal' operations, when combined with the 'illegal' activities of the *Mossad* and others based in Istanbul made it the

366. Dina Porat, *Entangled Leadership*, pp. 221–222.
367. Dina Porat, *Entangled Leadership*, pp. 225–232.
368. Dalia Ofer, 'The Jewish Agency Delegation in Istanbul', *Rescue Attempts during the Holocaust* (Jerusalem, 1977), pp. 435–439.

principal center of Palestinian *yishuv* activities to assist and rescue its co-religionists throughout the continent of Europe, though constant bickering over leadership and financing added to their difficulties and limited their accomplishments. The Revisionist agent in Bucharest during the war, William Perl, wrote subsequently:

> The group in Istanbul was run primarily by the Mossad, though our Josef Klarman–supported by Eri Jabotinsky, who had come for that purpose to Turkey–was recognized to be a most valuable team member. It was the Mossad which provided the funds required for the operation, and it was also the Istanbul group which, on the strength of the new British promises, obtained from the Turks the necessary transit visas and arranged for rail transportation from Istanbul to Palestine . . . . [369]

The 'Rescue Committee' members based in Istanbul carried out numerous activities to assist and at times rescue Jews being persecuted through Nazi-occupied Europe.[370] First and foremost, they maintained regular communications with most parts of eastern and northern Europe. Bader stated that 'our role is to simply establish an address to which people in occupied Europe could apply to when necessary'.[371] Moshe Shertock is said to have described the Istanbul office as a 'peep hole to the other side'.[372] Indeed, from the first days that the Istanbul office was established, Bader led its members in writing hundreds of letters to Jews in the occupied territories asking about conditions and what could be done to assist them.[373] After a time answers came back, revealing the full horror of the Final Solution. At first, correspondence went through the regular Turkish mail

---

369. William Perl, *The Four-Front War* (New York, Crown, 1989), p. 359.

370. These activities are treated in some detail in Yehuda Slutsky, *History of the Hagana, vol. III: From Resistance to War* (Tel Aviv, 1972), pp. 172–174, as well as in Dina Porat, *Entangled Leadership, passim*.

371. Ehud Avriel, *Open the Gates*, p. 119.

372. Dina Porat, *Entangled Leadership*, p. 239.

373. Eliahu Stern, 'The Contacts between the Delegation in Istanbul and Polish Jewry', (in Hebrew), *Yalkut Moreshet*, no. 39 (May 1985), pp. 135–136. Ariel Horwitz, 'Menahem Bader's Mission in Istanbul and the Contacts of Hashomer-Hatzair with European Jewry', (in Hebrew) *Yalkut Moreshet* no. 35 (April 1983), pp. 152–202. Copies of some 7,000 of these letters are kept at the *Lochame Hegata'ot* (The Ghetto Warriors) Museum, Tel Aviv, in file 2/1063.

system, which remained part of the international postal organization, with the Turkish post office at times intervening to supply additional postage and registration as required for the mail to go through. After a time, however, the official mails became increasingly irregular, and many letters both from and to the Istanbul office seem never to have reached their destination due to Nazi intervention. Starting early in 1943, then, Bader began to use as private couriers to carry both mail and money, people who were able to move relatively freely in the Nazi-occupied territories, particularly Turkish businessmen and truck drivers, a few diplomats, and couriers sent by the Papal representative in Istanbul, Angelo Roncalli, later Pope Paul XXIII,[374] who were sympathetic to the Jewish Agency's work and to the plight of Europe's Jews.[375] When news came of deaths in the Nazi concentration camps, letters of condolence were sent to relatives and friends with the hope that their tragedies would stimulate them to provide even more news about what was going on around them. Information was also gathered from the refugee Jews arriving in Istanbul. In an effort to establish trust and confidence with the British, in the vain hope that they would in return lower their restrictions on Jewish immigration to Palestine, much of this information was shared with British Intelligence and Foreign Office officials both in Istanbul and Haifa.[376]

The second principal means of opening and maintaining lines of communication as well as helping Jews in the occupied countries was to send them packages of food, clothing, and other supplies, sometimes through the mail but more often through the private couriers as well as channels maintained by the International Red Cross. At first Britain pressured the Turkish government not to allow such packages to be sent on the theory that they would most likely fall into the hands of the enemy and assist their war effort. Turkey in any case was hesitant in fear that such shipments would strain even further its own critical shortages of food and clothing. Starting in August 1943, however, the entry of the American Jewish Joint Distribution Committee into this area, and the American diplomatic support that went with it, convinced the British to withdraw their objections. As a result, starting in January 1944 Turkey facilitated the shipment of hundreds of packages of food and clothing from Istanbul, sometimes by post but more

---

374. On Roncalli's important contributions, see p. 277 and *passim* .

375. Turkish Ministry of Foreign Affairs to Turkish Embassy to Paris (Vichy), no. 556/28, 31 April 1941; Dina Porat, *Entangled Leadership*, pp. 241–242.

376. Dina Porat, *Entangled Leadership*, pp. 242–245.

often through the Red Cross, to Jews in most of the countries of Eastern Europe. While the shipments stimulated some objections from Turks already suffering considerable shortages of food, the Turkish government insisted on approving them once it had received American assurances, never entirely fulfilled, that supplies would subsequently be sent to replace them as soon as possible.[377]

Hard currency often was sent both in letters and packages, and sometimes to help European Jews bribe local officials to exempt them from anti-Jewish regulations, sometimes to purchase food and clothing as well as train or boat tickets for transportation to Palestine via Turkey. Some of the money came from Palestine itself, for the most part deposited in Turkish banks and then withdrawn as needed with the permission of the Turkish Ministry of Finance.[378] Sometimes wealthy Jews resident in Istanbul arranged government permission for bank loans to add to the funds arriving from Haifa.[379] A great deal of money came from Jewish organizations in Turkey and the United States, particularly from the American Jewish Joint Distribution Committee, most of which was smuggled through Turkey to Eastern Europe in order to avoid the delays caused by Turkish restrictions against the transfer of hard currency outside the country without special permission.[380] In the end, however, approximately half of the funds raised to finance the immigration of European Jews to Palestine during the war came from the Jewish community in Palestine, while the other half came from the United States, South Africa, England, Turkey and elsewhere.[381] Some of the money, food, passports and other documents sent to Jews in Poland was carried by Poles who had lived in Hungary before the war as well as members of the Polish underground, through their agents in Istanbul, who were used despite grave misgivings as to their intentions due to the Polish anti-Semitism which Jews had long endured.[382] Hungarian and German

---

377. Turkish Ministry of Foreign Affairs to Turkish Embassy to Paris (Vichy) no. 6731/67, 15 April 1944. Archives of the Turkish Embassy (Paris).

378. Turkish Ministry of Foreign Affairs to Turkish Consulate to Marseilles (Grenoble) no. 922/26, 1 January 1944. Archives of the Turkish Consulate (Paris); Eliahu Stern, 'The Contacts between the Delegation in Istanbul and Polish Jewry', (in Hebrew), *Yalkut Moreshet*, no. 39 (May 1985), pp. 136–138.

379. Avneri, *From 'Velos' to 'Taurus'*, p. 334–335.

380. Dina Porat, *Entangled Leadership,* pp. 249–250.

381. Avneri, p. 335.

382. Eliahu Stern, pp. 144–145.

spies also acted for a time as couriers for the Jewish Agency to reach Jews in Germany in particular.[383]

The money sometimes went directly to those for whom it was intended in the Nazi-occupied countries. Sometimes it was given to agents who were responsible for making sure that it was used only for assistance and rescue activities. It was not always possible to secure receipts for the payments, and confirmations were often received only after a very long time if at all. Under these conditions Barlas and his associates were faced with the option of going ahead and sending the money, with the distinct risk that it would be lost or stolen, or that it would actually fall into the hands of the Nazis, or to give up and stop helping altogether, but they felt they simply could not pursue the latter course, and that financial help had to continue to be sent regardless of the risk.[384]

The Istanbul office of the Jewish Agency, considerably more than that in Geneva, often sent documents that European Jews needed to travel or to gain exemption from persecution or deportation, either passports or at least certificates of nationality issued by neutral countries, particularly those in Central or South America.[385] Sometimes these documents were obtained in return for substantial payments to greedy consular officials. Sometimes they were obtained free from idealistic officials who realized how much the Jews were suffering and wanted to help. Many came from Catholic priests stimulated to help by the appeals of Monsigneur Roncalli in Istanbul. Sometimes these were obtained directly from the Turkish or other consulates or embassies in the countries concerned, particularly in France, Belgium and Switzerland. Sometimes they were obtained in Ankara or Istanbul and then sent on. When the refugees had such documents, they traveled legally and left their countries with the permission of the Nazi authorities. When they were unable to obtain them, or when the Nazis or local Balkan countries refused to honor them, agents sent from Istanbul or Geneva arranged escape roads across the borders of France to Spain or Switzerland, or in Eastern Europe from Czechoslovakia, Lithuania and Poland to Hungary, from there through Rumania or Bulgaria to the Black Sea, and then by via Turkey to Palestine.

Members of the Rescue Committee at times traveled into Nazi-occupied territory, particularly to Greece, Poland, Austria, Rumania,

---

383. Eliahu Stern, p. 146.
384. Barlas, p. 74.
385. Eliahu Stern, pp. 141–143.

Hungary and Slovakia, not only to assist Jews when they could and to make sure that they knew that they had not been forgotten by the outside world, but also to directly gather information on what was being done, given them by many Jews in occupied Europe who feared that they would disappear under Nazi persecution without anyone even knowing what they were going through, and also in the hope that knowledge of these conditions in Palestine, Britain and America might stimulate the Western Allies to do something to save them before it was too late. Much of this information also was transmitted from Istanbul to Jewish communities in countries not yet occupied by the Nazis, like Rumania and Hungary, sometimes transmitted privately by sympathetic members of the Turkish diplomatic delegations in those countries,[386] to forewarn them as to what might happen when and if the Nazis took over. The information also was used to plan subsequent campaigns to help and rescue those Jews who were being persecuted and also to agitate to secure international pressure against implementation of the Final Solution. Much of the hard currency sent to help the Jews being persecuted by the Nazis was supplied by the Turkish Ministry of Finance.

Many of these activities were materially assisted by Monsigneur Angelo Giuseppi Roncalli, the future Pope John XXIII, who after acting as Papal delegate to Bulgaria from 1925 to 1934 served as Apostolic Delegate to Greece and Turkey and Apostolic Administrator for the Latin Christians of Constantinople (Istanbul) from 5 January 1935 until the middle of 1944. Roncalli had from the start of his mission attempted to point local Christians in Turkey toward reconciliation with the Turks despite the hostility resulting from Christian opposition to the Ottoman war effort during World War I as well as the subsequent Turkish War for Independence and consequent bloody clashes between Christians and Muslims which had taken place, using again and again in his private meditations and public speeches the phrase which he repeated in his *Journal of the Soul*: 'I Love the Turks'. (*io amo i turchi*).[387] By the outbreak of World War II, he had reconciled most Turks to his presence, and greatly increased his influence with the government in Ankara, by learning Turkish, reciting the Christmas mass in Turkish, introducing Turkish into local liturgy

---

386. See, for example, Namık Kemal Yolga, Turkish Consul in Paris, to the Turkish Consulate in Bucharest, April, 1943. In Archives of the Turkish Embassy (Paris), dossier 6127.

387. *Giovanni XXIII. Il Pastore. Corrispondenza dal 1911 al 1963 con i preti del Sacro Cuore di Bergamo* (Padova, 1982), pp. 256, 261; Roberto Morozzo della Rocca, 'Roncalli Diplomatico in Turchia e Grecia, 1935–1944', *Cristianesimo nella Storia*, VIII/2 (1987), pp. 33–72, particularly pp. 55–56, 58.

and prayer, and advising all his Parishioners, including Armenians and Latins, to apply 'Christian charity' to past problems and to work together with Turkish Muslims to build the new and modern state.[388] In his conversations with local Jewish leaders, moreover, he promised to do all he could to eliminate the passages in Catholic liturgy which had encouraged anti-Semitism and caused so many Blood Libel attacks on Jews during previous centuries, an ambition which culminated following his elevation to the Papacy in 1958 in his assigning the Secretariat for Promoting Christian Unity in 1960 with the task of preparing a new declaration dealing with the Jewish People, which resulted in the introduction of significant changes in the Vatican II Council that followed.

Without any encouragement from the Vatican, moreover, Roncalli arranged with the Turkish government for food to be sent to starving Jews and Greeks in Greece during the winter of 1941–42, a shortage caused as much by Greek hoarding and the British blockade as it was by German confiscations and looting.[389] Roncalli also arranged for the Holy See to use its influence in Germany to attempt to prevent deportations of Jews to the East for extermination as well as to get it to allow Jews to leave for Palestine, at least if they had valid immigration certificates issued to the British or by the Jewish Agency on British authority.[390]

Even as Turkey moved to facilitate the passage of Jewish refugees on their way to Palestine, however, in one of the darkest moments in British history, His Majesty's Government moved to limit or halt the rescue movement, basing its Palestine policy on the consideration that if it angered

---

388. Morozzo della Rocca, p. 56.

389. Peter Hoffmann, 'Roncalli in the Second World War: Peace Initiatives, the Greek Famine and the Persecution of the Jews', *Journal of Ecclesiastical History*, XL (1989), pp. 77–84.

390. Aside from ignoring Papal orders not to assist the Jewish refugees coming to Turkey, Roncalli also intervened in Bulgaria to convince its King and Parliament not to accept German demands to deport all their Jews to Auschwitz. Gilbert, *Auschwitz*, p. 122 and Barry Rubin, *Istanbul Intrigues*, pp. 47–48, 93–94, 213–214; Peter Hoffmann, 'Roncalli in the Second World War: Peace Initiatives, the Greek Famine, and Persecution of the Jews', *Journal of Ecclesiastical History* XL (1989), 74–99; Saul Friedlander, *Pie XII et le IIIe Reich* (Paris, Seuil, 1964); John Morley, *Vatican Diplomacy and the Jews during the Holocaust, 1939–1943* (New York, Ktav,1980); Peter Hebblethwaite, *Pope John XXIII: shepherd of the modern world* (New York, 1985), pp. 141–143; and Vittoro Ugo Righi, *Papa Giovanni sulle rive del Bosforo* (Padua, Italy, 1971); Ira Hirschmann, *Caution to the Winds* (New York, 1962), pp. 179–185; Roberto Morozzo della Rocca, 'Roncalli Diplomatico in Turchia e Grecia, 1935–1944', *Cristianesimo nella Storia*, VIII/2 (1987), pp. 33–72.

the Arabs, they could always change sides and go over to the Nazis, for whom many Arab nationalists had already expressed considerable sympathy because of common hostility to the Jews, whereas the latter had nowhere to go. Thus N. Butler, of the North American Department of the British Foreign Office, stated:

> If we antagonize the Arabs, they are free to change sides so to speak, and throw in their lot with the Axis who will certainly be ready to welcome them. If on the other hand we antagonize the Jews, they have no such alternative, and will be forced still to adhere to our cause, since the whole of their racial future is wrapped up in our victory. Every Jew must realize this, including the Zionists in the U.S.A.[391]

In order to pacify the Arabs, then, descendants of those who had come out of the Arabian peninsula to conquer Palestine and other parts of the Middle East in the seventh century A.D.,[392] Great Britain refused to allow Jewish refugees to enter Great Britain 'unless in some quite rare and exceptional cases it can be shown that the admission of the refugee will be directly advantageous to our war effort',[393] or to provide more than a small number of them with visas which would enable them to enter Palestine[394] or

---

391. Public Record Office (London), Foreign Office Archives 371/32680/W3963, quoted in Ofer, *Escaping the Holocaust*, p. 361.

392. Ian Henderson minute in the Foreign Office on 23 December 1943: 'The question at issue is one of balancing the advisabilities of helping the State Department and Treasury to meet Jewish electoral pressures and of their avoiding a crescendo of US criticism about our Palestine policy, and, on the other hand, of meeting the requirements of the Colonial Office in relation to practical politics and Arab wishes'. Public Record Office, FO 371/36747, W. 17687, quoted in Gilbert, *Auschwitz*, p. 168.

393. British Home Secretary Herbert Morrison to Cabinet, 23 September 1942. Public Record Office, Cabinet papers 66/29/18, quoted in Gilbert, *Auschwitz*, p. 77. The most useful analyses of British Foreign Policy regarding the Middle East at this time are Bernard Wasserstein, *Britain and the Jews of Europe, 1939–1945*, Oxford, 1979), and Martin Gilbert, *Auschwitz and the Allies* (New York, 1981)

394. Britain adhered to the limit of 75,000 Jewish immigrants yearly, as set out in its prewar White Paper on Palestine. Thus on 1 February 1941, in the face of the desperate need of thousands of Jews to flee Eastern Europe to Palestine, it certified the admission of no more than 4,500 refugees from Rumania, Hungary, Greece, Yugoslavia, Bulgaria, Switzerland, and Sweden, as reported by A. Whittall, H.M. Passport Control Officer, to the Passport Control Office, British Embassy, Istanbul, on 19 March 1941 (Barlas, *ibid.*, p. 235).

any other Mediterranean area which it controlled. In addition, it pressured Turkey and the countries of southeastern Europe to refuse them entry and to turn back those arriving by ship, train or land,[395] going on then to blame Turkey when, in the light of constant threats of German invasion and consequent budgetary problems, the Turkish Prime Minister declared that he would admit them only if they were allowed to go on to Palestine.

Insofar as the British Government was concerned, there was no point of rescuing these Jews since there was no place to put them. As the British Ministry of Economic Warfare informed the United States Embassy in London on 15 December 1943, 'The Foreign Office are concerned with the difficulties of disposing of any considerable number of Jews should they be rescued from enemy occupied territory. . . .'[396] Britain thus, albeit for its own reasons, actively cooperated with German implementation of the Final Solution by using all its influence to enforce the German prohibition against Jewish emigration from Europe so that they could be exterminated in the camps then being set up in the East. Turkey, however, saved the lives of most of these refugees by recognizing visas for Palestine issued by the Jewish Agency in Istanbul which, since the British in many cases would not honor them when they went beyond the annual quotas for Jewish immigrants established by the 1939 White Paper, meant that they would be allowed to remain in Turkey through the remainder of the war or at least until means were provided for them to immigrate 'illegally' from the ports along the coast of southern Turkey across the Mediterranean to Palestine, evading the British naval blockade, landing secretly on the shores of the Holy land, and vanishing into friendly Jewish settlements and houses throughout the country.[397]

This British policy led to a number of terrible disasters in which ships loaded with Jewish refugees sank on the high seas, with terrible loss of life, including the *Salvador*, which sank in the Sea of Marmara on 12 December 1940, about which T. M. Snow, Director of the British Foreign Office Refugee Section, stated: 'There could have been no more opportune disaster from the point of view of stopping this traffic',[398] and most disastrous of all, the 200-ton ship *Struma*, which sank in the Black Sea not far from the

---

395. Porat, *Entangled Leadership*, pp. 290–291.

396. Bernard Wasserstein, *Britain and the Jews of Europe, 1939–1945* (London and Oxford, 1979), p. 247. Quoted in Gilbert, *Auschwitz,* p. 167.

397. Charles Barlas, *ha Atasala biyinei a son* (Hebrew, Tel Aviv, 1975), p. 12.

398. Public Record Office, London, FO 371/25242, W 2451, f. 229, quoted in Gilbert, *Auschwitz,* p. 21.

Bosporus in late February 1942, with the loss of 769 refugees from Rumania, all of whom would have been saved had not strong pressure from the British government, and in particular British refusal to allow the ship pass through its blockade to land its cargo in Palestine, prevented Turkey from allowing the ship through the Straits after it had waited for ten weeks offshore while the diplomatic exchanges went on.[399]

The Turkish Grand National Assembly had just passed the new law that formally granted the right of transit through Turkey to Jewish refugees from Nazi persecution anywhere in Europe so long as they held visas which would allow them to enter the countries to which they were going.[400] Even when such refugees arrived without visas, moreover, the Turkish authorities were not expelling them, but instead were interning them until places could be found to which they could go. In this case, however, the British were saying that since Palestine could not take these refugees, it was Turkey's obligation to do so even though its economy was strained to the limit because of wartime conditions. The British excuses were legion. British High Commissioner in Palestine, Sir Harold MacMichael, wrote the Foreign Office that:

> Palestine cannot afford to increase the unproductive element in the population, and reports indicate that the Struma passengers are largely of the professional class.[401]

So it was that although Turkey allowed Istanbul's Jewish community to send food and other supplies to the refugees waiting in the *Struma* outside Istanbul harbor,[402] and it continuously declared its readiness to allow the ship to pass through the Straits into the Mediterranean just as soon as the British agreed to allow it to land in Palestine, the British maintained their refusal to allow the ship to pass out of the Dardanelles. Insofar as Britain

---

399. Turhan Aytul, 'Struma Faciası' *Milliyet,* 30 June–6 July 1985. Dalia Ofer, *Escaping the Holocaust* (New York and Oxford, 1990), pp. 147–166; Avneri, *From 'Velos' to 'Taurus',* ppp. 311–318; Jurgen Rohwer, *Die Versenkung der Judeischen Fluchlingstransporte Struma und Mefkura im Schwarzen Meer Feb. 1942–Aug. 1944* (Frankfurt, Graefe, 1964) explains that neither Germany nor Turkey sank the *Struma,* that in fact a Turkish freighter was also sunk nearby at the same time, as shown by archival records from the USSR. He also shows that no German warships were in fact active in the Black Sea as early as 1942.

400. See page 264.

401. Sir Harold MacMichael to Foreign Office, 16 February 1942. FO 372/29162, quoted in Dalia Ofer, *Escaping the Holocaust,* p. 162.

402. Dalia Ofer, *Escaping the Holocaust,* p. 164.

was concerned, it was up to Turkey not only to rescue the refugees but to house and feed them indefinitely.

British Ambassador to Turkey, Sir Hughe Knatchbull-Hugessen, at the suggestion of Turkish Foreign Minister Numan Menemencioğlu, finally proposed to his government that, rather than forcing the ship to sail back into the Black Sea, it might be allowed to sail through the Straits so that 'if they reached Palestine, they might despite their illegality receive humane treatment',[403] but the idea was vetoed by the British Colonial Secretary, Lord Moyne, in charge of Palestine, who informed Foreign Secretary Anthony Eden:

> The landing of seven hundred more immigrants will not only be a formidable addition to the difficulties of the High Commissioner. . but it will have a deplorable effect throughout the Balkans in encouraging further Jews to embark on a traffic which has now been condoned by Her Majesty's Ambassador. We have good reason to believe that this traffic is favoured by the Gestapo, and the Security Services attach the very greatest importance to preventing the influx of Nazi agents under the cloak of refugees. As to Knatchbull-Hugessen's humanitarian feelings about sending the refugees back to the Black Sea countries, it seems to me that these might apply with equal force to the tens of thousands of Jews who remain behind and who are most eager to join them . . . I find it difficult to write with moderation about the occurrence which is in flat contradiction of established Government policy, and I should be very glad if you could perhaps even now do something to retrieve the position and to urge the Turkish authorities should be asked to send the ship back to the Black Sea, as they originally proposed.[404]

Lord Moyne attempted to further justify his opposition to admitting the refugees by stating that there was a threat that German spies would be

---

403. Sir Hughe Knatchbull–Hugessen to Foreign Office, Public Record Office (London), Colonial Office 733/449/P3/4/30, quoted in Gilbert, *Auschwitz*, p. 22.

404. Minutes of Colonial Office officials S. E. V. Luke and E. B. Boyd, Public Record Office, Colonial Office papers 733/449/P3/4/30, quoted in Gilbert, *Auschwitz*, pp. 22–23. Gilbert goes on to point out that no Nazi agent was ever found among these refugees, as shown in the Ph.D. dissertation by R. W. Zweig, *British Policy to Palestine, May 1939 to 1943*, (Cambridge University, 1978).

smuggled into Palestine along with them, a ludicrous contention.[405] Just how much the British were frustrated by Turkey's refusal to stop this flow of 'illegal' Jewish refugees was shown by a further comment by one of Moyne's assistants at the Colonial Office, S. E. V. Luke, who on 23 December 1941, in reaction to Knatchbull-Hugessen's proposal, noted that:

> This is the first occasion on which, in spite of numerous efforts, the Turkish Government has shown any signs of being ready to help in frustrating these illegal immigrant ships, and then the Ambassador goes and spoils the whole effect on absurdly misjudged humanitarian grounds.[406]

The Bulgarian Captain of the *Struma* refused to sail his ship from Istanbul into the Mediterranean, since it was registered under the flag of Panama, which was at war with the Axis, making any voyage through the Mediterranean extremely dangerous unless the British navy was willing to guarantee its safety.[407] It was therefore forced to go back into the Black Sea, where it was sunk by a Soviet submarine a few days later with the loss of almost all on board.[408] To compound absurdity upon absurdity, the official British Report on the *Struma* affair blamed the Turkish government for the disaster, though more fully documented investigations show that Turkey was willing to allow and even help the *Struma* on its way through the Straits to Palestine, and that it was the pressure applied by the highest levels of the British government which compelled the ship to meet disaster back in the Black Sea.

Even after the *Struma* disaster, when two survivors attempted to go from Istanbul, where they were given refuge, to Palestine, they were refused admission by the British authorities on the grounds that they were enemy

---

405. Bernard Wasserstein, *Britain and the Jews of Europe, 1939-1945* (Oxford, 1979), pp. 144–146.

406. Minute by S.E.V. Luke, 23 December 1941, in Colonial Office papers (Public Record Office, London) 733/449/P3/4/30, cited in Gilbert, *Auschwitz*, p. 22; Wasserstein, *Britain and the Jews of Europe, 1939–1945*, p. 145, and Joan Peters, *From Time Immemorial* (New York, Harper, 1984), p.368.

407. William R. Perl, *The Four-Front War* (New York, 1979), pp. 350–351.

408. Avneri, *From 'Velos' to 'Taurus'*, pp. 314–315.

aliens,[409] so they remained in Istanbul through the remainder of the war with the permission of the Turkish government.

Britain continued to follow a policy that:

> no facilities can be granted to Jewish refugees who may become stranded in Turkey or in other neutral countries while attempting to enter Palestine from enemy-occupied territory.[410]

Soon afterwards, Chaim Weizmann led a mass protest demonstration in London, blaming the British government entirely for the disaster.[411] In the Parliamentary debates that followed, British government speakers excused their refusal to allow Jewish refugees to enter Britain on the grounds that, by doing so, they were preventing the spread of anti-Semitism in that country, a truly astonishing pretext for what they had done.[412]

British High Commissioner for Palestine Sir Harold MacMichael subsequently recommended rejection of the efforts of the Jewish Agency to get it to admit refugees from Bulgaria to Palestine, stating:

> I fear that if the Bulgarian Government were to know that we were prepared to accept Jews, they would send out as many as the trains could hold without regard to numerical or other qualifications. There could be no process of selection in connection with immigrants, and we could not send back any who came out of Bulgaria. It seems to me that the door would then be thrown open to any number and condition of Jews whom any Axis country felt disposed to get rid of, with or without German instigation, nor could we any longer maintain our refusal to facilitate the journey to Palestine of illegal immigrants who arrive in Turkey.[413]

---

409. Public Record Office, Colonial Office 733/446/76021/40, fol. 63, quoted in Gilbert, *Auschwitz*, p. 25.

410. Public Record Office, War Cabinet 64 (1942), Public Record Office, Cabinet papers 65/26, and Central Cabinet Archives (Israel) Z4/14908, quoted in Gilbert, *Auschwitz*, pp. 37–38.

411. *Jewish Chronicle*, 13 March 1942, quoted in Cohen, ed. *Weizmann*, p. 269n. Also Barnet Litvinoff, *Weizmann, Last of the Patriarchs* (London and New York, 1976), p. 224.

412. Gilbert, *Auschwitz*, pp. 138–140.

413. Sir Harold MacMichael to Colonial Office, Public Record Office, FO 371/32.698, W. 15197. Quoted in Gilbert, *Auschwitz*, p. 80.

The British government finally decided in May 1942 that:

(1) In pursuance of the existing policy of taking all practicable steps to discourage illegal immigration into Palestine, nothing whatever will be done to facilitate the arrival of Jewish refugees in Palestine.

(2) Future shiploads of illegal immigrants who nevertheless succeed in reaching Palestine will be landed, placed in detainment camps, and those who pass the securing and economic absorptive capacity checks will gradually be released against the current half yearly quotas granted under the White Paper . . . . Refugees who reach Palestine in immigrant ships will be landed and will be passed through a check for security to the satisfaction of both the civil and the military authorities, it being understood that the onus of proof of bona fides will, as far as possible, be placed on the individual detainee. If the individual passes this check, he will, subject to the application of the overriding principle of economic absorptive capacity, be released from detention . . . . While His Majesty's Government are satisfied that the arrangements described above will not infringe the provisions of the White Paper relating to immigration into Palestine, they feel that, in their efforts to avoid a recurrence of the 'Struma' disaster, they have now gone as far as is possible within the limits of the policy approved by Parliament. Finally, in view of the extremely delicate position in the Middle East, His Majesty's Government are anxious that the new arrangements should have the minimum of publicity. It is not intended, therefore, that there should be anything in the nature of a public declaration or announcement concerning them, either in this country or in Palestine. I shall be glad if you will observe similar reticence, though I realize that you will no doubt find it necessary to communicate in confidence with Dr. Weizmann and the Executive of the Jewish Agency in Jerusalem, and others whom it may seem to you essential to inform. In your communication to Dr. Weizmann, you will no doubt stress the importance of avoiding publicity in the American Press . . . . [414]

---

414. Cranborne, Colonial Office, London, to Mr. Locker, 22 May 1942, quoted in Barlas, *ibid.*, pp. 235–237.

There were many instances throughout the war when British refusal to allow refugee groups coming from Eastern Europe to enter Palestine or to go on to refuge in Britain because of its own very strong internal anti-Semitism,[415] resulted in their being sent back to face death at the hands of the Nazis,[416] though in many such cases Turkey, for humanitarian reasons, agreed to allow them to remain until the end of the war, despite continuous pressure to the contrary by Britain and Germany.

Even when the Gestapo in May 1944 offered the Jewish Agency in Istanbul an opportunity to exchange as many as a million Jews from Hungary, Czechoslovakia, Rumania and Poland, who would otherwise have been sent to Auschwitz for execution, for trucks, food or foreign money, the offer was rejected by Britain, at least partly because of the consideration that a 'large evacuation' of Jews through Turkey:

> . . . would involve our being pressed to receive unmanageable numbers into Palestine, and thereby introduce the dangerous complication that the immigration quota would be exceeded at a particularly critical time.[417]

To propose admitting Jewish refugees to the British islands or colonies 'would be an embarrassing development', because of food shortages and other problems.[418]

On 1 April 1943, the British War Cabinet Committee on Refugees, chaired by subsequent Prime Minister, Clement Attlee and including Home Secretary Herbert Morrison, agreed to try to persuade the United States and others in Africa and North and South America to take the refugees, but on condition that efforts would be made 'to make quite sure that these refugees would stay in Turkey, and would not be passed on, e.g. to Palestine.' [419] Turkey, thus, would have to keep the Jewish refugees because

---

415. Statement to the British Cabinet by Home Secretary Herbert Morrison: Public Record Office, War Cabinet, 23 September 1942. Cabinet papers 66/29/18, quoted in Gilbert, *Auschwitz*, p. 77.

416. Gilbert, *Auschwitz*, pp. 74–76.

417. War Cabinet Committee on the Reception and Accommodation of Refugees, 31 May 1944. Public Record Office, Cabinet Papers 95/15, quoted in Gilbert, *Auschwitz*, p. 218.

418. Meeting of all the British departments at the Foreign Office, 25 March 1943. Public Record Office, Cabinet papers 95/15, quoted in Gilbert, *Auschwitz*, pp. 127–8.

419. War Cabinet Committee on the Reception and Accomodation of Refugees, 1 April 1943, Public Record Office, Cabinet Papers, 95/15, quoted in Gilbert, *Auschwitz*, p. 128.

no-one else wanted them, and if Turkey were to refuse to accept more refugees, it would be criticized for a lack of humanity.

Nor was the United States, because of its developing oil interests in the Arab Middle East, much more sympathetic than Great Britain to the idea of either admitting Jewish refugees to its own country or allowing them to go on to Palestine. When in November 1941 the Turkish Minister to Bucharest proposed to the American Minister that 300,000 Rumanian Jews then being subjected to persecution by the Iron Guard as well as the dictatorial government of Antonescu, be shipped to safety in Palestine, the American State Department strongly opposed the plan.[420]

Despite persistent British as well as German efforts to get Turkey to close the Jewish Agency office in Istanbul, then, it continued to be allowed to use Turkish facilities to smuggle diamonds, gold coins, and currency into the Nazi-occupied lands to help feed and house Jews who were not able to leave, with the Turkish ambassadors and consular representatives at times helping and even arranging for Jews to flee to Turkey. All of this activity took place at a time when British assistance of money and food to the persecuted Jews of Hungary and Bulgaria was strongly opposed by Foreign Secretary Anthony Eden, who stated that 'The majority of the adults who would benefit are Jews, and the political difficulties involved in this are obvious . . . ,' and who went on to even oppose a public British declaration condemning the Nazi atrocities against the Jews because ' . . these repeated threatenings might debase the currency'.[421] German and British pressure on Greece, Bulgaria and Yugoslavia to limit the Zionists' ability to charter ships for the dangerous trip through the Black Sea to Turkey and Palestine or to allow the ships of other nations to carry Jewish refugees through their territorial waters severely limited their ability to transport refugees, since all these nations put up very little resistance.[422]

Greece, which had remained as virulently anti-Semitic ever since it had separated from the Ottoman Empire during the Greek War for Independence as it had been in previous centuries,[423] and which had used

---

420. *Foreign Relations of the United States of America, 1941* II, 875–876.

421. Memorandum by Eden to the War Cabinet, 13 March 1944. Public Record Office, Cabinet papers 95/15, quoted in Gilbert, *Auschwitz*, p. 178.

422. Ofer, *Escaping the Holocaust*, pp. 131–133.

423. Steven Bowman, 'Jews in Wartime Greece', *The Nazi Holocaust. 4. The 'Final Solution' Outside Germany, volume 1,* ed. Michael Marrus (Westport and London, Meckler, 1989), pp. 297–314, particularly p. 298; Moyse Konstantine, *He Symbole ton Hebraion eis ton*

the violent events in Macedonia during and after World War I to drive the Jewish community out of its Ottoman center at Salonica,[424] outdid the Nazis and the British in working to prevent the escape of Jewish refugees from the Nazis, prohibiting use of ships flying its flag for anything connected with the *Aliyah*. Britain also got all the other nations of southeastern Europe to prohibit their nationals from serving on refugee ships sailing through the Black Sea, severely limiting *Mossad*'s ability to operate them on a regular basis.[425]

Turkey, however, resisted similar pressure, refusing to close the Straits to refugee ships on the grounds that this would violate the basic principles of freedom of navigation to which all the nations involved had subscribed before the war. When Nazi and British pressure at times forced Turkey to overtly limit these Zionist rescue activities by closing the Jewish Agency office and limiting Jewish immigration into and through Turkey, the Turkish government allowed the same Zionists to maintain the unofficial *Aliyah Bet* organization established by the *Mossad* committee to continue to bring in Jewish refugees and send them on to Palestine on an 'illegal' basis.

Apeleutheritikon Agona ton Hellenon (The Contribution of the Jews to the Greek War of Independence) (Athens, 1971), quoted in Bowman, p. 310.

424. Bowman, *ibid.*, pp. 299–300. See also Rena Molho, 'Venizelos and the Jewish Community of Salonica, 1912–1919', *Journal of the Hellenic Diaspora*, XIII/3–4 (1986), pp. 113–123, who explains how the Greek Prime Minister Venizelos, after conquering Salonica during the first Balkan War, attempted to change the general pro-Turkish attitudes of its Jewish population to emulate into the Greek-like racial hatred by emphasizing Greek nationalism and promoting Zionism, and that it was only after this failed, and the Greek Jews continued to moarn for the old days of Turkish rule that Greece began its campaign to drive the Jews out of Salonica so as to establish a Greek majority for the first time since the Ottoman conquest.

425. Ofer, *Escaping the Holocaust*, p. 134, on the basis of a communication from Samuel Hoare (Bucharest) to R. Campbell (Belgrade), 30 January 1940 (Public Record Office, FO 371/25238/W1384/38/48), concludes ' . . . in a memorandum from the head of the Near East Department of the Colonial Office, Harold Downie, to the head of the Refugees Department in the Foreign Office, J. E. Carvell. Downie wrote concerning the refusal of the Turkish government to make involvement in illegal Jewish immigration a punishable offense. The Turks would go no further than to issue stern admonitions. Downie felt this was insufficient and asked the Foreign Office to exert maximum pressure on the Turks and not limit itself to polite requests. Carvel pointed out that although many of the Turks' excuses were weak, their unwillingness to violate freedom of commerce was in fact well-grounded. . . .'

Turkey moreover helped rescue non-Turkish Jews in Rumania and Hungary, where almost a million and a half Jews had lived when the war began. Both were ruled by Fascist governments, in various forms of alliance with Germany, so that though they were not occupied by the Germans, they instead undertook their own means of persecuting their Jews. In both countries the Turkish diplomats worked to help protect Jews of all nationalities, even though most were not Turkish citizens. It was not that easy for the refugees to escape. Even after they had secured both a certificate permitting them to enter Palestine and a visa allowing them to transit through Turkey, wartime conditions made the problem of securing transportation at times almost impossible to overcome, particularly since Bulgaria was loathe to allow such refugees to pass through its territory to Turkey and beyond. Trains, however, were found, and Turkish and other ships carried hundreds of refugees from the coasts of Rumania and Bulgaria, sometimes to Istanbul, sometimes to the Black Sea port of Samsun or the Aegean port of Izmir, and from there to Palestine.[426]

Transportation of Jewish refugees through the Black Sea to Istanbul and beyond was made extremely difficult by a combination of German and British pressure on Hungary, Rumania and Bulgaria to prevent them from passing through their Black sea ports. A German naval force in the Black Sea operated, moreover, to stop refugee ships and take off their passengers, at times carrying out orders to sink them, with substantial loss of life, when it proved impossible to capture them.[427] Starting in January 1943, however, train cars of refugee Jewish children began arriving Istanbul. When British-occupied Iraq and Egypt refused to admit them,[428] or even grant them transit visas, Turkey allowed them to go on by small boat from its southern ports at Mersin and Antalya, across the Mediterranean to Palestine.

Turkey often allowed Jewish refugees from Eastern Europe to pass through its territory on their way to Palestine even when they arrived without proper documents or visas. Thus Charles Barlas wrote American Ambassador Laurence Steinhardt regarding such an action on the part of Turkish Foreign Minister Numan Menemencioğlu:

---

426. See, for example, the testimony of Michael Geteniu regarding his experiences in one of these small transports taking him from Salonica to Turkey, and from there to Palestine. Moreshet Archives, Givat Haviva center at Kibbutz Artzi near Hadera in Israel. Testimony archives no. A 337.9. Also the testimony of Zvi Markus in the same archive, no. A 410..

427. Ofer, *Escaping the Holocaust*, p. 192–194.

428. Gilbert, *Auschwitz*, pp. 112–113, 118.

As the result of the personal visits I made to the Turkish Minister for Foreign Affairs, the Bulgarian S/S Milka was allowed to enter the port of Istanbul without proper documents and although previously declared unseaworthy by the International Red Cross. In my first talk with the Turkish Minister for Foreign Affairs, he stated that as the Jewish refugees on board the S/S Milka had not been cleared by any authorities, were without Turkish visas, and without Palestine entry certificates, he would not under any circumstances permit them to land in Turkey as to do so would be to encourage the illegal traffic in refugees. He said that it was only by refusing entry into Turkey to refugees who arrived without Turkish transit visas that he could avoid a flood of illegal entries . . In the course of my second talk with him which lasted for over an hour and a half, I finally succeeded in persuading him to allow the refugees from the S/S Milka to land. After he had agreed to make this concession, he telephoned the Minister of Communications in my presence and requested him to provide the necessary four or five railroad cars immediately to transport the refugees from the Milka to Syria. After having made this friendly gesture, he stated to me categorically that he had done so as an exception and as a courtesy to me and that he wished to make it clear that he could make no further exceptions and that if any further refugees arrived Turkish visas that he would refuse them entry into Turkey. He added that he had done and was doing everything within his power to assist me in arranging for a large legal movement, and that he would see Von Papen as soon as possible in an endeavor to obtain safe conduct for the S/S Tara, but that as long as he was engaged in increasing the legal entry and movement of refugees into Turkey he would not tolerate any attempt to what he described as 'forcing his hand' by having refugees arrive in Turkish ports or at the Turkish frontier without Turkish transit visas . . . . Insofar as concerns transit facilities, as you are aware the Turkish authorities have agreed to increase them within the limits of the carrying capacity of the single track railroad from Istanbul to the Syrian frontier. Thus far the number of refugees has been within the carrying capacity of the railroad with its two trains weekly. Should the number increase beyond the carrying capacity of the railroad, it will be necessary to deal with this situation by means of a shuttle service by boat between Istanbul and a Syrian or Palestine port.... [429]

Thousands of refugees arrived in Turkey by boat and train and on foot during the remainder of 1943 and 1944 from Greece, Bulgaria, Rumania, Poland and Hungary, particularly after the latter was occupied by Germany in March 1944 and as the gas chambers of Auschwitz and elsewhere geared up to carry out the Final Solution.[430]

It was only in early 1944 that the United States government finally realized the extent of the Holocaust and moved to provide substantial support to the task of rescuing the surviving Jews in Eastern Europe. In response to increasing political pressure for action in the United States, American Ambassador to Turkey Laurence Steinhardt, himself a Jew, was asked by the Secretary of State whether the limited number of refugees who were arriving was due to Turkey's blocking their passage, and whether it might be possible to get Turkish assistance for the transport of Jews coming from southeastern Europe as well as camps to house them in Turkey until they were sent on to Palestine.[431] Steinhardt responded that the failure of large numbers of Jewish refugees to pass through Turkey previously was due not to Turkish reticence but to the refusal of the Balkan countries to allow them to leave as well as the difficulty they had encountered in finding adequate transportation even when they had received permission to move on. It was not that Turkey was unwilling to give them transit visas. It always had been willing to do so if only Britain would allow them to go on to Palestine. Turkey, moreover, was even ready to provide ships to transport

---

429. United States Ambassador Lawrence A. Steinhardt (Ankara) to Charles Barlas, Jewish Agency for Palestine, Pera Palace Hotel, Istanbul, 3 April 1944. Central Zionist Archives (Jerusalem). Frances Nicosia, ed. *Archives of the Holocaust, vol. 4. Central Zionist Archives Jerusalem, 1939–45* (New York and London, Garland, 1990), doc. 84, pp. 220–222.

430. The details of these operations are given in Ofer, *Escaping the Holocaust*, pp. 218–318, a brilliant study, though it suffers considerably from its failure to use Turkish sources or to acknowledge the Turkish contribution to these operations. See also Randolph Braham and Bela Vago, *The Holocaust in Hungary: Forty Years Later* (New York, Columbia University Press, 1986); John Conway, 'Der Holocaust in Ungarn: Neue Kontroversen und Uberlegungen', *Vierteljahrshefte fur Zeitgeschichte* XXXII (1984), pp. 179–212. Sari Reuveni, 'Special dispatches and late trains from Hungary to Auschwitz, 1944', *Yalkut Moreshet* XXXIX (1985), pp. 123–134; Tsvi Erez, 'Hungary–Six Days in July 1944, *Holocaust and Genocide Studies* III/1 (1988), pp. 37–53.

431. United States Department of State, Decimal Archives 840.48/5041, State Department to Steinhardt, 25 January 1944.

them from the Bulgarian and Rumanian coasts. It had already done so. But it was a poor country which would be using a substantial part of its merchant marine in the effort, and it needed guarantees that if the ships were sunk, the United States would provide replacements.

As a direct result of Steinhardt's report, on 22 January 1944 President Franklin Delano Roosevelt established the War Refugee Board (WRB), composed of representatives of the departments of State, Interior and War, to facilitate this task.[432] British Prime Minister Winston L. S. Churchill regarded the Middle East a primary British sphere of influence and an important element in maintaining the British Empire, so he deeply resented this American entry into the area. Due to the need to maintain Anglo-American cooperation in Europe and elsewhere in the world, however, the British had no choice but to cooperate and to change their policy to one of issuing group visas for these refugee groups massed in Istanbul so that they could go on to Palestine without further difficulty.[433] On 29 January 1944, the British Embassy at Ankara therefore informed the Turkish Ministry of Foreign Affairs:

> (1). Assurance is being given to the effect that Jewish immigrants arriving to Turkey under the scheme of 5,000 certificates will be granted visas to Palestine within twenty-four hours of their arrival in Istanbul.
>
> (2). Mr. Barlas, Representative of the Jewish Agency in Turkey, will be responsible for the arrangements regarding transportation of the immigrants to Palestine as well as their maintenance during their stay in Istanbul.
>
> (3). It is being understood that the transportation will be arranged in groups of seventy five children (including five adults as conveyors) every ten days, according to an itinerary to be agreed on.[434]

The War Refugees Board immediately moved to send its own agents to Istanbul to arrange for contacting the countries under Axis control and to provide transportation for their Jewish refugees to Turkey, to establish

---

432. Henry Feingold, *The Politics of Rescue. The Roosevelt Administration and the Holocaust, 1938–1945* (New Brunswick, N.J., 1970).

433. Ofer, *Escaping the Holocaust*, pp. 267–270.

434. Haim Barlas Archives, Jerusalem, quoted in Barlas, *ibid.*, p. 248.

transit camps in Turkey to receive refugees coming from southeastern Europe, and to provide transportation for them onward to Palestine.[435] The first WRB agent to arrive in Istanbul was an American Jewish businessman, Ira A. Hirschmann, an executive at Bloomingdale's department store in New York City, who remained through most of 1944 with instructions both to initiate rescue projects and to assist the agencies already in the field in those programs which they were already carrying out. He was joined in this effort by Ari Jabotinsky, son of the famous Ze'ev Jabotinsky, who represented the Zionist revisionist movement *EZEL* as well as the emergency committee of the *Irgun* in the United States,[436] Dr. Judah Magnes, who had been sent from Palestine especially to support what now had become the most important group then operating to support and rescue European Jewry, and Joseph Schwartz and Reuben Resnick, who represented the American Joint Distribution Committee.

Hirschmann's mission was initially opposed by Ambassador Steinhardt who feared that the former's direct and at times crude and uninformed approaches might alienate the Turkish officials with whom he had been working, but their difficulties were worked out in a luncheon meeting in Ankara on 2 July 1944. Hirschmann therefore gained the Ambassador's full support in the organizational meeting held on July 10 at the office of the American Office of War Information at the American Consulate, Istanbul, under the sponsorship of the Jewish Agency. The members of the Rescue Committee as well as other groups which had been active in Istanbul during the previous two years were formed into two groups, a united Rescue Council including representatives of all the groups, which acted as an advisory committee, and a smaller operating committee responsible for day-to-day operations. Together they acted as an umbrella group, coordinating the continued activities of the Rescue Committee as well as the American Jewish Joint Distribution Committee, resolving their differences and contradictory policies before approaches were made to the Turkish government [437]

---

435. Secretary of State to Ambassador Laurence Steinhardt, 25 January 1944. United States Department of State Archives (National Archives, Washington, D.C.), Decimal File 840.48/5041. Ofer, *Escaping the Holocaust*, p. 270.

436. William Perl, *The Four-Front War* (New York, Crown, 1979), pp. 359–360.

437. Ofer, *Escaping the Holocaust*, pp. 270–271; Barlas, pp. 44–46. Ira Hirschmann, *Life Line to a Promised Land* (New York, Vanguard, 1946); Ari Jabotinsky, *My Father Ze'ev Jabotinsky*, pp. 196–202; Haim Lazar-Litai, *Despite it All: the Aliye Bet of the Jabotinsky*

Steinhardt and Barlas had for some time been urging that the various relief organizations coordinate their efforts in rescuing the persecuted Jews in Eastern Europe. They had stated again and again that the independent actions of these groups, such as competitive bidding for food and ships, independent applications to various Turkish authorities without regard to what others had done before, as well as conflicting reports and projects, had made very difficult the work of the American Embassy as well as the Rescue committee, both in their relations with Washington and the individual organizations as well as with the responsible Turkish officials.[438] Turkish government officials supported these complaints about the uncoordinated activities of the various Jewish agents from Palestine. They were tired of receiving the many contradictory appeals for help and permission, as well as complaints about each other, from the different groups attempting to rescue European Jews, insisting instead that Barlas be recognized as their central leader, through whom all communications would pass between them and the various branches of government.

Though very insulting to his Turkish hosts, whom he seems to have viewed as inferior beings,[439] very much as Steinhardt originally feared, between July and October 1944 Hirschmann was very successful in getting all the different Jewish rescue groups in Istanbul to cooperate to achieve their common goal in a series of meetings held in Istanbul.[440] Once this was accomplished the Turkish officials became much more willing to agree to their requests. Hirschmann therefore was able to write to Barlas that the Turkish Government now was ready to provide the ship needed to carry Jewish refugees from Rumania through the Black Sea to Turkey:

---

movement (Tel Aviv, 1988). Avneri, *From 'Velos' to 'Taurus'*, p. 352–354; William Perl, *The Four-Front War* (New York, Crown, 1979), pp. 310–312 and *passim*.

438. Hirschmann report to the meeting of 'Representatives of Relief Organizations in Istanbul', held at the offices of the Office of War Information in Istanbul on 10 July 1944, in John Mendelson, ed., *The Holocaust*, vol. 14, p. 22.

439. See pp. xiii.

440. The minutes of the meetings which he chaired in Istanbul while accomplishing this, located at the Franklyn Delano Library in Hyde Park, New York, as part of the War Refugee Board archives, Box 41, volume 9, are published in John Mendelsohn, ed., *The Holocaust: 14. Relief and Rescue of Jews from Nazi Oppression, 1943–1945* (New York and London, Garland, 1982), pp. 22–94.

. . . I can tell you positively and from the highest source that a passenger ship will be ready in Istanbul in ten days to sail to Constanza in order to transit 1,500 children. This is definite and final. Do not make any other plan other than the arrangements for the 1,500 passengers in ten days. It is important that there be no delays. We have contributed our share, the rest is for you to finish. You know what this means concerning responsibility for the future. All of the United States government's influence has been implemented in order to bring about this outcome, and it cannot fail because of a defect in operations . . . . The thousands of lives that are about to be saved depend on that.[441]

Turkish Foreign Minister Numan Menemencioğlu offered the liner *Tari*, which had a capacity of approximately 1,500 passengers, so long as the belligerents were willing to guarantee its safety and promises were made to replace it if it were sunk. Ambassador Laurence Steinhardt wrote Barlas:

The ship Tari, a passenger ship prepared to sail at sea with a capacity of 1,500 passengers, and equipped with the necessary rescue equipment, has been handed to me by the Turkish government for the purpose of sailing from Istanbul to Constanza, or if necessary from Burgas or Varna to Haifa, in order to transit Jewish refugees from the Balkan states. While the details of the contract are still being negotiated between H. Block, from the Transportation by Ships Bureau of the United States, and the General Manager of the Turkish Steamship Company, most of the obstacles were removed in a conversation with the Foreign Minister, and I am sure that the contract will be signed. Indeed, negotiations concerning Safe Conduct are being held with the Russian Ambassador in Ankara and the American Ambassador in Moscow, as well as for a German Safe Conduct, concerning which negotiations are being conducted by H. Simon, representative of the International Red Cross in Geneva.[442]

Agreement was delayed, however, by the refusal of the Allied naval authorities to promise any sort of guarantee to the owners in case the ship

---

441. Barlas, p. 45.
442. Barlas, p. 46.

was lost beyond a vague promise to substitute some sort of freighter in place of this passenger liner, or to assist the work of transporting the refugees through the Black Sea and the Mediterranean, and by various obstructionist tactics of the Bulgarian government .

At this point Menemencioğlu complained that while Turkey was making the *Tari* available to carry refugees, had declared its readiness to allow the Jews into Turkey without any visas or other papers, and was willing to put the neutral Turkish flag on any ship which the Allies were willing to supply to carry the refugees from Turkey to Palestine:

> . . . the American and British governments, insofar as he was aware, had thus far taken no step to aid in the evacuation of refugees from the Balkans to Palestine other than to demand that others do so . . . . The two richest countries on earth, which own or control practically all the shipping of the world . . , were insisting that the Turk Government dedicate sixteen percent of its passenger fleet to the movement of refugees.[443]

Hirschmann, however, also did not seem to be listening to the Foreign Minister, since he caused even more delays with his complaint that the rental asked for the boat by its Turkish owners, quite high in the light of the danger involved, was excessive, while resolution was further delayed by German refusal to guarantee the safety of the ship.[444]

In a strange turnabout, the Jewish Agency committee at this point was very concerned about the possibility that Turkey would sever its relations with Germany and join the Allies, since this would most certainly cause an end to German permission for Jewish refugees to leave Nazi-occupied countries. Ankara was therefore urged to delay its entry into the war until most of the refugees could be saved, though of course in the process it would be criticized by others for not joining the war effort against the Axis.[445] In response Turkish Prime Minister Şükrü Saraçoğlu urged

---

443. Steinhardt and Hirschmann to War Refugee Board, 4 April 1944. National Archives, Record Group 59, Decimal series 840:48. Refugees /5537; and Steinhardt to War Refugee Board, 12 April 1944. National Archives, Record Group 59, Decimal Series 840:48 Refugees/5606, quoted in Hoffmann, p. 94.

444. Ofer, *Escaping the Holocaust*, pp. 194–195.

445. Meeting of the Operating Committee of Relief Organizations, United States Consulate, Istanbul, 31 July 1944, minutes in John Mendelsohn, ed. *The Holocaust*, XIV, 44–45.

Hirschmann to establish a 'bridge of ships' sailing regularly with refugees between Varna and Istanbul in place of the sporadic voyages which had been undertaken previously, so that all could be evacuated before the imminent Turkish entry into the war.

In the end, the *Tari* itself never did sail as a result of all these problems, but the small boats which the *Mossad* had been using in consequence of Saracoğlu's request, and with Turkish help and support, continued to carry 'illegal' Jewish refugees through the Black Sea and the Straits to southern Turkey and from there to Palestine.[446]

Hirschmann worked closely with Papal representative in Istanbul, Monsigneur Angelo Roncalli, in helping and rescuing the Jews of Hungary, who had been placed in mortal danger by Germany's occupation of the country in 1944. Using *Aliyah* agents as well as papal representatives and official diplomatic couriers, Roncalli also relied heavily on the communication networks and establishments of the Sisters of Zion, who had residences in both Tarabya on the Bosporus and in Budapest, to send thousands Turkish visas and Palestine immigration certificates, and even 'temporary' baptismal documents, some genuine and most forged, to Hungarian Jews that enabled them to join those who were fleeing through Turkey to Palestine as a result of the efforts of the *Aliyah* agents themselves. Hirschmann later wrote of Roncalli:

Roncalli is a fascinator. Charming, vocal, amusing, political, friendly—he wins everyone. His Palace at Principo is a gem, old stately rooms, pictures, etc. He has helped the Jews in Hungary and I beseech his further help. He reminded me so forcefully of La Guardia with his charm and humor and cleverness that it seemed uncanny. His little eyes sparkled and rolled; his stomach protruded, his body swayed. He protested in the name of God his lack of differentiation between peoples.[447]

---

446. Ofer, *Escaping the Holocaust*, pp. 273–275. Ofer's failure to use Turkish sources has resulted in serious errors in an otherwise excellent study. For one thing, she consistently refers to the Turkish foreign minister as A. Neumann, perhaps an intentional effort to indicate that the country was under German influence. The Turkish Foreign Minister was, however, Numan Menemencioğlu, a distinguished member of one of Turkey's most distinguished diplomatic families. .

447. Ira Hirschmann Diary, 31 July 1944: Franklin Delano Roosevelt Library, Hyde Park New York, Ira Hirschmann papers, box 1: 'Diary, Feb–Oct. 1944', quoted in Hoffman, *ibid.*, p. 90.

Largely as a result of Roncalli's leadership and encouragement, large numbers of 'conversions of convenience' were arranged by nuns and priests in Hungary to enable its Jews to escape deportation and death.[448] On 12 August, 1944, Ira Hirschmann reported to the War Refugee Board in Washington on Roncalli's contributions to saving Hungarian Jews:

> The Catholic Church in Hungary has taken an active part in rescuing many Hungarian Jewish citizens by means of the technical device of conversion of Jews to Christianity. Nazis have attempted in numerous ways to oppose these measures to which the church and especially the Dominicans who have been most sympathetic, responded they have authority to baptize immediately any person who is in imminent danger of death. During air raids hundreds of Jews are baptized in air raid shelters. When religious classes for Jews were held in churches, groups of Hungarian Nazis entered and broke up the classes which resulted in most of the baptisms now taking place in the shelters. It is reported that in the past month more Jews have been converted to Christianity than during the last 15 years.[449]

On 1 August 1944 Turkey severed its relations with Germany and joined the Allies in the war despite the urgings of Hirschmann that it delay this move further to allow more refugees to escape. In response to his urgings, however, the Turkish government issued instructions to its consuls in Burgas, Constanza and Budapest to give up to four hundred transit visas every ten days to permit voyages to Turkey by sea by all Jews able to flee from Hungary, Rumania and Bulgaria.[450] Similar instructions subsequently were sent authorizing the issuance of transit visas for land travel from Rumania and Bulgaria to Turkey. Hirschmann sent one thousand Palestine certificate confirmations to the *Aliyah* agents in Hungary and Rumania, authorizing individual refugees to enter Palestine in accordance with the British quotas, thus providing the Turkish consular authorities with the

448. Hoffmann, *ibid.*, pp. 90–92.

449. Ira Hirschmann to War Refugee Board, 12 August 1944, from National Archives (Washington), Record Group 59, Decimal System 840:48/Refugees 8–1244, quoted in Hoffmann, *ibid.*, p. 93.

450. British Embassy (Ankara) to Foreign Office, 9 August 1944, quoted in Barlas, *ibid.*, pp. 248–250.

authorization needed for them to issue transit visas to enter Turkey either by land or sea. He promised that more would be sent as needed.[451]

Soon afterwards three small Turkish ships hired by *Mossad*, the *Bulbul*, the *Marina*, and the *Mefkure*, left the Rumanian port of Constanza with another 1,000 Jews escaping to Palestine, with Turkish transit visas provided as a result of the certificates which Barlas had sent.

While the German flotilla stationed between the Rumanian coast and the Bosporus initially allowed it to sail into the Black Sea, the *Mefkure* was fired on and sunk, with heavy loss of life, apparently because the Germans thought that Polish and Serbo-Croatian partisan leaders had been included among the refugees in order to enable them to join the Allied forces fighting against the Germans in North Africa.[452]

In August 1944, Hirschmann and his committee decided to send large numbers of Palestine admission certificates to Jewish refugees in Yugoslavia and Rumania as well as Bulgaria, most of whom were fleeing from Hungary after the Nazis started to deport most of its Jews to the death camps, while the Turkish Foreign Ministry immediately instructed its consulates in those countries to provide transit visas as required.[453]

On many occasions, after the refugees reached Istanbul, they remained much longer than was initially expected or authorized in their transit visas, as a result of transportation difficulties as well as continued British efforts to restrict their further progress to Palestine. The Turkish government, however, extended the transit visas of such refugees so that many in fact remained in the country until the end of the war.[454]

Britain continued to strongly resent American intervention in what it considered to be it's affairs,[455] but in the light of the efforts of the WRB and

451. Meeting of the Operating Committee of Relief Organizations, Office of the War Refugee Board, United States Consulate, Istanbul, 21 August 1944, minutes in John Mendelsohn, ed. *The Holocaust*, XIV, 56–57.

452. M. Resel, *Tik Mefkura* (The Mefkura File) (Tel Aviv, 1981), quoted in Ofer, *Escaping the Holocaust*, pp. 197, 367. See also Ofer, pp. 263–264.

453. Turkish Foreign Ministry (Ankara) to Turkish consulates in Bucharest and Sofia, 27 August 1944; copy in archives of Turkish Embassy (Paris); Meeting of Relief Organizations at the Office of the War Refugee Board, Istanbul, 25 August 1944. Minutes in John Mendelsohn, ed., *The Holocaust*, pp. 68–69.

454. Turkish Foreign Ministry (Ankara) to Turkish Embassy to Paris (Vichy), no. 671/33, 5 September 1944. Archives of the Turkish Embassy (Paris). Meeting of Relief Organizations at the Office of the War Refugee Board, Istanbul, 4 September 1944. Minutes in John Mendelsohn, ed., *The Holocaust*, pp. 79–81.

455. Ofer, *Escaping the Holocaust*, pp. 281–282.

of Ira Hirschmann in particular, it was compelled to continue to relax its immigration policies and support the effort to rescue the Jews.[456]

On 19 May 1944, the British Passport Control Officer in Istanbul, A. Whitall, informed Barlas:

> . . . I confirm that, in accordance with instructions from the Foreign Office, Jewish refugees arriving in Turkey from occupied Europe may now be granted visas for Palestine on application, i.e. without reference to London or Jerusalem . . .[457]

The British Embassy reported to the Foreign Office:

> We have now reached agreement with (Turkish) Ministry of Foreign Affairs for the immediate institution of the following comprehensive arrangements which will cover admission into Turkey in transit of Jewish refugees from Hungary, Roumania and Bulgaria. . . .
>
> The (Turkish) Ministry of Foreign Affairs have undertaken to request Ministry of the Interior tomorrow to admit into Turkey henceforth without delay and without reference to Ankara any persons arriving at Turkey's land frontiers without Turkish visas . . . . This should mean in practice that almost every Jew arriving without a Turkish visa will be admitted . . . .[458]

American Ambassador Laurence Steinhardt, wrote Reuben Resnik:

> American Embassy, Ankara, June 15, 1944
>
> Mr. Reuben B. Resnik,
> c/o American Consulate-General, Istanbul
> Dear Rube,
> Thank you for your two letters of June 14th. Since last seeing you, I have had a talk with the Secretary General of the Foreign Office who agreed not only to inform the Turkish Minister in

456. Timothy P. Maga, 'Operation Rescue: the Mefkure Incident and the War Refugee Board, *American Neptune*, XLIII/1 (1963), pp. 31–39.
457. Haim Barlas Archives, Jerusalem, quoted in Barlas, *ibid.*, pp. 247–248.
458. Barlas, *ibid.*, pp. 248–249.

Bucharest that the Turkish Government desired the movement of Jewish refugees from Rumania to Istanbul and Palestine facilitated, but that he would give the necessary instructions to make at least two and perhaps more similar Turkish vessels available to operate without safe conduct between Rumanian and Bulgarian ports and Istanbul. The only point that bothered him was the criticism to which the Turkish Government might be subjected if a Turkish vessel was sunk and a large number of refugee lives lost while operating without safe conduct. I replied that the plight of the Jewish refugees in the Balkans was now so desperate that I was sure they would be willing to take the risk involved of passage without safe conduct rather than be left to the tender mercies of the Nazis, and intimated–without saying so–that if there should be a disaster we would do everything within our power to make it clear to the American public that it had been the result of a humanitarian act by the Turkish Government which could in no sense be held morally responsible for the loss of lives growing out of an attempt to save these same lives. I have sent a lengthy explanatory telegram this morning to the Department of State outlining our difficulties under Turkish law in obtaining the consent of the Ministry of Finance to purchase Turkish pounds at the diplomatic rate for your exports, explaining the situation with respect to UKGG and urging the Department to request London to telegraph UKCC in Istanbul to accord you the favorable rate. I expect to see the Minister for Foreign Affairs within the next two days, and will press him again to accord you the favorable rate direct, but have less confidence that he will be able to persuade the Minister of Finance–who is extremely hard-boiled–than I have that you will get the rate through UKCC. It also occurs to me that the rate that UKCC can give you if authorized may be even more favorable than the diplomatic rate, but as to this I am not certain. In any event it will not be less favorable, of that I am sure.

With kind personal regards,

Sincerely yours,

Laurence A. Steinhardt[459]

---

459. Laurence Steinhardt Archives, Library of Congress, Washington, D.C.; copy in Archives of the American Joint Jewish Distribution Committee, *Turkey, 1943–1945* (New York)

The Turkish Ambassador to Rumania throughout the war, Hamdullah Suphi Tanrıöver, played an important role in stopping Rumanian plans to send its 600,000 Jews to the Nazi death camps.[460] The Turkish Red Crescent and the Jewish Agency in Istanbul sent medical supplies and clothing to Eastern Europe on a regular basis, but at times Bulgaria refused to allow these supplies to be given to its Jewish citizens. In addition, starting in the summer of 1940, the Turkish government sent trucks, trains, and the steamship *Sakarya* on regular rescue missions through the Black Sea, bringing several hundred Jewish refugees from throughout eastern Europe to Istanbul on each trip. Similar rescues were made by the steamships *Europa, Vitornal, Pacific* and *Atlantic* as well as many small motor boats and sail boats sent from Turkish ports on the Black Sea. The refugee ships were allowed through Turkish waters by the authorities whether or not they had regular papers, or even when the latter were obviously forgeries or invalid documents sold to the *Aliyah Bet* agents, for the most part by clerks in the consulates of many of the countries of Central and South America.[461]

Most of the refugees landed at the Black Sea port of Samsun, from which they were sent overland to Konya, Niğde and Mersin, where they remained while passport and visa formalities were completed for their subsequent passage to Palestine. Other refugees from Yugoslavia, Bulgaria and Greece as well as many fleeing from the death camps at Bergen-Belsen and Vittel and a few from Denmark, Sweden, Switzerland and Slovakia came by sea from Salonica across the Aegean to Izmir, and from southern Greece, Rhodes and the eastern Mediterranean islands to southern Anatolia's Mediterranean ports of Antalya, Bodrum, Iskenderun and Mersin. From there they went on in groups to Palestine on steamers and small boats arranged by the Jewish agency and the Turkish government as well as overland through Syria by trains of the Turkish railroads.

On 1 February 1941, Haim Barlas estimated that about 4,594 Jewish refugees from Eastern Europe had received Turkish visas as a result of thirty lists submitted to the Ankara government: [462]

---

460. Tilavi, *Yeudei Romania be Maavak als Atmala* (Jerusalem, 1962), quoted in Avner Levi, p. 166. In the end 330,000 Jews died in Rumania during the war, with only women and children surviving.

461. Dr. Baruch Konfino, *Illegal Immigration from the Shores of Bulgaria, 1948-1940, 1947–1948* (Jerusalem, 1965), p. 49.

462. Barlas, *ibid.*, p. 235.

FROM	NUMBER OF PASSPORTS	REFUGEES
Kaunas	474	720
Bucharest	1105	2006
Budapest	398	590
Salonica	28	60
Zagreb	268	309
Geneva	199	373
Riga	17	42
Sofia	17	23
Stockholm	450	450
Individual cases, Lvov, etc.	18	21
Totals	2944	4594

Thousands more came in subsequent years, though exact figures lack for the years before 1944. The American Jewish Joint Distribution Committee reported that between January and October 1944, they helped 4,404 Jewish refugees go to Turkey, of whom 691 were from Bulgaria, 160 from Hungry, 2,732 from Rumania, 539 from Greece, and 282 from Holland. All came by the following steamers: the Milca (239 passengers); Maritza (334), Bella Cita (153), Milca (272), Maritza (318), Kazbek (752), Morina (308), Bulbul (391), Turkish Railroads (35), and five saved from the steamship *Mefkure*, which was sunk.[463] In the final analysis, a total of 16,474 'official' Jewish immigrants passed through Turkey during the war on their way to Palestine, in addition to approximately 75,000 'unofficial' refugees, while the Jewish Agency in Istanbul and its affiliated groups distributed some 523,547 pounds sterling to Jews in Nazi-occupied Europe in 1943 and 1944.[464] According to American figures, a total of $215,000 was distributed in Turkey for Jewish refugees by various American relief organizations from January 1944 until February 1945, much of which was raised in emotional campaigns led by Hirschmann after he returned to the United States.[465]

---

463. American Jewish Joint Distribution Committee, Archives 1943–1945 (New York).

464. Ofer, *Escaping the Holocaust*, pp. 320–321.

465. This included $150,000 from the American Jewish Joint Distribution Committee, $35,000 from the International Rescue and Relief Committee, $25,000 from the Vaad Hahatzala Emergency Committee, and $5,000 from the Emergency Committee to Save the Jewish People of Europe. 'Treasury Department licenses for relief and rescue issued persuant to recommendations of the War Refugee Board up to February 5, 1945', in Franklin D. Roosevelt Library, Records of the War Refugee Board, Box 15, Folder: Jewish Labor

Turkey's role in the war went beyond its help to Europe's suffering Jews. It was through the Jewish agents in Istanbul that Adolph Eichmann's offer came to liberate the surviving Jews of Hungary, in return for war equipment and money.[466] It was through these same agents that the offer of Helmuth von Moltke, representing the underground German anti-Nazi opposition, for an early peace immediately after the failure of their attempt against the life of Adolph Hitler, was passed on to the Allies in October 1943, through the agency of one of the leading refugee professors, politicall scientist Alexander Rüstow.[467] Similarly, it was to Istanbul in February, 1944 that agents from Hungary came to offer a separate peace if only their nation could be rescued from the deadly Nazi embrace.[468]

Moshe Shertock later stated that from the Jewish perspective, Istanbul was far more important as a base for gathering information and providing refuge for Jews fleeing from the Nazis than were the other neutral centers in Europe, since only it provided direct connections between European Jewry and the Yishuv in Palestine. Zionists active in Istanbul during the war remain convinced that, in the absence of help from the great Jewish communities of Britain, America and South Africa, it was their activities alone, done with the full knowledge and silent support of the Turkish government, that provided European Jews with the feeling that some people still remembered them and were trying to help them.[469]

Committee to Licenses, published in John Mendelsohn, *The Holocaust. vol. 14. Relief and Rescue of Jews from Nazi Oppression, 1943–1945* (New York and London, 1982), pp. 153–192. On Hirschmann's role in raising funds in the United States to help the relief operations based in Turkey, see Henry Feingold, *The Politics of Rescue* (New York, 1970), p. 289.

466. Alex Weissberg, *Advocate for the Dead: The Story of Joel Brand* (London, 1958); Gilbert, *Auschwitz*, pp. 212–213; Hilberg, *Destruction of the European Jews* III, 1133–1138.

467. Peter Hoffman, *The History of the German ResisTance, 1933–1945* (Cambridge, Mass., MIT Press, 1977), pp. 225–226; Barry Rubin, *Istanbul Intrigues*, pp. 175–176; Michael Balfour and Julian Frisby, *Helmuth von Moltke: A Leader against Hitler* (London, 1972), pp. 269–274, 278–279; Ger van Roon, *Neuordnung im Widerstand: Der Kreisauer Kreis innerhalb der deutschen Widerstandsbewegung* (Munich, 1967), pp. 317–322; Melmuth J. Graf von Moltke, *A German of the Resistance: The Last Lettes of Count Helmuth James von Moltke* (Oxford University Press, London, 1948); Heinz Höhne, *Canaris* (New York, Doubleday, 1979), pp. 482–486; Michael Balfour and Julian Frisby, *Helmuth von Moltke: A Leader against Hitler* (Macmillan, London, 1972), pp. 269–277. .

468. Barry Rubin, *Istanbul Intrigues*, pp. 143–144.

469. Rubin, *Istanbul Intrigues,* and Tevet, 436–437.

Conclusion

Turkey most certainly did not remain neutral during World War II in order to save the Jews of Europe. It did so because it was allied with Britain and France, which were unable to promise assistance if its entry into the war led to a German invasion. The resulting Turkish neutrality, however, did make it possible for its diplomatic agents in Nazi-occupied Europe to significantly assist in saving thousands of Jews from persecution and death and for Turkey to constitute the most important bridge for Jewish refugees fleeing from Eastern Europe on their way to Palestine. This belies the claim, so often heard, that the Wealth Tax reflected anti-Semitism or constituted a conscious effort to drive the Jews out of Turkey. If anything, as we have seen, it constituted a desperate effort to solve the financial problems caused by the need to defend the nation against the threat of Nazi invasion from Greece combined with resentment at excessive wartime profits and fear that the alliance of some Armenian nationalists with the Nazis was aimed at taking advantage of the German invasion of the Soviet Union to create an Armenian state in the southern Caucasus and eastern Anatolia.

Whatever lingering doubts that may have remained from the Wealth Tax were dispelled soon after the war when Prime Minister Recep Peker firmly declared in 1947 that:

> Every individual in this nation is part of an indivisible whole on the basis of common language and destiny born from living together in this land and is equal in sharing duty, privilege and honor . . . . Anti Semitism will remain the shame of the twentieth century, and if in our legislation there are anti-minority provisions they will be amended . . . .[470]

Jewish Turks have continued to live in Turkey in peace and prosperity to the present. Turkey moreover has remained an important place of refuge to which those fleeing from persecution in the Middle East have been able to go, whether Kurds from Iraq, Jews and Bahais from Khomaini's Iran, or Turks from Greece, Armenia, Azerbaijan, Greek Cyprus and Bulgaria.

---

470. Speech at University of Istanbul, reported in *Ulus*, 29 March 1947. Quoted in Kemal Karpat, *Turkey's Politics* (Princeton, 1959), pp. 257-258.

Bibliography

Otto Abetz, *Das offene Problem. Ein Rückblick auf zwei Jahrzehnte Deutscher Frankreichpolitik* (Cologne, 1951).

Otto Abetz, *Histoire d'une politique franco-allemande, 1930–1950: Memoires d'un Ambassadeur* (Paris, 1953).

Otto Abetz, *D'Une Prison* (Paris, 1950).

Michel Abitbol, *The Jews of North Africa during the Second World War* (Detroit, Wayne State University Press, 1989).

Michel Abitbol, 'The Jews of Algeria, Tunisia and Morocco, 1940–1943', (in Hebrew), *Pe'amim*, no. 28 (1986), pp. 79–106.

Yitzhak Abrahami, 'The Jewish Communities of Tunisia during the Nazi Conquest', (in Hebrew), *Pe'amim*, no. 28 (1986), pp. 107–125.

Uwe Dietrich Adam, *Judenpolitik im Dritten Reich* (Düsseldorf, 1972).

H. G. Adler, *Der Verwaltete Mensch: Studien zur Deportation der Juden aus Deutschland* (Tübingen, 1974).

Jacques Adler, *The Jews of Paris and the Final Solution* (New York and Oxford, 1987).

Samet Ağaoğlu, *Demokrat Partinin Doğuşu ve Yükseliÿ Sebepleri* (The Reasons for the Birth and Rise of the Democratic Party) (Istanbul, 1972).

Reuben Ainsztein, *Jewish Resistance in Nazi-Occupied Eastern Europe* (London, 1974).

Rıdvan Akar, *Varlık Vergisi* (The Wealth Tax) (Istanbul, Belge, 1992).

Alexis Alexandris, *The Greek Minority of Istanbul and Greek-Turkish Relations, 1918–1974* (Athens, Center for Asia Minor Studies, 1983).

L. Algisi, *Papa Giovanni XXIII* (Turin, 1981).

Helmut Allardt, *Politik vor und hinter den Külissen* (Düsseldorf, 1979).

David Alvarez, 'The Embassy of L.A. Steinhardt. Aspects of Allied-Turkish Relations, 1942–1945', *East European Quarterly*, 1975/1.

Abraham Shaul Amarillio, 'The Great Talmud Torah Society in Salonica', (in Hebrew), *Sefunot* XIII (1978), pp. 274–309.

American Jewish Committee, *The Jewish Communities of Nazi-Occupied Europe* (New York, 1982).

Ettore Anchieri, *Costantinopoli e gli Stretti nella politica russa ed europea* (Milano, 1948).

Rabbi Marc Angel, *The Jews of Rhodes* (New York, 1980).

Zvi Ankori, 'Greek Orthodox-Jewish Relations in Historic Perspective: The Jewish View', *Journal of Ecumenical Studies*, XIII (1976), pp. 17–57

M. Ansky, *Les Juifs d'Algérie du Décret Crémieux à la libération* (Paris, 1950).

Ismail Arar, *Hükümet Programları, 1920–1965* (Government Programs, 1920–1965) (Istanbul, 1968).

Benjamin Arditti, *The Jews of Bulgaria during the Years of Nazi Occupation, 1940–1944* (in Hebrew, Tel Aviv, 1969).

Fahir Armaoğlu, *Siyasi Tarih, 1789–1960* (Political History, 1789–1960) (2nd ed., Ankara, 1973).

Fahir Armaoğlu, *Yüzyil Siyasi Tarihi, 1914–1980* (Political History of the Century, 1914-1980) (Ankara, 1983).

Sarkis Atamian, *The Armenian Community. The Historical Development of a Social and Ideological Conflict* (London and New York, 1955).

Falih Rifki Atay, *Yolcu Defteri* (Travel Book) (Ankara, 1946).

Phyllis Auty and Richard Clogg, *British Policy towards Wartime Resistance in Yugoslavia and Greece* (London, 1975).

Aryeh Levi Avneri, *From Velos to Taurus: The First Decade of Jewish 'Illegal' Immigration to Mandatory Palestine, 1933–1944* (in Hebrew), Tel Aviv, Hakibbutz Hame'uhad, 1985).

Yitzhak Avneri, *The Zionist Organization and Illegal Immigration to Palestine from the British Conquest to the Second World War* (in Hebrew) (Unpublished Ph.D. dissertation, Tel Aviv, 1979).

Haim Avni, 'Spanish Nationals in Greece and their Fate during the Holocaust', *Yad Vashem Studies on the European Jewish Catastrophe and Resistance* VIII (1970), pp. 31–68.

Haim Avni, *Spain and the Jews in the days of the Holocaust and the Emancipation* (in Hebrew) (Tel Aviv, 1975).

Haim Avni, *Spain, the Jews and Franco* (Philadelphia, Jewish Publication Society, 1980).

Ehud Avriel, *Open the Gates* (New York, Random House, and London, 1975). Hebrew edition published in Tel Aviv, 1976.

Şevket Süreyya Aydemir, *Ikinci Adam: Ismet Inönü* (The Second Man: Ismet Inönü) (2 vols, 2nd edn, Istanbul, 1966 –68)

Şevket Süreyya Aydemir, *Suyu Arayan Adam* (Istanbul, Remzi, 1965).

Cihat Baban, *Politika Galerisi* (The Political Gallery) (Istanbul, Remzi, 1970).

Menahem Bader, *Sad Missions* (in Hebrew) (Tel Aviv, 1954, 2nd revised edn, Tel Aviv, 1978).

John A. Bailey, *Lion, Eagle and Crescent: the Western Allies and Turkey in 1943. A Study of British and American Diplomacy in a Critical Year of the War* (Unpublished Ph.D. dissertation, Georgetown University, 1969).

Michael Balfour and Julian Frisby, *Helmuth von Moltke: A Leader against Hitler* (London, Macmillan, 1972).

Elisabeth Barker, *British Policy in South-East Europe in the Second World War* (London, 1976).

Haim (Charles, Chaim) Barlas, *Rescue in the Days of the Holocaust* (in Hebrew: *Hatzala Bi'yemey ha-sho'ah*) (Tel Aviv, Bet-Lohame ha-geta'ot/Hakibbutz Hameuhad Publishing House, 1975).

Haim Barlas, 'Operation Lithuanian Aliyah', (in Hebrew), *Research Papers on the Holocaust and Resistance. New Series, Collection A* (Tel Aviv, Hakibbutz Hameuhad, 1970), pp. 246–255.

Haim Barlas, 'Meetings in Istanbul', (in Hebrew) *Masua* 4 (April 1976), pp. 125–133.

Michael Barsley, *Orient Express* (New York, 1967).

Faik A. Barutçu, *Siyasi Anılar* (Political Memories) (Istanbul, Milliyet, 1977).

Ilhan Başgöz ve Howard A. Wilson, *Türkiye Cumhuriyetinde Eğitim ve Atatürk* (Education in the Turkish Republic and Atatürk) (Ankara, 1968).

Yehuda Bauer, *A History of the Holocaust* (New York, 1982).

Yehuda Bauer, *Flight and Rescue: Brichah–The Organized Escape of the Jewish Survivors of Eastern Europe, 1944–1948* (New York, Random House, 1970).

Yehuda Bauer, *From Diplomacy to Resistance: A History of Jewish Palestine, 1930–1945* (New York, Atheneum, 1973).

Yehuda Bauer, *American Jewry and the Holocaust: The American Jewish Joint Distribution Committee, 1939–1945* (Detroit, Wayne State University Press, 1981).

Yehuda Bauer and Jacob Robinson, eds, *Guide to Unpublished Materials of the Holocaust Period* (6 volumes, Jerusalem, Yad Vashem, 1970–1981).

Judith Tydor Baumel, ed., *Israel State Archives, Jerusalem* (New York, Garland, 1991).

Alfred Bäumler, *Alfred Rosenberg und der Mythos des 20. Jahrhunderts* (Munich, 1943).

Celal Bayar, *Celal Bayar Diyorki, 1920–1950* (Celal Bayar says, 1920–1950) (Ankara, 1964).

Ertuğrul Baydar, *İkinci Dünya Savaşı İçinde Türk Bütçeleri* (Turkish Budgets during the Second World War) (Ankara, Maliye, 1978).

François Bédarida, *La Politique Nazie d'Extermination* (Paris, Albin Michel, 1989).

J. G. Beevor, *SOE: Recollections and Reflections, 1940–1945* (London, 1981).

J. Bowyer Bell, *Terror out of Zion: Irgun Zvai Leumi, Lehi and the Palestine Underground, 1929–1949* (New York, 1977).

Eliahu Ben-Elissar, *La Diplomatie du IIIe Reich et les Juifs 1933–1939* (Paris, 1969).

Norman Bentwich, *The Rescue and Achievement of Refugee Scholars. The story of displaced scholars and scientists, 1933–1952* (The Hague, Martinus Nijhoff, Holland, 1953).

Anne Benveniste, *Le Bosphore à la Roquette: La communaute judeo-espagnole à Paris (1914–1940)* (Paris, 1990).

Jean Jacques Bernard, *Le Camp de la mort lente (Compiègne, 1941–1942* (Paris, Albin Michel, 1944).

John Bierman, *Odyssey: The Last Great Escape from Nazi-Dominated Europe* (New York, Simon and Schuster, 1984).

Joseph Billig, *Le Commissariat Général aux questions Juives, 1941–1944* (3 volumes, Paris, Centre de Documentation Juive Contemporaine, 1955–1960).

J. Billig, *Alfred Rosenberg dans l'action idéologique, politique et administrataive du Reich hitlérien: Inventaire commenté de la collection de documents conserves au Centre de Documentation Juive Contemporaine provenant des Archives du Reichsleiter et Ministre A. Rosenberg* (Paris, 1963).

Joseph Billig, *L'Institut d'Étude des Questions Juives: Officine française des autorités nazies en France. Les inventaires des archives du Centre de Documentation Juive Contemporaine* (Paris, CDJS, 1974).

Joseph Billig, 'La Condition des Juifs en France', *Revue d'Histoire de la Deuxieme Guerre Mondiale* VI (1956), pp. 23–55.

Faruk Hakan Bingün, *Nazi Almanyasından Kaçarak Türkiye'ye sığınan Alman bilim Adamı ve Sanatçılar* (German intellectuals and artists who fled from Nazi Germany to Turkey) (Ankara Üniversitesi Sosyal Bilimler

Enstitüsü Uluslararası Ilişkiler Anabilim Dalı, Yüksek Lisans Tezi, 1990).

Andreas Biss, *A Million Jews to Save* (New York, Barnes, 1975).

Cyril Black, *Floyd Black, 1888–1983: A Remembrance by his Son* (Princeton, New Jersey, 1984).

Edwin Black, *Transfer Agreement* (New York, Macmillan, 1984).

Pierre Blet, Robert A. Graham, Angelo Martini and B. Schneider, *Actes et Documents du Saint Siege Relatifs à la Second Guerre Mondiale* (Rome, 11 volumes).

Louis Botrel, *Histoire de la franc-maçonnerie française sous l'Occupation (1940–1945)* (Paris, Detrad, 1988).

Philippe Bourdrel, *Histoire des Juifs de France* (Paris, Albin Michel, 1974).

Tom Bower, *Klaus Barbie: The Butcher of Lyons* (New York, Pantheon, 1983).

Steven Bowman, 'Jews in Wartime Greece', *Jewish Social Studies* XLVIII/1 (1986) 48(1), pp. 45–62, reprinted in *The Nazi Holocaust,* ed., M.R. Marrus, *4. The Final Solution Outside Germany, volume 1* (Westport and London, Meckler, 1989), pp. 297–314.

R. L. Braham, ed., *The Destruction of Hungarian Jewry* (2 vols, New York, World Federation of Hungarian Jews, 1963)

R. L. Braham, *The Politics of Genocide: The Holocaust in Hungary* (2 vols, Columbia University Press, New York, 1980)

Ernest Bramsted, *Goebbels and National Socialist Propaganda, 1925–1945* (London, 1965).

Joel Brand, *Desperate Mission* (New York, Grove, 1958).

Martin Broszat, 'Das deutsch-ungarische Verhältnis und die ungarische Judenpolitik in der Jahren 1938–41', *Gutachten des Instituts für Zeitgeschichte* I (1958), 183–200.

Martin Broszat, 'Das dritte Reich und die rumänische Judenpolitik', *Gutachten des Instituts für Zeitgeschichte* I (1958), 102–183.

Christopher Browning, *The Final Solution and the German Foreign Office: A Study of Referat D III of Abteilung Deutschland 1940–1943* (New York and London, Holmes and Meier, 1978).

Christopher Browning, 'Unterstaatssekretär Martin Luther and the Ribbentrop Foreign Office', *Journal of Contemporary History* XII (1977), 313–344.

Vicki Caron, 'Prelude to Vichy: France and the Jewish Refugees in the Era of Appeasement', *Journal of Contemporary History* XX (1985), pp. 157–200.

Daniel Carpi, 'The Italian Government and the Jews of Tunisia in World War II (June 1940–May 1943)', (in Hebrew), *Zion* LII (1987), pp. 57–106.

Daniel Carpi, 'Notes on the History of the Jews in Greece during the Holocaust Period. The Attitude of the Italians (1941–1943)', *Festschrift in Honor of Dr. George S. Wise* (Tel Aviv, 1981), pp. 25–62.

Daniel Carpi, 'The Jews of Greece in the Holocaust period (1941–43) and the behavior of the Italian occupation authorities', (in Hebrew), *Yalkut Moreshet*, no. 31 (1981), pp. 7–39.

Daniel Carpi, 'The Diplomatic Negotiations over the Transfer of Jewish Children from Croatia to Turkey and Palestine in 1943', *Yad Vashem Studies on the European Jewish Catastrophe and Resistance* (Jerusalem) XII (1977), 109–124.

Daniel Carpi, 'Nuovi Documenti per la Storia Dell'Olocausto in Grecia: L'Atteggiamento degli Italiani (1941–1943)', Michael, *On the History of the Jews in the Diaspora* VII (1981), pp. 119–200.

Daniel Carpi, 'The Italian diplomat Luca Pietromarchi on his activities for the Jews of Croatia and Greece', (in Hebrew), *Yalkut Moreshet* no. 33 (1982), pp. 145–152.

Daniel Carpi, 'The Mufti of Jerusalem, Haj Amin el-Huseini, and his Political Activity during the Second World War', (in Hebrew), *Hazionut* 9 (1984), pp. 286–316.

Robert Cecil, *The Myth of the Master Race: Alfred Rosenberg and Nazi Ideology* (London, Batsford, 1972).

Central Zionist Archives, *List of Archives and Collections of Documents Kept in the Central Zionist Archives* (Jerusalem, 1965).

Centre de Documentation Juive Contemporaine, *Les Juifs sous l'Occupation: Recueil des Textes Officiels Français et Allemands, 1940/1944* (Paris, 1982).

Centre de Documentation Juive Contemporaine, *L'Activité des Organisations Juives en France sous l'occupation* (Paris, 1983).

Centre de Documentation Juive Contemporaine, *Le Statut des Juifs de Vichy: Documentation,* ed. Serge Klarsfeld (Paris, Association Les Fils et Filles des Déportés Juifs de France, 1990).

Centre de Documentation Juive Contemporaine, *Drancy, 1941–1944* (Paris, 1991).

Centro di Documentazione Ebraica Contemporanea (Milan), *Ebrei in Italia: Deportazione, resistenza* (Florence, 1975).

Frederick Chary, *The Bulgarian Jews and the Final Solution, 1940–1944* (Pittsburgh, Pa., 1972).

Bibliography

Asher Cohen, 'Le Peuple Aryen vu par le Commissariate General aux
Questions Juives', *Revue d'Histoire de la Deuxieme Guerre Mondiale et
des Conflits Contemporains* , XXXVI/141 (1986), pp. 45–58.

N. W. Cohen, *Not Free to Desist: The American Jewish Committee, 1906–
1966* (Philadelphia, Pa., 1972).

E. H. Cookridge, *The Orient Express* (New York, 1969).

Lewis Coser, *Refugee Scholars in America* (New Haven, Connecticut, 1984).

Jan Cremer and Horst Przytulla, *Exil Türkei: Deutschprachtige Emigranten
in der Türkei 1933–1945* (Karl Lipp, 1981).

Alexander Dallin, *German Rule in Russia 1941–1945: A Study of Occupation
Policies* (New York, 1956).

Rae (Rachel) Dalven, *The Jews of Ioannina* (Philadelphia, Cadmus, 1990)

Rachel Dalven, 'The Holocaust in Janina,' *Journal of Modern Greek Studies*
(May 1984), pp. 87–103.

Lucy Davidowitz, *The War Against the Jews, 1933–1945* (London, 1975).

Basil Davidson, *Special Operations Europe: Scenes from the Anti-Nazi War*
(New York, 1981).

Louis de Jong, *Die deutsche Fünfte Kolonne im Zweiten Weltkrieg* (Stuttgart,
1959).

Renzo de Felice, *Storia degli ebrei italiani sotto il fascismo* (Turin, 1972).

D. J. Delivanis, 'Thessaloniki on the Eve of World War I', *Balkan Studies*
XXI/2 (1980), pp. 191–201.

Selim Deringil, *Turkish Foreign Policy during the Second World War: an
'active' neutrality* (Cambridge University Press, Cambridge and New
York, 1989).

David Diamant, *Les Juifs dans la Résistance française, 1940–1944* (Paris,
1971).

Zanvel Diamant, 'Jewish Refugees on the French Riviera', *Yivo Annual of
Jewish Social Science* VIII (1953), pp. 264–280.

Maria Antonia di Casola, *Turchia Neutrale (1943–1945): La Difesa degli
Interessi Nazionali dalle Pressioni Alleate* (2 vols, Milano, 1984).

Eliyahu Dobkin, *Immigration and Rescue in the Years of the Holocaust* (in
Hebrew) (Jerusalem, Arachim, 1946).

François Georges Dreyfus, *Histoire de Vichy: Vérités et Légendes* (Paris,
Perrin, 1990).

Robert Dunn, *World Alive* (New York, 1956).

Nathan Eck, 'The Rescue of Jews with the Aid of Passports and Citizenship
Papers of Latin American States', *Yad Vashem Studies,* no. 1 (1957),125–
152.

Blake Ehrlich, *Resistance: France 1940–1945* (Boston, Little Brown, 1965).

Amos Elon, *Timetable* (Garden City, New York, 1980).

Adolf von Ernsthausen, *Wende im Kaukasus. Ein Bericht* (Neckargemünd, Germany, 1958).

Philipp W. Fabry, *Die Sowjetunion und das Dritte Reich. Eine dokumentierte Geschichte der deutsch-sowjetischen Beziehungen von 1933–1941* (Stuttgart, 1971).

Carlo Falconi, *The Silence of Pius XII* (Boston, Little Brown, 1970).

S. Fauch, 'Das deutsch-bulgarische Verhältnis 1939–44 und seine Reckwirkung auf die bulgarische Judenpolitik', *Gutachten des Instituts für Zeitgeschichte* II (1966), 46–59.

Henry Feingold, *The Politics of Rescue. The Roosevelt Administration and the Holocaust, 1938–1945* (New Brunswick, N.J., Rutgers University Press, 1970).

Mary Felstiner, 'Commander of Drancy: Alois Brunner and the Jews of France,' *Holocaust and Genocide Studies* II /1 (1987), pp. 21–47.

W. Filchenfeld, D. Michaelis and L. Pinner, *Ha'avara Transfer nach Palastia und Einwanderung Deutschen Juden, 1933–1939* (Tübingen, 1972).

Stephen Fischer-Galati, 'Fascism, Communism and the Jewish Question in Romania', *Jews and Non-Jews in Eastern Europe, 1918–1945*, ed. Bela Vago and George Mosse (New York and Jerusalem, 1974).

Donald Fleming and Bernard Bailyn, eds. *The intellectual migration. Europe and America, 1930–1960* (Cambridge, Mass., Harvard University Press, 1969).

Etienne Fouilloux, 'Extraordinaire Ambassaeur. Mgr. Roncalli a Paris (1944-1953)', *Revue Historique*, vol. 279 (1), pp. 101–128.

Hizkia M. Franco, *Les Martyrs juifs de Rhodes et de Cos* (Elisabethville, Katanga, 1952).

Henry Friedlander and Sybil Molton, ed., *Archives of the Holocaust: An international Collection of Selected Documents* (18 vols, New York, Garland, 1990).

Henry Friedlander and Sybil Milton, eds., *Bundesarchiv of the Federal Republic of Germany, Koblenz* (New York, Garland, 1992).

Henry Friedlander and Sybil Milton, eds, *Zentrale Stelle der Landesjustizverwaltungen, Ludwigsburg* (New York, Garland, 1992).

Saul Friedlander, *Pie XII et le IIIe Reich* (Paris, Seuil, 1964); *Pius XII and the Third Reich* (New York, Knopf, 1966).

Philip Friedman, 'The Karaites under Nazi rule', *On the Track of Tyranny* (London, 1960), pp. 97–123, and *Roads to Extinction: Essays on the*

Holocaust, ed., Philip Friedman and Ada June Friedman (New York and Philadelphia, Jewish Publication Society of America, 1980), pp. 153–175.

Saul Friedman, *No Haven for the Oppressed: United States Policy Toward Jewish Refugees, 1938–1945* (Detroit, Michigan, 1973).

Cevat Geray, *Türkiye'den ve Türkiye'ye Göçler ve Göçmenlerin Iskânı: 1923–1961* (Migrations and the Settlement of Migrants going from and to Turkey, 1923-1961) (Ankara, Ankara Universitesi Siyasal Bilgiler Fakültesi Maliye Enstitüsü Yayını, 1962).

Benjamin Gil, *Aliyah Pages: Thirty Years of Immigration to Eretz Israel, 1919–1949* (in Hebrew) (Jerusalem, Jewish Agency Aliyah Department, 1950).

Martin Gilbert, *Auschwitz and the Allies* (New York, 1981).

Johanes Glasneck, *Methodender Deutsch Faschistestchen Propaganda-tätigheit in der Türkei vor und Wahrend des Zweites Weltkrieges* (Halle, 1966). (translated into Turkish as: *Türkiyede Faşist Propagandası*, Ankara, n.d.).

Mahmut Goloğlu, *Milli Şef Dönemi* (The Era of the National Chief) (Ankara, 1974).

Peter Gosztony, *Hitlers Fremde Heere: Das Schicksal der nichtdeutschen Armeen im Ostfeldzug* (Vienna, 1976).

W. P. Green, 'The Fate of Oriental Jews in Vichy France', *Wiener Library Bulletin*, XXXII (1979), no. 49, pp. 40–50.

W. P. Green, 'The Nazi Racial Policy toward the Karaites', *Soviet Jewish Affairs*, VIII/2 (1978), pp. 36–44.

A. A. Gretschko, *Die Schlacht um den Kaukasus* (Berlin, 1969).

Natan Grinberg, *Hitleriskiyat natisk sa unishtojavone na evreite ot Bulgaria* (Tel Aviv, 1961).

Moşe Grosman, *Dr. Markus (1870–1944)* (Istanbul, As, 1992).

Kurt Grossmann, *Emigration: Geschichte der Hitler-Flüchlinge 1933–45* (Frankfurt/Main, 1969).

Yitzhak Gruenbaum, *In Days of Destruction and Holocaust* (in Hebrew) (Jerusalem, 1946).

Naim Güleryüz, 'Temmuz 1944-Rodos: Selahattin Ülkümen ve Matilde Turiel', *Şalom*, 25 April 1990

Naim Güleryüz, 'Türk Konsolosu'nun ölümden döndürdüğü 42 Yahudi', *Yaşam* (monthly supplement to *Şalom*), August 1986, pp. 10–13.

Lewis Hagen, *The Secret War for Europe* (New York, 1968).

Peter Hebblethwaite, *Pope John XXIII* (New York, 1985).

Anthony Heilbut, *Exiled in Paradise: German Refugee Artists and Intellectuals in America from the 1930s to the Present* (New York, Viking, 1983).

Jonathan Helfand, ed., *Yeshiva University of New York* (New York, Garland, 1991).

Ivo Herzer, Klaus Voigt and James Burgwyn, eds., *The Italian Refuge: Rescue of Jews During the Holocaust* (Washington, D.C., Catholic University of America Press, 1989).

Raul Hilberg, *The Destruction of the European Jews: Revised and Definitive Edition* (3 vols, New York and London, Holmes and Meier, 1985).

Raul Hilberg, *La Destruction des Juifs d'Europe* (Paris, Fayard, 1988).

Andreas Hillgruber, *Die Räumung der Krim 1944* (Frankfurt/Main, 1959).

Andreas Hillgruber, *Der Einbau der verbündeten Armeen in die Deutsche Ostfront, 1941–1944* Frankfurt/Main, 1960).

F. H. Hinsley, *British Intelligence in the Second World War* (3 vols, London, 1979-1984).

Ernest E. Hirsch, *Üniversite Kavramı ve Türkiyedeki Gelişimi* (The Concept of the University and Reform in Turkey) (Istanbul, Fakülteler Matbaasi, 1979).

Ernst E. Hirsch, *Hâtıralarım* (My Memories) (Ankara, 1985).

Yair Hirschfeld, *Deutschland und Iran in Spielfeld der Machte, Internationale Beziehungen unter Reza Schah, 1921–1941* (Dusseldorf, 1980).

Ira Hirschmann, *Caution to the Winds* (New York, 1982)

Ira Hirschmann, *Life Line to a Promised Land* (New York, Vanguard, 1946).

Lukasz Hirszowics, *The Third Reich and the Arab East* (London, Routhledge Kegan Paul, 1966).

Peter Hoffmann, *The History of the German Resistance, 1933–1945* (Cambridge, Mass., 1977).

Peter Hoffmann, 'Roncalli in the Second World War: Peace Initiatives, the Greek Famine and the Persecution of the Jews', *Journal of Ecclesiastical History*, XL (1989), pp. 74–99.

Gary Hogg, *Orient Express* (New York, 1969).

Ariel Horwitz, 'Menahem Bader's Mission in Istanbul and the Contacts of Hashomer-Hatzair with European Jewry', (in Hebrew) *Yalkut Moreshet* no. 35 (April 1983), pp. 152–202.

Heinz Höhne, *The Order of the Death's Head* (London, 1970).

Heinz Höhne, *Canaris* (New York, 1979).

Hans-Joachim Hoppe, 'Bulgarian Nationalities Policy in Occupied Thrace and Aegean Macedonia', *Nationalities Papers*, XIV/1–2 (1986), pp. 89–100.

Hans-Joachim Hoppe, 'Germany, Bulgaria, Greece: their Relations and Bulgarian Policy in Occupied Greece', *Journal of the Hellenic Diaspora* XI/3 (1984), pp. 41–54.

H. Stuart Hughes, *Prisoners of Hope: The Silver Age of the Italian Jews, 1924–1974* (Cambridge, Mass., Harvard University Press, 1983).

Paula Hyman, *From Dreyfus to Vichy: The Remaking of French Jewry, 1906–1939* (Columbia University *Press*, New York, 1979).

Carol Iancu, *Les Juifs en Roumanie, 1966–1919* (University de Provence, France, 1978).

Eri Jabotinsky, *The Sakariya Expedition: A Story of Extra-Legal Immigration into Palestine* (Johannesburg, South Africa, 1945).

Hans-Adolf Jacobsen, *1939–1945 Der Zweite Weltkrieg in Chronik und Dokumenten* (Bonn, 1961), translated into Turkish as *1939–1945 Kronoloji ve Belgelerle Ikinci Dünya Savaşı* (Ankara, 1989). References are to Turkish translation.

Hans-Adolf Jacobsen, *Nationalsozialistische Aussenpolitik, 1933–1938* (Frankfurt and Berlin, 1968).

Eberhard Jaeckel, *Frankreich in Hitlers Europa. Die deutsche Frankreichpolitik im Zweiten Weltkrieg* (Stuttgart, 1966).

Gotthard Jäschke, *Die Türkei in den Jahren 1935–1941* (Leipzig, 1943).

Gotthard Jäschke, *Die Türken in Den Jahren 1942–1951*(Wiesbaden,, 1955).

Gotthard Jäschke, *Türkiye Kronolojisi (1938–1945)* (Chronology of Turkey, 1938–1945) (Ankara, Türk Tarih Kurumu, 1990).

Yeshayahu Jelinek, 'The Holocaust and the Internal Policies of the Nazi Satellites in Eastern Europe: A Comparative Study', *The Nazi Holocaust*, ed., M.R. Marrus, 4. *The Final Solution Outside Germany, volume 1* (Westport and London, Meckler, 1989), pp. 291–296.

Jewish Agency, *Report on Activities in the years 1940–1946* (in Hebrew). Report to the 46th Zionist Congress at Basel in 1947 (Jerusalem, 1947).

(Pope John XXIII), *Giovanni XXIII, Il Pastore. Corrispondenza dal 1911 al 1963 con i preti del Sacro Cuore di Bergamo* (Padova, 1982).

Carlos Caballero Jurado, *Foreign Volunteers of the Wehrmacht, 1941–1945* (London, Osprey, 1983)

Isaac Kabeli, 'The Resistance of the Greek Jews', *YIVO Annual of Jewish Social Sciences* VIII (1953), pp. 281–288.

David Kahn, *Hitler's Spies: German Military Intelligence in World War II* (New York, 1978).

Yakup Kadri Karaosmanoğlu, *Politikada 45 yıl* (Forty Five years in Politics) (Ankara, Bilgi, 1968).

Kemal Karpat, *Turkey's Politics: The Transition to a Multi-Party System* (Princeton, N.J., 1959)

R. Kashani, *The Jewish Communities in Turkey* (in Hebrew) (Jerusalem, 1968).

André Kaspi, Serge Klarsfeld and Georges Wellers, *La France et le Question Juive* (Paris, Messinger, 1981).

Robert Katz, *Black Sabbath. The Politics of Annihilation. The Harrowing Story of the Jews of Rome, 1943. A Journey through a Crime against Humanity* (London, Barker, 1969).

Nathanian Katzburg, 'British Policy on Immigration to Palestine during World War II', Yad Vashem, *Rescue Attempts during the Holocaust* (Jerusalem, 1977), pp. 183–203.

Arslan Kaynardağ, 'Üniversitelerimizde ders veren Alman felsefe profesörleri', (German philosophy professors teaching in our universities), Türkiye Felsefe Kurumu, *Türk Felsefe Araştırmalarında ve Üniversite Öğretiminde Alman Filozofları* (German Philosophers in Turkish philosophy researches and University teaching) (Ankara, 1986), pp. 1–31.

Andreas Kazamias, *Education and the Quest for Modernity in Turkey* (London, 1966).

Nissim Kazzaz, 'The Influence of Nazism in Iraq and Anti-Jewish activity, 1933–1941', (in Hebrew) *Pe'amim* no. 29 (1986), pp. 48–71.

Yitzhak Kerem, 'Efforts to Rescue the Jews of Greece during the Second World War', (in Hebrew), *Pe'amim* no. 27 (1986), pp. 77–109.

Yitzhak Kerem, 'Immigration Patterns from Greece to the Ottoman Empire in the 19th century', VIIIth Symposium of the Comité International d'Etudes Pre-Ottomanes et Ottomanes, University of Minnesota, 14-19 August 1988, to be published as 'The Influence of Anti-Semitism on Jewish Immigration Patterns from Greece to the Ottoman Empire in the 19th century,' in the papers of the conference.

Yitzhak Kerem, 'The Bulgarian Deportation of the Jews of Macedonia, Pirot and Thrace,' Association for Jewish Studies Annual Conference, Boston, Massachusetts, 17-19 December 1989.

Jon Kimche and David Kimche, *The Secret Roads: The Illegal Migration of a People, 1938-1948* (London, Secker and Warburg, 1951).

Alexandros Kitroeff, 'Documents: The Jews in Greece, 1941–1944: Eyewitness Accounts', *Journal of the Hellenic Diaspora* XII/3 (1985), pp. 5–32.

Serge Klarsfeld, *Memorial to the Jews Deported from France, 1942–1944: Documentation of the deportation of the victims of the Final Solution in France* (New York, Beate Klarsfeld Foundation, 1983).

Serge Klarsfeld, *Vichy-Auschwitz: Le Role de Vichy dans la Solution Finale de la Question Juive en France, 1943–1944* (2 vols, Paris, Fayard, 1985).

Serge Klarsfeld, *Drancy, 1941–1944* (Paris, 1988).

Serge Klarsfeld, *1941: Les Juifs en France: Préludes a la Solution finale* (Paris, 1991).

Ruth Kluger and Peggy Mann, *The Last Escape: The Launching of the Largest Secret Rescue Movement of all Times* (New York, Doubleday, 1973, Los Angeles, Pinnacle, 1978).

Hughe Knatchbull-Hugessen, *Diplomat in Peace and War* (London, 1949, 2nd ed., 1968).

Cemil Koçak, *Türkiyede Milli Şef Dönemi, 1938–1945* (The Era of the National Chief in Turkey) (Ankara, 1989)

Teddy Kolleck, *One Jerusalem* (in Hebrew) (Tel Aviv, Maariv Bookshop, 1979).

Barukh Konfino, *Illegal Immigration from the Shores of Bulgaria, 1938–1940* (in Hebrew) (Tel Aviv, 1965).

Bilge A. Köksal-Ilkin Rasih, *Türkiyede Iktisadi Politikanın Gelişimi (1923–1973)* (The Development of Economic Policies in Turkey, 1923-1973) (Istanbul, Yapı ve Kredi Bankası, 1973).

W. Krausnick, *Anatomy of the SS State* (London, 1970).

Lothar (Ludwig) Krecker, *Deutschland und die Türkei im Zweiten Weltkrieg* (Frankfurt/Main, 1964).

Bruce Kuniholm, *The Origins of the Cold War in the Near East* (Princeton, New Jersey, 1978).

Uri M. Kupferschmidt, 'The Maronite Patriarch Arida and the Jews persecuted by the Nazis', (in Hebrew), *Pe'amim*, no. 29 (1986), 72–80.

Yuluğ Tekin Kurat, *Ikinci Dünya Savaşında Türk-Alman ticaretindeki iktisadi siyaset* (Economic Policy in Turkish-German trade during the Second World War) (Ankara, 1961).

Th. Lavi, *Yeudei Romania be Mouvak al ha Atsala* (Hebrew, 1962).

Th. Lavi, 'The Background to the Rescue of Romanian Jewry during the Period of the Holocaust', *Jews and Non-Jews in Eastern Europe, 1918–*

1945, ed. Bela Vago and George Mosse (New York and Jerusalem, 1974).

Th. Lavi, 'Documents on the Struggle of Rumanian Jewry for Its Rights during the Second World War', *Yad Vashem Studies* IV (1960), 261–315.

Haim Lazar-Litai, *Despite It All: The Aliyah Bet of the Jabotinsky Movement* (in Hebrew) (Tel Aviv, 1988).

Lucien Lazare, *La résistance juive en France* (Paris, Stock, 1987).

Jenny Lebel, 'The Holocaust in Yugoslavia—Communities in Macedonia, Pirot and Kossovo', (in Hebrew), *Pe'amim* no. 27 (1986), pp. 62–76.

Paul Leverkuehn, *German Military Intelligence* (London, Weidenfeld and Nicolson, and New York, 1954).

Paul Leverkühn, *Der geheime Nachrichtendienst der deutschen Wehrmacht im Kriege* (Frankfurt, 1957).

Avner Levi, 'The Jews of Turkey on the Eve of the Second World War and During the War', (in Hebrew), *Pe'amim* no. 27 (Tel Aviv, 1986), pp. 32–47.

Claude Levy and Paul Tillard, *La Grande Rafle du Vel d'Hiv (16 juillet 1942)* (Paris, Laffont, 1967).

Günter Lewy, *The Catholic Church and Nazi Germany* (London, 1964).

Chaim Lipschitz, *Franco, Spain, the Jews and the Holocaust* (New York, Ktav, 1983).

Zdenko Löwenthal, *The Crimes of the Fascist Occupants and their Collaborators against Jews in Yugoslavia* (Belgrad, 1957).

E. Ludsuveit, 'Der deutsche Imperialismus in der Türkei während des Zweiten Weltkrieges,' *Studien zur Kolonial geschichte und Geschichte der nationalen und kolonialen Brfreiungsbewegung* vol. X/XI (1964).

James Mandalian, 'Dro–Drastamat Kanayan', *The Armenian Review* II (1958).

James Mandalian, 'Geregin Nezhdeh', *The Armenian Review* I (1957).

Meir Mardor, *Strictly Illegal* (London, 1964).

Michael R. Marrus and Robert O. Paxton, *Vichy et les Juifs* (Paris, Calmann-Lévy, 1981)

Michael R. Marrus and Robert O. Paxton, *Vichy France and the Jews* (New York, Basic Books, 1981, Schocken, 1983).

Michael R. Marrus, ed., *The Nazi Holocaust: Historical Articles on the Destruction of European Jews* (15 vols in 9, Westport and London, Meckler, 1989).

Michael R. Marrus and Robert O. Paxton, 'The Nazis and Jews in Occupied Western Europe, 1940–1944', *Journal of Modern History* LIV (1982), 687–714.

René Massigli, *La Turquie devant la guerre. Mission à Ankara* (Paris, Plon, 1964).

John Masterman, *The Double Cross System in the War of 1939 to 1945* (New Haven, Conn., 1972).

Alexander Matkovsky, 'The Destruction of Macedonian Jewry in 1943', *Yad Vashem Studies* III (1959), pp. 203–258.

Alexander Matkovsky, *A History of the Jews in Macedonia* (Skopje, 1982).

Mary Matossian, *The Impact of Soviet Policies in Armenia* (Leiden, 1962).

Guiseppe Mayda, *Ebrei sotto Salo: La persecuzione antisemita 1943-1945* (Milan, 1978).

Richard Meinertzhagen, *Middle East Diary, 1917–1956* (London, 1959).

John Mendelsohn and Donald Detwiler, eds, *The Holocaust: Selected Documents* (18 vols, New York, Garland, 1982)

John Mendelsohn, ed., *Deportation of the Jews to the East* (New York, Garland, 1991).

John Mendelsohn, 'The Holocaust: Records in the National Archives on the Nazi Persecution of the Jews', *Prologue* XVI (1984), pp. 23–29.

Ali Kemal Meram, *Ismet Inönü ve Ikinci Cihan Harb* (Ismet Inönü and the Second World War) (Istanbul, n.d.)

Lucillo Merci, Joseph Rochlitz and Menachem Shelach, 'Excerpts from the Salonika Diary of Lucillo Merci (February-August 1943)', *Yad Vashem Studies*, VIII (1987), pp. 293–323.

Ahmet Meriç, *Varlêk Vergisinin Satılmış Kahramanı Faik Ökteye Açık Mektup* (Open Letter to Faik Ökte. the purchased hero of the Wealth Tax) (Istanbul, 1951).

Meir Michaelis, *Mussolini and the Jews. German-Italian Relations and the Jewish Question in Italy, 1921–1945* (London, Institute for Jewish Affairs, New York, Oxford University Press, 1978).

Meir Michaelis, 'The Holocaust in Italy, 1943–1945', (in Hebrew) *Pe'amim*, no. 28 (1986), pp. 5–27.

Meir Michaelis, 'The Attitude of the Fascist Regime to the Jews in Italy', *Yad Vashem Studies* no. 4 (1960), pp. 7–41.

Marshall Miller, *Bulgaria during The Second World War* (Stanford, California, 1975).

Sybil Milton and Roland Klemig, eds. *Bildarchiv Preussischer Kulturbesitz Berlin* (2 vols, New York, Garland).

Sybil Milton, ed. *American Jewish Joint Distribution Committee, New York* (3 vols, New York, Garland, 1992)

Maurice Moch et Alain Michel, *L'étoile et la francisque: Les institutions juives sous Vichy* (Paris, Cerf, 1990).

M. Molho and J. Nehama, *In Memoriam: Hommage aux Victimes Juives des Nazis en Gréce* (2nd expanded edition, Salonica, 1973).

Anne Morelli, 'Les diplomates italiens en Belgique et la question juive, 1938–1943', *Bulletin de l'Institut Historique Belge de Rome* LIII–LIV (1983–4), pp. 357–407.

Aryeh Morgenstern, The Agency's Joint Rescue Committee, 1943–1945, (in Hebrew), *Yalkut Moreshet* XIII (June 1971), pp. 60–103.

John Morley, *Vatican Diplomacy and the Jews during the Holocaust, 1939–1943* (New York, Ktav,1980).

Amnon Netzer, 'Anti-Semitism in Iran, 1925–1950', (in Hebrew) *Pe'amim* no. 29 (1986), pp. 5–31.

Roberto Morozzo della Rocca, 'Roncalli Diplomatico in Turchia e Grecia (1935–1944)', *Cristianesimo nella Storia*, VIII/2 (1987), pp. 33–72

V. A. Muradiak *et al*, eds, *Sovetskaya Armeniia v Gody Velikoi Otechestevennoi Voiny, 1941–1945: Sbornik Dokumentov i materialov* (Erivan, 1975).

Nadir Nadi, *Perde Aralığından* (From Amidst the Curtain) (Istanbul, 1964).

Nicholas Nagy-Talavera, *The Green Shirts and Others: A History of Fascism in Hungary and Rumania* (Stanford, California, 1970).

Fritz Neumark, *Zuflucht am Bosphor* (Frankfurt, 1980). Translated into Turkish as *Boğaziçine sığınanlar: Türkiye'ye iltica eden Alman Ilim Siyaset ve Sanat Adamları, 1933–1953* (Those who took refuge on the Bosporus: German scientists and scholars who fled to Turkey, 1933-1953) (Istanbul University, 1982).

Francis Nicosia, *The Third Reich and the Palestine Question* (London, Tauris, 1985).

Rudolf Nissen, *Erinnerungen eines Chirurgen* (Stuttgart, 1969).

Dalia Ofer, *Escaping the Holocaust: Illegal Immigration to the Land of Israel, 1939–1944* (New York, Oxford University Press, 1990).

Dalia Ofer, 'The Activities of the Jewish Agency Delegation in Istanbul in 1943', *Rescue Attempts during the Holocaust: Proceedings of the Second Yad Vashem International Historical Conference, Jerusalem, April 8–11, 1974* (Jerusalem, Yad Vashem, 1977), pp. 435–450.

Dalia Ofer, 'Aid and Rescue Activities of the Palestinian Delegation in Istanbul, 1943', (in Hebrew), *Yalkut Moreshet* XIV (November, 1972), pp. 33–58.

Nissan Oren, 'The Bulgarian Exception: A Reassessment of the Salvation of the Jewish Community', *Yad Vashem Studies* VII (1968), pp. 83–106.

Dietrich Orlow, *The Nazis in the Balkans* (Pittsburgh, Pa., 1968).

Faik Ökte, *Varlık Vergi Faciası* (The Tragedy of the Capital Tax) (Ankara, 1951)

Zehra Önder, *Die Türkische Aussenpolitik im Zweiten Weltkrieg* (Munich, 1977).

Kâzım Öztürk, *Türkiye Cumhuriyeti Hükümetleri ve Programları* (The Governments and Programs of the Republic of Turkey) (Istanbul, 1968).

George Paloczi-Horvath, *The Undefeated* (London, 1959).

Jean-Louis Panicacci, 'Les Juifs et la question juive dans les Alpes-Maritimes de 1939 à 1945', *Recherches régionales Côte d'azur et contrées limitrophes: Bulletin trimestriel* (Archives Départmentales des Alpes-Maritimes, n.d., pp. 239–330.

Franz von Papen, *Memoirs* (London, Deutsch, 1952).

Robert O. Paxton, *Vichy France: Old Guard, New Guard* (Princeton University Press, 1966).

William R. Perl, *The Four-Front War: From the Holocaust to the Promised Land* (New York, Crown, 1979).

David Wingeate Pike, 'Les Forces Allemandes dans le Sud-Oest de la France, Mai–Juillet 1944', *Guerres Mondiales et Conflits Contemporains*, XXXVIII/152 (1988), pp. 3–24,

Max Pinl and Lux Furtmuller, 'Mathematicians under Hitler', *Leo Baeck Institute Yearbook* XVIII (1973), pp. 129–182.

Edward Pinsky, 'Cooperation Among American Jewish Organizations in their Efforts to Rescue European Jewry during the Holocaust, 1939–1945', Unpublished Ph.D dissertation, New York University (1980).

A. Pinto and D. Pinto, *Stradanje Sarajevskih Jevreja pod Ustashkim Rezhimom* (Sarajevo, 1974).

I. S. O. Playfair, *The Mediterranean and the Middle East* (6 vols, London, 1954–1987).

Leon Poliakov and Jacques Sabille, ed., *Jews under the Italian Occupation* (Paris, 1955).

Leon Poliakov and Josef Wulf, eds., *Das Dritte Reich und seine Diener: Dokumente* (Berlin, 1956).

Dina Porat, *An Entangled Leadership: the Yishuv and the Holocaust, 1942–1945* (in Hebrew) (Tel Aviv, Am Oved, 1986).

Dina Porat, *The Blue and the Yellow Stars of David: The Zionist Leadership in Palestine and the Holocaust, 1939–1945* (Cambridge, Mass., Harvard University Press, 1990).

Y. Porath, *The Palestinian Arab National Movement* (2 vols, London, 1977).

Pearl Liba Preschel, *The Jews of Corfu*, Unpublished Ph.D. dissertation, New York University, 1984.

Luigi Preti, *Impero fascista ed ebrei* (Milan, 1968).

Roman Rainero, 'I rapporti italo-turchi nel periodo fascista', *Il Veltro* XXIII/2–4 (March–Aug 1979).

Maurice Rajsfus, *Drancy: Un camp de concentration très ordinaire, 1941–1944* (Paris, Manya, 1991).

David A. Recanati, ed., *Zikhron Saloniki: Grandezi i Destruyicion de Yeruchalaim del Balkan* (Tel Aviv, 1971–1972).

Gerald Reitlinger, *The Final Solution* (2nd revised ed., London, 1968).

Gerald Reitlinger, *The SS: Alibi of a Nation, 1922–1945* (Englewood Cliffs, N.J., 1981).

George Rendell, *The Sword and the Olive. Recollections of Diplomacy andthe Foreign Service, 1913–1954* (London, Murray, 1957).

Rescue Activities from Istanbul, 1940–1945 (in Hebrew) (Jerusalem, 1969).

Moshe Resel, *The Mefkure File* (in Hebrew) (Tel Aviv, 1981).

Ernst Reuter, *Schriften-Reden, Zweiter Band: Artikel, Frief, Reden 1922 bis 1946*, ed. Hans J. Reichhardt (Berlin, 1973).

Vittoro Ugo Righi, *Papa Giovanni XXIII sulle rive del Bosforo* (Padova, Italy, 1971).

Emmanuel Ringelblum, *Polish-Jewish Relations during the Second World War* (Jerusalem, Yad Vashem, 1974, New York, Fertig, 1976).

Michel Roblin, *Les Juifs de Paris* (Paris, Picard, 1952).

Jurgen Rohwer, *Die Versenkung der Jüdischen Flüchtlingstransporter Struma und Mefkura im Schwarzen Meer Februar 1942–August 1944* (Frankfurt/Main, Graefe, 1964).

Iasha Romano, *Jevreji Jugoslavije 1941–1945. Zrtve Genocida i Ucesnici NOR* (The Jews of Yugoslavia, 1941–1945. Victims of Genocide and Participants in the War of National Liberation) (Belgrade, 1980).

Etienne Rosenfeld, *De Drancy à ces camps dont on ne parle pas* (Paris, Harmattan, 1991).

Dominique Rossignol, *Vichy et les Francs-Maçons* (Paris, Lattès, 1981).

Cecil Roth, 'The Last Days of Jewish Salonica', *Commentary* no. 10 (July 1950), pp. 49–55.

Werner Röder and Helbert Strauss, *Biographisches Handbuch der Deutschsprachigen Emigration nach 1933/International Biographical Dictionary of Central European Emigrees, 1933–1945* (Institüte für Zeitgeschichte München and Research Foundation for Jewish Immigration, New York), vol. I (Munich, New York, London and Paris, 1980).

Barry Rubin, *The Arab States and the Palestine Conflict* (Syracuse, N.Y., 1980).

Barry Rubin, *Istanbul Intrigues: A True-Life Casablanca* (New York, 1989).

Arthur Ruppin, *Three Decades of Palestine* (Westport, Conn., 1975).

Alexander Rustow, *Freedom and Domination* (Princeton, New Jersey, 1980).

Donna Frances Ryan, 'Vichy and the Jews: The Example of Marseilles', Unpublished Ph.D. dissertation, Georgetown University, 1984.

Giacomo Saban, 'Ebrei di Turchia,' *La Rassegna Mensile di Israel*, XLIX (Jan–Apr. 1983).

Giacomo Saban, 'Ebrei di Turchia (2): Gli Anni Difficili,' *La Rassegna Mensile di Israel*, LVI (Jan.–Aug. 1990), pp. 161–189.

Jacques Sabille, *Les Juifs de Tunisie sous Vichy et l'Occupation* (Paris, 1954).

Jacques Sabille, 'Attitude of the Italians to the Jews in Occupied Greece', *The Jews under Italian Occupation*, ed. Leon Poliakov and Jacques Sabille (Paris, 1955).

Yasmut Savas, *Biographische Studien zu Bedeutenden Deutschprachigen Arzten in der Türkei* (Giessen, 1987).

J. Schechtman, *The Life and Times of Vladimir Jabotinsky* (New York, 1961).

H. D. Schmidt, 'The Nazi Party in Palestine and the Levant, 1932–1939', *International Affairs* XXVIII/4 (October 1952), pp. 460–469.

Ehrengard Schramm-von Thadden, *Griechenland und die Grossmächte im Zweiten Weltkrieg* (Wiesbaden, 1955).

P. E. Schramm, *Kriegstagebüch des Oberkommandos der Wehrmacht* (Frankfurt/m., 1965).

Bernard Schröder, *Deutschland und der Mittlere Osten im Zweiten Weltkrieg* (Göttingen, 1975). .

Zekeriya Sertel, *Hatırladıklarım* (What I Remember) (Istanbul, 1977).

Moshe Sevilla-Sharon, *Türkiye Yahudileri* (The Jews of Turkey) (Istanbul, Iletişitim, 1992).

Errikos Sevillias, *Athens, Auschwitz* (Port Jefferson, N.Y, Cadmus, 1984 and New York, Lycabettus, 1987).

Stanford J. Shaw and Ezel Kural Shaw, *History of the Ottoman Empire and Modern Turkey* (2 vols, Cambridge University Press, 1976 and later editions).

Stanford J. Shaw, *The Jews of the Ottoman Empire and the Turkish Republic* (London, Macmillan, and New York, New York University Press, 1991).

Menahem Shelah, 'The Holocaust in Yugoslavia–The Communities in Serbia and Croatia', (in Hebrew) *Pe'amim*, no. 27 (1986), pp. 31–61.

A. J. Sherman, *Island Refuge: Britain and Refugees from the Third Reich, 1933–1939* (London, 1973).

Gérard Silvain, *La Question Juive en Europe, 1933–1945* (Paris, Clattes, 1985).

Rachael Simon, 'The Jews of Libya on the Eve of the Holocaust', (in Hebrew) *Pe'amim*, no. 28 (1986), pp. 44–78.

Ruggero Simonato, 'Il Carteggio tra A.G. Roncalli e C. Costantini (1936–1956', *Cristianesimo nella Storia*, VII/3 (1986), pp. 515–552.

Yehuda Slutsky, *History of the Haganah* (in Hebrew) (Tel Aviv, 3 vols, 1967–1973), vol. III, *From Resistance to War* (Tel Aviv, Am Oved Publishers, 1972).

Jacqueline Soferman, 'Anti Jewish Legislation in Bulgaria, 1940–1942, and the Response it Aroused', (in Hebrew) *Pe'amim*, no. 27 (1986), pp. 143–168.

Aryeh Steinberg, *International Aspects of Jewish Immigration From and Through Rumania, 1938–1947* (in Hebrew) (Unpublished Ph.D. dissertation, Haifa University, 1984).

Lucienne Steinberg, *Les Allemands en France, 1940–1944* (Paris, Albin Michel, 1980).

Maxime Steinberg, *L'Etoile et le Fusil: 1942: Les Cent Jours de la Deportation des Juifs de Belgique* (Bruxelles, 1984).

Eric Steiner, *The Story of the 'Patria'* (New York, Holocaust Library, 1982).

Eliahu Stern, 'The Contacts Between the Delegation in Istanbul and Polish Jewry', (in Hebrew) *Yalkut Moreshet* no. 39 (May 1985), pp. 135–152.

Fritz Stern, *Ernst Reuter* (Berlin, 1976).

Herbert A. Strauss, 'Jewish Emigration from Germany: Nazi Policies and Jewish Responses', *Leo Baeck Inst. Year Book* (Great Britain), XXV(1980) pp. 313–361.

Zosa Szajkowski, *Analytical Franco-Jewish Gazeteer, 1939–1945* (Paris, 1966).

Zosa Szajkowski, *Jews and the French Foreign Legion* (New York, 1975).

T. C. Dişişleri Bakanlığı, *Türkiye Dış Politikasında 50 yıl: Ikinci Dünya Savaşı Yılları (1939–1946)* (Fifty Years in Turkish Foreign Policy: The Years of the Second World War, 1939–1946) (Ankara, Turkish Ministry of Foreign Affairs, Directorate of Research and Political Planning, n.d.).

A. Mennan Tebelen, *Carnet d'un Diplomate* (Paris, 1951).

Yahya Tezel, *Cumhuriyet Döneminin Iktisadi Tarihi, 1923–1950* (Economic History of the Republican Period, 1923-1950) (2nd edn, Ankara, 1986).

Jurgen Thorwald, *The Illusion: Soviet Soldiers in Hitler's Armies* (New York, Harcourt Brace, 1975).

Lise Tiano, *L'Immigration et l'installation en France des Juifs grecs et des Juifs turcs avant la Second Guerre Mondiale* (unpublished thesis, Paris X, 1981).

Heinz Tillmann, *Deutschlands Araberpolitik im Zweiten Weltkrieg* (Berlin, 1965).

Jean Tournox, *Le royaume d'Otto* (Paris, 1982).

Isaiah Trunk, *Judenrat: The Jewish Councils in Eastern Europe under Nazi Occupation* (New York, Macmillan, 1972).

Pars Tuğlacı, *Çağdaş Türkiye* (Contemporary Turkey), (3 vols, Istanbul, 1987–1990).

Feridun Fazıl Tülbentçi ve Münir Müeyyet Berkman, *Ikinci Cihan Harbi Kronolojisi (1939–1944)* (Chronology of the Second World War, 1939–1944) (Ankara, 4 vols, Başvekalet Basın ve Yayın Umum Müdürlüğü, 1943–1945).

Bela Vago, 'Political and Diplomatic Activities for the Rescue of the Jews of Northern Transylvania, June 1944–February 1945', *Yad Vashem Studies*, VI (1967).

Nadejda S. Vasileva, 'On the Catastrophe of the Thracian Jews', *Yad Vashem Studies* no. 3 (1959), pp. 295–302.

Eberhard von Mackensen, *Vom Bug zum Kaukasus: Das III. Panzerkorps im Feltzug gegen Sowjetrussland 1941/42* (Neckargemünd, Germany, 1967).

Patrick von zur Muhlen, *Zwischen Hakenkreuz und Sowjetstern. Der Nationalismus der sowjetischen Orientvolker im Zweiten Weltkrieg* (Dusseldorf, Droste, 1971).

Maurice Voutey, 'Les Persecutions raciales en Cote d'Or: Contribution a l'Etude des Arrestations', *Revue d'Histoire de la Deuxieme Guerre Mondiale* (France), XXXI (1981), pp. 17–30.

Bernard Wasserstein, *Britain and the Jews of Europe, 1939–1945* (Oxford and London, Institute of Jewish Affairs, 1979).

David Weinberg, *Les Juifs à Paris de 1933 à 1939* (Paris, Calmann-Lévy, 1944).

Edward Weisband, *Turkish Foreign Policy, 1943–1945* (Princeton University Press, Princeton, N.J., 1973).

Alex Weissberg, *Advocate for the Dead: The Story of Joel Brand* (London, 1956, 1960).

Michael Weissmandl, *From the Straits* (in Hebrew) (Jerusalem, 1960).

Chaim Weizmann, *The Letters and Papers of Chaim Weizmann. vol. XX, series A. July 1940–January 1943*, ed., Michael J. Cohen (New Brunswick, N.J., 1974)

Georges Wellers, *De Drancy à Auschwitz* (Paris, 1946).

Horst Widmann, *Exil und Bildungshilfe: Die deutschsprachige akademische Emigration in die Türkei nach 1933, mit einer Bio-Bibliographie der emigrierten Hochschullehrer in Anhang* (Bern/Frankfurt (Main), 1973). Translated into Turkish as *Atatürk Üniversite Reform* (Atatürk's University Reform) (Istanbul, 1981).

World Zionist Organization, *The Central Zionist Archives* (Jerusalem, 1970).

David Wyman, *The Abandonment of the Jews: American Policy and the Holocaust, 1941–1945* (New York, Pantheon, 1984).

Yad Vashem, Bibliographical Series (YIVO), vol. I, J. Robinson and P. Friedman, *Guide to Jewish History under Nazi Impact* (Jerusalem, 1960).

Leni Yahil, *The Holocaust: The Fate of European Jewry 1932–1945* (in Hebrew), (Jerusalem, Schoken, 1987).

Leni Yahil, 'Select British Documents on the Illegal Immigration to Palestine (1939–1940),' *Yad Vashem Studies* X (1974).

Ahmet Emin Yalman, *Yakın Tarihte Gördüklerim ve Geçirdiklerim* (What I saw and experienced in recent history) (4 vols, Istanbul, 1971).

Ahmed Emin Yalman, *Turkey in My Time* (University of Oklahoma Press, Norman, Oklahoma, 1956).

Çetin Yetkin, *Türkiyede Tek Parti Dönemi, 1930-1945* (The Era of the Single Party in Turkey, 1930-1945) (Istanbul, Altin, 1983).

David Yisraeli, 'The Third Reich and the Transfer Agreement', *Journal of Contemporary History*, VI/2 (1971), pp. 129–148.

Susan Zuccotti, *The Italians and the Holocaust: Persecution, Rescue and Survival* (New York, Basic, 1987).

Ronald Zweig, *Britain and Palestine during the Second World War* (London, Royal Historical Society, 1986).

Archives, Newspapers and Interviews

Archives

Archives of the Turkish Embassy and the Turkish Consulate (Paris), and the Turkish Foreign Ministry (Ankara).

Archives of the Turkish Prime Minister's Office (*Başbakanlık Arşivi*), Republican Archives (*Cumhuriyet Arşivi*), Yenimahalle, Ankara.

Archives of the *Ministère des Affaires Etrangères* (*Quai d'Orsay*, Paris). *Archives Diplomatiques, Guerre 1939–1945. Sous serie G-Vichy-Afrique-Levant. Sous Serie C-Etat Francais*, no. 139–143: *Question Juive, 1940–1948*; no. 149–150, Foreigners in France, 1942–1944; no. 151–154: Inspection of camps, 1940–1943; no. 158: Foreign internees in France, 1940–1943; no. 161: Foreign worker groups, 1941–1944.

Politisches Archiv des Auswärtigen Amtes (Bonn), and microfilms at University of California, Berkeley and National Archives (Washington, D.C.). See George O. Kent, ed., *Catalogue of Files and Microfilms of the German Foreign Ministry Archives, 1920–1945* (3 vols, Stanford, California, 1962–1966); and Günther Sasse, *Das Politische Archiv des Auswärtigen Amtes, Almanach 1968* (Cologne, 1967), pp. 125–137.

Archives of the *Centre de Documentation Juive Contemporaine* (Paris).

Archives of the United States Department of State, National Archives, Washington, D.C.

Archives of the British Foreign Office, War Office, Colonial Office and War Cabinet, Public Record Office, Kew Gardens, London.

Archives of the India Office, Commonwealth Relations Office, London.

Archives of the American Joint Distribution Committee (New York), *Turkey, 1943–1945*.

Archives of United States Ambassador to Turkey during World War II, Laurence A. Steinhardt (Library of Congress, Washington, D.C.).

Archives of Moreshet (*Givat Haviva* near Hadera, Israel): Istanbul Unit, Menachem Bader Collection, C.6, D.1. (Consulted by authors of several works used in this study).

Central Zionist Archives (Jerusalem): *Archives of the Zionist Executive and Jewish Agency for Palestine:* S 6 : Files of the Aliyah Immigration Department, 1919–1948; S 24–S 25: Files of the Political Department, 1921–1948; S 26: Files of the Rescue Committee, 1939–1948; S 71: Press Cuttings, 1939–1961; *Archives of the World Zionist Central Office:* Z 4 series: Executive of Zionist Organization and Jewish Agency for Palestine in London, 1917–1955; *Archives of branches of Zionist Organization and Jewish Agency;* L 5 series: Zionist Agency office in Istanbul, 1909–1917; L 15 series: Immigration Office in Istanbul, 1940–1946. (Consulted by authors of several works used in this study).

Newspapers

Journal d'Orient
Cumhuriyet
Tan
Ulus
Son Telegraf
Kurun
Vatan

Interviews

Rabbi Haim Nahum Efendi: Grand Rabbi of Ottoman Empire, 1909–1920, Chief Rabbi of Egypt, 1923–1960. Interview in Cairo, March–April 1956.

Avram Galante: Historian of Ottoman Jewry. Interview on Heybeliada, Istanbul, March 1957.

Kâmuran Gürün: Secretary General of the Turkish Foreign Ministry, Ambassador to Greece. Interview on 21 April 1991.

Melih Esenbel: Third Secretary in the Turkish Embassy (Vichy), 1941–1945. Interview on 27 April 1991.

Namık Kemal Yolga: Vice-Consul at Turkish Consulate-General, Paris, 1940–1945. Interview on 25 April 1991. Letter from Ambassador Yolga to Stanford J. Shaw, 5 July 1991, containing his memories of Paris during World War II.

Mina Türkmen: Daughter of Fikret Şefik Özdoğancı, Turkish Consul-General in Paris, 1942–1945. Interview on 29 April 1991.

Necdet Kent: Account of his experiences as Turkish Vice Consul at Marseilles and Grenoble during World War II, given to the Quincentennial Foundation, Istanbul.

Hayim Eliezer Kohen: Director of Protocol at the Chief Rabbinate in Istanbul, who, along with Simon Brod, was in charge of receiving and caring for the Jewish refugees arriving in Istanbul from various places in western Europe during World War II. Interview on 16 December 1991.

Appendix 1

TURKISH DIPLOMATIC AND CONSULAR PERSONNEL IN FRANCE AND GREECE DURING WORLD WAR II

---

1. FRANCE

(a) Turkish Embassy in Paris and Vichy :

Behiç Erkin. Ambassador in Paris from 13 July 1939 (arrived 30 August 1939) to 10 September 1940.

Behiç Erkin. Ambassador to Paris at Vichy from 10 September 1940 until retirement on 13 July 1943.

Kenan Gökart. *Chargé d'Affaires* at Vichy from 13 July to 27 September 1940.

Ali Şevket Berker. *Chargé d'Affaires* at Vichy, 28 September 1943 to 12 December 1944.

Numan Rifat Menemencioğlu, Ambassador at Vichy and Paris from 30 November 1944 until 2 November 1956.

Melih Esenbel, Third Secretary at Vichy.

(b) Turkish consuls general at Turkish Consulate-General, Paris, located at 170 Boulevard Haussmann, Paris VIIIème

Behçet Şefik Özdoğancı, Consul-General from 2 March 1939 until 8 August 1939.

Cevdet Dülger, Consul-General from 9 August 1939 to 30 April 1942.

Namık Kemal Yolga,[471] Chancellor and later Vice Consul, 17 April 1940–27 January 1945, Acting Consul-General, 30 April–17 August 1942.

---

471. Born on 23 November 1330/1914 in Elaziz, Turkey, the son of retired *Kaymakam* Zülfi Yolga. Graduated from Ankara University Political Science Faculty in 1936. After serving as a clerk in the Foreign Ministry, he passed his examinations and became a regular official in December 1938. From January 1939 until April 1940 he served as a Secretary in the Economics and Trade Department at the Ministry. He served in the Turkish Consulate-

Fikret Şefik Özdoğancı, from 17 July 1942 until 9 May 1945.
Halil Ali Ramazanoğlu, from 9 May 1945 until 8 December 1947.

(c) Turkish consuls general at Marseilles/Grenoble :

Basri Reşit Danişmend, Consul-General from 24 July 1936 until 20 March 1940.
Bedi'i Arbel, Consul-General from 1 April 1940 until 31 May 1943.
(Mehmed) Fuad Carım, from 1 June 1943 until 20 May 1945. [472]
Münir Pertev Subaşı, Consul-General from 18 June 1945 until 31 March 1947.
Necdet Kent, Vice Consul and later Consul at Marseilles (Grenoble) from 1941 until 1945.[473]

General in Paris, from 17 April 1940 until April 1945, first as Secretary and Chancellor, then as Acting Consul-General from 30 April until 17 July 1942, then after the arrival of Behçet Şefik Özdoğancı, as Vice-Consul until his departure from Paris in April 1945. He served subsequently as First Secretary and later Chief Councellor to the Ambassador to Rome (July 1947–July 1949), and as First Seretary and later Counsellor at the Turkish Embassy at Damascus (July 1949–August 1951). After service at the Ministry in Ankara, he became Turkish Ambassador to France (1953–1959), Secretary General of the Ministry of Foreign Affairs (1960–1963), Ambassador to Rome (1963–1965), Paris (1966), Caracas, Venezuela (1966–1969), Tehran (1969–1972), and the Soviet Union (1976–1979). He now lives in retirement in Ankara.

472. Born in Aleppo in 1892. Graduated from School of Political Science (*Mülkiye Mektebi*) in 1913. Active member of *Ittihat ve Terakki*. Served as deputy to Grand National Assembly during War for Independence, and also served at front. Went with Ali Fuad Cebesoy to Moscow in 1921. Served as Consul-General in Copenhagen (1938), Milan (1939), Marseilles (1943–1945), as Ambassador to Cidde (1945) and Argentina (1950), and General Secretary of the Foreign Office (1948–1950); Retired in 1957 and still living in Istanbul in 1969.

473. Born in Istanbul in 1911 and entered the Turkish Ministry of Foreign Affairs in 1937. He served as Third Secretary and later Second Secretary of the Turkish Embassy in Athens, 1940–1941, Vice Consul of the Turkish Consulate-General in Marseilles, 1941–1945, First Secretary of the Turkish Embassy in London (1945–6), Director of the Cabinet of the Minister of Foreign Affairs, (1945–1950), Consul-General in New York (1950–1953), Liverpool (1955-1956), Ambassador to Bangkok Thailand (1958–1960), New Delhi, India (1960–1962), Teheran Iran (1964-1966), Stockholm, Sweden (1969–1972), and Warsaw, Poland (1972–1976). He now lives in retirement in Istanbul.

2. GREECE

(a) Turkish Embassy at Athens: Ambassador from October 1939 until 13 July 1945: **Mehmed Enis Akaygen.**

(b) Turkish Consulate-General at Athens/Piraeas: Consul-General **Inayetullah Cemal Özkaya**, 25 March 1940–12 April 1945

(c) Turkish Consulate-General at Salonica: **Idris Çora**, 12 September 1938–27 November 1943; **none** from 1943 until 1946

(d) Turkish Consulate at Rhodes: **Salahuddin Ülkümen**, 1943–1945.[474]

(e) Turkish Consulate at Gümülcine: **Tevfik Türker**, 13 August 1939–18 August 1943; **Muzaffer Kamil Görduysus**, 1 October 1943–22 December 1947

(f) Turkish Consulate at Midilli:
Ahmed Nesib Tulgay, 1 October 1937–11 November 1941;
Hasan Tahsin Mayatepek, 11 November 1941–30 April 1942;
Talat Acarer, 30 May 1942–9 June 1942;
None: 1942–1945

---

474. Born in Istanbul in 1911 and entered the Turkish Ministry of Foreign Affairs in 1937. He served as Third Secretary and later Second Secretary of the Turkish Embassy in Athens, 1940–1941, Vice Consul of the Turkish Consulate-General in Marseilles, 1941–5, First Secretary of the Turkish Embassy in London (1945–6), Director of the Cabinet of the Minister of Foreign Affairs, (1945–1950), Consul-General in New York (1950–1953), Liverpool (1955–1956), Ambassador to Bangkok Thailand (1958–1960), New Delhi, India (1960–1962), Teheran Iran (1964–1966), Stockholm, Sweden (1969–1972), and Warsaw, Poland (1972–1976). He now lives in retirement in Istanbul.

Appendix 2

AMBASSADOR ILTER TÜRKMEN REPORTS ON RESEARCH INTO PARIS EMBASSY ARCHIVES ON JEWISH TURKS IN FRANCE DURING WORLD WAR II

Archives of the Turkish Embassy (Paris) and of the Turkish Foreign Ministry (Ankara)

> Republic of Turkey, Paris Embassy
> No. 0504/M–1665–734, By courier
> 5 August 1988
>
> Regarding the sending of Jews to Turkey
> To the Ministry of Foreign Affairs
> Ref: communication of 11 June 1988

It is well known that our government and our missions in France were very much involved in sending from France to Turkey Jews who were Turkish citizens who had asked for our help in various ways in order to rescue them from the persecution and destruction policies to which they were being subjected before and during World War II in execution of Nazi doctrines in the areas under their occupation.

All the documents found in the archives of our embassy relating to the years 1933 until 1945 have been examined in this context, and many requests from Jewish Turks in France have been found asking our embassy and our Consulate-Generals to intervene in order to prevent them and their families from being sent to concentration camps. Study of these dossiers, however, shows that the policy of protection applied after 1942 only to Turkish citizens and only to Jews who were properly registered at our Consulate-Generals.

A large number of documents were found in our archives regarding applications to the French local authorities, the Vichy government, and the German Embassy in Paris regarding those Jewish Turkish subjects whose citizenship was in proper order who wished to return to Turkey. These documents indicate that as a result of agreement with the Vichy government which was under the control of Hitler's Germany as well as with German authorities, our Consulate-Generals were able to supervise the sending in caravans back to Turkey of Jewish citizens living in areas where their lives were threatened.

The evaluation and execution of the requests made by Jewish citizens in France, as well as the task of answering them, was handled mainly by our Consulate-Generals at Paris and Marseilles, even for those requests which initially were made to our embassy.

The efforts of the embassy were most successful in securing the release of Jewish citizens sent to concentration camps when they involved applications to the Foreign Ministry of the Vichy government, regarding Jewish Turks still in concentration camps in France, but we have not been able to determine what happened to the Jews whom the Gestapo quickly sent to camps within Germany.

Study of our dossiers has not been able to confirm protection after 1939 for Jewish Turks whose citizenship status was not regular and who had not maintained contact with the consulates. However a communication from our Consulate-General in Marseilles to our Embassy in Paris indicates that our Honorary Consulate in Lyon distributed certifications of Turkish citizenship illegally to Jews in its district. There can be no doubt that Jews who obtained certificates of Turkish citizenship in this way were saved from the Gestapo. While we have not encountered any documents showing that non Turkish Jews were saved in this manner, some documents give some idea that such instances did exist.

With my best wishes,

(**signed**) Ilter Türkmen, Ambassador

Appendix 3

TESTIMONY OF RETIRED AMBASSADOR NAMIK KEMAL YOLGA REGARDING JEWISH TURKS IN FRANCE DURING WORLD WAR II

Ankara, 5 July 1991

SOME SHORT NOTES WHICH I HAVE PREPARED FOR THE USE OF PROFESSOR STANFORD SHAW ON SUBJECTS WHICH WE RECENTLY DISCUSSED BY TELEPHONE.

The Paris Consulate of the Republic of Turkey during the years of the German Occupation.

1. *ADDRESS*: During these years, the Consulate-General in Paris was in an apartment complex at 170, Boulevard Haussmann, at the corner of Rue de Courcelles, which served both as Chancery and Residence .

2. *PERSONNEL*:

a. PROFESSIONAL OFFICIALS:

1) **Cevdet Dülger,** Consul-General, 9 August 1939–30 April 1942

2) **Fikret Şefik Özdoğancı**, Consul-General 17 July 1942–9 May 1945

3) **Bahri Engin,** Vice Consul, transferred to Turkish Embassy in Vichy during spring, 1940

4) **Namık Kemal Yolga,** Chancellor, later promoted to Vice Consul, 17 April 1940–27 January 1945, Acting Consul-General, 30 April–17 July 1942

b. LOCAL CLERKS:

1) ***Tcherna Frisch:*** French citizen, member of Jewish family that immigrated from Poland. Worked continuously at the Turkish consulate from the time it first opened as a Vice Consulate in 1924 until her death in the 1950s. Mademoiselle Frisch was a very wise and experienced person who with her great knowledge of the affairs of the Consulate-General was the pillar of the Chancery operations.

2) **Germaine Guicheteau**: A French citizen, Mademoiselle Guicheteau started at the Consulate-General before World War II and served there for about ten years. She was an extremely valuable and energetic colleague, liked by everyone, and knew more about what was going on than anyone else.

3) **Recep Zerman***:* A Turkish citizen who served at the Consulate-General from before World War II until the 1950s.

4) **Janine Bousquet**. A French citizen, who entered the service of the Consulate-General in the time of the late Fikret Şefik Özdoğancı.

Aside from the late Recep Zerman, there were quite a few Turkish citizens who worked at the Consulate-General with the title of Local Clerk (*Mahalle Kâtip*), but they were appointed for short periods of time and did not play important roles in carrying out the duties of the Consulate-General. For all practical purposes, the entire work of the Paris Consulate-General was carried out by two professional officials and four local clerks.

3. PHOTOGRAPHS
I am sending six photographs which I believe will be useful:

a. The Staff of the Consulate-General on the occasion of the celebration of Turkish Republic Holiday (*Cumhuriyet Bayramı*) in 1941. From left to right: Chancellor Namık Kemal Yolga, Consul-General Dülger, and Local clerks Guicheteau, Frisch, and Zerman.

b. The Staff of the Consulate-General on the occasion of the celebration of Turkish Republic Holiday in 1943. From left to right: Guicheteau, Local Clerk Refik Ileri, who after the war became a professional Foreign Service Official, but died at a young age; Consul-

General Fikret Özdoğancı's daughter Mina;[475] Consul-General Fikret Özdoğancı, and his wife Nüzhet Hanım, Vice Consul Yolga, Frisch, Local Clerk Nerma Özdoğancı, niece of the Consul-General, Zerman and Bousquet.

c: Photographs of the undocumented (*gayrimuntazam*) Jewish Turks standing in line in front of the Consulate-General at different times.

Situation of our Jewish fellow citizens during the occupation years:

The German persecutions of Jews in occupied France did not begin immediately following the occupation, but by the middle of 1941, protection of our fellow countrymen of Jewish origin was our most important and pressing task. The actions of the Consulate-General in this respect were not just a matter of obeying our Constitution, which made no distinction among our fellow citizens based on religion or anything else–there is no such prejudice in our national character. That is, the Anti-Semitism which can be seen in many countries in various degrees has never existed in Turkey at any time in history. To the contrary, Jewish Turks have never been mistreated by the state; they have lived amidst their fellow citizens of Turkey with friendship and love. Thus it was natural from all points of view that the Consulate-General's task of protecting Turkish citizens should be applied to Jewish Turks as it was to Turks of other religions.

I can say objectively that the political situation at the time greatly eased our task. We had not entered the war. And Turkey was not merely another neutral country. The Hitler regime was conducting its relations with us with considerable and special care. And this applied also to the occupation authorities in France. For example, Though just a young consular official, I was able to personally undertake missions at the Paris branch of the German Embassy and at the Gestapo, whose address changed at different times. On one occasion I was able to literally take off the train which was to deport them to Germany three Jewish Turks from the Drancy concentration camp–I assert with pride and thankfulness that the policy followed by the late President Ismet Inönü during the Second World War, along with all of Turkey, was to rescue all our fellow citizens living in all the countries under German occupation.

---

475. Author's note: Now Mrs. Mina Türkmen.

With the help of the political situation, but most importantly as a result of the tremendous efforts of our Consulate-General, the Jewish Turks living in 'occupied' France at the time escaped many of the extremely dangerous situations of those years. There was only one exception that I know of, one family living in Bordeaux was sent to Germany before we could protect them. Our Consulate-General also had to provide protection on the economic side. The occupation forces attempted to 'Aryanize', that is to confiscate and place in the hands of non-Jewish Frenchmen, the shops and other economic establishments belonging to Jews. Our Consulate-General was able, however, to secure the appointment of other Turkish citizens as administrators (*gérant*) of the places of business belonging to Jewish Turks, with the selections in fact being made by me. And this was only a matter of form. In fact the businesses were thus not 'Arianized', and they continued to be managed by their original Jewish owners.

A matter which took up a great deal of our time was the situation of our 'irregular' (*gayrimuntazam vatandaş*) fellow citizens, the term which we applied to those who were unable to secure the Certificates of Citizenship (*vatandaşlık ilmühaberi*) which we provided to those Turkish citizens who regularly registered at the Consulate-General while living for long periods of time in France. The area of France which the Paris Consulate-General was responsible for included the immediate area of Paris and vicinity, where most of the Turks in France were located. When the occupation authorities began persecuting Jews in France, the 'irregular' Turkish citizens stormed into the Consulate-General, at first crowding into the Chancery on the second floor, then filling the staircases which led up from the entrance hall, with the latecomers backing onto the sidewalk along Boulevard Haussmann, as can be seen in the photographs. Initially I would stand on the staircase landings, later on a chair at the building entrance, giving them information about the procedures that they had to follow and asking them to bring all the documents which they could find which documented their Turkish citizenships. I remember that on a few occasions the only documents some of them could bring were receipts for taxes paid in Ottoman times. We then gave them documents of 'attestation', which stated that they had applied to the Consulate-General to regularize their citizenship situation and that these requests had been sent to Ankara. They were able to use these documents like Certificates of Citizenship which, I believe, were accepted for registration with the police. This was our normal procedure for our 'irregular' fellow citizens.

Our relations with our Jewish fellow citizens at that time were not just official, they also were personal. For example, our Consul-General, the late Cevdet Dülger, who was a bachelor and therefore gave great importance to being with other people, met almost every day with eight to ten friends, of whom three were leaders of our community of Jewish Turks, namely L. Fresko, S. Kohen, and R. Vidal, who had a carpet shop at the south corner of Saint Augustin square—I remember him with great affection. Dülger's successor as Consul-General, Fikret Şefik Özdoğancı, maintained the same friendships.

I would like to emphasize that material considerations absolutely played no role whatsoever in our official and personal relationships with our Jewish fellow citizens, as God and thousands of Turkish citizens will bear witness. Personally, I was very meticulous about this, with whatever proposals made to benefit me in fact bearing against the persons involved.

(**signed**) *Namık Kemal Yolga*

Appendix 4

TESTIMONY OF RETIRED AMBASSADOR NECDET KENT REGARDING HIS RESCUE OF JEWISH TURKS AT MARSEILLES DURING WORLD WAR II

I was appointed Vice Consul at the Marseilles Consulate-General of the Turkish Republic in 1941, and after subsequently being promoted to the rank of Consul remained at my post in Marseilles until 1944. While I was there, I served under Consul-Generals Bedi'i Arbel, Münir Pertev Subaşı, and Fuat Carım, all of whom are now deceased.

At that time there were two kinds of Jewish Turks in France. The first group consisted of Jews who at the conclusion of World War I left Turkey, mostly with the French occupying forces, and settled in France. Many of these no longer had Turkish passports, or if they still possessed them, they had expired. Many of them had no documents other than their Birth Certificates, in Old Turkish, issued by the Ottoman administration before the establishment of the Turkish Republic. They were considered to be 'without nationality' (*tabiyetsiz*) by the Turkish consulates. Since the French administration was very liberal on such matters before World War II, it did nothing about this problem, and therefore these people did not bother to apply to the Turkish consulate to regularize their situation.

The second group of Jewish Turks consisted of those who had left Turkey with valid passports but who for various reasons, particularly because of the outbreak of the war, could not return home; they were considered 'regular' (*régulier*) Turkish citizens.

When Nazi Germany occupied northern France, many Jewish Turks, like others as well, fled to unoccupied Vichy France, and therefore entered the district to which our consulate was assigned. The French referred to all those who came from the north as *repliés*, or 'people who had retreated.' Matters continued normally for some time after this exodus. But when the Nazis occupied southern France, then things got much worse. Their first act was to load all the Jews they could capture into cattle cars and send them off to Germany. In response to complaints about this coming from Turkish citizens, we went into action. If the status of the Turkish Jew applying for assistance to the Consulate was 'regular', a Certificate of Citizenship document was immediately given to him. In addition, a statement of his Turkish citizenship and that his place of business was under the protection of Turkey, was affixed in a prominent place which could be seen at the front of the establishment. At first, the Nazis left this sort of Turkish citizens in peace. Even for those Jewish Turks whose status was not regular, after they filled out an application (*beyanname*), they were given a document which stated that it was known that they were Turkish citizens and that procedures had been started to provide them with the necessary documents. By this method we saved many people from the Nazis. However with the passage of time, and with changes in the district Gestapo chiefs, the attacks by the Nazis increased. During that time we had to go to Gestapo headquarters as many as three or four times daily in order to rescue our Jewish fellow citizens who had been arrested and detained, often by threatening the Nazis. And just as bad, the Italians, who up to then had treated the Jews in their zone reasonably well, began to emulate the Germans. One day I spent close to two hours arguing with the Italian Consul trying to get him to abandon his inhuman actions. Reports which came to me indicated that I was somewhat successful with the Italians.

Every day the Germans found new ways to persecute the Jews in our district. Towards the end, they would surround a Jew in the middle of the street, force him to lower his trousers and show whether or not he was Jewish by whether he was or was not circumcised. As a result of this method, many Muslim as well as Jewish Turks were arrested and brought to Gestapo headquarters, and many of these were sent to Germany. Whenever such arrests took place, I immediately went to Gestapo headquarters to explain the situation. I explained that circumcision in itself was not limited to Jews. When I saw in their eyes that they did not understand, I told them that I would be ready to myself be examined by a physician. By such means I was able to rescue a number of innocent persons from the police.

Our Consul-General was on leave for a time. One evening, a Turkish Jew from Izmir named Sidi Iscan, who worked at the Consulate as a clerk and translator, (he has also passed away, may God give him rest) came to my house in a state of considerable excitement. He told me that the Germans had gathered up about eighty Jews and had taken them to the railroad station with the intention of loading them onto cattle wagons for shipment to Germany. He could hardly hold back his tears. Without stopping to express my grief, I immediately tried to calm him and then took the fastest vehicle available to the Saint Charles railroad station in

Marseilles. The scene there was unbelievable. I came to cattle wagons which were filled with sobbing and groaning people. Sorrow and anger drove everything else from my mind. The most striking memory I have of that night is the sign I saw on one of the wagons, a phrase which I cannot erase from my mind: 'This wagon can be loaded with twenty head of large cattle and five hundred kilograms of hay.' Within each wagon there were as many as eighty people piled on top of one another. When the Gestapo officer in charge of the train station heard that I was there, he came to me and in a very cross manner asked me what I was looking for. With as much courtesy as I could force myself to summon, I told him that these people were Turkish citizens, that their arrest had been a mistake, and that it should be remedied at once by their release. The Gestapo officer said that he was carrying out his orders, and that these people were not Turks but were just Jews. Seeing that I would get nowhere by making threats which could not be carried out if they were not fulfilled, I returned to Sidi Iscan and said, 'Come on, lets board the train ourselves', and pushing aside the German soldier who tried to block my way, I boarded one of the wagons with Sidi Iscan beside me. This time it was the turn of the Gestapo officer to cry and even plead. I couldn't listen to anything he said, and amidst the crying glances of the Gestapo officer, the train began to move. Since it was a long time ago, I cannot remember too well, but I remember that the train came to a stop when we came either to Arles or Nimes. A number of German officers climbed onto the car and immediately came to my side. I received them very coldly and did not even greet them. They told me that there had been a mistake, the train had left after I had boarded, the persons responsible would be punished, as soon as I left the train I could return to Marseilles on a car that would be assigned to me. I told them that it was not a mistake, that more than eighty Turkish citizens had been loaded onto this cattle wagon because they were Jews, that as a citizen of a nation as well as the representative of a government which felt that religious beliefs should not be the reason for such treatment, there could be no question of my leaving them alone, and that was why I was there. The officers said they would correct whatever mistakes had been made and asked if all those in the wagon were Turkish citizens. All the people around me, women, men, and children, stood petrified while they watched this game being played for their lives. Most likely because of my refusal to compromise, as well as an order received by the Nazi officers, we all descended from the train together. After a time the Germans left us alone. I will never forget what followed. The people who had been saved threw their arms around our necks and shook our hands, with expressions of gratitude in their eyes. After sending them all on their way to their homes, without even glancing at the Mercedes-Benz which the Nazis had provided for us, Sidi Iscan and I rented an automobile which operated by wood and returned to Marseilles. I have rarely experienced in my life the internal peace which I felt as I entered my bed towards morning of that day.

I have received letters from time to time over the years from many of my fellow travelers on the short train ride of that day. Today who knows how many of them are still in good health and how many have left us. I remember them all affectionately, even those who may no longer remember me.

Statement by His Excellency retired Ambassador Necdet Kent to the Quincentennial Foundation, Istanbul, translated by Stanford J. Shaw and published by courtesy of the Foundation.

Appendix 5

BUSINESSES AND PROPERTIES BELONGING TO JEWISH TURKS IN PARIS ADMINISTERED BY TURKISH AGENTS UNDER DIRECTION OF TURKISH CONSULATE-GENERAL IN 1943

1. Administrator Mr. Huseyin Nakib, 178 Boulevard Berthier, Paris

Mr. David Cohen: 55 Avenue de la Grande Armée, Paris XVII, two apartments

Mr. Isak Elnekave: 30 Rue d'Auteuil, Paris XVI, hosery shop

Madame Kohen, 45-47 Rue d'Hauteville, Paris X, lighting and automobile accessories

Mr. Rafael Levi, 55 Champs Elysées, Paris VIII, *Elysées Scieries*

Mr. Isak Penoel, 8/12 Rue Immeubles Industriels, Paris II, furniture

Etz Michon, 100 Rue de la Folie Mericourt, Paris XI, automobile lamps

Mr. Rifat Acubel, 13 Rue d'Alexandrie, Paris III, textiles

Mr. Merkado Gabay, 5 Rue Saulnier, Paris IX, Commercial Bank Mundia

MM. Castro and Negrin, 42 Avenue d'Orleans, Paris XIV, textiles

M. Hatem, 11 Foubourg Poissonerie, *La Lampe Moderne*

2. Administrator Mr. Niyazi Gerede, 19 Rue Poncelet, Paris

Mr. Samuel Levi, 110 Rue Réaumur, Paris II, part owner of knitting factory

Mr. Albert Avigdor, 7 Passage des Ptes Ecuries, Paris X, lamps

Mr. Mizrahi, 60 Rue de Cléry, Paris

Mr. Mizrahi, 8 Rue Poissonière, Paris

MM Asseo and Bitran, 25 Rue du Caire, Paris, buttons, large hooks[476]

Mr. D. Eskenazi, 7 ter Passage des Petites Ecuries, Paris, manufacturers' representative

Mr. D. Policar, 26 Rue du Four, Paris, hosery and shirt shop

---

476. Turkish consular note: 'Asseo has died. His daughter is in the unoccupied zone.' Bitron has gone to Turkey.

M. Razon, 6 Cité de Paradis, Paris X, lighting materials
Madame Barzilay, 167 Boulevard Montparnasse, Paris. Sté Barlay, hosery
Ets Arditti, 13 Rue de l'Entrepôt, Paris, sinks and furs
Mr. Karel, 20 Rue du Caire, Paris, hosery shop
Mr. S. Guerson, 5 Rue Royale, Paris, carpets and objects of art
Maison Jean Lambert (Josef Bitran), 37 Rue du Chateau d'Eau, Paris
Maison Gattegno, 20 Rue Notre Dame de Recouvrance, Paris, cutlery,
    materials for hair dressers
Maison Rissel (Abravanel), 22 Rue Caumartin, Paris, fashion clothes
Maison Suzy (Krespi), 254 Rue de Vaugirard, Paris, hosery and novelties
Maison Ray (Jak Tarika), 73 Champs Elysées, Paris, stockings
Maison Violette (Madame Hasson), 136 Boulevard Voltaire, Paris,
    novelties and hosery
Mr. Levi, 350 Rue St. Honoré, Paris. *The Silk Shop*, silks

3. Administrator Ali Topçubaşı, 4 Rue Ollier, Paris

Mr. Jak Soustiel, 7 Rue des Messageries, Paris, articles of Paris
Mr. S. Matalon, 103 Rue de Vanves, Paris, shirt and hosery shop
Mr. L. Hillel, 55 Rue de Bretagne, exports

4. Administrator Tevfik Şükrü, 37 Boulevard Saint Martin

Madame Sara Hulon (partner), 59 Rue Turbige, Paris, hosery shop
Mr. Receb,146 Rue Lafayette, Paris, hosery shop
Mr. Mercan, 26 Rue de l'Ouest, Paris, hosery shop

5. Administrator Fethi Nevzad, 22 Foubourg du Temple

M. Tiano (associate), 34 Rue Greneta, Paris, confections for women
Mr. Isak Pinto, 319 Rue des Pyrenées
Mr. Vitali Avigdor, 19 Rue Fontaine, Paris, hosery shop
Mr. Avram Menase, 83 Rue de Clery
Mr. Fresco, 96 Rue des Travilliers, bank

6. Administrator Recep Zerman, 34 Rue St. Jacques

Mr. Vitali Baruh, 69–71 Rue de Clichy, furniture
Mr. David Gabay, 10 Rue Chauchat, *Proche Orient Commissaire*

7. Administrator Arif Tomruk

Ets Bear, 51 Rue d'Hautefille, Paris, lighting equipment
Isak Halfon, 41 Rue Lecombe

8. Administrator Vefik Azer, 24 Rue Saint Lazare, Paris

Mr. Nahum Weismann, 11 Rue de Chateaudun, Paris, dye works
Mr. Nisim Kohen, 17 Rue du Chateau d'Eau

9. Administrator Sinan Essad, 18 Passage des Petites Ecuries, Paris

Ets Hillel, 18 Passage des Petites Ecuries, Paris, lights for motorcycles
S. Treves, 3 Rue d'Abeville, Paris, electrical equipment

Appendix 6

SUMS DEPOSITED WITH TURKISH CONSULATE-GENERAL[477] (PARIS) FOR TRANSFER TO TURKEY BY JEWISH TURKS BEING REPATRIATED TO TURKEY FROM FEBRUARY TO APRIL 1944

PASSPORT/ DOSSIER NUMBER TURKISH ADDRESS	NAME	AMOUNT PAID (FRENCH FRANCS)
1994 TP	Leon Levy	100,000
Istanbul: Taksim Hocazade no. 12/3 c/o Sabetay Kohen		
1941 TP	David Levy	125,000
Istanbul: Tomruk Sokak c/o Sami Hillel		
1381 TP	Nesim Kohen	100,000
Istanbul: Galata Yazıcı Sokak-Küçük Dikoş Han		
1989 TP	Hayim Kohen	20,000
Istanbul: Beyoğlu-Tozkoparan Cami Sokak no. 25, c/o Bayan Fanni Pappo		
1508 TP	Marko Kohen	100,000
Istanbul: Tünel Pasaji no. 9 c/o Bay Dr. Hodara		
905 TP	Ester Mitrani	25,000
Istanbul: Şişli-Rumeli Caddesi no. 41, c/o Razon family		
1651 TP	Rafael Gare	30,000
Istanbul: Beyoğlu-Istiklal Caddesi Aykut Han no. 451/21		

477. Turkish Consul-General (Paris) Fikret Şefik Özdoğancı, to Turkish Embassy to Paris (Vichy) no. 497/19, 14 April 1944. In Archives of Turkish Embassy Paris)

1497 TP   Hayim David   100,000
Istanbul: Sabuncu Han Caddesi no. 86, c/o Alber Eliya Finzi

1806 TP   Adut Yuda Saranga   25,000
Istanbul: Taksim-Lamartin Caddesi, Yeni Falson Apt. 28
c/o Bayan Behor Pinhas

456 TP   Merkado Eskenazi   80,000
Istanbul: Posta Kutusu 307, c/o Albert Niyogo

1379 TP   Tuti Benezra   15,000
Istanbul: Şişli-Bomonti Etempaşa apt.. no. 5, c/o Bay Barzilay

MARSEILLES   Yasef Kohen   84,918
Istanbul: c/o Selanik Bankası director Bay Levi

MARSEILLES   Yuda Yul Shoef   150,000
Istanbul; Galata, Kuledibi Şakulu Kakopulos apt. 46, c/o Mordo Şoef

MARSEILLES   Yako Şoef   170,000
Istanbul: Galata Kuledibi Şakulu-Klakopulos apt. 46, c/o Mordo Shoef

1164 TP   Aneta Ojalvo   40,000
Istanbul: Galata-Refik Saydam Caddesi-Deniz apt. no. 11, c/o Mois Markos

1936 TP   Lor Aboaf   30,000
Istanbul: Beyoğlu-Kibli Sokak Apergi Han

1108 TP   Isak Illel   30,000
Istanbul: Tahtakale-Prevoyana Han no. 4, c/o Daniel Behar

MARSEILLES   Yasef Baruh   150,000
Istanbul: Nişantaş-Demir Apt. no. 2, c/o Nesim Abuaf

218 TP   Nisim Arditi   30,000
Istanbul: Sirkeci Köprülü Han no. 30, c/o Demetro Yohannidis

1787 TP   Sinyoru Mazliyah   15,000
Izmir: Tire Kapısı-Karataş Karakol, c/o Bayan Meri Asher

277 TP   Josef Bitran   60,000
Istanbul: Şişli-Osmanbey-Rumeli Caddesi no. 88

2150 TP   Fortune Bear   70,000
Istanbul: Şişli-Osmanbey-Rumeli Caddesi no. 41. c/o Razon

2212 TP   Ilya Arditi   4,000
Istanbul: Sirkeci-Ebussuutefendi Caddesi no. 20

832 TP   Jak Tarika   70,000
Izmir: Posta Kutusu no. 5, c/o Alazraki

MARSEILLES   Isak Naum   15,000
Istanbul: Beyoğlu-Meşrutiyet Caddesi no. 2, c/o Ibraim

MARSEILLES   Sabetay Mis   50,000
Istanbul: Birinci Vakıf Han no. 31

Appendix 7

NATIONALITIES OF DEPORTEES FROM DRANCY CONCENTRATION CAMP [478]

America 10
Argentina 25
Armenia 4
Austria 2,217
Belgium 412
Bolivia 3
Brazil 2
Bulgaria 140
Chile 5
China 1
Costa Rica 21
Czechoslovakia 595
Danzig (Poland) 18
Denmark, 2
Ecuador 10
Egypt 27
England 324
Estonia 4
Finland 2
France:
    Born in France 14,469
    Naturalized citizens 7,724
    French protectorates 156
    Other French subjects 342
Germany 6,222
Greece 1,499
Guatemala 1
Haiti 4
Holland 587

478. Serge Klarsfeld, *Memorial to the Jews Deported from France, 1942–1944* (New York, 1983), p. xxxvi.

Honduras 50
Hungary
    Unrecognized by Hungarian Embassy 244
    Recognized by Hungarian Embassy 758
Iran 8
Iraq 13
Ireland 1
Italy 109
Latvia 130
Lebanon 2
Lithuania 276
Luxembourg 105
Mexico 2
Nicaragua 5
Norway 1
Palestine 53
Paraguay 121
Peru 22
Poland 14,459
Rumania
    Those unrecognized by Rumanian Embassy 242
    Those recognized by Rumanian Embassy 2,716
Russian refugees 2,716
Saarland (Germany) 3,290
San Marino (Italy) 1
Soviet Union 589
Spain 145
Sweden 3
Switzerland 39
Syria 17
Tahiti 1
Turkey
    Those unrecognized by Turkish Embassy 333
    Those recognized by Turkish Embassy 949
Uruguay 8
Venezuela 133
Stateless (*Apatrides*) 2,698
To be determined 154
Unknown 5124

Appendix 8

SHORT BIOGRAPHIES OF LEADING REFUGEE
SCHOLARS, PROFESSORS AND SCIENTISTS
DISMISSED FROM THEIR POSITIONS BY THE NAZIS
AND BROUGHT TO TURKEY DURING THE 1930s.[479]

I. ISTANBUL

ISTANBUL UNIVERSITY

SOCIAL SCIENCES AND HUMANITIES

Alfred Isaac (Cologne 1888–Nuremberg 1956). Jewish German economist. Professor in the Nuremberg Polytechnic School of Economic and Social Sciences starting in 1928 until forced retirement by Nazis in 1934. Came to Turkey with wife in 1937. Headed business course as Professor at Economics Faculty (*Iktisat Fakültesi*) of Istanbul University, 1937–1951. His knowledge of Turkish improved so rapidly that he was lecturing in Turkish within two years after his arrival. In addition to training hundreds of Turkish

---

479. These biographies are based on information found in personnel dossiers held by the archives of the Turkish Ministry of Education, Museum of Ethnography, Ankara, and the following studies: Werner Röder and Helbert Strauss, *Biographisches Handbuch der Deutschsprachigen Emigration nach 1933* (Institüte für Zeitgeschichte München and Research Foundation for Jewish Immigration, New York), vol. I (Munich, New York, London and Paris, 1980); Horst Widmann, *Exil und Bildungshilfe: Die deutschsprachige akademische Emigration in die Türkei nach 1933, mit einer BioBibliographie der emigrierten Hochschullehrer in Anhang* (Bern/Frankfurt (Main), 1973); Pars Tuğlacı, *Çağdaş Türkiye* (Contemporary Turkey), (3 vols., Istanbul, 19871990); Jan Cremer and Horst Przytulla, *Exil Türkei: Deutschprachige Emigranten in der Türkei 1933-1945* (Karl Lipp, 1981); Ernst E. Hirsch, *Hâtıralarım* (My Memories) (Ankara, Sevinc, 1985). Yasmut Savas, *Biogographische Studien zu Bedeutenden Deutschprachigen Arzten in der Türkei* (Giessen, 1987); and Fritz Neumark, *Zuflucht am Bosphor* (Frankfurt, 1980).

economists and financial experts, he advised the government regarding the organization of the Ministry of Labor as well as laws on social insurance. Among his students were Orhan Tuna and many other leading Turkish economists. Isaac returned to Nuremberg in 1950.

Alexander Rüstow (Wiesbaden, Germany 1885–1963). Economist and sociologist. Rüstow was a legal expert in German Ministry of Economy, preparing the first German law on cartels, later served as administrative director of the German Machine Manufacture Society and Dozent at Berlin Higher Trade School. He strongly opposed the Nazis following their rise to power and led one of last efforts to prevent Hitler from assuming the Chancellorship, so he had to leave Germany, coming to Turkey in 1933 and settling in Istanbul with wife, daughter, and son Dankwart Rüstow. Almost immediately he began teaching Economics and Economic Geography at Istanbul University, subsequently also starting courses on the History of Philosophy. Though he lived in Turkey a long time, he never learned much Turkish, but he inspired his students, and also worked against the Nazis in Turkey on behalf of the American and British governments. In 1950 he returned to Germany and began teaching at Heidelberg University until his retirement in 1953. His son Dankwart attended Istanbul schools and Istanbul University between 1933 and 1946 and for many years has been a Professor of Political Science in the United States, first at Princeton University and later at the Graduate Division, City University of New York.

Hellmut Ritter (Hessich-Lichtenau, Germany 1892–Oberursel, Germany, 1971). Ritter became an Orientalist in consequence of his service in the German army during World War I in Istanbul and on the Iraq and Palestine fronts. He served as Professor of Oriental Languages at Hamburg University 1919–1926. He went to Turkey in 1926 to buy books for the German Oriental Society and remained there until 1948, living mostly in the Bosporus suburb of Bebek. Ritter founded the German Archaeoloogical Institute in Istanbul in 1929 and served as its director as well as as Professor of Arabic, Turkish, and Persian Philology at Faculty of Arts of Istanbul University from 1935 to 1948. His research on Turkish shadow puppets resulted in his publication of *Karagöz. Türkische Schattenspiele* (Istanbul, 1924–1953). He also founded the International Oriental Society and published its journal *Oriens* starting in 1948. He returned to Germany in 1948 as Professor of Eastern Languages at Frankfurt University, remaining there until retiring in 1957. He then returned to Turkey, where he did research at the Institute of Oriental Studies, Istanbul University.

Wilhelm Röpke (Schwarmstedt, Germany 1899 –Genoa 1966). Was Ordinarius Professor of Economics at Marburg University. Though he was not Jewish he hated the Nazis so in 1933 he fled to Turkey with his wife and three daughters, living at Kadıköy near Neumark, Rüstow and Isaac, and later Dobretsberger. Professor of Sociology and Economics, Istanbul University 1933–1937. Head of Social Sciences Institute of Istanbul University. In 1937 he went to *Institut Universitaire de Hautes Etudes Internationales* in Geneva.

Leo Spitzer (Vienna 1887–Italy 1960). Professor of Roman and Comparative Philology at Cologne University 1930–1933. Came to Turkey with wife and child in 1933, subsequently serving as Professor of Roman Languages and Literatures at Istanbul University, where he established courses in philology. He also established the School of Foreign Languages at Istanbul University, which later was continued by Erich Auerbach. He immigrated to the United States in 1936, becoming Professor at Johns Hopkins University until his death in 1960.

Erich Auerbach (Berlin 1892–New Haven 1957). Professor of Roman Philology at Marburg University 1929–1935. Came to Istanbul with wife and child in 1936 where he became Professor of Roman Philology in *Edebiyat Facultesi* of University of Istanbul and Director of its School of Foreign Languages, where his assistants included a number of scholars who later became well-known Orientalists, including Robert Anhegger, Kurt Laqueur, and Andreas Tietze. In 1947 he went to the United States, teaching first at Pennsylvania State University, serving as Visiting Professor at Institute for Advanced Studies at Princeton in 1949, and then as Professor of French and Roman Philology at Yale University until his death in 1957.

Andreas Bertalan Schwarz (Budapest 1886–Freiburg 1953). Practicing attorney in Weimar Germany. Professor of Roman Law at Zurich University and later at Freiburg University in Germany between 1926 and 1930. Because of Nazi persecution, he went to Turkey in 1934 at the recommendation of the Swiss government, to teach Roman and Civil Law due to changeover to western legal systems by Turkish Republic. He played an important role in developing the modern Turkish legal system and training many Turkish students including Türkan Rado and Hifzi Veldet Velidedeoğlu.

Ernst E. Hirsch (Friedberg 1902–). Dozent in private and international law starting in 1930, first at the University of Göttingen, then at Frankfurt, but left Germany in 1933 due to the rise of the Nazis. He was offered a position in International Trade Law at Amsterdam University, but preferred the offer to became Professor of Trade Law in Faculty of Law of Istanbul University, where he remained from 1933 to 1943, being the youngest professor invited to Istanbul University from outside the country. He learned Turkish well, and both lectured and wrote books in Turkish. Deprived of German citizenship by the Nazis, he became a Turkish citizen in 1943. Hirsch moved to Ankara in 1943, serving as Professor at Law Faculty of Ankara University, 1943–1952, teaching insurance and naval law, legal philosophy and legal sociology. He was a major figure in trade law and legal sociology in Turkey, in particular influencing the development of Turkish trade law.

Gerhard Kessler (East Prussia 1883–Kassel 1963). Taught sociology and economics as Professor at Leipzig University from 1927 to 1933. Active in political action against Nazis and arrested as a result soon after they came to power. He then went Istanbul with his wife and four children, serving as director of the course and program in Sociology and Social Politics at Istanbul University Economics Faculty until 1951, later also teaching in the law and literature faculties as well. He trained hundreds of Turkish students, including Orhan Tuna, Cavit Orhan Tütengil, Muhlis Efe, and Ziyaeddin Fahri Fındıkoğlu. In 1946 he joined Orhan Tuna in founding the first Turkish labor union, while working to develop a social democratic political party as well. Kessler returned to Göttingen University in 1951.

Fritz Neumark (Hannover 1900–1991). Became professor of Economics at Frankfurt/Mainz university in 1932, but driven out by Hitler a year later, immediately going to Turkey with his wife, two children and his mother. Neumarck served as Professor of Economics and Finance at Istanbul University for twenty years, 1933–1952, first at Faculty of Law, later at the Faculty of Economics, and also founding and directing the Finance Institute at Istanbul University starting in 1946. Among his students were Nedim Yahya, Sabri Ülgener, Orhan Dikman and Memduh Yasa. He returned to Germany in 1952, teaching finance at Frankfurt University, where he was twice chosen as Rector.

Walter Gottschalk (Aachen 1891–). Orientalist and librarian. Head of Oriental Section of Prussian State Library in Berlin, 1923-1935. Went to Turkey with wife in 1941. Served as Istanbul University Library Specialist starting in 1941 and Professor of Library Science at Istanbul University, 1941–1954. Retired in Frankfurt after 1954.

Clemens Bosch (1899 Cologne–1955 Istanbul). Privat Dozent and Chief Assistant in the Archaeological Institute at Halle/Saale University from 1932–1935, but he was removed from this position because his wife was not Arian. Bosch came to Turkey in 1935, with his wife and five children. where he worked as numismatic expert at Istanbul Archaeological Museum, 1935–1940, and from 1940 to 1955 as Professor of Ancient History at Istanbul University, where he remained until his death.

Hans Reichenbach (Hamburg 1891–Los Angeles 1953). Professor of Physics at Berlin University 1926–1933. Went to Turkey with his wife and two children, serving as Professor of Philosophy at Istanbul University, 1933–1938. He subsequently became Professor of Philosophy at University of California, Los Angeles from then until his death in 1953.

Andreas Tietze (1914–) Turcologist. Trained in Vienna where his father was Professor of Art History. Doçent and lecturer at Istanbul University, 1937–1958, where he worked with Erich Auerbach at the School of Foreign Languages, later becoming Professor of modern Turkish at the University of California Los Angeles (1958–1978). In 1978 he returned to the University of Vienna as Director of the Oriental Institute.

SCIENCES

Fritz Arndt (Hamburg 1885–Hamburg 1969). Assistant in Chemistry at universities of Greifswald and Kiel. He originally came to Istanbul during World War I, and from 1915–1918 was Professor of Chemistry at University of Istanbul (*Darulfünun*), founding the Yerebatan Chemistry Institute which introduced modern chemical research methods to Turkey. Dozent and Professor at University of Breslau from 1919 until 1933. He fled from the Nazis to Istanbul with his wife and two children in 1934; serving as Professor and Director of the Institute he had founded during World War I, the General Chemistry Institute, Istanbul University, from 1934 until he retired in 1955. He then returned to Germany after his retirement and became Honorary Professor at Hamburg University, 1956–1969. His Turkish students included Muvaffak Seyhan (Istanbul), Muzaffer Acarbay (Izmir), and Cemil Dikmen (Ankara). His son, M. Werner Arndt, was student of Linguistics at Istanbul University and later an Assistant in Linguistics at the same University from 1942 to 1949.

Friedrich L. Breusch (Pforzheim (Baden) 1903–). Head of Chemistry Division at Pathology Institute of Freiburg University from 1930–1935. Fled from the Nazis, first to Switzerland in 1936, later spent one year in Hungary. Starting in 1937 he was at Istanbul University, first in the Medical Faculty working with Haurowitz, then in Fen Fakültesi, where he taught a whole generation of Turkish chemists. After 1940 was Professor and Director of the Second Chemistry Institute which he established remaining there until he retired in 1971, after which he went to Basel.

Leo Brauner (Vienna 1898–). Professor at Jena University from 1932 until Nazis removed him in 1933. Came to Istanbul with wife and both parents and became Professor of Botany at Istanbul University and Director of the Botanical Physiology Institute in October 1933, remaining until 1955, when he returned to Germany.

Alfred Heilbronn (Fürth, Bavaria, Germany 1885–Münster, Germany 1962). In 1912 went to University of Münster as Dozent, and in 1919 became Professor there. Administrator of Münster Farmabotanik Institute and Professor of Botany at Münster University, 1919–1933; removed by Hitler in 1933 because he was Jewish, coming to Turkey with his wife and three children Heilbronn quickly learned and taught in Turkish and served as Professor of Botany at Natural Sciences Faculty of Istanbul University and Director of Botanical Institute, 1933–1956. He also established the Istanbul Botanical Garden, which he directed until 1956, when he retired and returned to Germany.

Hugo Braun (Prague 1881–Munich 1962). Worked at the Hygene Institute of Prague University from 1905–1909, then taught methods of toxicology and physical chemistry at the Pharmacological Institute of the same University in 1908–1909. From 1910 to 1912 he worked as Assistant of

Pathology at Medical Faculty of Frankfurt University. He went to German East Africa to study Trypanosomas in 1912–1913, taking up German citizenship on his return. He became Professor of hygene at Frankfurt University at start of World War I and served as Medical Advisor to the German 18th Army during the war, developing special serums against cholera and typhus. He was given the title of Dozent in 1916 and Professor in 1918 at the Hygene and Microbiology at the Medical Faculty of Frankfurt University, where he taught courses in immunology and seriology. In 1931 he won the Paul Ehrlich Prize for research in Microbiology and especially in metabolism of bacteria, but he was dismissed from University in April 1933 because he was Jewish. He went to Turkey in October of the same year with his wife. In July 1933 he was appointed to Istanbul University as Ordinarius Professor of Microbiology and Epidemology and Director of the Institute for Microbiology. In July 1934 the Director of the Institute of Parasitology Ordinarius Professor Ismail Hakki Çelebi left because of a dispute with directors of Istanbul University and Medical Faculty. Braun replaced him as Director, uniting the two institutes as Institute for Microbiology and Parasitology. There he taught students from the medical faculty, dentistry and pharmacological schools. He lived at first in Nişantaşı and later in Ortaköy on the Bosporus. After many years of service in Turkey in 1949 he returned to Germany as professor of Hygene and Bacteriology at University of Munich, rebuilding the institutes which had been destroyed during the War.

Philipp Schwartz (Werschetz, Hungary, 1894–1978). Assistant Physician at Pathological Anatomical Institute in Frankfurt starting in 1920, becoming Dozent in 1923 and Professor in 1927, the youngest Professor in Germany at the time. He was Professor of General Pathology and Pathological Anatomy at Frankfurt University 1927–1933 before fleeing from the Nazis. Established Society for German scientists outside Germany in Switzerland, helping many refugee professors go to Turkey starting in 1933. In September 1933 he went to Istanbul with wife and two children. There he was appointed to Istanbul University as Professor of General Pathology and Pathological Anatomy and director of Pathological Institute. Schwartz was a major figure in reorganization of Istanbul University along modern lines starting in 1933. He became Professor at Frankfurt University after 1951, then Pathologist at Warren State Hospital in Pennsylvania starting in 1953.

Wilhelm Peters (Vienna 1880–). Professor of Psychology at University of Jena. In 1933 fled from Nazis with his wife and two children and taught at University of London for a time before going to Turkey, where he served as Professor of Psychology at Istanbul University, 1937–1952 and also Director of the Pedagological Institute which he established.

Friedrich Dessauer (Aschaffenburg, Germany 1881–Frankfurt 1963). Studied electrotechnics and physics at the Munich Technical University as well as at Darmstadt and Frankfurt/Main. He got his Ph.D. at the University of Frankfurt with thesis on X-Rays. Professor and Director of Medical Physics at University of Frankfurt after 1922 until 1933, also Member of Parliament after 1924 as member of the Catholic German Center Party. Specialized in X-rays, starting under the direction of W.C. Röntgen. Removed by Hitler for political reasons. Came to Turkey in 1934 with his wife and two children, immediately being appointed as Professor and Director of the Radiology and Biophysics Institute of Istanbul University. Made major contributions to developing use of radiology in Turkey. Remained until 1937 before returning to Switzerland.

Wolfgang Gleissberg (Breslau, 1903–). Assistant in Astronomy at Breslau University before 1933, when he was removed by Nazis. He went to Turkey later the same year, there working as assistant in research and teaching to Professor Erwin Freundlich at Istanbul University Astronomy Institute before assuming direction of the Astronomy course starting in 1948. Gleissberg returned to Germany in 1958 as Honorary Professor at Frankfurt University, but returned to Turkey as visiting Professor at Ankara University in 1965–1966.

Erich Frank (Berlin 1884–Istanbul 1957). Appointed Professor of Internal Medicine at the University of Breslau in 1919. Chief Physician at the State Hospital in Breslau from 1928 to 1933, but was removed by Hitler because he was Jewish. Frank came to Turkey with his wife, a son and a daughter in the fall of 1933. He served as Director of the Internal Illness Clinic at Istanbul University and Professor of Internal medicine, from 1933 until 1957, teaching in Turkish after his early years and training hundreds of Turkish physicians, medical professors, docents and assistants. He played a major role in the expansion of modern medical practices in Turkey, serving also as a very popular physician. He died in Istanbul in 1957, and was buried at the famous Rumelihisari Cemetary, near Bebek on the Bosporus.

Felix Haurowitz (Prague 1896–). Professor of Biochemistry at the German University in Prague until 1939, when Germans occupied Czechoslovakia and he fled to Istanbul. He was immediately appointed Professor of Biochemistry at Istanbul University and Director of its Biochemistry Institute, where he served from 1939 to 1948, when he went to the United States, where he became Professor of Chemistry at Indiana University, retiring in 1968.

Karl Hellmann (Würzburg (Bavaria) 1892–Israel 1959). Privat dozent and chief physician at Eyes-Ears-Nose Institute at Würzburg University in Germany starting in 1928, but because of his dismissal by the Nazis in 1933, he went into private practice in Germany. In 1936 he was invited to Turkey, where he became Professor of Eyes, Ears, and Nose at Istanbul University, also replacing Austrian Professor Erich Rutin as Director of Eyes Ear Nose Section of *Güreba* Hospital of Istanbul University. He was particularly known for developing the larinxektomi technique, which made operations less difficult and dangerous.

Julius Hirsch (Hannover 1892–Basel 1963). From 1919 to 1923 Assistant Physician at Kaiser Wilhelm Chemical Institute. Went to University of Berlin Hygene Institute in 1923. Became Professor of Hygiene at Berlin University from 1929 to 1933. Driven out by Nazis and came to Istanbul with wife and two children. Became Professor of Hygiene and Director of Hygiene Institute at Istanbul University, 1933–1948. Learned some Turkish, but it was difficult for him and he continued to teach in German despite the stipulations of his contract.

Joseph Ingersheimer (Frankfurt 1879–Boston 1965). Professor of Ophthalmology at Frankfurt University from 1925 until 1933. Driven out of Germany by Nazis. Brought to Istanbul with Liepmann and Niesen by Schwartz. Became director of Istanbul University Eye Clinic and Ordinarius Professor of Ophthamology at Istanbul University, playing active role in reforming the University. Had close contact with government due to success in operating on eyes of a minister. He went to the United States in 1939 where he became professor at Tufts University, remaining there until his death.

Alfred Kantorowicz (Posen 1880–Bonn 1962). Ordinarius Professor at Dental Faculty at Bonn University from 1923–1933. Established system for looking after childrens' teeth in German schools. Dismissed by the Nazis in 1933. Came to Istanbul with his wife. Became Professor of Dentistry and Director of Dental School starting in 1933, remaining until 1948. His Turkish students included Prof. Pertev Ata and Prof. Lem'i Belger. He later returned to Germany.

Wilhelm Liepmann (Danzig 1878–Istanbul 1939). Professor of Medicine at Berlin Medical Faculty starting in 1921. Professor of Gynecology at Berlin University and Director of Cecilienhaus Women's Illness and Birth Hospital at Charlottenburg after 1925 until driven out by Hitler in 1933. Went to Turkey with his wife and three children. There he directed the Clinic for Womens Illnesses at Haseki Hospital of Istanbul University Faculty of Medicine and also was Professor of Gynecological Medicine, 1933–1939. He made major contributions to developing modern gynecology in Turkey.

Werner Lipschitz (Berlin 1892–United States 1946). Professor of Phamacology and Director of Pharmacological Institute at Frankfurt University from 1929–1933, when he was dismissed by the Nazis. Went to Turkey with wife and two children the same year where he became Professor of Physiological Chemistry and Director of Physiological Chemical Institute at Medical Faculty of Istanbul University. Went to United States in 1938 where he became Research Director of Lederle Laboratories.

Curt Kosswig (Berlin, 1903–1982). Professor of Genetics at Braunschweig Technical University and Director of its Natural History Museum. Driven from Germany by Nazis. Professor of Zoology at Istanbul University, and Director of the Istanbul University Institute of Zoology and Hidrobiological Research 1937–1955. Professor of Zoology and Director of the State Zoological Institute and of the Zoological Museum in Hamburg in 1955 until he retired in 1969. He returned to Turkey and lived in Istanbul after retirement.

Rudolf Nissen (Schlesien, Germany 1896–Basel 1981). Professor of Surgery at Berlin University 1930–1933. Driven out in 1933, and with his wife and colleague Ord. Prof. Phillip Schwartz came to Turkey in August 1933. Headed I Surgical Clinic at Istanbul University Medical Faculty (Cerrahpaşa) 1933–1939, training many Turkish professors and physicians.

Worked to bring other refugee professors from Germany before emigrating to the United States in 1939.

Hans Winterstein (Prague, 1879–Munich 1963). Dozent Professor at Rostock University Medical Faculty in 1910, and Ordinarius Professor in 1911. Went to Breslau University later. English wife and two sons. Fled from Nazis with wife in 1933, went to Turkey where he founded and headed Physiology course in Istanbul University Medical faculty, and became head of its Physiology Institute, 1933–1956. Became Turkish citizen, retired in 1953, after which he returned to Germany.

Siegfried Oberndorfer (Munich 1876–Istanbul 1944). In 1911 became Professor of Pathology at Munich University and Head of Pathology Section at Munich Schwabing Hospital, remaining there until 1933, when he fled to Turkey with his wife. From 1934–1944 was Director of General and Experimental Pathology Institute at Istanbul University, also serving as head of its Cancer Institute from 1938 until 1944.

ISTANBUL FINE ARTS ACADEMY

ARCHITECTURE

Gustav Oelsner (Posen 1879–Hamburg 1956). Architect and city planning specialist. Was City Architecture Director in Hamburg/Altona when dismissed by Nazis in 1933 because he was Jewish. He first fled to the United States. Came to Turkey at invitation of Turkish government in 1937, becoming Advisor to Ministry of Economics and City Planning Professor at *Istanbul Yüksek Mühendis Mektebi* (Higher School of Engineering), 1939–1951. After 1944 he also was a Professor at the Istanbul Technical University, teaching courses on city planning until his return to Hamburg in 1951.

Rudolf Belling (Berlin 1886–Munich 1972). He had been been Professor of Sculpture at Berlin Fine Arts Academy in 1930 until removed by Hitler in 1933. He worked privately for a time in Berlin, 1933–1936 until he was invited to Turkey by Atatürk himself, who appointed him head of the Sculpture Department of the Fine Arts Academy (*Güzel Sanatlar Akademisi*) in Istanbul starting on 7 January 1937. He also joined the Istanbul Technical

University starting in 1950. He sculpted many sculptures and statues in Turkey, including that of Ismet Inönü at Maçka section of Istanbul. Among his students were the well-known Turkish sculptors Hüseyin Gezer, Mahir Tomruk, and Ilhan Koman. He returned to Germany in 1967.

Clemens Holzmeister (Austrian born in Fulpmes (Tirol) in 1886). Administrator of Architectural Section of Fine Arts Academy in Vienna before 1938; also Rector of the school from 1933–1937. Forced to leave when Nazis arrived in 1938. Settled in Turkey with wife and child from 1938–1954; became Director of Architectural Section of Istanbul Technical University and Professor of Architecture from 1940 to 1954. Among other major buildings which he designed and whose constructed he directed were in Ankara the Ministry of National Defense (1931), the Higher Institute of Agriculture (1928), the Army House (1933), the General Staff Building (1930), the ministries of Agriculture, Trade and Interior, and the new Turkish Grand National Assembly building (1938). He returned to Vienna as Professor at the Fine Arts Academy in 1954.

Bruno Taut (Königsberg, Germany 1880Ankara 1938). Professor at the Berlin-Charlottenberg Technical University in 1931–1932, went to Moscow in 1932 and worked as architect in Japan in 1933. After 1936 was employed by Turkish government as architect for important buildings constructed in Ankara. Also served as Professor of Architecture at Istanbul Technical University and also at the Academy of Fine Arts Istanbul, 1936–1938, when he died. Founded the Turkish-German Culture Center in Istanbul shortly before his death.

PAINTING

Léopold Lévy (Paris 1882–1966). Attended the School of Fine Arts in Paris in 1889, where he absorbed the work of contemporaries like Manet, Cézanne, Renoir, and Rodin. Invited by Turkish government in 1936 to direct Painting Section of Fine Arts Academy in Istanbul, where he reformed instruction and established a special studio for engraving. Among his students were Nurullah Berk, Bedri Rahmi Eyüboğlu, Sabri Berkel, and Zeki Faik, all of whom became major artists in the postwar years. He regularly gave public lectures in Istanbul, Ankara and Beirut. Lévy returned to Paris in 1949.

II. ANKARA

ANKARA UNIVERSITY FACULTY OF LANGUAGE, HISTORY AND GEOGRAPHY

HUMANITIES

Benno Landsberger (Friedek, Germany, 1890–Chicago, 1968) Assyriologist and Semitist. Professor at Leipzig University in Assyrology and Semitics starting in 1929 until dismissed by Nazis. Came to Faculty of Language, History and Geography of University of Ankara (*Dil ve Tarih-Coğrafya Fakültesi*) in 1935 as Professor of Assyriology and founder of Sumerian Institute. Landsberger played an active role in organizing and building the Faculty and its library. He remained as Professor of Ancient Near Eastern Languages and Cultures at until 1948, when he went to the University of Chicago Oriental Institute. Among his students in Turkey were famous archaeologists Kemal Balkan, and Emin Bilgiç.

Hans Güterbock (b. Berlin-Charlottenburg, 1908–). Head of Near East Section of Berlin State Museum in 19331935. During the summers he went to the Boğazkoy archaeological excavations in Turkey carried out by the German Oriental Institute. He came to Turkey as a refugee with wife in 1935, joining Benno Landsberger at the Ankara University Faculty of Language History and Geography as Professor of Hittitology from 1935/6 to 1948. His principal students in Turkey were Raci Temizer, Emin Bilgiç, Kemal Balkan, and Muazziz Çığ, all of whom have become major archaeologists. Güterbock has served as Professor at the University of Chicago's Oriental Institute since 1949.

Georg Rohde (1899 Berlin, Germany–1960 Berlin). Privat Dozent at Marburg University in 1931, teaching classic philology, but was forced to leave Germany because of Hitler. Came to Turkey in 1935 with wife and two children. Appointed Professor of Philology of Ancient Languages at *Dil ve Tarih-Coğrafya Fakültesi* of Ankara University starting in 1935. Founded

Classical Philology Institute at Ankara University Faculty of Language History and Geography. With help of Minister of Education Hasan Ali Yücel his students began teaching Latin in many Turkish secondary schools, and he began publishing Turkish translations of many Latin classics and other world literary classics, a series which has remained in print to the present. Rohde learned and taught in Turkish within a short time after his arrival in the country. He returned to Germany in 1949, became Professor of Classical Philology at Free University of Berlin until his death. Among his Turkish students was the renowned Turkish archaeologist Ekrem Akurgal.

Walter Ruben (Hamburg, 1899–). Linguist and philologist. Taught Indian Philology at universities of Bonn and Frankfurt until 1933, when he fled to Turkey with wife and two children. Came to Ankara Faculty of Language History and Geography as Professor of Indology in 1935, remaining until 1948 when he went to Chile. His student Abidin Itil carried on Indological studies at Ankara University after his departure.

Wolfram Eberhard Born in Potsdam, Germany in 1909. Assistant Professor of Sinology at Peking University, 19341936; After 1936 was Director of the Museum of the East Asian Peoples (Grassi Museum). Eberhard came to Turkey in 1937 with his wife and two children. He was not a real refugee, but he worked and associated with them. In 1937 he replaced Anna Marie von Gabain as Professor of Sinology at Ankara University, when she returned to Germany. He remained in Ankara as Professor of Chinese language and Literature until 1948 when he went to the University of California, Los Angeles as Professor of Sociology, later moving to the University of California, Berkeley.

SOCIAL SCIENCES

Ernst Reuter (Apenrade, Germany 1889–Berlin 1953). Had been a prisoner in Russia during World War I, when he became a Communist. Later represented German Social Democratic Party in the Reichstag in 1932–1933. Mayor of Magdeburg and Member of German Parliament in 1931–1933. Arrested by Nazis, spent two years in a concentration camp, fled via Holland to England in 1935. Came to Ankara with wife and child in June 1935 through the intermediary of Fritz Baade, who had been with him in Social Democratic Party. Became trade expert for Turkish Ministry of Economics and later worked for the Ministry of Transportation. Starting in

November 1938 also became Professor of Political Science at *Mülkiye Mektebi*/Political Science Faculty, presenting new course in city planning. His letters written while in Turkey, including exchanges with other important German exiles, are found in Ernst Reuter, *Schriften-Reden, Zweiter Band: Artikel, Brief, Reden 1922 bis 1946*, ed. Hans J. Reichhardt (Berlin, 1973), pp. 453–687. After World War II he returned to Berlin in November 1946 and became its mayor during the Berlin Airlift Crisis.

SCIENCES

Wilhelm Salomon-Calvi (Germany 1868–Ankara, 1941). Professor of Geology and Director of the Geological-Paleontological Institute at Heidelberg University. He retired in 1934 in anticipation of being dismissed because he was Jewish and came to Ankara with his daughter the same year. There he became Professor at the Higher Institute of Agriculture, 1934–1941. Also served as director of the new Geology section that he established. Did successful research for many years at the Technical Research Institute for minerals/*Maden Teknik Araştırma Enstitüsü* in Ankara.

Edward Melchior (Dortmund, Germany 1883–Tessin/Switzerland). Professor of Surgery and Chief Physician at Breslau's *Wenzel Hanke* City Hospital until 1935, when he fled from the Nazis because he was Jewish and came to Turkey with his wife and three children. Became Director of Ankara *Nümüne Hastanesi* Surgery Division in 1936–1954, and after it was created, Professor of Surgery at Ankara University Medical Faculty in 1945. Had major influence in Turkish medicine, particularly in surgery while he was in Turkey, treating many people as physician.

Albert Eckstein (Ulm, Germany, 1891–Hamburg, 1950). Professor of Children's Illnesses at the Pediatrics Clinic at Dusseldorf, becoming its director in 1932, only to be dismissed by the Nazis in 1935. He came to Turkey with his wife, three children, and his mother later the same year, working as a physician in the Childrens Illness Section of the *Ankara Numune Hastanesi* (Ankara Hospital). Eckstein was appointed Professor at the Ankara University Medical Faculty when it was established in 1945. He played a major role in developing Turkish pediatrics, establishing institutes and clinics for Turkish children, mainly in rural areas, contributing in a major way to reducing the death rate among rural children. His students included Professor Ihsan Doğramacı, for many years an outstanding pediatrician, founder of Ankara's Hacettepe University, and later Chairman of Turkey's Higher Education Council. Eckstein later returned to Hamburg.

Otto Gerngross (Vienna, 1882–Ankara, 1966). Professor of Chemistry and Techology of Proteins at the Berlin Charlottenburg Technical University from 1923 to 1933. After being dismissed and driven out of Germany by Nazis, he came to Turkey with his wife and two children, becoming an Professor at the Higher Institute of Agriculture in Ankara/*Yüksek Ziraat Enstitüsü* starting in 1933. He was Professor at Ankara University after it was established, from 1938–1943. He went to Palestine in 1943 as practical chemist, but returned to Ankara in 1947 and taught at the *Fen Fakültesi* (Science Faculty) of Ankara University until his death there in 1966.

ANKARA CONSERVATORY

The Ankara Conservatory was preceeded by *Musiki Muallim Mektebi* (School for Music Teachers) established in the Cebeci district of Ankara in 1924 under direction of State Orchestra Director Osman Zeki Ungor. In 1933 Minister of Education Yusuf Hikmet Bayur established *Devlet Muzik Yüksek Okulu* (State High School of Music), which became *Devlet Musiki Akademisi* (State Music Academy) in 1934 and Ankara State Conservatory in 1939.

Carl Ebert. (Berlin 1887–Los Angeles, 1990). Theatrical producer and director. Started at Actor at Max Reinhardt's German Theater in Berlin from 1909 to 1914, appearing also on the stage at the Frankfurt and Berlin state theaters. At the same time he began to develop a career as theatrical administrator, presenting contemporary German writers plays at the Darmstadt City Theater from 1927–1931. He rose to be director of the Berlin City Opera Company in 1931–1933 when Nazis came to power, causing him to leave Germany and to work for a time in Switzerland, Austria and Italy before going to Argentina, where he produced operas at the Teatro Colon from 1933–1936. He helped Rudolph Bing and Fritz Busch organize the Glyndbourne Festival in England in the late 1930s. At the same time he was invited to Turkey, first in 1936 to organize stage affairs for Atatürk's Presidential Philharmonic Orchestra in Ankara. He later was brought to Turkey a second time, along with his wife and three children, by Minister of Culture Hasan Ali Yücel, remaining from the fall of 1939 until

March 1947, mainly in Ankara. Ebert was the founder of modern opera in Ankara, establishing and directing the Ankara State Opera company, which still remains as Turkey's foremost musical organization. He also assisted in planning the curricula and lessons at the Turkish State Conservatory (*Musiki Muallim Mektebi*), particularly its Theater and Opera sections and administered all theater and opera organizations in Ankara for the Ministry of Education until 1947. He was directly responsible for producing in Turkey many European operas as well as classical European and Turkish plays. He left Turkey and went to the University of California, Los Angeles in 1948–1954, where he directed its opera program. Ebert returned to head the Berlin State Theater between 1954 and 1962, but then retired in Los Angeles, where he died in 1990.

Paul Hindemith (1895–1963). Became first violinist of Frankfurt Opera in 1915, and Chief of Orchestra in 1923. Teacher of composition in Berlin Higher Enstitute of Music from 1927 to 1935, when he was declared *persona non grata* and dismissed by the Nazis. Between 1935 and 1937 he came to Turkey four times at the recommendation of Wilhelm Furtwangler, to help found the Turkish State Conservatory of Music in Ankara. He provided a number of reports on development of the Turkish orchestra and conservatory and recommended a number of musicians who remained to contribute significantly to the development of western music in Turkey.

Dr. Ernst Praetorius (Berlin 1880–Ankara, 1946). General Director of Music in Weimar until he resigned in protest against the Nazis in 1933. In October 1935 he came to Turkey and, upon the recommendation of Paul Hindemith, became director of the President's Philharmonic Orchestra from 1939 until his death, serving also as administrator and teacher in the Ankara Conservatory and as conductor of numerous operas and concerts in Ankara.

Eduard Zuckmayer (Nackenheim/Main 1890–Ankara 1972). Came to Ankara at invitation of Hindemith in 1936, becoming Orchestra Director and teacher of music at Musical Teachers School/*Musiki Muallim Mektebi* in Ankara. He later moved to the Ankara State Conservatory where he remained until his death in 1972, training hundreds of Turkish musicians and music teachers. After 1938 was also Professor at *Gazi Terbiye* Institute. In 1944–5 was interned at Kırshehir with other Germans after Turkey declared war against Germany, but in 1945 returned to teach at the *Gazi Eğitim Enstitüsü*, where he remained until his death.

Appendix 9

AMERICAN DIPLOMATIC REPORT ON NAZI ACTIVITIES IN TURKEY BEFORE WORLD WAR II

REPORT ON NAZI ACTIVITIES IN TURKEY.

J.V.A. MacMurray, United States Embassy, Istanbul, Turkey, to the Secretary of State, no. 74, 14 July 1936. (State Department archives Decimal File 867.4016).

I have the honor to transmit the following information, as of possible interest to the Department, regarding the activities of the German Nazi Party organization in Turkey. The German colony in Turkey is estimated at roughly 1,000 grown persons, according to a statement which the German Consul-General recently made to a member of my staff. Of this number, information obtained from the Press and from other sources is that only slightly more than 500 were present on the German vessel which on March 20 last sailed from Istanbul to the Black Sea, where they took part in the German national plebiscite, this in spite of the fact that free transportation to Istanbul was provided for those who resided in the interior. The Press added that 9 votes were cast against Herr Hitler on this occasion, and an anti-Nazi source is the authority for the report that 50 per cent of the votes cast were blank. Whether that report is true is of course questionable, but it seems to be the general opinion that a large number of the Germans of Istanbul, including some of the most prominent in business, were not in entire sympathy with the Nazi cause, though most of the non-sympathizers have identified themselves with Nazi organizations for reasons known only to themselves and perhaps to the local Nazi leaders.

Whatever may be the number of sincere believers in the Nazi principles, there is no doubt that the Party chiefs completely dominate the colony, and it is understood that, apart from the German-Jews (perhaps a hundred in number) who have left their country for political reasons and have settled temporarily in Istanbul, 99 percent of the Germans in Turkey have officially adhered to the Nazi Party or to other Nazi organizations. The most conspicuous among the exiled Jews are the 35 professors in the University of Istanbul, some of whom were formerly leaders in their professions in Germany. The sentiments most frequently heard expressed by these scholars and scientists, however, are not those of revenge against the regime that is responsible for their exile, but of dissatisfaction at being in any country other than Germany whose customs and habits are theirs and where their forebears have lived for generations. It is also significant to note that, of the two managers of the local branch of the Deutsch Bank, one is a non-German Jew who the Nazi manager insists must be retained if the bank is to function. Consular officers in Istanbul have remarked that this Jewish manager is often present at social functions given by the German Consul-General for his colleagues.

In Turkey, the vocal and active opposition to the Nazis springs from the local colony of Levantine Jews. They occupy positions of prominence and influence in the retail trade and in the banking profession and are said to make every effort to injure the Nazis, especially by trying to kill German trade. They do not appear to be well organized, however, and as they do not control the wholesale and the importing business, or the large purchases made abroad by the Turkish Government itself, their efforts to boycott German goods have not been successful; and Germany's importance in Turkish foreign commerce has gradually increased until it is now estimated that over fifty per cent of Turkey's imports come from that country. Germany's strong political position in Turkey for many decades, and the importance which she has recently acquired in Turkey's foreign trade, are undoubtedly responsible for the fact that Nazi activities in this country have been confined to the German Colony, and every effort has been made to present a united German front to the Turks. It may be noted, however, by any foreign resident of Istanbul that the German colony lives more to itself than it did several years ago, and that its members seem to have their time well occupied with Colony activities. The principal German Club, the Teutonia, used to have many members of non German nationality, but all of the latter have now resigned, and the club has become the center of Nazi activities. Likewise, the Ausflugsverein, an organization which promotes excursions and picnics, formerly had many non Germans associated with it, whereas it has now become a purely German organization in which nature study has become subordinated to such practices as carrying many kilos of sand and gravel in their packs for long distances so as to harden the members. The only organization which the Germans share with others is the German High School, which has for many years had such an excellent standing in all the diverse national groups which make up the population of Istanbul that it has apparently not yet been thought wise to destroy its value in promoting German culture among all peoples in this part of the world. Incidentally, over 50 per cent of the students in the German High School are followers of the Jewish faith.

Within the German colony, strict discipline is said to be exercised over the life of the members. Any recalcitrance is punished, the greatest penalty apparently being to place the name of the guilty one on a sort of black list, which involves loss of citizenship rights, passport, et cetera, and of one's job, if the Nazi chiefs can arrange it. The most powerful Nazi organization in Turkey is said to be a local branch of the Gestapo, headed by the German Consul-General, Dr. Axel Toepke. This officer was from 1931 to 1934 German Consul-General at Memel, where he is reported to have made himself persona non grata to the Lithuanian Government and was considered with apparently good reason to have been directly responsible for the anti-Lithuanian propaganda which culminated in the notorious Memel Nazi trials. The intelligence service of the Gestapo is said to be conducted both among refractory Germans who are expected to adhere to the Nazi organizations, and among the political exiles, emigrated Jews, et cetera. The Organization has furthermore been known to collect funds under threats from local German firms, and also to make reports to the Turkish Government for the obvious purpose of causing difficulties to recalcitrant Germans.

The leader who is considered individually the most powerful in local Nazi circles is a German by the name of Uhlig. He is said to have been formerly a superintendent of a concentration camp, and to have been sent here by the Government at Berlin for the purpose of organizing Nazi activities in the colony. He heads an organization which is devoted to the military training of the colony. Exercises are regularly conducted by him in the grounds of the Teutonia Club and also in the German Embassy building in Istanbul, which are said to be exactly in line with the exercises of the German army; and the rough handling to which some of the less militaristic have been subjected has probably contributed toward the general fear and dislike with which Herr Uhlig is regarded.

Another important member of the Nazi organization is a Herr Sechser, President of the Arbeitsfront. He is a former mechanic, specializing in motor cylinder installations, who has been awarded the degree of 'Engineer' by his Party. All members of the colony must join his organization, which procures jobs for members, supports destitute Nazis, sees that persons on the black list lose jobs and income, if this can be arranged, and collects fees from all members.

The Sturm Abteilung and the Sturm Staffel are reported to have branch organizations in Istanbul. Other organizations to which the members of the German colony are encouraged to devote their time are the *Hitlerjugend*, the *Jungvolk*, the *Bund Deutscher* ???, the *Nazi* ???*bund*, the *Bund der Auslandsdeutschen*, the *Arbeitsdeinst*, the *Sportsverein*, the *Turnverein*, and *Allemania*. The last mentioned, which was formerly a club of professionals and workmen whose members were absorbed by the Teutonia but are charged a smaller membership fee than the better-paid members of the latter club, is now a welfare organization for Nazis. In summary it may be said that, although the German colony in Turkey contains many elements who are believed not to be sympathetic with Nazi principles, yet the Party has succeeded in obtaining the adherence of practically all Germans who are here, keeps their time occupied with a number of organizations and clubs, and subjects them to strict discipline by means similar to those understood to be employed in Germany. These activities, however, seem to be confined completely to the colony, there being no evidence that German internal politics are allowed to interfere with the country's relations with Turkey.

Appendix 10

AMERICAN REPORTS ON SITUATION OF JEWS IN TURKEY BEFORE WORLD WAR II

1. Interview of Mr. Mandil (Istanbul) with Mr. Robert Newbegin, Third Secretary of the American Embassy in Istanbul, 6 February 1939.[480]

SUBJECT: Treatment of Jews in Turkey

PARTICIPANTS: Mr. Mandil, an American merchant established in Turkey, and Mr. Robert Newbegin, 2nd, Third Secretary of Embassy

PLACE AND DATE OF CONVERSATION: Mr. Mandil's shop, 4 February 1939.

When I called at Mandil's on February 4th, I took the opportunity to discuss with him the situation regarding Jews in Turkey. I asked him particularly if any cases of anti-Jewish feeling had come to his attention. He said that none had, and that he felt that the Jews here were treated as well as they were in any other country. He mentioned a number of Jews who had been forced to leave Turkey recently on short notice,[481] and stated that this was merely a special occurrence affecting only a few Jews because of the uncertain status of their nationality. He said that no Jews of Turkish nationality had experienced any difficulties recently. He pointed out that as far as he knew, the only opposition in this country to the Jews of Turkish nationality was aimed at that group who persisted in talking the Spanish language. He said that while some of these Jewish families had been in Turkey for over 400 years, they had made no effort to learn Turkish. He felt, however, that the full blame for this situation did not attend them alone, but to the Turkish authorities as well in that the latter had not in the past provided adequate schooling. He felt that gradually this language question would take care of

---

480. enclosed in J. V. A. Macmurray to Secretary of State, 20 February 1939. Decimal File 867.4016 JEWS/30.

481. 'German and Italian Jews who were expelled when their citizenship was revoked in their home countries, a mistake which was corrected within a few weeks.'

itself, but that any feeling in connection with the use of Spanish here was a perfectly normal and natural one.

He said that in the past when any anti-Jewish articles had appeared in the press, the editors had been severely reprimanded, and that he had no reason to expect a change in this respect. He called attention to the fact that recently the Government had expressed its willingness to allow relatives of Jews residing in Turkey to come here as visitors. In referring again to those who had recently been forced to leave the country because of their nationality status, he said there had been considerable uneasiness on the part of the Italian Jews here. However, pressure had been brought to bear on the Italian Government, which had finally agreed to extend their passports. They therefore seemed to be in no immediate danger. He felt that paid anti-Jewish propaganda from the outside was responsible for any minor anti-Jewish articles. He contended, on the other hand, that he felt that this in no way reflected the attitude of the population in general.

In closing, he reiterated his belief that the Jews in Turkey were treated as well here as they were in any other country. R.N.

2. Department of State, Division of Near Eastern Affairs, 15 March 1939.[482]

    A-M- Mr. Messersmith:

    U - Mr. Welles:

    S - Mr. Secretary

A few weeks ago, Dr. Weizmann, President of the World Zionist Organization, discussed with the Turkish authorities in Ankara a proposal for the immigration of 100,000 German Jewish refugees into Turkey in return for a large loan to be made to Turkey. There has never been any strong likelihood that this proposal would succeed, but discussion of it and other questions pertaining to Jews in Turkey has caused considerable speculation as to the attitude of the Turkish authorities towards both alien and Jewish Turks. In order to let the Turkish Government's position be known, the Turkish Prime Minister recently issued a statement to the press in Turkey stating that since the Jewish question had been mentioned, he wished to say that Jews of Turkish nationality, established in the country,

---

482. United States State Department Archives, National Archives, Decimal File 867.4016 JEWS/32

'are our genuine fellow-citizens. Their legal rights are guaranteed to them.' He added, however, that Turkey would not permit the immigration of Jews who are being driven out of other countries in Europe. He said that the Jewish refugees already employed in Turkey as specialists (doctors and professors) would be permitted to remain with their families until their contracts have expired.

A prominent American Jewish merchant established in Turkey has expressed to our Embassy his confidence that there is no particular cause for concern regarding the future treatment of Jews already in Turkey. He believes that Jews in Turkey are being treated as well as anywhere else in the world. These statements indicate that there is little active anti-Semitism in Turkey, at least for the present. With large numbers of Jews clamoring for admission into many of the smaller European countries, several of those countries, notably Greece and Turkey in our area, have let it be known that they are not prepared to serve as a refuge for persons oppressed elsewhere. These statements, however, have not denoted any animosity towards the oppressed. In the case, there are indications that the German Government has been pressing Athens to adopt an active anti-Semitic policy, and in spite of the fact that neither the Greek people or the Greek Government are naturally inclined to be anti-Semitic, the German pressure may result in stronger measures against the Jews than the present regulations, which extend merely to immigration restrictions.

Appendix 11

CHRONOLOGY, 1931–1945

---

10 April 1931, Mustafa Kemal Atatürk establishes the Turkish Historical Society (*Türk Tarihi Tetkik Cemiyeti*, later renamed *Türk Tarih Kurumu*).

12 July 1932. Mustafa Kemal Atatürk establishes the Turkish Language Society (*Türk Dili Tetkik Cemiyeti*, later renamed *Türk Dil Kurumu*) to modernize Turkish language.

18 July 1932. Turkey becomes 56th member of the League of Nations.

18 July 1932. Turkish Ministry of Religious affairs orders that Muslim call to prayer be recited in Turkish instead of Arabic.

26 September 1932. First Turkish Language Congress opens at Dolmabahçe Palace in Istanbul. Start of campaign for everyone in Turkey to use Turkish as primary language of communication.

30 January 1933. Hitler establishes National Government in Germany composed of National Socialists and German nationalists.

9 February 1933. Signature of Balkan Entente among Turkey, Greece, Yugoslavia and Rumania. Bulgaria and Albania stay out due to claims of territory from Greece and Rumania.

28 February 1933. Law for Protection of German State and People abolishes individual rights, establishes bases for concentration camps.

5 March 1933. German National Socialist Party gets 288 of the 647 seats in National Assembly, German Nationalist Party gets 52.

24 March 1933. Law of Authority gives German government right to issue laws without permission of parliament.

28 March 1933. Nazis prohibit Jews in German businesses, professions, schools. Start of emigration of Jewish professors and scientists to Turkey.

31 March 1933. Abolition of state governments in Germany.

14 April 1933. Anti-Jewish regulations issued in Japan on Nazi model.

24 April 1933. Establishment of Department of Secret State police as political police in Prussia.

2 May 1933. Abolition of German Labor unions.

31 May 1933. Abolition of old Faculty of Arts (*Darülfünun*) in Istanbul. Replaced by Istanbul University on 1 August 1933.

3 July 1933. Nazis begin to dismiss Jews from German civil service.

14 July 1933. Law prohibits establishment of new political parties in Germany, paving way for one party state.

20 July 1933. *Concordato* between Vatican and Germany signed.

20 July 1933. Nazis arrest 300 leading Jews at Nuremberg.

1 August 1933. Establishment of Istanbul University (*Istanbul Üniversitesi*) in place of old *Darülfünun*. Followed by major University reforms, dismissal of aged or incompetent teachers, their replacement by younger and more competent professors, including many German Jews dismissed by the Nazis, who begin to arrive in Turkey later the same year.

3 October 1933. Germany withdraws from League of Nation.

17 October 1933. Albert Einstein arrives at Princeton, New Jersey after canceling plans to take refuge in Turkey.

1 December 1933. Law for Security of State and Party Unity in Germany gives National Socialist Party a monopoly of power.

2 February 1934. Alfred Rosenberg becomes chief of Nazi racial philosophy programs.

9 February 1934. Balkan Pact signed among Turkey, Rumania, Yugoslavia and Greece, but excluding Bulgaria.

20 April 1934. Heinrich Himmler made Chief of Secret State Police in Prussia.

16 June–2 July 1934. Iranian Shah Riza Pahlevi visits Turkey.

20 June 1934. SS created as independent police organization in Germany.

21 June 1934. All Turkish citizens required to take last names. Mustafa Kemal given name Atatürk by Grand National Assembly on 24 November, and Ismet Paşa given name Inönü on 26 November 1934.

24 June 1934. Start of anti-Jewish riots in Eastern Thrace. Suppressed by Turkish government action in mid July 1934.

25 July 1934. Nazi coup in Austria unsuccessful, Prime Minister Dollfuss killed.

2 August 1934. Death of German President Paul von Hindenberg. Hitler made both President and Prime Minister of Germany. Armed forces swear loyalty to Führer.

18–23 August 1934. Second Turkish Language Congress (*Türk Dil Kongresi*) reinforces campaign for all Turks to speak Turkish as primary language.

1 October 1934. German military strength increased from 100,000 to 240,000 men.

24 November 1934. All Turks required to take family name.

26 November 1934. Mustafa Kemal given name Atatürk by Turkish Grand National Assembly.

26 November 1934. Grand National Assembly abolishes all Ottoman titles of honor and rank.

26 November 1934. Nazis dismiss Jewish and non-Jewish professors in German universities who refuse to take Nazi loyalty oath.

3 December 1934. Grand National Assembly prohibits wearing of religious garments outside of places of worship.

5 December 1934. All Turkish women given the right to vote and hold office.

14 December 1934. Vote granted to Turkish women.

25 January 1935. Aya Sofya mosque in Istanbul transformed into museum.

6 February 1935. Turkish women vote in elections for first time.

16 March 1935. Germany starts open rearmament toward 36 divisions. Renounces Treaty of Versailles.

12 April 1935. German Chamber of Writers excludes Jews and all other non-Aryan writers.

2 May 1935. Franco-Soviet Assistance Pact signed for 5 years.

May 1935–20 November 1938. Second German Ambassador to Turkey von Keller.

14 June 1935. Turkish Grand National Assembly creates Faculty of Language, History and Geography (*Dil ve Tarih-Coğrafya Fakültesi*) in Ankara as first element of Ankara University.

18 June 1935. German-British Naval Agreement.

15 September 1935. Nürnberg Laws against German Jews.

3 October 1935. Italy invades Abyssinia.

7 November 1935. Signature of 10 year Treaty of Friendship and Non Aggression between Turkey and Soviet Union.

5 November 1935. Abolition of Turkish Masonic Society. Restrictions against operation of foreign organizations in Turkey.

1 December 1935. Non Aggression pact signed among Iran, Iraq, Turkey and Afghanistan.

2 January 1936. Germany rejects League of Nations protest regarding its mistreatment of Jews, stating that this is 'internal affair.'

9 January 1936. Opening of Faculty of Language, History and Geography in Ankara. Staffed by German Jewish refugee professors as well as Turks.

7 March 1936. Germany occupies Rhineland in violation of Locarno agreement.

9 March 1936. Jews prohibited from voting in German plebiscite supporting Hitler policies.

6 May 1936. Founding of Turkish State Conservatory in Ankara. Staff includes many Jewish and non-Jewish musicians from Germany.

17 June 1936. Heinrich Himmler appointed head of German police.

18 July 1936. Start of Spanish Civil War.

20 July 1936. Montreaux Treaty on Straits signed by Turkey, Bulgaria, France, England, Japan, Rumania, Yugoslavia, Greece and Soviet Union. Italy joins on 2 May 1938.

24–31 August 1936. Third Turkish Language Congress accepts 'Sun Language Theory', stressing Turkish contributions to civilization.

7 September 1936. Germany confiscates 25 percent of large fortunes owned by German Jews.

25 October 1936. Italy completes Abyssinia occupation, establishes Berlin-Rome Axis.

25 November 1936. Anti-Comintern Pact between Germany and Japan signed as move against international Communism.

14 December 1936. Opening of Economics Faculty (*Iktisat Fakültesi*) of Istanbul University.

5 January 1937. Article 2 of Turkish Constitution altered to read 'The State of Turkey is Republican, Populist, Statist, Laic and Revolutionary'.

12 January 1937. Grand Mufti of Jerusalem demands end to Jewish immigration to Palestine.

5 March 1937. United States Secretary of State Cordell Hull apologizes to Nazi government for attacks on its policies by New York mayor Fiorello Laguardia.

28 May 1937. Neville Chamberlain becomes British Prime Minister.

7 July 1937. Report of Peel Commission recommends end to British mandate over Palestine and its division between Arabs and Jews. Accepted by World Zionist Congress on 2 August 1937, rejected by Pan Arab conference on 8 September 1937.

8 July 1937. Saadabad Pact of Friendship signed among Turkey, Afghanistan, Iran and Iraq

1 November 1937. Ismet İnönü replaced as Prime Minister of Turkey by former General Director of the 'Business Bank' (*İş Bankası*) Minister of Economics Celal Bayar. İnönü remains deputy to Grand National Assembly from Malatya until chosen President after death of Atatürk in November 1938. Bayar government includes Şükrü Saraçoğlu as Minister of Justice, Şükrü Kaya as Minister of the Interior, Tevfik Rüştü Aras as Foreign Minister.

6 November 1937. Italy joins anti-Comintern Pact with Germany and Japan.

4 January 1938. Britain postpones partition of Palestine recommended by Peel Commission, appoints new commission chaired by Sir John Woodhead.

12 March 1938. German forces occupy Austria.

27 May 1938 Signature of Turkish-British Trade Treaty.

1 July 1938. Italy places restrictions on Jewish writers.

8 July 1938. Violent Arab protests against British policies in Palestine.

22 July 1938. All German Jews required to carry special identity cards.

3 August 1938. Italy forbids Jews to attend public schools, intermarry with non Jews.

17 August 1938. Second German law requiring German Jews to change original names to those dictated by Ministry of the Interior. If they use names other than these, after 1 January 1939 men must use name Israel and women Sara. Foreign Jews in Germany exempted.

1 September 1938. Italy orders expulsion of all Jews who came after 1919.

29 September 1938. Signature of Munich Agreement among England, France, Italy and Germany. Sudetenland part of Czechoslovakia left to Germany.

3 October 1938. Germany occupies Sudetenland.

5 October 1938. Nazi law requires that passports of all Jews living in Germany be annulled in accordance with Article 5 of the First Regulation of the Passport Law of 14 November 1935. They must be surrendered within two weeks, and Jews on German passports must return to Germany within two weeks. Passports held by Jews outside the country should be stamped with letter J to revalidate them.

9 November 1938. Crystal night in Germany. Burning of Synagogues and destruction of Jewish organizations.

9 November 1938. Woodhead commission declares partition of Palestine impossible. Accepted by Arabs, rejected by Zionists.

10 November 1938. Death of Mustafa Kemal Atatürk at the Dolmabahçe Palace in Istanbul.

11 November 1938. Turkish Grand National Assembly elects Ismet İnönü President of Turkey, with Celal Bayar remaining as Prime Minister. Refik Saydam is Minister of Interior, Hilmi Uran Minister of Justice, Şükrü Saraçoğlu Foreign Minister.

12 November 1938. Jews not allowed to benefit from or use German culture.

15 November 1938. New law prohibits Germans from giving any lessons to Jewish children. Jewish children prohibited from attending German schools, compelled to go to special Jewish schools.

20 November 1938. German Ambassador to Turkey von Keller retires, leaves Turkey. No new German ambassador appointed until 1939.

21 November 1938. Britain offers German Jews opportunity to settle in Uganda instead of Palestine.

3 December 1938. All driving licenses for German Jews to be withdrawn by order of SS Leader and Director of Security in Ministry of Interior Heinrich Himmler. Jews living in Germany forbidden from driving any sort of automobile

4 December 1938. By order of Himmler, after 6 December 1938 all Jews of German citizenship are prohibited from appearing on roads or harbors or using automobiles. Jews in Berlin are prohibited from being in theaters, cinemas, cabarets, concert and conference salons, museums, lunaparks, exhibition halls, sports buildings, and the like. They are forbidden from being in public baths and private bath establishments; they are forbidden from being on Kaiser Wilhelmstrasse from the Leipzig Strasse to Unterderlinden. They are forbidden from Vossstrasse from Hermann Göring Strasse to Kaiser Wilhelm Strasse. They are forbidden from all state monuments along the north of Unterderlinden from the University to the Arsenal. This does not include Jews of foreign citizenship. Within a short time they will be forbidden from all main streets and auto streets of Berlin.

3 December 1938. Law on Jewish use of property in Germany.

8 December 1938. Jews dismissed from all German higher schools in accordance with regulations of Ministry of Education and Nürnberg Laws. Previous exceptions to these laws are now abolished.

28 December 1938. Hasan Ali Yücel becomes Turkish Minister of Education.

17 January 1939. Germany prohibits Jews to practice as dentists, chemists and veterinarians, causing new large-scale exodus of Jewish scientists to Turkey and elsewhere.

18 January 1939. Turkish Grand National assembly accepts the Defense of the Nation Law (*Milli Korunma Kanun*), most important economic law enacted in Turkey during World War II. Government given wide powers to rearrange economy.

24 January 1939. Heydrich given assignment of clearing all Europe of Jewish influence by evacuation.

25 January 1939. Resignation of Celal Bayar as Turkish Prime Minister. Replaced by Interior Minister and General Secretary of the Republican People's Party Dr. Refik Saydam. Tevfik Fikret Silay (Konya Deputy) appointed Justice Minister, Şükrü Saraçoğlu Foreign Minister, Hasan Ali Yücel Minister of Education.

25 January 1939. Prime Minister Saydam tells Republican People's Party congress press conference that he opposes European Jews coming to

Turkey in large groups but that Turkey will protect Jewish Turks from persecution.

1 February 1939. Czechoslovakia expels all foreign Jews within six month period.

7 February 1939. Opening of London conference on Palestine.

21 February 1939. In accordance with article 14 of 3 December 1938 German Law on Jewish use of Property, Jews must deliver all gold, platinum and silver objects and precious stones to official sales places established by the state.

25 February 1939. Germany orders one hundred Jews to be expelled from the country each day.

2 March 1939. Election of Pope Pius XII.

4 March 1939. Laurence Steinhardt appointed United States Ambassador to Soviet Union.

14 March 1939. Slovakia declares independence.

15–16 March 1939. Bohemia and Moravia enter under German protection. End of independent Czechoslovakia.

26 March 1939. New election of deputies to Turkish Grand National Assembly.

27 March 1939. Spain joins anti-Comintern Pact. Britain declares general mobilization.

28 March 1939. End to Spanish Civil War. Franco enters Madrid.

31 March 1939. Britain and France declare guarantee for Poland.

1 April 1939. Signature in Ankara of Turkish-American Trade Agreement; to go into effect as of 5 May.

3 April 1939. Second Refik Saydam government formed in Turkey following elections to Grand National Assembly. Şükrü Saraçoğlu remains Foreign Minister and Hasan Ali Yücel as Minister of Education.

3 April 1939. Grand National Assembly re-elects Inönü as President of the Republic.

7 April 1939. Italy begins occupation of Albania.

10 April 1939. British fleet sails into eastern Mediterranean as guarantee of Greece and Turkey from possible Italian invasion from Albania.

12 April 1939. German Propaganda Minister Joseph Goebbels arrives in Turkey.

13 April 1939. British and French declare guarantee of Greece and Rumania.

18 April 1939. Franz von Papen appointed new German Ambassador to Turkey, arrives in Ankara 27 April 1939.

3 May 1939. Anti Jewish laws enacted in Hungary, with declared intention of expelling 300,000 Jews within a year.

8 May 1939. Signature in Ankara of new Turkish-German trade agreement.

12 May 1939. Signature of Turkish-British joint declaration of friendship and mutual assistance in case of aggression or war in the Mediterranean area.

12 May 1939. German ambassador Von Papen gets Turkey to ship chrome to Germany as alternative to breaking of relations.

19 May 1939. Istanbul newspaper *Ikdam* advocates prohibition of speaking of non-Turkish languages in public places.

20 May 1939. Secret German-Russian negotiations begin in Moscow.

22 May 1939. *Stahlpact*/German-Italian military alliance.

23 May 1939. British Parliament approves plan for independent Palestine after ten years, unified government to be shared by Arabs and Jews. Jewish immigration to be limited to 75,000 refugees during subsequent five years, after which it would stop.

26 May 1939. Fethi Okyar becomes new Turkish Minister of Justice.

6 June 1939. Cuba refuses to allow Hamburg American liner St. Louis to land 907 Jewish refugees from Germany, declaring that it already has accepted 9,300 refugees and can accept no more. United States rejects request that ship be allowed to land in one of its ports.

23 June 1939. Turkey and France sign nonaggression pact in Paris and Ankara. France agrees to return Alexandretta (Hatay) to Turkey. Agreement on mutual assistance if war breaks out in Mediterranean area.

24 June 1939. Brazil allows 3,000 German Jews to enter country as refugees.

30 June 1939. Turkish Grand National Assembly annexes Hatay. French withdrawal completed on 23 July.

6 July 1939. All German Jews forced to join Union of Jews.

9 July 1939. Hamdi Suphi Tanrıöver appointed Turkish Ambassador to Rumania.

13 July 1939. Behiç Erkin appointed Turkish Ambassador to France. Arrives in Paris on 30 August 1939.

18 July 1939. New German Ambassador Franz von Papen speech at Tokatlian hotel in Tarabya (Istanbul), warns Turkey against honoring recent defense agreements with Britain and France: 'forthcoming events in Europe will very soon convince Turkey of the value of remaining neutral.'

8 August 1939. Panama registered ship Parita carrying 600 Jews from Czechoslovakia refused right to land at Izmir.

9 August 1939. Appointment as Turkish Consul-General in Paris of Cevdet Dülger, who remains until 30 April 1942.

23 August 1939. Signature of German-Soviet secret Alliance.

23 August 1939. Signature in Paris of Turkish-French Trade Treaty.

25 August 1939. Great Britain agrees to guarantee Poland.

26 August 1939. Franz Von Papen meets President Ismet Inönü at Florya summer presidential palace, warns him against Turkey's joining Britain and France against Germany.

30 August 1939. New Turkish Ambassador to France Behiç Erkin arrives in Paris. Serves in Paris from 13 July 1939 until 10 September 1940 and at Vichy from then until 13 July 1943.

31 August 1939. Hitler gives order to invade Poland.

31 August 1939. New Turkish Ambassador to Hungary Reşat Ekrem Ünaydın arrives in Budapest.

1 September 1939. German invasion of Poland.

1 September 1939. German Jews prohibited from being outside their homes after 9 p.m. every evening in Germany.

2 September 1939. Germany guarantees territorial integrity of Norway.

3 September 1939. France and Britain declare war on Germany.

3 September 1939. Turkey declares neutrality in war.

4 September 1939. New Turkish Ambassador to France Behiç Erkin presents credentials in Paris.

4 September 1939. New Turkish law prohibits export of raw materials.

4 September 1939. Arrival in Berlin of Hüsrev Gerede as new Turkish Ambassador to Germany. Appointed on 1 August 1939.

5 September 1939. United States declares neutrality in war.

7 September 1939. Turkey prohibits export of raw materials due to war crisis.

8 September 1939. Turkey calls up military reserves for training in case of need. Turkish university students studying in Europe called home.

11 September 1939. First British forces land in France.

11 September 1939. Turkish Prime Minister Saydam tells Grand National Assembly that it will remain neutral for the time being, though talks are going on with Britain and France on how Turkey should fulfill its alliance with them while under threat of German invasion.

17 September 1939. Soviet forces invade eastern Poland.

18 September 1939. Ankara imposes regulations against possible German air raids.

23 September 1939. Prohibition against export of precious metals outside Turkey.

26 September 1939. All Communist societies and organizations dissolved in France by government decree.

27 September 1939. Warsaw surrenders to Nazis and Soviets.

27 September 1939. New Turkish Ambassador Hüsrev Gerede received by Hitler.

29 September 1939. Germany and Soviet Union divide Poland. German persecution and extermination of Polish Jews begins.

29 September 1939. German Jews required to turn over all their radios to Police Department.

30 September 1939. Switzerland proclaims neutrality in war.

3 October 1939. Turkish military mission led by Kâzim Orbay arrives in England. Received by King George VI.

4 October 1939. Turkish Prime Minister Saydam receives German Ambassador Franz von Papen, who again warns him against joining Britain and France.

6 October 1939. Hitler proposes peace to France and England; rejected by France on 10 October, by England on 12 October 1939.

8 October 1939. Arrests of French Communist deputies begin.

17 October 1939. Turkish Prime Minister Saydam reports to Republican People's Party parliamentary group that Russian government is making demands on Turkey to change Straits Convention, but that relations remain friendly.

18 October 1939. Special Turkish author Yakup Kadri Karaosmanoğlu arrives in Amsterdam as new Turkish Ambassador to the Hague. Appointed on 3 September 1939.

19 October 1939. British-French-Turkish Fifteen Year Mutual Assistance and Alliance Pact signed in Ankara. Approved in Turkish Grand National Assembly on 8 November 1939. Allies agree that Turkey will remain neutral until they are able to assist it to resist possible German attack.

19 October 1939. Turkey suspends exports of chrome to Germany.

October 1939. Poland divided between Germany and Russia.

26 October 1939. German Governor appointed for Poland. Start of Nazi persecution of Jews–concentration in Ghettos, restrictions on movements outside, clothing and food restrictions.

31 October 1939. Fall of Ciano government in Italy.

1 November 1939. Turkish President Ismet Inönü declares Turkey will remain neutral while retaining friendship with Great Britain and Soviet Union.

3 November 1939. American Congress passes Lend-Lease law to provide military assistance to Great Britain.

8 November 1939. Attempt on Hitler's life at Bürgerbraeukeller in Munich.

8 November 1939. Turkish Grand National Assembly approves Treaty of Mutual Assistance between Turkey, Britain and France.

17 November 1939. Last German military advisor leaves Turkish army.

20 November 1939. Turkish Foreign Minister Menemencioğlu leads Turkish economic delegation to London and Paris for purpose of increasing trade with Britain and France. Turkey starts negotiations for trade agreement with Germany.

30 November 1939. Start of Soviet invasion of Finland.

8 January 1940. Turkey signs secret Economic Agreements with England and France, agreeing to supply them with chrome in return for loans and other financial concessions.

18 January 1940. Grand National Assembly passes the National Defense Act (*Milli Korunma Kanunu*). Places restrictions on Turkish economy.

20 January 1940. French National Assembly expels Communist deputies.

3 February 1940. Turkey signs new trade agreement with Great Britain.

6 February 1940. German Jews can manufacture and sell clothing only with permission.

11 February 1940. German-Soviet Economic agreement.

21 February 1940. Germany begins construction of concentration camp at Auschwitz as principal German labor and extermination center for European Jews.

10–11 March 1940. Ribbentrop visits Rome.

20 March 1940. Fall of Daladier government in France; replaced on 21 March 1940 by Paul Reynaud.

1 April 1940. Appointment of Bedi'i Arbel as Turkish Consul-General at Marseilles. Remains until 31 May 1943.

8 April 1940. Turkish President Inönü orders mobilization of Turkish forces around Adana and Izmir in fear of German or Italian attack.

9 April 1940. Germany starts to occupy Norway and Denmark. Denmark surrenders without resistance.

14 April 1940. British land at Narvick in Norway.

17 April 1940. Appointment to Turkish Consulate-General (Paris) of Namık Kemal Yolga, who remains until 27 January 1945.

10 May 1940. German invasion of the West begins. Invasion of Belgium, Holland, Luxembourg. Air attacks on Rotterdam, Bruxelles.

10 May 1940. Winston Churchill replaces Chamberlain as British Prime Minister.

10 May 1940. Germany starts to kill people with mental illnesses in accordance with Law of 1 September 1939. After 70,000 killed in this way, killing is ended in August 1941.

14 May 1940. Holland surrenders to Germany.

17 May 1940. Brussels surrenders to Germany without resistance.

17 May 1940. German forces invade northern France.

17 May 1940. Turkey begins fifty percent increases of excise and income taxes in efforts to meet costs of mobilization .

20 May 1940. Turkish Grand National Assembly passes law to establish State Conservatory. Musical and theatrical divisions later established.

22 May 1940. Turkish Grand National Assembly passes law allowing establishment of Martial Law when necessary.

28 May 1940. Belgium surrenders. British evacuation from Dunkerque begins, completed on 4 June 1940.

28 May 1940. Turkish Grand National Assembly authorizes Transaction Tax (*Muamele Vergisi*) on businesses in new effort to meet costs of mobilization included in 1940 Budget Law.

31 May 1940. Turkish Grand National Assembly authorizes creation of local Price Control Commissions (*Fiat Murakebe Komisyonları*) throughout the country to control prices. Composed of local businessmen with some municipal and district officials.

31 May 1940. Turkish Grand National Assembly authorizes sale of goods left unclaimed in Customs Houses to provide funds for mobilization.

4 June 1940. British evacuate Dunkirk.

5 June 1940. Turkish President Ismet İnönü inspects Turkish defenses in Eastern Thrace in fear of German attack from Greece.

7 June 1940. Republican Peoples Party orders end to listening to German Propaganda radio broadcasts in its own club houses and cafes. Asks others to follow its lead.

10 June 1940. Norway surrenders to Germany.

10 June 1940. Italy declares war on Great Britain and France.

10 June 1940. French government abandons Paris.

12 June 1940. Spain declares neutrality in war.

12 June 1940. Turkish cabinet meeting under chair of President Ismet Inönü declares Turkey's intention to remain neutral during war. Says that Britain and France agree on this step since they are in no position to provide military assistance if Turkey is attacked by German forces coming from Greece.

14 June 1940. Signature in Ankara of new Turkish-German Trade Agreement.

14 June 1940. German army occupies Paris without resistance.

14 June 1940. Republican People's Party parliamentary group declares Turkish friendship with Britain and France even though it is unable to join them in the war.

15 June 1940. German army occupies Lithuania, immediately starts rounding up Jews.

17 June 1940. German army occupies Latvia and Estonia.

17 June 1940. Pétain government asks Germany for Armistice for France. Rejects British proposal to unite Britain and France to fight on.

17 June 1940. Marshall Pétain forms Cabinet at Bordeaux and asks Germans for conditions of armistice.

18 June 1940. General de Gaulle declares Free French Committee. Britain recognizes him as leader of Free French on 28 June 1940.

22 June 1940. Signature of French-German armistice at Compiègne.

24 June 1940. Signature of Italian-French armistice.

26 June 1940. Turkish Prime Minister Saydam says Turkey will enter war only if attacked.

28 June 1940. Soviet army occupies Rumanian Bessarabia and Bukovina. Rumania in turn mobilizes army against Hungary.

29 June 1940. Signature of Turkish-German treaty.

29 June 1940. Marshall Pétain establishes Government of 'unoccupied' France at Vichy as compromise between Versailles and Paris.

29 June 1940. Russia invades Rumania.

1 July 1940. Government of unoccupied France moves to Vichy.

2 July 1940. French government for unoccupied France established at Vichy.

4 July 1940. British fleet destroys French fleet at Oran. Marshall Henri-Philippe Pétain becomes Vichy Premier, Pierre Laval Vice-Premier.

4 July 1940. Berlin Police regulation that German Jews can buy or sell food only between 4 and 5 every afternoon.

5 July 1940. French Pétain government breaks diplomatic relations with Britain.

9–10 July 1940. French National Assembly gives full powers to Marshall Pétain by revising Constitution.

11 July 1940. Foundation of the French State (*l'Etat Française*) at Vichy.

11 July 1940. Lord Halifax tells British House of Lords that Britain understands why Turkey is remaining neutral.

mid July 1940. Rumanian Iron guard attacks Jews, and legal restrictions begin against Rumanian Jews.

15 July 1940. Lithuania, Estonia and Latvia vote to join Soviet Union., which annexes them on 21 July 1940.

16 July 1940. Vichy government deprives naturalized French Jews of citizenship.

22 July 1940. Edirne and Eastern Thrace declared martial law zone; foreigners not allowed to remain more than one night. Foreign airplanes forbidden to overpass area.

24 July 1940. All foreigners in Turkey ordered to register with police within twenty four hours of arrival.

25 July 1940. Signature of Turkish-German trade barter agreement. Turkey to export chrome and other raw materials to Germany in return for manufactured goods.

25 July 1940. Turkish Ministry of Trade prohibits bargaining in marketplace; orders fixed prices.

1 August 1940. Recall of Turkish students from France and Belgium.

9 August 1940. Completion of Berlin to Baghdad railroad.

16 August 1940. Amendment of Law on residence and travel of foreigners in Turkey. Report by J.V.A. MacMurray, United States Embassy (Istanbul), no. 1534, 16 August 1940. (Decimal File 867.111/242). Law no. 3529 of 5 January 1939 was relative to the residence and travel of foreigners in Turkey; went into force on 16 July 1938. Law no. 3900 amended Articles 16, 20 and 30 of that law; enacted by Grand National Assembly on 24 July 1940. The main changes are: (1) The government is authorized to extend when it considers it necessary, to visits of a private nature the obligation to furnish police authorities within 24 hours of certain information regarding the visitor; and (2) Council of Ministers may subject to the authorization of the police the travel or residence of foreigners in zones other than those where travel or residence is now forbidden by law.

Resmi Gazete no. 4575 of 31 July 1940;

Law no. 3900, accepted on 24 July 1940.

English text in U.S. report:

Law Modifying certain articles of Law no. 3529 relative to the residence and travel of foreigners in Turkey.

Article 1. Articles 16, 20, and 30 of Law no. 3529 are modified in the following manner:

Article 16: Persons or establishments admitting a foreigner into their homes or into premises under their management for a stay, visit or any other purpose, are obliged to notify within twenty four hours, the nearest police or gendarme station of the name and surname, citizenship and profession of such foreigner, the nature, date and number of the identification document in his possession, also to indicate the persons accompanying him. Visits of a private nature not connected with business and which do not exceed seven days are exempt from this provision. However, the Government may, whenever it may deem it necessary, extend to private visits the obligation to give notice within twenty four hours, specified in paragraph 1.

Article 20: The Council of Ministers may prohibit the residence or travel of foreigners, individually or in groups, to certain zones of the country other than those where their travel or residence is already prohibited by law, and it may also subject such residence or travel to the authorization of the police.

Article 30: Persons failing to comply, without a reasonable excuse, with the provisions of Articles 7, 14, 15, 16, 18 and 19 and with the obligation to notify the authorities specified in Article 17, shall be liable to a light imprisonment up to three months and to a light fine from 5 to 100 Turkish pounds.

Article 2. The present law enters into force on the date of the publication.

Article 3. The Council of Ministers is charge with the application.

30 July 1940

5–19 August 1940. Italy occupies British Somaliland.

19 August 1940. First issue of newspaper *Vatan*, edited by Ahmet Emin Yalman.

19 August 1940. Vichy outlaws Masonic lodges in its territory.

21 August 1940. Turkish Grand National Assembly modifies laws relating to treason by spying, actions to harm national future, military defense, with treason trials to be conducted by military Martial Law courts.

25 August 1940. Hüseyin Cahit Yalçin declares in *Yeni Sabah* that although Turkey is neutral, it wants Britain to win the war.

30 August 1940. Rumania forced to give Bessarabia and northern Bukovina to Soviet Union and part of Transylvania to Hungary.

4 September 1940. General Ion Antonesco becomes President of Rumania following political disputes over cession of land to Soviet Union.

6 September 1940. King Carol abdicates throne of Rumania in favor of son Michael.

8 September 1940. Rumania surrenders South Dobruca to Bulgaria. Arranged by Germany to provide Bulgaria with outlet to Aegean sea through Black Sea and Straits.

9 September 1940. New Rumanian King Michael I decrees anti-Semitic laws.

27 September 1940. Second German anti-Jewish regulation in France.

27 September 1940. Signature of military and economic alliance of Germany, Italy and Japan (Axis).

3 October 1940. First Anti-Jewish Law issued in Vichy France: *Statut des Juifs*. Followed by anti-Jewish legislation in Belgium.

3 October 1940. On occasion of celebration of Jewish New Year in Istanbul synagogues, Jewish community in Turkey promises that from this time forward its members will abandon the use of Judeo-Spanish and speak only Turkish.

4 October 1940. Hitler meets Mussolini at Brenner Pass. Inauguration of Rome-Berlin Axis.

8 October 1940. German troops invade Rumania, ostensibly to protect oil fields.

12 October 1940. German Military mission goes to Bucharest. Followed by establishment of German army units in Rumania.

15 October 1940. Mussolini gives order to invade Greece.

18 October 1940. Vichy government prohibits Jews from civil service as well as management positions in communication media and industries.

22 October 1940. Portugal prohibits Jews from passing through its country in flight from Nazis. Leaves Turkey as main refuge.

28 October 1940. Italian invasion of Greece begins.

22–24 October 1940. Hitler meets with Laval, Franco and Marshall Pétain.

28 October 1940. Italy invades Greece.

29 October 1940. British land in Crete.

30 October 1940. Marshall Pétain blames Jews for French collapse, urges French people to collaborate with Germans.

1 November 1940. Turkish President Ismet Inönü declares that Turkey will remain neutral in war.

4 November 1940. Greek counter attack takes Koritza in Albania.

5 November 1940. Roosevelt elected for third term.

12 November 1940. In accordance with Law of 12 November 1938 which prohibited German Jews from using or benefiting from German culture, German Jews not allowed to buy or rent books.

14 November 1940. Start of German blockade of 350,000 Jews in Jewish quarter of Warsaw.

15 November 1940. Turkish Council of Ministers declares martial law in the six provinces bordering the Bosporus and Dardanelles Straits: Istanbul, Edirne, Kırklareli, Tekirdağ, Çanakkale and Kocaeli, because of fear of imminent German invasion.

20 November 1940. Hungary joins Axis.

21 November 1940. Greek counter attack captures Koritza in Albania.

22 November 1940. Martial Law imposed in Turkey due to threat of invasion.

23 November 1940. Rumania enters Triple Pact (Axis)

24 November 1940. Slovakia enters Triple Pact (Axis)

25 November 1940. Bulgaria refuses to join Axis.

9 December 1940. First British counter attack in Egypt led by General Wavell.

12 December 1940. Hungarian-Yugoslav Friendship pact.

13 December 1940. Marshall Pétain removes Pierre Laval as Prime Minister of Vichy government.

27 December 1940. Turkish law no. 3955 permits French Embassy in Turkey to use blocked currency held by Turkish Central Bank for purposes in Turkey, including compensation to Jewish Turks for funds blocked in France.

29 December 1940. Roosevelt speech that US must be Arsenal of Democracy.

13 January 1941. Greece rejects sending of British force to help against Germans.

14 January 1941. Hitler-Antonescu discussions followed by slaughter of Jews on streets of Bucharest by Iron Guard.

19–20 January 1941. Hitler meets Mussolini. Decision for German to attack Greece to help Italy.

24 January 1941. Thousands die in anti-Semitic riots in Bucharest, Rumania.

28 January 1941. German Security Police chief in Paris Helmut Knochen demands, on the basis of the recommendations of his Gestapo expert on Jewish questions, Theodor Dannecker, to create internment camps in the occupied zone of France to collect foreign Jews.

17 February 1941. Signature of Turkish-Bulgarian non aggression pact.

20 February 1941. *Talimatname* issued by Turkish cabinet allowing issuance of transit visas for Jewish refugees if they have visas to enter other countries following departure from Turkey.

24 February 1941. British cabinet decides on expedition to Greece.

1 March 1941. Bulgaria joins Axis. German army occupies Sofia. Followed by anti-Jewish legislation in Bulgaria.

2 March 1941. Turkey closes Dardanelles to all ships without Turkish captains.

5 March 1941. British forces leave Egypt for Greece. Land at Piraeus 7 March 1941.

9 March 1941. Italy renews attack on Greece.

13 March 1941. Hitler issues secret order for invasion of Soviet Union.

25 March 1941. Yugoslavia joins Axis.

25 March 1941. Turkish-Russian Joint Declaration of non intervention, arranged by Great Britain to keep Turkey out of German hands. Russia disclaims desire for Straits, eastern Turkey.

27 March 1941. Military revolt in Belgrade, overthrows government, renounces agreement with Germany.

29 March 1941. Vichy government creates *Commissariat general aux Questions Juives* (CGQJ), under the direction of Xavier Vallat, to 'recognize and eliminate Jews from all interference in the vital domains and public life, then administer the Jews and their properties under the direction of a central service until they are evacuated . . . and for that purpose to create a 'Central Jewish Office.' (1) To propose to the government all legislative and regulatory measures needed to carry out decisions made by the government in principle on the state of the Jews, their civil and political capacity, their right to exercise functions, employment and professions; (2) to assure coordination needed between different departments of the government to apply these laws and decisions; (3) to arrange the administration and liquidation of Jewish properties and businesses, as prescribed by law, taking into account the needs of the national economy; (4) to designate agents for these operations and to supervise their operations; and (5) to ultimately provoke police measures regarding Jews.'

1 April 1941. Rashid Ali pro-Nazi coup takes power in Baghdad. Suppressed by full British military occupation of Irak.

4 April 1941. Chief of German Military Administration in France Best asks Xavier Vallat, head of the *Commissaire Général aux Questions Juives*, to take preliminary measures to arrange for the internment and deportation of French Jews, starting with the first five thousand.

5 April 1941. Treaty of Friendship between Soviet Union and Yugoslavia.

6 April 1941. Start of German attack on Yugoslavia and Greece. Turkey declares eastern Mediterranean to be war zone. Turkey blows up railroad bridges leading to Greece and Bulgaria at Edirne and Üzünköprü.

6–17 April 1941. German invasion of Yugoslavia. Joined by Bulgaria, which on 31 July occupies Yugoslav and Greek Macedonia and Thrace after fighting is over.

6–27 April 1941. German occupation of Greece as British withdraw.

9 April 1941. Germans break Metaxas line and occupy Salonica.

10 April 1941. German forces occupy Zagreb. Croatia declares independence and neutrality.

12 April 1941. Hungary joins Germans in war.

12 April 1941. Turkish Ministry of Education to facilitate voluntary transfer to Anatolia of elementary and high school students in Thrace area threatened with German invasion.

12–13 April 1941. Germans occupy Belgrade, invade remainder of Yugoslavia.

17 April 1941. Surrender of Yugoslav army. Germans start persecuting Yugoslav Jews.

17 April 1941. British troops occupy Iraq to end Rashid Ali revolt.

19 April 1941. Bulgaria invades Greek Western Thrace and Macedonia. Establishes neutral zone along Turkish border.

19 April 1941. Istanbul University closes term early due to war emergency.

20 April 1941. Germans occupy Belgrade.

23 April 1941. Greek army surrenders to Germans. Persecution of Greek Jews begins.

24 April 1941. British forces leave Greece. Start loading troops and leave on 30 April 1941.

26 April 1941. Third German anti-Jewish regulation in France, modifying that of 27 September 1940, which said Jews are those who belong or belonged to Jewish religion or who had more than two Jewish grandparents. New German definition now says that anyone who has three Jewish grandparents is Jewish; or any grandparent who was Jewish and was a member of the Jewish religion or married to a Jew.

27 April 1941. Germans occupy Athens.

27 April–15 May 1941. Germans occupy southern Greece and Greek islands.

28 April 1941. Turkish Grand National Assembly passes law to fight smuggling.

7 May 1941. Churchill accepts Turkish refusal to close Straits in Germany on grounds of its neutrality.

8 May 1941. Anti-Jewish Ordonnance enacted by Germans for Jews in occupied France.

11 May 1941. Inauguration of *Institut d'études des Questions Juives* in Paris, directed by Captaine Sézille.

14 May 1941. Arrest of 3,700 Jews in Paris. Ordered to go to police stations to 'examine their situations', with identity papers, then arrested. Included 3,430 Polish Jews, 123 stateless (*apatride*) Jews and 157 Czech Jews. 5,000 Jews aged between 18 and 40 taken to the concentration camps at Pithiviers and Beaune la Rolande (Loiret). These taken constituted the bulk of the first four convoys of deportees to the East from France sent in June 1942.

20 May 1941. German planes bomb Crete in preparation for 1 June 1941 occupation.

29 May 1941. General Turkish tax increase to meet costs of mobilization.

31 May 1941. British occupy Baghdad and end Rashid Ali revolt.

1 June 1941. Germany occupies Crete.

2 June 1941. Second Anti-Jewish *Statut des Juifs* Law issued by Vichy France. Replaces the First Statut issued on 3 October 1940. Pétain as Marshall of France decrees that any person with three Jewish grandparents is Jewish or anyone who practices the Jewish religion and who had two

Jewish grandparents. New regulation eliminates French Jews from all public functions, liberal professions, commercial, industrial and artisan positions. No Jews allowed in the press, with internment decreed for violations. Followed by anti-Jewish legislation and persecution in French North Africa under Vichy control.

2 June 1941. Vichy law orders census within one month of all Jews in France, as defined by the second *Statut des Juifs*.

8 June 1941. Syria occupied by British forces with assistance of Free French forces under direction of Charles de Gaulle.

12 June 1941. Germany denies that it has asked Turkey for right to transit troops through Anatolia to help Rashid Ali revolt against British in Iraq.

13 June 1941. Vichy government announces that 12,000 Jews have been sent to concentration camps for opposing French cooperation with Germans.

18 June 1941. Signature in Ankara of Turkish-German Treaty of Friendship and non-Intervention. Approved in Turkish Grand National Assembly on 25 June 1941.

June 1941. Germany starts promoting Turanian movements in Turkey to raise Turkic peoples of Central Asia in revolt against Russia, led by Enver Pasha's uncle Halil Pasha and professors Zeki Velidi Togan and Ahmet Caferoğlu. Aim at regaining Baku to deprive Russia of needed oil. Makes agreement with Turkey to establish autonomous Turkish states in Russian Central Asia as they are conquered by Germans. Turkic soldiers imprisoned by Germans during invasion of Russia to form autonomous Muslim units in German army invading Russia, to include Georgian and Armenian prisoners as well.

June 1941. Slaughter of Jews at Jassy, in northern Rumania.

22 June 1941. German forces invade Poland, starting invasion of Soviet Union. Turkey declares its neutrality in conflict. German soldiers begin mass extermination of Jews in occupied territories of Eastern Europe, often assisted by local Slavic population.

2 June 1941. Turkey declares neutrality in Russo-German war.

25 June 1941. Turkish Grand National Assembly accepts Turkish-German Friendship and Non Aggression Pact.

1 July 1941. Gestapo Chief of Service of Jewish Affairs in France Theo Dannecker reports that in the region of Paris there are 139,981 Jews, of whom 50,388 were French Jewish adults and 16,514 French Jewish children, 55,036 were foreign Jewish adults and 18,043 foreign Jewish children. Census of Jews in Vichy France in December 1941 said there were about 140,000 Jews, but many were Jews who had been in occupied France at the time of the German census and who therefore were counted twice.

8 July 1941. Germany and Italy divide Yugoslavia, with Croatia becoming independent under German 'protection.' Start of anti-Jewish persecutions.

16 July 1941. New regulation in France that no more than two percent of lawyers can be Jews.

22 July 1941. French Vichy Law on Jewish enterprises, property and belongings. 'To eliminate all Jewish influence in the national economy, the CGQJ can name a provisional administrator to all industrial, commercial, immobiliere or artisan enterprises; all *immeuble, droit immobilier* or *droit au bail*; all *bien meuble, valeur mobiliere* or *droit mobiliere*, if they belong to or are directed by Jews.'

29 July 1941. Start of required census of Jews in France.

31 July 1941. Heydrich obtains from Göring a new decree enlarging his anti-Jewish mission to include not only clearing all Europe of Jewish influence by evacuation, as ordered on 24 January 1939, but also by annihilation.

31 July 1941. Bulgaria occcupies Macedonia and Thrace by agreement with Germany. Though it protects Bulgarian Jews, it persecutes Jews in occupied territories in return for German support.

12 August 1941. Pétain blames Jews in France for 'evil wind' which causes resistance against collaboration with Germans.

13 August 1941. German regulation orders confiscation of all radios in Jewish hands in France.

20 August 1941. Official opening of Drancy Concentration Camp in Paris.

20–25 August 1941. First raffle of Paris Jews in 11th district of Paris to decide who will be interned and deported. 2,894 Jews arrested on the street and Drancy concentration camp northeast of Paris opened to hold them. On 21 August operations extended to the 10th, 18th, and 20th districts of Paris, and 600 more Jews arrested. On 22 August 1941, 325 Jews arrested in 3rd, 4th, 10th, 11th, 18th, 19th and 20th districts. Total arrested in this sweep were 4,232 Jews, of whom 1,500 were French. Forty Jewish lawyers also were arrested by special German order, and 21 of these were deported. Remainder sent to Drancy Concentration camp.

25 August 1941. England and Soviet Union occupy Iran jointly.

1 September 1941. German regulations introduced requiring all German Jews over 6 years of age to wear a Jewish star with six points on their clothing, with the word *JUDE*, and made of yellow cloth. They cannot leave their areas without written permission of local police. They cannot wear medals, decorations and other marks of this sort.

5 September 1941. Start of *Le Juif et la France* exposition at Palais Berlitz in Paris under direction of Wuster, who had organized *The Eternal Jew* exposition in Germany. Goes on until 11 January 1942.

21 September 1941. Great fire in Fener, Greek quarter of Istanbul along Golden Horn, partly destroying Greek Patriarchate (repairs completed in summer of 1990).

24 September 1941. New regulation says no more than two percent of architects in France can be Jews.

2–3 October 1941. Many Paris synagogues burned, 3 synagogues blown up.

October 1941. German capture of Belgrade followed by slaughter of Belgrade Jews.

5 October 1941. Jews prohibited from traveling in France. Many railroad stations are full of Jews being sent to concentration camps.

9 October 1941. Signature in Ankara of German-Turkish Trade Agreement. Turkey to ship copper and chrome to Germany in return for war equipment.

15 October 1941. Creation of *Police aux Questions Juives* under direction of Vichy Ministry of the Interior, attached to *Commissariat Général aux Questions Juives*.

15 October 1941. Turkish Generals Ali Fuad Erden and Husnu Emir Erkilet visit German headquarters on Eastern Front in company of Hitler.

16 October 1941. German troops capture Odessa on Black Sea.

17 October 1941. Yunus Nadi declares in his newspaper *Cumhuriyet* that both Germany and England accept the logic of the Turkish policy of remaining far from the conflict.

23 October 1941. Solution of 'Jewish Question' by forced emigration officially changed to deportation and murder in the East. German Gestapo Chief informs Gestapo officials in France that Himmler prohibits all Jewish emigration except for special cases representing a real interest for the Rich and submitted for permission to Berlin. Gestapo takes measures to prevent emigration of Jews from occupied to unoccupied France.

1 November 1941. First issue of anti-Jewish monthly in Paris, *Cahier Jaune*, published by the EIQJ.

13 November 1941. Germans invade Crimea, advance toward Black Sea port at Sevastopol, threaten Turkey from new direction. Conquest completed on 1 July 1942.

21 November 1941. Yunus Nadi's newspaper *Cumhuriyet* starts campaign of publicizing arrests of Jewish war profiteers while ignoring similar arrests of Armenian, Greek and Muslim businessmen. Examples in *Cumhuriyet*, 21 November 1941.

25 November 1941. French law prohibits Jews from serving on juries.

25 November 1941. Bulgaria joins Axis.

28 November 1941. Foreign male Jews who took refuge in France after 1 January 1936 and are aged 18 to 55 must join cadres of foreign workers, subsequently to facilitate their grouping and arrest in Vichy France starting in August 1942 and their transfer to Drancy as a first step to deportation.

29 November 1941. French law organizes *Union général des Israélites de France*, by CGQJ, to assure representation of all Jews with the authorities, especially to arrange assistance. All Jews resident in France required to affiliate with it. It is given legal status, all Jewish organizations are dissolved and their properties are turned over to the UGOF except for legal Jewish cultural and religious groups.

7 December 1941. Japanese attack on Pearl Harbor.

10 December 1941. Issuance of *Ordonnance Relative du Controle des Juifs*. Based on and replacing the 3 October 1940 *Statut des Juifs*, the 2 June 1941 law prescribing a census of Jews in France, the law of 22 July 1941 on Jewish enterprises and properties. Jews of both sexes, French or foreign, must submit to periodic control to be communicated by the press or in meetings. Jews living in the Department of the Seine must always have in their possession an identity card visaed by the Préfect of Police after 1 November 1940 and bearing a cachet stating '*Juif*' or '*Juive*' in a prominent place. Jews coming to Paris from the provinces must come in person to the Police of the Department of the Seine with their identity cards and documents showing their military situation. Jews changing their domicile, even within the Department of the Seine, must report to the police of their old and new districts, with the police authorizing such changes only in serious or exceptional cases. People who rent to Jews, even for no payment, must report the arrival of the Jew to the police within twenty four hours. The property of Jews cannot be moved outside the Department of the Seine. All changes in family situation–births, marriage, death, children reaching the age of fifteen, must be reported to the local préfect of police. Severe punishment provided for violations.

11 December 1941. Germany and Italy declare war on United States.

11 December 1941. Signature in Berlin of Alliance between Germany, Italy and Japan. War declared between Germany and United States and Britain.

12 December 1941. Istanbul Martial Law extended for six months.

12 December 1941. Arrest of 743 leading French Jews in Paris.

15 December 1941. Steamship *Struma* carrying 769 Rumanian Jews refused right to land passengers at Istanbul after British Ambassador declares that ship will not be allowed to exit Dardanelles in order to go to Palestine. Set out again into Black Sea on **23 February 1942** and sank following explosion on **24 February 1942.**

17 December 1941. Price of bread in Istanbul almost doubled, from 9 to 16.5 piasters. Bread rationing introduced.

19 December 1941. Turkish Grand National Assembly strengthens the National Defense Act (*Milli Korunma Kanunu*). Government given the right to confiscate anything needed to meet the requirements of the people or defend the nation, to search and siege as needed, with severe penalties for people found hoarding food or other supplies.

26 December 1941. Decree that no more than two percent of pharmacists in France can be Jews.

7 January 1942. Laurence Steinhardt (Moscow) appointed United States Ambassador to Turkey.

10 January 1942. German Jews required to turn over all materials and clothing made of fur and wool, except for clothing needed in kitchen.

13 January 1942. Start of rationing of bread in Turkey.

20 January 1942. Wannsee conference (Berlin) discusses implementation of Final Solution of exterminating European Jewry.

21 January 1942. Turkish Military conscription term of service extended to three years, two years for University students.

25 January 1942. Istanbul newspaper *Tasviri Efkar* criticizes Jews for not speaking Turkish.

28 January 1942. Salaries of all Turkish civil servants increased by twenty five percent to match inflation.

1 February 1942. Prime Minister Refik Saydam condemns hoarding as cause of shortages of food and other essentials.

14 February 1942. Rauf Orbay appointed Turkish Ambassador to London. Arrives in London 28 March 1942.

17 February 1942. Jews in France are prohibited from using newspapers, magazines and law bulletins sold by post, publisher or street sellers without special permission.

20 February 1942. Start of internment of Japanese in United States.

24 February 1942. Steamship *Struma* sinks in Black Sea by Soviet submarine after British refusal to allow it to enter Mediterranean or land Jewish refugees from Rumania in Palestine.

24 February 1942. Failure of attempt by two staff membes of Russian Embassy to assassinate German ambassador to Turkey Franz von Papen in Ankara.

28 February 1942. Daily Turkish bread ration lowered to 300 grams per day.

10 March 1942. American Ambassador Laurence Steinhardt presents credentials to Turkish President Ismet Inönü.

11 March 1942. United States and Britain agree to send war equipment to Turkey to help it defend against possible Nazi invasion.

15 March 1942. Three British planes from Iraq send war equipment to Turkey to counter German efforts to gain Turkish support, bomb Turkish city of Milas, killing several people. Britain apologizes and agrees to pay damages.

26 March 1942. Beginning of mass extermination of Jews at Auschwitz, Sobibor, Treblinka, and other concentration camps in Eastern Europe.

26 March 1942. German order that starting on 15 April 1942 Jewish houses in France must bear Jewish star in black on white background.

27 March 1942. Beginning of 'racial deportation' convoys from France to extermination camps in East.

20 April 1942. Jews working for Turkish news agency *Anadolu Ajansı* dismissed following demands by von Papen.

8 May 1942. Germans invade Caucasus with assistance of 812th Armenian Legion to capture Azerbaijan oil centered at Baku, encircle Turkey from the East.

15 May 1942. German Jews forbidden to raise house animals, cats, dogs, birds and the like.

29 May 1942. German Jews are forbidden to act as barbers in shops or homes.

29 May 1942. Jews in Paris required to wear yellow star.

June 1942. Establishment in Ankara of British-American Coordination Committee to arrange to send supplies to Turkish army on regular basis. American arms assistance to Turkey begins on large scale in autumn of 1942.

11 June 1942. German Jews forbidden to purchase or smoke cigarettes or cigars in public.

19 June 1942. German forces commanded by General Erwin Rommel conquer Libya, approach Egyptian border.

19 June 1942. German Jews ordered to turn over all electric instruments, like stoves, record players, records, typewriters, bicycles, film and projection equipment.

26 June 1942. Beginning of Turkish-British military coordination.

July 1942. Start of large-scale deportation of Jews from France and Belgium to death camps.

1 July 1942. Completion of German conquest of Crimea with assistance of Armenian brigade in Wehrmacht.German threat to eastern Turkey mounts to fulfill promises to Armenian nationalists.

7 July 1942. Turkish Prime Minister Dr. Refik Saydam dies suddenly in Istanbul of heart attack.

9 July 1942. Şükrü Saraçoğlu appointed new Turkish Prime Minister while remaining as Foreign Minister. Hasan Ali Yucel remains as Minister of Education.

13 July 1942. Prime Minister appointed as Assistant General Secretary of Republican People's Party.

16–17 July 1942. Raffle to chose Jews for deportation to East carried out at Val d'Hiver in Paris.

30 August 1942. French Monsigneur Saliège publicly condemns persecution of Jews in France in speech at Toulouse.

4 September 1942. British halt Axis advance into Egypt.

7 September 1942. Soviet army pushes Germans back from Stalingrad. Start of general German retreat in Russia.

12 September 1942. German occupying forces authorize evacuation of Jewish citizens of neutral countries from France, setting deadline at 31 January 1943. Deadline subsequently extended to 25 May 1944.

18 September 1942. German Jews are not allowed to have meat, eggs, wheat products, milk and the like without special permission. No cocoa or marmalade may be purchased for children over the age of six. For those under six years of age, they may have only one half liter of fresh milk each.

18 September 1942. Turkish-Rumanian trade agreement signed.

8 November 1942. American-British invasion of North Africa begins in Morocco and Algeria. Capture of Algiers. Vichy France breaks diplomatic relations with United States.

11 November 1942. Germans occupy 'unoccupied' Vichy France.

11 November 1942. Wealth Tax (*Varlık Vergisi*) law no. 4305 passed by Turkish Grand National Assembly.

15 November 1942. Admiral Darlan takes command of 'unoccupied France' with capital at Algiers, with Marshall Pétain ceding powers to him on 16 November 1942.

17 November 1942. Pierre Laval given full powers by Marshall Pétain as Admiral Darlan is dismissed.

27 November 1942. Stalin joins Britain and United States in trying to get Turkey to openly join western Alliance.

8 January 1943. Turkish Grand National Assembly passes law to give free bread to poor families.

13 January 1943. French Foreign Ministry informs Turkey that it cannot protect Jewish Turks from anti-Jewish laws imposed by Nazis much longer, and that best way to save Jewish Turks was to send them back to Turkey.

14–26 January 1943. Roosevelt, Churchill and Stalin meet at Casablanca. Agree to increase efforts to get Turkey to join Alliance against Germany as part of Churchill's Balkan plan.

20 January 1943. Expiration of period for payment of Wealth Tax. Arrests and deportation to Aşkale labor camp begins for those who fail to meet obligations.

30 January 1943. O.S. Orhon states in *Çınaraltı:* 'The Turks are neither racists nor enemies of the Jews nor imperialists'.

30–31 January 1943. Adana Conference. Britain represented by Churchill and Ambassador to Ankara Hughe Knatchbull-Hugessen, Turkey by President Inönü, Prime Minister Saraçoğlu, Foreign Minister Numan Menemencioğlu, Cemal Erkin and Chief of Staff Fevzi Çakmak. Churchill discusses British-American arms aid to Turkey with Ismet Inönü at Adana. Churchill presents messages from King George VI and Franklin Roosevelt to Inönü. Says that Turkish entry into war will end Soviet danger to Turkish territory. *Anadolu Ajansı* reports on 1 February that they reached agreement on postwar plans. Reuter reported on 2 February that agreement was reached on strengthening Turkey's defenses. However Turkey did not agree to enter war at this time due to fears of secret British promises to Russia regarding Straits, Turkish territory.

1 February 1943. Germans destroy old Port and Jewish quarter in Marseilles.

2 February 1943. German army at Stalingrad surrenders.

24 February 1943. Hitler announces plan to annihilate Jews in Europe in Nazi party program.

28 February 1943. Secondary and final elections to Turkish 7th Grand National Assembly completed on 28 February 1943, first meeting of new parliament held on 8 March 1943. Among deputies who lose seats are pro-Nazi Yunus Nadi Abalioğlu, owner and editor of Istanbul newspaper *Cumhuriyet*, and famous authors Hüseyin Rahmi Gürpinar and Yahya Kemal Beyatli. Among better known candidates elected for first time were Ismail Hakki Baltacioğlu (Professor at the Faculty of Arts and Letters,

Ankara), Yavuz Abadan (Professor at University of Istanbul), Prof. Ahmed Hamdi Tanpinar (Professor of Turkish Literature at University of Istanbul), Bodrumlu Avram Galante (Professor of Ancient History at University of Istanbul), Celal Esat Arseven (Professor of Ottoman Art and Architecture, Istanbul Academy of Fine Arts).

March 1943. Beginning of Nazi deportations of Salonica Jews to death camps.

8 March 1943. Second Saraçoğlu government formed following elections. Numan Menemencioğlu made Foreign Minister.

15 March 1943. Turkish Consulate-General (Paris) sends first train caravan of Turkish Jewish refugees from Paris back to Istanbul.

18 March 1943. Germans abandon offensive in Caucasus, begin disastrous retreat.

April 1943. British military advisory committee comes to Ankara to fulfill Adana Conference promises of additional military aid to Turkey.

3 April 1943. Germans begin to leave Tunisia.

17 April 1943. Germans demand that Hungarian Regent Admiral Horthy intern all Jews in Hungary. Start of rescue operations to send Hungarian Jews through Turkey to Palestine.

19 April 1943. Signature in Ankara of new Turkish-German trade Agreement.

12 May 1943. End to German/Italian resistance to Allied forces in North Africa.

14 May 1943. Foreign Minister Numan Menemencioğlu on occasion of inauguration of the Turkish Institute of International Law at University of Istanbul, includes in speech that it is 'contrary to the essence of our régime that individuals, that is to say, those who call themselves Turks, should be deprived of their rights even in the name of the hypothetical interests of the community.' Reported by U.S. Ambassador Laurence A. Steinhardt, no. 359,

18 May 1943 (U.S. National Archives, Department of State Archives, Decimal File 867.00/3259).

1 June 1943. Appointment as Turkish Consul-General at Marseilles (Grenoble) of Fuad Carım. Remains until 30 May 1945.

19 June 1943. Goebbels declares that Berlin is now officially free of all Jews.

9 July 1943. German police authorized to directly carry out punishments against Jews. When a Jew dies, his entire property passes to the German state. But when heirs are non Jews living in Germany, they may receive inherited property.

10 July 1943. American and British forces invade Sicily.

25 July 1943. Mussolini overthrown in Rome, flees to refuge with Germans. Replaced by Marshal Pietro Badoglio as Prime Minister. Fascist party dissolved, armistice negotiations with Allies begin.

24 August 1943. Russian troops occupy northern Rumania.

2 September 1943. Allies invade southern Italy. Germans occupy northern Italy as Italy signs armistice with Allies and leaves the war. Germans start persecution of Jews in Italy.

8 September 1943. Germans occupy Italian zone of southeast France, start persecution of Jews who took refuge there.

10 September 1943. Germans occupy Rome.

17 September 1943. Pardon by Turkish Grand National Assembly law no. 4501, modifying law no. 4305, for those delinquent in paying Wealth Tax. (*Sicilli Kavanin* 24 (1943), p. 740).

28 September 1943. Turkish *Chargé d'Affaires* at Vichy Ali Şevket Berker until 12 December 1944.

9 October 1943. Last German troops driven out of Caucasus.

21 October 1943. Free French leader Charles de Gaulle decrees restoration of citizenship of Algerian Jews.

18 November 1943. German troops evacuate Sofia.

28 November–1 December 1943. Teheran Conference gives new impetus to Allied efforts to get Turkey to enter war. Stalin opposes Turkish entry due to fear that execution of Churchill's Balkan invasion plans would increase British influence at Russian expense.

20 November 1943. Opening of Istanbul Technical University.(*Istanbul Teknik Üniversitesi*)

2 December 1943. Pardon and freeing of those Turks who were sent to forced labor at Aşkale for failure to pay Wealth Tax.

4–7 December 1943. Second Cairo Conference of Roosevelt, Churchill and Ismet İnönü. Failure of Russian delegate Andre Vishinsky to attend alarms Turkish delegation as to Russian intentions. Americans assure Turkey that Germany no longer has strength to attack it if Turkey joins war with Allies.

4 January 1944. Advancing Russian troops enter Poland.

4 February 1944. Turkey seizes three steamships belonging to Barzilay ve Benjamin steamship company as result of their bankruptcy due to Wealth Tax.

8 February 1944. First 1944 Turkish train caravan of Turkish Jewish refugees sent by Turkish Consulate-General leaves Paris for Istanbul with 61 Jewish Turks.

1 March 1944. Britain asks Turkey to join war. Turkey asks guarantees against invasion by Russian forces, which are now approaching Rumania. Jewish Agency asks Turkey to postpone entry until more Jewish refugees can be evacuated through Turkey from Hungary and Rumania.

15 March 1944. Turkish Grand National Assembly Law no. 4530 on final settlement of Wealth Tax, pardoning remaining balances owed. *Sicilli*

Kavanin 25 (1944), pp. 97–98. It still secured revenue of TL 316 million; efforts abandoned to collect the remaining TL 110 million still owed.

18 March 1944. Russian troops enter Rumania. Turkey repeats demands for Allied guarantees against Russian invasion as prerequisite for entry into war.

22 March 1944. Germany occupies Hungary, establishes pro-Nazi government. Persecution and massacre of Hungarian Jews begins.

28 March 1944. Second 1944 Turkish train caravan of Turkish Jewish refugees sent by Turkish Consulate-General leaves Paris for Istanbul with 52 Jewish Turks.

10 April 1944. Russian troops capture Odessa on Black Sea from Germans, demand Turkish permission to send ships through Straits. Turkey again asks British guarantee against Russian aggression.

14 April 1944. Britain and United States ask Turkey to stop shipping chrome to Germany. Turkey agrees, suspends shipments on 21 April 1944.

13 May 1944. Hitler authorizes full German withdrawal from Soviet Union.

15 May 1944. Beginning of deportations of Jews from Hungary to Auschwitz.

16 May 1944. Seventh 1944 Turkish train caravan of Turkish Jewish refugees sent by Turkish Consulate-General leaves Paris for Istanbul with 42 Jewish and 12 non Jewish Turks.

18 May 1944. Turkish government announces that homes of leading pan Turkists Zeki Velidi Togan, Nihal Atsız, and Reha Oğuz Türkkan were searched and documents incriminating them of illegal activities were found, leading to their arrest.

23 May 1944. Last train caravan of Jewish Turks sent from Paris to Istanbul by Turkish Consulate-General. with 39 Jews and 8 non Jewish Turks.

4 June 1944. Allies occupy Rome.

6 June 1944. Allies invade Normandy.

15 June 1944. Numan Menemencioğlu resigns as Turkish Foreign Minister after cabinet rejects the guarantees he had given to Von Papen over allowing German warship Kassel to sail through Straits to Germany. Ship inspected outside Dardanelles by British navy, found to be warship and seized. Turkish-German trade relations reduced thereafter. Menemencioğlu sent as Turkish Ambassador to France, where he remains until 1958. Şükrü Saraçoğlu takes over Foreign Ministry himself until Hasan Saka is appointed Foreign Minister on 13 September 1944.

7 July 1944. Russian submarine sinks Turkish ship Şemsi Bahri in Bosporus.

12 July 1944. Opening of Istanbul Technical University.

19 July 1944. Turkish Consul Selahhatin Ülkümen rescues Jewish Turks on Rhodes.

31 July 1944. Last convoy of Jews sent to Auschwitz leaves Drancy Camp.

2 August 1944. Turkish Grand National Assembly severs diplomatic and economic relations with Germany. 3,000 German citizens resident in Turkey ordered to leave within ten days.

5 August 1944. Ankara Radio states that the Turkish government remains ready to help Jewish refugees.

5 August 1944. German ambassador Franz von Papen goes by train from Ankara to Istanbul. Leaves Turkey on 5 August 1944.

20 August 1944. New Soviet offensive begins in Ukraine.

21 August 1944. American forces commanded by General Patton enter Paris.

23 August 1944. Rumania signs armistice with Soviets, declares war on Germany.

30 August 1944. Charles de Gaulle forms provisional French government in Paris.

31 August 1944. Soviet forces occupy Bucharest.

7 September 1944. Start of trial at Istanbul Martial Law court of 23 leading pan-Turianians. Convicted of illegal activities on 29 March 1945.

8 September 1944. Bulgaria signs armistice with Soviet Union.

14 September 1944. Hasan Saka appointed Turkish Foreign Minister.

13 October 1944. Allies occupy Athens.

20 October 1944. Soviet forces occupy Belgrade.

30 November 1944. Appointment of former Foreign Minister Numan Rifat Menemencioğlu as Turkish Ambassador at Vichy. Remains there, and after French return, to Paris until 2 November 1956.

13 December 1944. Laurence Steinhardt appointed American Ambassador to Czechoslovakia.

3 January 1945. Turkey breaks relations with Japan.

20 January 1945. Hungary signs armistice agreement with Allies.

21 January 1945. Soviet army invades Germany.

4–11 February 1945. Yalta Conference asks Turkey to declare war on Germany and Japan, delayed by Turkish government due to appeals of Jewish Agency. Makes it condition for Turkey to join San Francisco Conference, scheduled to meet on 25 April 1945 to organize United Nations.

13 February 1945. Soviet army captures Budapest.

23 February 1945. Turkish Grand National Assembly declares war on Germany and Japan and its intention to join the United Nations Declaration of 1 January 1942.

23 February 1945. Signature of first Treaty of Mutual Assistance between United States and Turkey.

19 March 1945. Soviet Union unilaterally renounces Turkish-Soviet non-aggression pact of 1925, demands territorial concessions in eastern Anatolia and revision of Straits conventions to provide greater Soviet control over Straits. Rejected by Turkey.

March 1945. Allied armies cross Rhine and enter Germany.

30 April 1945. Hitler commits suicide.

8 May 1945. Surrender of Germany.

26 June 1945. Turkey signs United Nations Agreement in San Francisco.

29 June 1945. Death of *Cumhuriyet* founder and owner Yunus Nadi.

10 August 1945. Japan surrenders. End of World War II.

Appendix 12

PRINCIPAL MEMBERS OF THE TURKISH
GOVERNMENT, 1923–1945

PRESIDENTS:
Mustafa Kemal Atatürk (1881–1938): 29 October 1923–10 Nov. 1938
Ismet Inönü (1884 –1973): 11 November 1938–22 May 1950

PRIME MINISTERS:
Ismet Inönü: 4 March 1925 –1 November 1937
Celal Bayar (1883–1986): 1 November 1937–25 January 1939
Refik Saydam (1881–1942): 25 January 1939–8 July 1942
Şükrü Saraçoğlu (1887–1953): 9 July 1942–12 August 1946

FOREIGN MINISTERS:
Tevfik Rüştü Aras: 5 March 1925–11 November 1938
Şükrü Saraçoğlu: 11 November 1938–12 August 1942
Numan Menemencioğlu: 12 August 1942–15 June 1944
Şükrü Saraçoğlu: 15 June 1944–13 September 1944
Hasan Hüsnü Saka: 13 September 1944–10 September 1947

INTERIOR MINISTERS:
Şükrü Kaya: 2 November 1927–11 November 1938
Refik Saydam: 11 November 1938–25 January 1939
Faik Öztrak: 25 January 1939–6 May 1942
Fikri Tüzer: 7 May 1942–17 August 1942
Receb Peker: 17 August 1942–20 May 1943
Hilmi Uran: 20 May 1943–5 August 1946

EDUCATION MINISTERS:
Reşit Galip (1897–1934): 19 September 1932–26 October 1933
Hikmet Bayur (1891–1980): 27 October 1933–8 July 1934
Abidin Özmen (1890–1966): 9 July 1934–9 June 1935
Saffet Arıkan (1888–1947): 10 June 1935–28 December 1938
Hasan Ali Yucel (1897–1961): 28 December 1938–5 August 1946